The Other Divide

There is little doubt that increasing polarization over the last decade has transformed the American political landscape. In *The Other Divide*, Yanna Krupnikov and John Barry Ryan challenge the nature and extent of that polarization. They find that more than party, Americans are divided by involvement in politics. On one side is a group of Americans who are deeply involved in politics and very expressive about their political views; on the other side is a group much less involved in day-to-day political outcomes. While scholars and journalists have assumed that those who are most vocal about their political views are representative of America at large, they are in fact a relatively small group whose voices are amplified by the media. By considering the political differences between the deeply involved and the rest of the American public, Krupnikov and Ryan present a broader picture of the American electorate than the one that often appears in the news.

Yanna Krupnikov is Professor of Political Science at Stony Brook University. She is the co-author (with Samara Klar) of *Independent Politics: How American Disdain for Parties Leads to Political Inaction*, which has won three APSA section awards. Her research has appeared in the New York Times, Washington Post, CNN and the Hidden Brain podcast.

John Barry Ryan is Associate Professor of Political Science at Stony Brook University. He is the co-author (with T.K. Ahn and Robert Heckfeldt) of *Experts, Activists, and Democratic Politics: Are Electorates Self-Educating?* His research has appeared in the *New York Times, Washington Post*, CNN and the Hidden Brain podcast.

The Other Divide

*Polarization and Disengagement in American
Politics*

YANNA KRUPNIKOV
Stony Brook University

JOHN BARRY RYAN
Stony Brook University

CAMBRIDGE
UNIVERSITY PRESS

University Printing House, Cambridge CB2 8BS, United Kingdom

One Liberty Plaza, 20th Floor, New York, NY 10006, USA

477 Williamstown Road, Port Melbourne, VIC 3207, Australia

314–321, 3rd Floor, Plot 3, Splendor Forum, Jasola District Centre,
New Delhi – 110025, India

103 Penang Road, #05–06/07, Visioncrest Commercial, Singapore 238467

Cambridge University Press is part of the University of Cambridge.

It furthers the University's mission by disseminating knowledge in the pursuit of
education, learning, and research at the highest international levels of excellence.

www.cambridge.org
Information on this title: www.cambridge.org/9781108831123
DOI: 10.1017/9781108923323

© Yanna Krupnikov and John Barry Ryan 2022

First published 2022

A catalogue record for this publication is available from the British Library.

Library of Congress Cataloging-in-Publication Data

ISBN 978-1-108-83112-3 Hardback
ISBN 978-1-108-92636-2 Paperback

To Ailis

Contents

Figures

Tables

Preface and Acknowledgments

During one of our early conversations about this project, Yanna said this book should be like *Freaks and Geeks* – the turn of the century, high school dramedy created by Paul Feig and Judd Apatow that Yanna has never seen. She has gleaned, however, that the program showed high school from a different perspective than other high school shows that center on the cool kids, the athletes, and the cheerleaders. While those shows were supposed to be about people for whom the teenage years might be a high point of their lives, *Freaks and Geeks* was about students who are generally uncomfortable with high school and how they relate to those other "cooler" kids. In theory, more people should recognize a part of themselves in *Freaks and Geeks* than in *Beverly Hills, 90210.*

Similarly, this book is not about politicians or their loudest supporters and detractors on social media. At the same time, we do not pretend those people do not exist and that those people are not important. Rather, our hope is that people at all levels of political engagement could read some of the quotes in it and say, "I understand where this person is coming from" even if at other points they read survey results that they cannot believe. Our goal was to present a broader picture of the American electorate than the one that often appears in the news.

If we succeeded in this goal in any way, we did so with the assistance of many people, some of whom may not even have known we were writing this book. As we debated over the book's contents, we would each invoke our mentors Bob Huckfeldt, Skip Lupia, and Nick Valentino knowing that mentions of these scholars would be especially persuasive. We are also tremendously grateful to Michael Boerner, the Stony Brook political science department business administrator; without the help of the best administrator in academia, this whole project would not have been possible.

We are tremendously thankful to those who took the time to read various drafts of the chapters in this book: Elizabeth Connors, Jessica Feezell, Eitan Hersh, Yphtach Lelkes, Matthew Levendusky, Matt Pietryka, and Stuart

Soroka. We are also grateful to Eitan for many conversations that have helped to shape this book. In addition, we were lucky to receive feedback and help on various stages of this project from people whose insights made the book much better: Talbot Andrews, James Druckman, Eric Groenendyk, Mirya Holman, Natalie Jackson, Samara Klar, Shannon McGregor, Kathleen Searles, Anand Sokhey, John M. Warner, the participants at Duke University's Behavior and Identities Workshop, and the participants at Wesleyan University's 2018 Election Conference. Moreover, we will always be indebted to research assistance from a number of graduate students: Romeo Gray, Maggie MacDonnell, Carlo Macomber, Jacob A. Martin, and Michael Yontz. Indeed, Jacob deserves special credit as he was essentially this book's main copy editor.

Finally, we want to thank the journalists we were fortunate to interview, who are quoted in Chapter 8. Although they remain anonymous, we sincerely thank them for their time and for broadening our perspective.

Of course, we must also thank Cambridge University Press for this opportunity. Robert Dreesen first expressed interest in this idea. We are especially grateful to Sara Doskow, the editor for this project, who made this book possible – we are fortunate to get the opportunity to work with her. We would also like to thank the two anonymous reviewers of our prospectus and early writing whose constructive, supportive feedback influenced how we completed the project.

As we (thought we) were finishing this project, the world was disrupted by the COVID-19 pandemic. Like so many things, the final product was shaped by the pandemic, and the completion of it was delayed as a result. Without the efforts of the wonderful staff at Stony Brook Child Care, we may still be working on this book. It is not possible to say enough about all they did to remain open in order to take care of the children of the employees and students of Stony Brook University and Stony Brook University Hospital.

We turn now to the delicate task of thanking pets. We are thankful to (and miss) Penny, the cat we had at the beginning of the project, and to Toast and Jackie Daytona, the cats who used to live at a PetSmart and live here now. And many of the friends we have already thanked know that Sebastian is one of the great dogs of our time.

Finally, we obviously owe a great debt to our families. Our parents – Svetlana, Vulf, Jeannette, and John – served as an example of hard work and sacrifice. We are also grateful to our grandparents. Our daughter serves as an inspiration and remains the most important collaborative work of our lives.

We are lucky people who have benefited so much from the sacrifices of others.

A House Divided against Itself?

We need some people who are active in a certain respect, others in the middle, and still others passive . . .. How could a mass democracy work if all the people were deeply involved in politics?

Berelson, Lazarsfeld, and McPhee (1954)

Much of the modern study of mass political behavior in the United States often returns to three books released during the Eisenhower administration. *Voting* by Berelson, Lazarsfeld, and McPhee (1954) approached its subject from a sociological perspective. Anthony Downs' (1957) *An Economic Theory of Democracy* is the foundational study of political decision-making from the rational-choice perspective. *The American Voter* by Campbell et al. (1960) pioneered the use of the mass survey for political research. These approaches to studying politics are ubiquitous now, but, at the time, these were pathbreaking methodological advances. The authors of these books were to the study of politics what Chuck Berry, Little Richard, and Elvis Presley were to popular music.

While these books are rightly praised for their insights, we want to briefly highlight their titles. The titles clearly state what the books are about and make it clear that these books are not shy in their ambitions. These books are about voting and democracy, and this is obvious to someone who can only see the spines of the books.

The title of this book is more of a mystery. What is the other divide? And if this book is about the *other* divide, this implies that another book could have been written about a different divide that is unstated but clearly important – after all, the divide at the center of this book is the *other* one and not the one that everybody is thinking about.

Since this is not a detective story, let us solve both of these mysteries at the start of the book. The *other* divide is the divide between those people who make politics a central part of their lives and those who do not. The unstated, more familiar divide is the partisan divide between Democrats and Republicans.

The partisan divide should be more familiar because there is no shortage of research articles offering evidence of its presence, most recently through the lens of affective polarization. Democrats and Republicans do not want to have dinner together (Chen and Rohla 2018); they appear to see the other party as less than human (Martherus et al. 2021); they would be upset if their child married someone of the opposing party (Iyengar, Sood, and Lelkes 2012); and they may even be happy if someone of the other party contracted a debilitating illness (Kalmoe and Mason 2019). Coverage of this partisan animosity has also become something of a news beat. Between the summer of 2018 and the summer of 2019, for example, *The Washington Post* published more than fifty articles invoking partisan polarization; *The New York Times* published nearly twice as many.

The other divide – the divide in people's focus on politics that is at the center of this book – is actually not less documented. In fact, the books we mentioned at the start of this chapter all allude to this divide through studies on political attention. Both *Voting* and *An Economic Theory of Democracy* suggest that differences in levels of political attention are important to democracy. In a section titled "Involvement and Indifference," Berelson, Lazarsfeld, and McPhee (1954) write that democracy functions better with "a distribution of voters than by a homogeneous collection of 'ideal' citizens" (315). Downs (1957) describes a division of labor in which masses of inattentive members of the public can free ride off the efforts of the smaller number of politically attentive citizens. On the other hand, the authors of *The American Voter* were less sanguine about the large proportion of the public who "pay much less attention to political events than is commonly realized" (Campbell et al. 1960, 182). They document the failures of the inattentive public, writing, "many people fail to appreciate an issue exists, others are insufficiently involved to pay attention to recognized issues, and still others fail to make connections between issue positions and party policy" (Campbell et al. 1960, 183).

Individually, some of the authors of *The American Voter* had still bigger concerns. Converse (1962), for example, worried that there were some people who were so "uninvolved" in politics that, even during elections, they received "no new relevant information" (587). He did not entirely blame the uninvolved for this outcome; media coverage of congressional candidates, he wrote, is "buried in such a remote section of the paper" that "it is no wonder that data that we have collected over the years show a large portion of citizens who fail to be aware of their congressional candidates as individuals at all" (Converse 1962, 586). He also wondered whether people who are so uninvolved in politics can engage in the type of self-governance that is required for the maintenance of American democracy (Converse 1964). For Converse, then, this divide in people's attention to politics was not the "other" divide – it was *the* focal divide.

Six decades later, times have changed for both divides. The American Political Science Association (APSA) of the 1950s was concerned that the parties were not divided enough (APSA Report 1950). In 2020, the presidents of APSA wrote an op-ed noting that "doubts about whether the election will be fair are being raised from all directions" – an outcome, they suggested, fueled at least in part by deep-seated partisan divisions in America (Aldrich et al. 2020). The emergence of new media technologies means that people no longer have to seek out what Converse (1962) had termed the "remote section" of their local newspaper to learn about their congressional candidates. It is now easier for even the most casual, most "uninvolved" news consumer to come across "relevant" political information. Yet, although increased media options give people many more ways to learn about politics, the diversification of media also makes it easier to avoid politics altogether (Prior 2007) – potentially exacerbating the divides in political attention. These differences between our modern era and the post-World War II time period set the stage for the thesis of this book: The growing partisan divide in America can only be understood in the context of the growing gulf between people who spend their day following politics and those who do not (i.e., the *other* divide).

As we will suggest in this book, people's focus on politics – which we will refer to as "involvement" – is best considered as a continuum. For the time being, however, it is easier to understand our argument if we can divide citizens into three groups. Some people are, to use Converse's (1962) term, "uninvolved"; they are like the Nebraska respondent in his study, who explained that they "don't just know what the parties have been up to lately" (587). Some people, a much larger group, are more likely to behave in the ways Hutchings (2005) suggests: They focus on politics when something happens that is important to them. Finally, there is a third group of people, a group whose focus on and attention to politics is outsized; they are, to foreshadow our core argument, *deeply involved* in politics (a term taken from Berelson, Lazarsfeld, and McPhee [1954]).

The divide between this third group, the deeply involved, and everyone else is key to understanding modern American politics. It would seem natural to think this third group has a lot in common with the second group – those who are sometimes involved in politics. Both of these groups know the basics, they likely know what is going on in the news, and they typically vote. But in this book, we will argue and show that the deeply involved group is unique in a variety of ways that are consequential to American politics.

It is this deeply involved group, we will argue, that has affected how many political observers evaluate the state of American politics. Many assume that the polarization that exists in modern America is experienced similarly by the vast majority of Americans. But this is not the case. Many Americans *do* dislike the political elites of both parties, but they do not necessarily direct this anger at ordinary voters. At times, these people may even perceive partisanship as unimportant and politics to be increasingly counterproductive. The loud, angry partisans who have come to define this modern political era of hyper-partisanship for so many, we show in this book, are largely concentrated in the group of the deeply involved.

In this way, the "other" divide is fundamental. On one side is a minority of Americans who are deeply involved in politics. On the other side is the majority of Americans who have much less investment in day-to-day political outcomes. These two groups have different social networks, different policy preferences, different ideas about family life and child-rearing, and, of course, different beliefs about political parties. The deeply involved minority does *genuinely* dislike rank-and-file members of the other party; this group may even wish ill on out-partisans. For many less involved Americans, political divisions are more complicated: They do not love the opposing party but are more likely to direct the bulk of this animosity at elites and party activists.

People who are deeply involved in politics are also more likely to express their opinions: They discuss politics with others, and they are more likely to raise their voices via social media. In turn, journalists have become drawn to exemplars of angry partisans, which means the information people get about American politics has become flooded with news about political hatred and partisan contempt. Though they form a minority, the amplified voices of the deeply involved are perceived as the voices of most – if not all – Americans. America appears profoundly divided by politics because when people visualize politics, the "pictures in our heads" (Lippmann 1922, 1) are of the deeply involved – and the deeply involved *are*, in fact, profoundly divided by politics.

1.1 AMERICA, DIVIDED BY POLITICS

In 2018, *The New York Times* ran a survey of 2,204 Americans. The main question in the survey – borrowed from the long-running General Social Survey (GSS) – began as follows:

We are all part of different groups. Some are more important than others when we think of ourselves.
    In general, which in the following list are **first, second and third most important to you in describing who you are?** (Badger and Bui 2018)

What followed was a list of possible identities that included such things as "my occupation," "my race or ethnic background," "my religion," "my role in the family," and "my political party or movement." The *Times* was especially interested in that last category – politics. They were conducting this survey in what they described as an "era of acrid partisanship" and wanted to compare the results of their survey to the 2004 GSS result. In 2004, only 4 percent selected "my political party or movement" as one of their top three most important descriptors. "We suspected those numbers might be higher today," wrote *New York Times* reporters, Emily Badger and Quoctrung Bui (2018).

The results seemed to surprise the reporters. In 2018, in the heat of a midterm election, 16 percent of survey respondents ranked politics in their top three most important identities. Of the ten possible identities given to people, politics came in second to last, followed only by social class. Only 3% of people ranked politics as their most important identity, compared to 39% who ranked family status first and 16% who placed religion first. Certainly, these patterns showed a considerable increase from 2004, but the importance of politics did not seem to increase "to a huge degree," Badger and Bui (2018) wrote.

Using a slightly different question, the *New York Times* survey also asked respondents to rate the importance of these different identities. Now, the respondents did not have to select just three identities from the set; they could, in theory, report that *all* ten identities were equally very important to them. Again, however, politics came in next to last: Just over 20 percent of the respondents reported that their political and partisan identities were very important to them, compared to more than 50 percent who reported that their family identities were very important.

The *New York Times* survey is not an anomalous result. In a different survey, Druckman and Levendusky (2019) asked a different sample of Americans to engage in a similar task: rating the importance of six different identities on a scale of 1 to 5. Looking at the average ratings, Druckman and Levendusky (2019) found that partisanship tied for last. Political identities, they wrote, were rated as "significantly less important than all other identities apart from [social] class" (Druckman and Levendusky 2019, S110).

Elsewhere, Karpowitz and Pope (2020) posed a similar question as part of the American Family Survey (AFS). Fielding their survey during a highly contentious presidential election, Karpowitz and Pope also asked respondents to rate the importance of a set of identities. Again, politics came in last – though 34 percent of people did report that their political party was either very or extremely important to them (Karpowitz and Pope 2020, 14). This is, notably, higher than the percentage who viewed politics and partisanship as very important in the *New York Times* survey. That being said, other comparable identities are also rated as more important in the AFS than the *New York Times* survey. In the AFS, 44 percent of respondents said that their religious identities were important, for example, relative to only about 35 percent in the *Times*. Still, while the actual percentage of Americans for whom political identities are important is an open question (likely, one highly dependent on measurement), a unifying pattern in these results is that political identities seem much less important to people than their other characteristics.

That politics seemed so much less important to people relative to their other identities surprised the *New York Times* reporters (the political scientists who found similar patterns seem less surprised). Indeed, much of the article about these results – "Americans Say Their Politics Don't Define Them. But It's Complicated" – offers possible explanations about why the data patterns are actually hiding just how important politics is to the American public. Identities are inherently contextual, and perhaps, the article posits, more people would have reported that their political identities were important to them had the survey begun with a political prime. Or perhaps, "other identities on this list – religion, race, gender, even occupation – have increasingly become intertwined with politics." People do not need to "explicitly prioritize their politics," Badger and Bui (2018) wrote, because "these other identities now offer a clearer window into their politics."

Badger and Bui (2018) are, without a doubt, correct. Indeed, they should be – their reporting on this topic relies not only on the survey but also on interviews with five different political scientists studying American political partisanship. Political parties have become better sorted (Levendusky 2009), and the result is a clearer division of the American public (Fiorina 2016). People are increasingly receiving social and political cues about the way others who are like them are supposed to behave in various political contexts (Barber and Pope 2019; Connors 2020; Druckman et al. 2021b). People are bringing politics to, ostensibly, nonpolitical contexts more than they have in the past (Iyengar et al. 2019). Politics is obviously *divisive*.

But there are two ways to consider the divisions that politics creates, and both are present in the *New York Times* article. Badger and Bui choose to focus on the one that they believe lurks beneath the surface of their survey: America is so divided that partisan divisions are inherent even in people's nonpartisan characteristics. Yet, the data also suggest the possibility of another political divide: There is a minority of people for whom politics is of clear, explicit importance.

Even if politics is inextricably linked to our other identities, there is likely a difference between people who select politics and partisanship when asked to pick just three most important identities and those who do not.

Spry's (2018) multidimensional approach to identities offers a useful way to think through this distinction. There is a difference, Spry argues, between belonging to a group (what she terms "membership"), identifying with a group ("identity"), and believing that what happens to other members of the group also affects you ("consciousness"). In Spry's framework, many people are group members, but only some people are what she calls "strong identifiers" – people for whom a personal identity is heavily connected with a particular group membership. What makes someone a strong identifier, Spry argues, is that "the self and the group are inextricably tied" (Spry 2018, 60). Extrapolating this idea to the *New York Times* survey, what Spry's theory first suggests is that we cannot conflate the idea of having a partisan team with the importance of that team for one's sense of self. Second, however, Spry's argument underscores the importance of self-categorization: There is something unique about a group of people who, when given a set of other identities, chose politics.

The New York Times acknowledges that the data suggest that "most Americans don't live and breathe politics the way Washington news fiends do (or, to be honest, the way we do)." Yet, *The New York Times* misses an important nuance. When asked to describe themselves, there are relatively few people for whom politics is primary. The authors of the article assume that this outcome is somehow a function of their measure being imprecise and failing to capture the fundamental place political and partisan divides hold for many Americans. But, to be a cliché of the terrible anonymous reviewer every academic has encountered, we suggest the data point to a different question: If so few people believe that politics is important to them, why does America seem so divided? The answer, as we will suggest throughout this book, is that there is a critical divide between those who believe politics holds a primary place in their lives and those who do not.

1.2 CAPTURING THE RELATIONSHIP WITH POLITICS

Imagine that there are two people, whom, for the sake of this example, we will call Chip and Dale. Imagine that Chip does not want to read any news about politics, nor does he want to hear his friends discuss political campaigns. Chip may know that an election is coming but has little interest in stories about the candidates; he knows next to nothing about politics. Dale, on the other hand, checks political news on an hourly basis, and he will specifically search out information about an ongoing campaign; he feels an odd sense of anxiety when he cannot follow political news. Dale is knowledgeable about politics, but, more than that, he seeks out social interactions that focus on politics and these social interactions often take the form of being vocal – he regularly posts news stories and shares his political opinions via social media. It makes Dale frustrated and angry when he sees people posting things about politics that he finds incorrect or contrary to his own position. It also makes him frustrated and angry to know how little attention Chip pays to politics. Were Chip and Dale to be asked about interest in and attention to politics in a survey, Chip would likely select the category that reflects the least interest and attention, while Dale would likely place himself in the top category of both measures. The survey measure, then, reflects the very clear distinction in how Chip and Dale relate to politics.

Now let's say we have a third person: Pete. Pete checks in with political news every day – though he never feels as anxious about it as Dale. Pete will discuss politics with some coworkers or friends and may even post "I voted!" via social media on Election Day. Pete feels some frustration when he sees others share opinions that he does not agree with, but he usually ignores those types of posts on social media and has never shared a post with his own political opinion. Pete believes he has enough political knowledge to feel comfortable with politics. In a survey, Pete would likely select response options that reflect that he is very interested in and pays a good deal of attention to politics – the same response options as Dale.

Pete and Dale end up in the same interest and attention categories, though their relationships with politics are markedly different. Politics is more important to Dale; he is much more *involved* in politics. Dale is more likely to be politically vocal. If one of these two people is going to end up in a protracted political argument, it is more likely to be Dale. When journalists turn to social media to consider the shape of political opinions on a topic (McGregor 2019), they are going to be much more likely to encounter Dale's opinion than Pete's. Just as Dale and Chip have different relationships with politics, so too do Dale and Pete. The difference between Chip and Dale is reflected in how they respond to survey questions about interest and attention; the difference between Pete and Dale, however, is less clear-cut.[1]

Chip, Dale, and Pete reflect two types of variation in measures that categorize people's levels of interest in and attention to politics. The first is the expected variation *across* the categories – for example, between Chip and Dale/Pete; the second, however, is the variation *within* categories – for example, between Dale and Pete. This second form of variation is certainly to be expected; there is no ordinal survey measure that can avoid within-category variation. Indeed, measures of attention and interest are likely better than many other ordinal measures in capturing relevant individual distinctions (see Prior 2019 for a discussion). Our argument is not a critique of these measures (in fact, we use these measures at various points in the book). Rather, our argument is that variation within the top categories of interest and attention hints at a meaningful but heretofore unexplored political divide between people like Pete and people like Dale.

Of course, our example is just hypothetical. As a next step, then, we turn to data from two national surveys. Our goal in the next sections is very simple: Given that there are different ways in which someone may engage with politics, can we observe variation *within* the response categories of interest and attention measures? In other words, do surveys offer any patterns that suggest that Petes and Dales end up in the same attention and interest categories?

1.2.1 Over-Time Patterns

If, as we suggested previously in this chapter, people are imagining an America where people are extraordinarily politically vocal, the implication is that people are also imagining an America where people are highly interested in and attentive to politics. There are glimmers of this possibility in some survey data. In a 2017 Pew survey, for example, 52 percent of Americans reported that they started paying more attention to politics after the 2016 election. Of course, paying more attention does not necessarily mean paying a *high* level of attention – after all, if one begins at no attention, even a slight shift is an increase. Also, an increase in attention may not necessarily reflect patterns in political interest.

---

[1] We note, however, that the actual Chip, Dale, and Pete are cartoon characters who pay no attention to American politics given that their primary residence is a magic kingdom.

When we track over-time patterns in interest using the American National Election Study (ANES) from 1956 to 2016, we do see some evidence of an increase in interest (Figure 1.1a). It is not an entirely clear increasing pattern – there is a dip in interest during the 1996 election and then an increase again in 2004 – but it is a line that generally trends upward. In 2016, about 50 percent of ANES respondents categorized themselves as "very much interested," compared to 29.6 percent in 1956.

To put this increase into a broader context, we also plot other variables that may reflect greater over-time engagement in politics. In Figure 1.1b, alongside the interest measure, we also plot the percentage of ANES respondents who engaged in any campaign activities over the course of the campaign. In 1952, 23.9 percent of ANES respondents reported undertaking some campaign activity, and in 2016, 23.4 percent reported doing so. Across the entire time period, campaign activities have always lagged behind levels of interest. What is more, in the three most recent campaigns with the highest interest levels – 2008, 2012, and 2016 – campaign activity lagged about 20 percentage points behind interest.

In Figure 1.1b, then, we see that people's attempts at influencing others have increased considerably over the time period. In 1952, 28.1 percent of people reported trying to influence someone's vote, compared to 48.9 percent in 2016. On the other hand, the patterns in postelection conversation (a measure that is only included on the ANES starting in 1992) are less clear. Generally, few people discuss politics after an election ends, though more than 40 percent

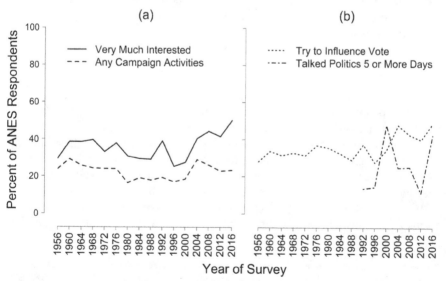

FIGURE 1.1 Changes in campaign interest and activity from 1952 to 2016
Source: Data from the American National Election Study cumulative file.

continued postelection political discussions in 2000 and 2016, likely reflecting the postelection challenges (in 2000) and a surprise outcome (in 2016).

The patterns in Figure 1.1, then, suggest that increases in interest do not always co-occur with increases in other forms of political engagement. We do not see similar shifts in campaign activities, for example, and shifts in postelection discussion behavior seem more reflective of the election context than of some intrinsic interests. In 2012, while 41.5 percent of ANES respondents reported being "very much interested," only 11.4 percent were still talking about politics after the campaign was over.

Our goal is not to explain these over-time patterns in levels of interest and other measures of engagement.[2] Rather, our goal is to suggest that the divergences in Figure 1.1 hint at the possibility that the "very much interested" category includes people who vary in their relationship with politics. In the next section, we examine the possibility of variation within this top category of interest more directly.

1.2.2 Variation in Top Categories

Focusing on over-time patterns, as we did in the previous sections, limits the measures that we can track. Therefore, in this section we rely on more recent data and look more directly at variation within interest and attention categories. Our goal, again, is not to critique these measures but merely to explore the possibility that the highest interest and attention categories include different types of people. We again rely on the ANES but, in this section, also include data from the 2018 Cooperative Congressional Election Study (CCES). Before we turn to the variation, we present the distributions of the different interest and attention measures we are using (Figure 1.2 a-c). As Prior (2019) demonstrates, interest is unidimensional, suggesting that the "Interest and Following Campaigns" measure (Figure 1.2a) and the "Interest in Public Affairs" measure (Figure 1.2c) are likely capturing similar ideas. In Figure 1.2b, however, it is possible that the attention measure is capturing a different aspect of people's approach to their political surroundings. The distributions in Figures 1.2 reflect the final data point in Figure 1.1: 50 percent of respondents, in both the ANES and the CCES, select the highest interest categories. The attention measure in Figure 1.2b looks somewhat different: Only 20.2 percent select the highest category, though 55.3 percent report that they pay attention either most of the time or all of the time.

Within these categories, however, we see considerable variation in other forms of engagement with politics (Figures 1.3–1.6). It is certainly clear that

---

[2] One question that may come up is whether people believe it is socially desirable to report that they are interested in politics. Prior (2019), however, demonstrates that this is unlikely to be the case; people, he concludes, do not seem to be "compelled to exaggerate their political interest" (42). People's self-categorization as "very much interested" seems genuine.

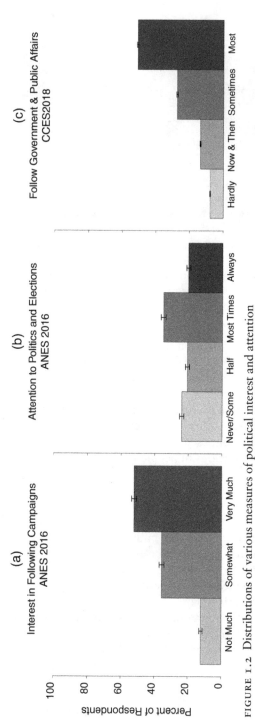

FIGURE 1.2 Distributions of various measures of political interest and attention

Source: Data from 2016 American National Election Study and the 2018 Cooperative Congressional Election Study. Error bars represent 95 percent confidence intervals.

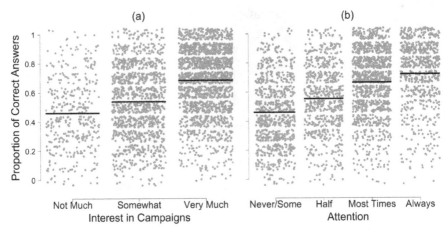

FIGURE I.3 Political knowledge levels by different levels of interest and attention
Source: Data from 2016 American National Election Study. Horizontal lines represent
the mean of political knowledge for that level of interest (panel a) or attention (panel b).
Random jitter is added to the scatterplot to make it easier to see the various respondents.

people in the highest interest and attention categories are much more
knowledgeable and engaged than those in the lowest categories. Yet, *within*
the highest categories of both interest and attention are people who seem to
have very different relationships with politics.

Some people who pay a lot of attention to and have a lot of interest in politics,
for example, are very knowledgeable – others are much less so (Figure 1.3).
Although being more interested in politics makes one more likely to take
a variety of political actions, the proportions of people who take those actions
is still on the lower end (Figure 1.4). Indeed, among those who report the highest
levels of interest and attention are people who are heavily engaged and spend
a good deal of time talking about politics, but there are also people who appear
much quieter (Figure 1.4). These differences in expression also translate to
social media patterns (Figure 1.5). Attention to politics increases people's
political engagement on social media, but, nonetheless, among respondents
who report that they pay attention to politics most of the time, about half
report that they never post on social media about politics.

In short, the patterns in the figures suggest that it is relatively easy to
distinguish between Chip, who pays no attention, and people like Dale and
Pete, who are attentive to politics. Variance patterns clearly show that at the
lowest levels of interest and attention are people who have less knowledge, take
fewer political actions, and are much less likely to engage in any political
expression. It is more difficult, however, to distinguish between Dale and Pete.
Whin the top categories are people for whom, like for Dale, interest and
attention co-occur not only with other political behaviors but also with high

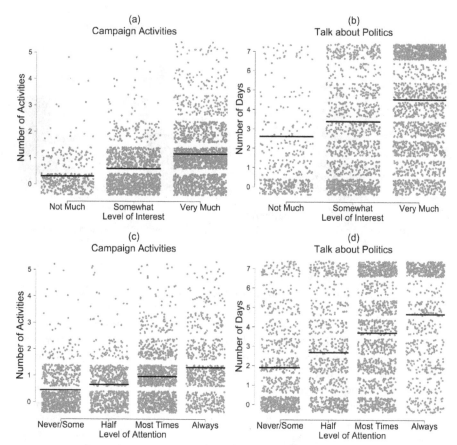

FIGURE 1.4 Campaign activities and political discussion by levels of interest and attention.

Source: Data from 2016 American National Election Study. In panels a and c, horizontal lines represent the mean number of activities for that level of interest (a) or attention (c). In panels b and d, horizontal lines represent the mean number of days a respondent discusses politics for that level of interest (b) or attention (d) Random jitter is added to the scatterplot to make it easier to see the various respondents.

levels of political expression. On the other hand, these top categories also include people like Pete: They *do* pay attention to politics, but they are not necessarily going to spend a part of each day engaging with political content or expressing their political opinions.

It is, without a doubt, important to distinguish between those who have a good deal of interest and attention and those who have none. This distinction offers a means by which we can determine who is likely to be entirely disengaged from politics. But we suggest that there is another divide that is hiding within the interest and attention measures: the divide between those who, like Pete, are

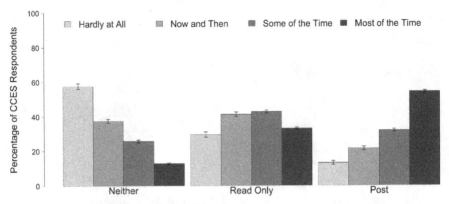

FIGURE 1.5 Social media use by attention levels
Source: Data from 2018 Cooperative Congressional Election Study. Error bars represent 95 percent confidence intervals.

merely interested and attentive and those who, like Dale, are deeply focused on politics.

We want to be clear that this is not merely a question of measurement. Survey measures of interest and attention reflect real, valid, and predictive differences among the electorate. Indeed, scholars have shown that interest and attention affect a variety of political outcomes and reflect a dispositional stability (Prior 2019). In this book, however, we will argue and show that there are more gradations to people's relationships with politics, and these gradations form an especially meaningful political divide in the highest categories of interest and attention. The dividing line in American politics may seem to be between Chip and Dale/Pete, but it is actually between Dale and the other two voters.

1.3   BEYOND POLITICAL INTEREST AND ATTENTION

Let's return to our three hypothetical exemplars: Chip, Dale, and Pete. Distinguishing between Chip and the other two is simple: Chip has no connection to politics at all, whereas Dale and Pete do. The more complicated part is, as we already suggested, distinguishing between Dale and Pete. Both Dale and Pete pay attention to political news, but only Dale feels anxious when he is in a context that does not allow him to follow political news (e.g., a meeting at work). Both Dale and Pete feel some frustration when they encounter people whose political opinions differ from theirs, but Dale is much more likely to voice his disagreement. Both Dale and Pete may read about politics on social media, but Dale is much more likely to post about his opinions and share political content.

Distinguishing between Dale and Pete is challenging. Both of them are clearly very interested in politics. Yet, Dale's relationship to politics seems very different from Pete's – politics seems much more of a focus for Dale. This idea of importance offers a starting point for differentiating these two people. What separates Dale and Pete, we will argue in this book, is their level of *involvement* in politics. Pete is interested in politics, but Dale is *deeply involved*.

Before we go any further, it is important to make clear that we do not claim any credit for introducing the term "involvement." The idea of involvement in politics has been part of political science for decades. In fact, in the previous sections of this chapter, we quoted several scholars who used the terms involved and uninvolved to distinguish between groups of Americans (Berelson, Lazarsfeld, and McPhee, 1954; Campbell et al. 1960; Converse 1962). In this early research on political behavior, involvement included a broad set of political predispositions – one of which was, notably, interest in politics (Campbell et al. 1960). The authors of *The American Voter*, however, point out that involvement was an idea beyond political interest. Rather, they suggested that it was a psychological predisposition, an idea that reflected an individual's "commitment" to politics (Campbell et al. 1960, 104). The authors of *The American Voter* also foreshadowed one of the results in this book: "[A] really intense commitment to politics is probably limited in American society to a small fraction" (104).

Although this book does not introduce the term "involvement" to political science, in Chapter 3 we do draw on research from political science, psychology, sociology, and marketing – all disciplines that have worked to capture what it means to be involved in and committed to something – to outline the psychology of political involvement. Our particular interest is in the psychology of the "deeply involved" (a term that has also been previously used in political science by Berelson, Lazarsfeld, and McPhee (1954)) or people who have an especially intense focus on politics as we explain in Chapter 3.

The deeply involved spend a good deal of time following politics. More than merely checking in with the news every morning or evening, those who are deeply involved pay attention to political news consistently throughout the day. The deeply involved feel anxious when they cannot follow politics. They can see the political consequence of even seemingly mundane, small political events. They are also likely to express and discuss their political opinions – often publicly.

Of course, political interest and attention are linked to involvement. Deeply involved people are certainly interested in and attentive to politics. Indeed, it would be difficult to imagine someone being deeply involved but completely uninterested in a topic (see e.g., Mittal 1995). Deep involvement, however, is a characteristic that describes a relationship with politics that is beyond that which is captured with higher levels of political interest. This is not a critique of either research on or measurement of political interest or attention. Rather, it is to underscore that deep involvement is a psychological characteristic that is different from interest; some people are very interested in politics, but others are deeply involved. It is the difference between those who are deeply involved and everyone else that forms the "other divide" in American politics.

We draw on research on the sociology and psychology of deep involvement to argue that people who are deeply involved have strong perceptions about the appropriate and inappropriate ways of being involved. Being engaged – even deeply so – in a topic is one thing, but it is important to engage with the topic in ways that are *correct*. Translating this idea to politics suggests the possibility of a relationship between deep involvement and people's political positions: For those who are deeply involved, it is equally important that people who are engaged belong to a particular party or even more specifically support a particular set of positions within that party. The implication, then, is that deep involvement in politics is likely to co-occur with animosity toward people who are politically different and greater affinity for your own political side – that is, higher levels of affective polarization.

Along with this stronger psychological commitment to politics comes a desire for social interaction about politics. The deeply involved are more likely to begin political conversations and engage in political conversations. This tendency is likely to be most visible via social media, as a key affordance of these platforms is broad, public expression of a person's views or thoughts. Social media platforms, then, allow the deeply involved an opportunity to share information, share their opinions, and correct people whose political positions or ideas they view as incorrect.

It is this intersection between deep involvement, animosity, and expression that not only forms the foundation of the "other divide" but also reinforces the image of the American public as one that is deeply divided. The people who are most engaged in politics – the deeply involved – know the most about day-to-day politics. They are also most likely to feel strongly about what is politically right and politically wrong, where "right" and "wrong" are political outcomes, rather than procedures and rules. Indeed, it is possible that a person who is deeply involved so strongly believes in the potential benefit of a given political outcome that they are willing to support processes that break with political rules and norms. Because the deeply involved are drawn to social interactions about politics, they are more publicly expressive, and their political views and positions are more likely to be amplified – first by their own voices and then by journalists and pundits as "exemplars" of ordinary voters (see e.g., Levendusky and Malhotra 2016). To restate our previous argument: America appears heavily divided along partisan lines because partisanship is, likely, the main division among the deeply involved. What we suggest in this book, however, is that once we broaden our scope to the entire electorate, the emerging division is often between those who are and those who are not deeply involved in politics.

1.4 PLAN OF THE BOOK

In what follows, our goal is to consider the various ways in which deep involvement in politics divides people. Before we can delve into this "other divide" in American politics, however, it is important to consider the political divide that has gotten the most attention in both contemporary politics and political science research: the partisan divide. After all, there is no "other" divide if there is no "main" divide. Therefore, in Chapter 2, we begin not with deep involvement but with affective polarization. In this chapter, we first track the evolution of affective polarization in political science research, the translation of this concept to media coverage, and its emergence as a critical political divide in America. Our goal in this chapter is to draw out the nuance inherent in political science research on affective polarization that is often missing from its translation to media coverage. Weaving together published research with new experiments, we suggest that research points to a complicated, conditional portrait of affective polarization in America. Some people are clearly polarized, but there are limitations to the power of overt polarization cues in politics (see e.g., Costa 2021). Levels of affective polarization have increased in the American electorate over time, but just how polarized America is also depends on how one measures people's feelings about the other party (Druckman et al. 2021b; Klar, Krupnikov, and Ryan 2018; Druckman and Levendusky 2019).

What emerges from Chapter 2 is that, without a doubt, there are people in America who harbor an unconditional animosity for the opposing party; there are likely more of these types of people at the time of this writing than there were two decades ago (Iyengar et al. 2019). For many people, however, most of their political animosity is directed toward partisan elites (Druckman and Levendusky 2019; Kingzette 2020) and members of the opposing party who are very vocal about their political positions (Druckman et al. 2021b). Some people seem to dislike the political opposition, but many other people seem to also dislike *politics*. Jointly, these two ideas set the stage for the remainder of the book. What if a dividing point in American politics is broader than just people's attachment to a party but is actually their attachment to *politics itself*?

We begin exploring this "other divide" in Chapter 3 through a theory of political involvement. Although we have already introduced the idea of "deep involvement" previously in this chapter, we define involvement with greater precision in Chapter 3. Relying on an interdisciplinary approach, we outline the characteristics of deep involvement: (1) spending a tremendous amount of time on a topic, (2) interpreting even mundane events as being highly important, and (3) seeking out social interactions related to politics. Although we discuss the relationships between these characteristics, we do not make a causal argument about their emergence – there is evidence suggesting that all three emerge simultaneously (Thorne and Bruner 2006), but there is also evidence suggesting that seeking out social interactions follows the emergence of the first two characteristics (Kozinets 2001). The key idea is that when someone is deeply involved, all three are present.

In the same chapter, we also discuss the implications of deep involvement for political behavior and political outcomes. We consider what deep involvement means for news habits and political discourse, and we also explore why people who are deeply involved in politics may be especially likely to harbor animosity toward the opposing party. Then, we turn to those who are not deeply involved in politics. Here, we use the psychology of self-categorization to consider what the amplified voices of the deeply involved mean for the way people perceive their own relationships with politics.

The deeply involved, we theorize in Chapter 3, are different from those who have lower levels of involvement. The four chapters that follow are devoted to analyzing just how different this group of people is from the majority of Americans. Specifically, we analyze a variety of political outcomes to track involvement divides in politics – differences between those who have a strong focus on politics and those who do not. These analyses, however, depend on a measure that allows us to determine gradations of political involvement, distinguishing those who are deeply involved from everyone else. Therefore, we begin Chapter 4 with a measure of involvement, developed based on the theoretic arguments in Chapter 3. In Chapter 4, we walk through the development and validation of our main measure, as well as the distribution of the measure across different types of samples. As we will stress in Chapter 4 (and throughout the book), the measure we develop does *not* include any items that are associated with measures of partisan strength, partisan identity, or affective polarization. Rather, it is a measure that is focused on behaviors toward *politics* rather than partisanship.

After the introduction of this measure, Chapter 4 focuses on a series of descriptive, exploratory analyses that track the relationship between involvement and traditional correlates of political behavior. First, we consider whether there are certain demographic characteristics that are more heavily associated with higher levels of involvement. Second, we turn to the relationship between involvement and affective polarization. Next, we analyze whether people who are deeply involved differ in which political issues they find most important. We conclude the chapter with a study that investigates whether there are involvement gaps in one of the most critical determinants of political behavior: political efficacy. Across these analyses, we find evidence that involvement divides the American public. Higher levels of involvement are, as anyone who has had a passing introduction to research in American politics may already suspect, associated with stronger partisanship, more ideological extremity, and greater affective polarization. In particular, while many people show animosity toward the opposing side, those who are deeply involved are unique in *their affinity for their own side*. Moreover, involvement also divides co-partisans – people who are deeply involved prioritize different political issues than those who are less involved. Finally, we find that those who are deeply involved have a much greater sense of political efficacy across a variety of indicators. People who are deeply involved are more likely to believe that they know what is best for American politics.

Building on the patterns in Chapter 4, in Chapter 5 we turn to a more challenging question: What might lead people to become deeply involved in politics? We begin Chapter 5 with a caveat, and it is a caveat we will note here as well – tracking the development of political predispositions is a difficult task. We cannot, for example, randomly assign life experiences and track their causal outcomes. Still, we rely on a foundation of research in political science and psychology to focus on one factor that scholars have long suggested is pivotal to people's political development – their socialization. Therefore, in Chapter 5, we consider how a variety of social experiences – family interactions, educational contexts, and friendship networks – relate to involvement. We find deep involvement is associated with more early-in-life political socialization; it is also more heavily associated with a very specific college experience. Turning to people's social networks, we find "involvement bubbles": People tend to associate with others who are equally as (un)involved as they are.

Jointly, Chapters 4 and 5 document involvement divides across a variety of fundamental political factors. People who are deeply involved have different relationships to partisanship and are more likely to be affectively polarized. Moreover, involvement divides people's feelings about issues *within* parties and bisects efficacy. We also see involvement gaps in people's networks and perceptions of social distance to others. People who are deeply involved, these chapters hint, are living different lives than those who are less politically involved. Chapter 6, then, turns to a more unusual context: parenting.

We consider the relationship between involvement and parenting because people's views on parenting are revealed preferences of their most fundamental values – people's thoughts about how children should spend their time speak to their beliefs about what is most important in a society (Darling and Steinberg 1993). From this perspective, parenting is an ideal test of people's beliefs about the role politics *should* play in American society. Focusing on overt political socialization, Chapter 6 relies on a series of experimental studies that manipulate parenting decisions. We find that, generally, people prefer parents who avoid politics – the participants in our studies seem uncomfortable with an explicit political socialization. The group that seems most comfortable with political parenting, however, is the deeply involved. Indeed, it is the deeply involved who are most likely to report that they would make the same decisions as the parents who introduce politics to their young children's lives. If people's beliefs about raising children are a form of revealed value preferences, then people who are deeply involved value politics much more than those who have lower levels of involvement.

The deeply involved are different. They are more confident in their political positions (Chapter 4); they have different social networks (Chapter 5); and they place a greater value on politics (Chapter 6). These differences become more important if they are exacerbated by unequal political voices. In other words, it is less important that involvement affects which issues co-partisans find important if people at all levels of involvement are equally likely to be heard by policy-makers. This, however, may not be the case. Indeed, in Chapter 3, we theorized that seeking out social interactions is a fundamental component of deep involvement; this need for social interaction, we argued, translates to greater expressiveness. This greater tendency toward expressiveness is something that, to this point in the book, we have not tested directly; we focus on expression in Chapter 7.

To address questions of political voice and expression, in Chapter 7, we modify our measure of involvement to ensure that there are no indicators within the scale that could, on their own, measure expression. Using this modified involvement measure, we rely on a series of tests to track whether people who are more involved in politics are more likely to discuss politics with others and more likely to post their positions on social media. Moving beyond relationships between involvement and expression, we next investigate what this tendency of the deeply involved to express their political positions means for people who are less involved. We find a notable tension. The deeply involved express their political positions because they believe that they are informing others about important political outcomes and events. Those who are less involved, however, see this form of political expression less charitably: They do not believe that political expression on social media is designed to inform but rather that it is designed to somehow bolster the status of the person doing the posting. Moreover, those who are less involved perceive people who post about politics on social media as more extreme but no more knowledgeable about politics. There are involvement gaps not only in people's willingness to express their political opinions on social media but also in how people perceive the political opinions they see shared.

Chapter 7 suggests a consequential outcome: The voices people are most likely to hear discussing politics are those of the deeply involved. These voices are not always perceived in the most positive manner by those who have lower levels of involvement. Chapter 8 tracks the broader implications of the involvement gaps documented in the previous chapters by exploring the possibility that the voices of the deeply involved are especially likely to be amplified by the media. Unlike previous chapters, which focus on the American public, Chapter 8 turns to a particular group of elites: political journalists. Weaving together research on journalistic practice, surveys of journalists, a content analysis, and qualitative interviews with journalists, we argue that journalists end up amplifying the deeply involved because they often focus on covering political polarization among the public. Because journalists often seek to create narratives that will be accessible and interesting to their readers, these stories are also likely to include exemplars of polarization – regular people who personify political divisions. Exacerbating these patterns is an increasing reliance on social media among journalists (see e.g., McGregor 2019) as social media over-represents the voices of the deeply involved.

We note in this introductory chapter and in Chapters 2 and 3 that the deeply involved have come to exemplify what it means to engage in politics and to be a partisan. We return to this idea in the final section of Chapter 8 through a discussion of co-authored research demonstrating that people overestimate both the extremity and the expressiveness of other Americans. In other words, people assume that most people are like the people amplified by media coverage of partisanship and polarization: strongly partisan and highly vocal about their political positions. Notably, people's *perceptions* of partisans differ starkly from the *actual* modal partisan – a moderate who rarely discusses politics. That modal partisan, however, is probably unlikely to make the news or appear in someone's social media feed sharing a (moderate) political opinion (Bode 2016).

We conclude in Chapter 9 by turning the spotlight on people who are *not* deeply involved. Not being involved, we argue, should not be confused with being apathetic and not caring about political outcomes – indeed, most of the people who voted in the 2020 election were likely not deeply involved. One should not assume deep involvement is synonymous with caring; rather, it reflects a very particular engagement with politics. We also return to the quote from Berelson, Lazarsfled, and McPhee (1954) that opened this chapter to consider what it would mean to have a public that is fully deeply involved and why the political uncertainty of the less involved may sometimes be valuable. We conclude, however, where we began: the relationship between the partisan divide and the "other" divide that is at the center of this book. Understanding growing affective polarization, we suggest, means seeing politics through the lens of involvement differences.

1.5 A WORD ABOUT THE DATA AND STATISTICAL ANALYSES

Before we begin, we want to set the stage for the data analyses that follow in the six of the remaining eight chapters. The data used in this book come in three forms. The bulk of the evidence comes from eight original studies ($N = 8{,}026$) conducted in 2019 and early 2020. In addition to these original studies, we also rely (as we did in this chapter) on archival data from studies conducted by other researchers (total $N = 115{,}855$). In addition, we also use data from four studies ($N = 10{,}105$) that we collected along with co-authors for previous projects.

Of the original studies included in this book, we want to highlight three surveys conducted on national samples, since they serve as the main studies for this project. The first survey ($N = 1{,}564$) was conducted in two waves by the survey company Dynata in April 2019. Throughout the text, we will refer to any study that was part of this large survey as being part of study "D19." The second survey ($N = 1{,}586$) was conducted in two waves by the survey company Qualtrics in the first two months of 2020. Throughout the text, we will refer to any study included as part of this survey as being part of study "Q20." The third survey ($N = 1{,}500$) was conducted in a single wave by YouGov in July 2020. Throughout the text, we will refer to any study included as part of this survey as being part of study "YG20."

In an appendix that follows at the end of the book, we have outlined which studies are part of which surveys. In that appendix, we also include information about the demographics of the respondents in these three main surveys, which includes information about how the respondents measure basic political variables (e.g., their partisanship). For greater detail on the studies, we direct you to the website we have created for this book: www.otherdividebook.com. The website has the full question wording and response options for each of the three main surveys.

The materials on the website also include the full results for the various models and statistical tests performed in this book. Throughout the book, we will primarily present the results from regression models in figures – typically, plotting the marginal effects of key variables or the predicted values of the dependent variables based on a particular set of values for the independent variables in the model. For this reason, we often do not discuss the coefficients for control variables. Therefore, we present full coefficient tables in the online appendix, organized by chapter and result.

We also want to note that many of the results in this book are descriptive; indeed, in many cases, we deliberately refer to outcomes as co-occurrences rather than using language that implies causality. Although the research we rely on to develop our theory makes a very clear causal link between involvement and animosity toward other people – we deliberately do not do so. Demonstrating causal relationships would mean manipulating levels of involvement. However, if our theoretic arguments are correct, and deep involvement is a type of intense focus on a topic that develops over time, then by definition, it would be likely impossible to manipulate involvement in an experiment. There are experiments that help demonstrate causality, but in those cases, involvement is moderating a treatment effect and is not the cause of the effect. Still, we believe that the results we demonstrate here do speak to the broader point of this book: There is a clear political divide between people who are deeply involved and those who are not.

2

Subtleties of Partisan Division

*If you write an explainer about how to argue with your straw-man family member
about impeachment over dinner, I will personally air drop a turkey on your house,
WKRP style. Very few people actually get into political arguments over
Thanksgiving!*
  Ariel Edwards-Levy, Senior Reporter and Polling Editor at the Huffington Post

In 1946, the American Political Science Association (APSA) established the
Committee on Political Parties, to be led by political scientist
E. E. Schattschneider. Four years later, this committee would produce a report
with a series of recommendations for American political parties – a report that,
in 2020 America, seems, at best, quaint. American parties, the report suggested,
needed to do more to distinguish their policy positions and do so with a greater
sense of party loyalty. Now, the parties need not go overboard: "It is here not
suggested, of course, that the parties should disagree about everything. Parties
do not, and need not, take a position on all questions that allow for
controversy" (APSA Report 1950, 20). Rather, the parties should offer what
the report termed "policy alternatives on matters likely to be of interest to the
whole country" (20).

Preemptively responding to the concern that working to distinguish party
platforms would lead to greater divisiveness, the writers of the report assured
that this would not be the case. Far from it, they suggested, clarity on party
platforms would allow for a "more reasonable discussion of public affairs"
(20). The authors of the report also turned to ideological divisions, writing:

*Nor is it to be assumed that increasing concern with their programs will cause the parties
to erect between themselves an ideological wall.* There is no real ideological division in
the American electorate, and hence programs of action presented by responsible parties
for the voter's support could hardly be expected to reflect or strive toward such division
[italics in original text] (20–21).

Decades after the completion of the report, the idea that the two parties ever needed to be reminded to differentiate themselves from each other may seem unthinkable. Yet, what is even more striking about the report is the authors' sense of optimism about parties and partisanship. In 1950, the report viewed political partisanship – both at the elite and mass levels – as a way of improving the state of American democracy.

Even at the time of the report's publication, not everyone agreed. "Much as he may desire change, the political scientist cannot invent new methods or ideas to meet specific problems without anticipating the by-products of his reforms," wrote Julius Turner in his response to the report (Turner 1951, 149). Unlike the authors of the report, Turner foresaw a coming political divisiveness. "The ideological and geographical polarization of the parties which would result if the Committee's tools are used would not necessarily lead to violent upheaval," he wrote, but added in a footnote to the sentence, "violent upheaval is nevertheless a possibility" (Turner 1951, 151, footnote 18).

At the present time, Turner's vision seems closer to the state of contemporary American political parties. Since the report's publication, American political elites have grown more and more polarized on political issues (Hetherington and Weiler 2009; Levendusky 2009). Extreme partisan fringe groups, such as the Tea Party, have further formed the shape of elite (and mass) partisan polarization (Parker and Barreto 2014). The public too has grown more divided along partisan lines (Iyengar et al. 2019). And, in January, 2021, a mob invaded the Capitol in Washington, DC, as part of a failed effort to overturn the electoral defeat of a president. Partisanship has not improved the state of American democracy (as the authors of the APSA report had hoped), but it has become a more powerful force in American politics. This partisan divide has moved beyond issue disagreement into affective polarization – Democrats and Republicans dislike each other for reasons that appear to have no root in ideology (Iyengar et al. 2019).

Although our book will focus on the involvement divide between those who focus on politics and those who do not (the "other" divide), as we argue in Chapter 1 this divide is inextricably linked to the better-known American political divide. Affective polarization within the American electorate, we suggest, co-occurs alongside the involvement divide. Therefore, in this chapter, we leave involvement aside for the moment and focus on affective polarization to set the context for what follows in the remainder of the book.

2.1 PLAN OF THE CHAPTER

As this chapter will soon make clear, there is a tremendous amount of research on the partisan divide in political science. Indeed, we began revisions on this chapter at around 10 a.m. on a Tuesday, and by 11 a.m. we had been alerted to two new working papers on partisan divisions. Moreover, the topic is of such importance that scholars in other disciplines have also increasingly begun to investigate how and why Americans have become so politically divided.

This research has focused on partisan divides among both political elites and the mass public. Both of these divides are important for American politics, but because our focus in this book is on the American public, this chapter addresses partisanship among the mass public. Even if we limit our focus to the mass public, the breadth of research investigating partisan differences is vast. There is research on differences in political beliefs (Hetherington 2001), relationships between ideology and partisanship (Jefferson 2020; Lupton, Smallpage, and Enders 2020), the social norms that reinforce partisanship (Klar 2014; White and Laird 2020), and other questions of partisan sorting (Fiorina 2016). This rich and important literature not only tracks partisan divisions, but the way these divisions relate to other dividing lines in America like race (Westwood and Peterson 2020; White and Laird 2020) and gender (Ondercin and Lizotte 2020).

In this chapter, and in this book, however, our focus is on *affective polarization* – the "tendency of people identifying as Republicans or Democrats to view opposing partisans negatively and co-partisans positively" (Iyengar and Westwood 2015, 691). Affective polarization has become especially important as it has transcended politics, bringing partisan divides into ostensibly nonpolitical contexts (Iyengar et al. 2019). We focus on affective polarization because this is the type of division that is especially likely to intersect with political involvement.

Here, we consider affective polarization in three parts. First, we establish the prominence of affective polarization in the discourse on partisanship. To this end, in Section 2.2 we consider the growing presence of research on affective polarization in political science and the translation of this research to media coverage of American politics. Second, we turn to the nuances in the research on affective polarization – nuances that are often absent in media coverage of polarization. Bringing together existing research and new studies, we show that despite growing affective polarization, many people still welcome compromise (e.g., Wolak 2020a) and are repelled by political elites who emphasize negative partisanship (e.g., Costa 2021). We also turn to a study that considers how people responded to a contentious partisan event – President Donald Trump's 2020 impeachment – and find that many people had negative views of their *own* party's elites.

Section 2.3 leads to an idea that will echo in the remainder of this chapter and the rest of the book: How do we reconcile America's growing affective polarization with more limited evidence of the phenomenon's political effects (e.g., Broockman, Kalla, and Westwood 2021)? In Section 2.4, we suggest one part of the answer lies in how we conceptualize affective polarization. Some people harbor *unconditional* animosity toward the other political side – they dislike a member of the opposing party because they belong to the opposing party; for others, however, survey responses that are interpreted as animosity actually reflect other types of feelings and beliefs (Yair 2020). Differentiating between those who are unconditionally affectively polarized and those whose political feelings are more conditional offers a clearer portrait of the scope of affective polarization in America.

Introducing conditionality to affective polarization suggests an important variation in how people feel about partisanship and politics. This variation hints at the presence of two groups: One that is divided by politics and one that is frustrated with partisan elites and perhaps politics more generally. The involvement divide is important because it intersects with these two groups.

2.2 POLARIZATION AT THE FOREFRONT

In a 2018 Public Religion Research Institute survey, 91 percent of participants agreed that the country is divided by politics; comparatively, 83 percent said that America was divided by race and ethnicity; and 77 percent agreed with a survey question that America is divided along religious lines (Najle and Jones 2019). Indeed, research shows that ordinary Americans now dislike the opposing side more than they have at any previous point in American history (Iyengar, Sood, and Lelkes 2012). This animus toward the other side is a key component of affective polarization (Iyengar et al. 2019).

The idea of affective polarization has become an important explanation of political dynamics in America. Affective polarization is now not only a foundational concept in political science research on partisanship, but it has also garnered media attention. In what follows, we establish the prominence of polarization for both researchers and journalists. For now, we track the presence of this concept; later in this chapter, we will consider the nuances in the research on affective polarization.

2.2.1 Polarization at the Forefront of Academic Research

To suggest that affective polarization has been an often-cited concept in political science research over the last decade would likely be an understatement. To date, Iyengar, Sood, and Lelkes (2012), which introduced the idea of affective polarization, has been cited 1,355 times.[1] An article by Iyengar and co-authors chronicling affective polarization research, published in the *Annual Review of Political Science* in 2019 – about a year ago as of this writing – already has 267 citations. For the sake of comparison, the average number of citations for the other articles in that same issue of *Annual Review* is eighteen.[2] In the years 2018–2020, there have been fifty-one articles using the term "affective polarization" in the *American Political Science Review*, *American Journal of Political Science*, *The Journal of Politics*, *Public Opinion Quarterly*, and *Political Behavior*. By comparison, there have been seventeen articles using the term "bipartisanship" in those journals over the same period.

---

[1] The citation count is obtained using Google Scholar in December 2020.
[2] The citation count is obtained using Google Scholar. We exclude the *Annual Review* article that is a conversation with a scholar rather than a review of the literature. Were we to include that article, the average number of citations would be 17.3.

In short, political science has turned its attention to affective divisions among the public.

2.2.2 Polarization in Media Coverage

The idea of a polarized America has also taken root in media coverage of American politics. Tracking references to polarization in American newspapers, Levendusky and Malhotra (2016) show an increase in what they term "general polarization" between 2000 and 2012. The authors find that while in 2000 and 2002 there were "only a few dozen articles" that mentioned political polarization, starting in 2004 "there were several hundred articles per year, far too many to code by hand" (Levendusky and Malhotra 2016, 284). Following a similar approach, Klar and Krupnikov (2016) also find increases in references to polarization, this time tracking the patterns through 2014.

Relying on the same methods as Levendusky and Malhotra (2016), we also consider the use of the word polarization in media coverage. In our approach, we extend the coding to the year 2016, using previous research as a basis for comparison. Unlike Levendusky and Malhotra (2016), however, we focus only on *The New York Times* (we do so following Boydstun 2013). Aside from this narrower focus, we use the same database as Levendusky and Malhotra, the same search terms, and exclude the same types of articles.[3]

Levendusky and Malhotra (2016) report that their initial set of results produces a population of 1,522 articles referencing polarization in American politics. This population of articles is across all seven years in their sample, across a wide set of American newspapers, which means that on average there were 217 stories invoking polarization per year across all American newspapers. Following the same procedures for the year 2016, however, but focusing *only* on *The New York Times* yields a population of over 250 articles that mention polarization. In other words, we see almost as many polarization references in one newspaper in 2016, as Levendusky and Malhotra (2016) see across a variety of American newspapers in earlier years. Certainly, one can argue that 2016 was an unusual year given an especially contentious and historically negative presidential campaign (Westwood, Peterson, and Lelkes 2019). Still, it is notable that the media coverage reflects the context of negativity via mentions of polarization.

Of course, not all inclusions of polarization in the news carry the same implications. After content-coding a sample of their articles, Levendusky and Malhotra (2016), for example, find increases in stories that refer to what they term as "general polarization" – or polarization across the breadth of politics rather than specific issues (see also Levendusky 2009; Klar and Krupnikov 2016). To consider the patterns in 2016, we follow Levendusky and Malhotra

---

[3] We follow the approach described in Levendusky and Malhotra (2016) and search for variants of polarization and American politics on LexisNexis.

(2016) and hand code a randomly selected sample of 100 articles.[4] We code these articles for variation in the type of polarization covered and the way that polarization was demonstrated.

We find that, first, most of the articles (71 percent) in our randomly drawn sample were not *about* polarization – rather, they mentioned polarization as part of establishing the context of American politics. An April 2016 *New York Times* article discussing then-Republican primary frontrunner Donald Trump's chances for victory in the general election, for example, noted that the "country's politics have become so sharply polarized that no major-party contender is likely to come near the 49-state defeats suffered by Democrats in 1972 and 1984" (Martin and Cohn 2016). A November 2016 article – published a day before the election – noted that if elected, then-Democratic nominee Hillary Clinton would inherit a "populace so polarized and full of loathing that it seems to be segregating. Her husband had it easy by comparison" (Mahler 2016). These mentions suggest that there is little need to explain what is meant by polarization as it is an understood state of the political context.

A plurality of the articles in our sample (46 percent) focuses only on *ideological* polarization, for example, issue divisions between the parties, with another 15 percent focusing on both affective and ideological divides.[5] Also, 41 percent consider polarization at both the elite and mass levels. Notably, however, articles that *focus* on polarization, not those that just mention this phenomenon, are more likely to consider polarization at the mass level. Moreover, nearly half of these polarization-focused articles include ordinary people as examples of polarization – a process that Levendusky and Malhotra (2016) term "exemplification"; in contrast, this only happens in 8.7 percent of articles that just mention polarization. The only references to political violence in our sample of articles are among those that focus on polarization (though, notably, these references to violence are very rare, at just 5 percent across the whole sample).

That ordinary people and mass polarization are more likely to appear in articles that *focus* on polarization is notable. While polarized elites are something that people may generally expect from American politics, "exemplars" of polarization among ordinary voters may have a greater effect on people. Research shows that exemplars are more likely to shape public opinion (Ross and Dumetrescu 2019). If, as Lippmann (1922) suggested, the news is responsible for the "pictures in our heads," then the picture of politics created by media coverage is one of clear, broad, partisan animosity. We will consider the implications of exemplification more directly in Chapter 8. Here,

---

[4] The article "population" was obtained via LexisNexis. Articles that were not about American politics were removed. Subsequently, articles were selected via a random number generator to form a sample for coding and then randomly assigned to one of two coders. Several randomly selected articles were then pulled to be coded by both coders and one of the researchers to obtain an intercoder reliability score.

[5] In 32 percent of the articles in the sample, coders could not ascertain clearly what type of polarization – affective or ideological – was being discussed.

however, our first step is to delve more deeply into the research on affective polarization and add some nuance to the partisan "pictures in our heads."

2.3 COMPLICATING THE "PICTURES IN OUR HEADS"

Tracking coverage over seven national elections, Levendusky and Malhotra (2016) conclude as follows:

> The mass media depict polarization as widespread, occurring across many issues, and accompanied by incivility and dislike of the opposition, not simply issue-based disagreement. Discussions of polarization also lament the lack of compromise and consensus in the contemporary political sphere. Finally, the media discuss polarization not via abstract statistics, but through the experiences of particular people (286).

The image that emerges in the media is supported by research in political science. The "incivility and dislike of the opposition, not simply issue-based disagreement" depicted in news stories are in line with evidence that some members of political parties do increasingly dislike each other (Iyengar and Westwood 2015; Mason 2015, 2018; Rogowski and Sutherland 2016), and that this dislike does not seem to have a parallel growing ideological polarization (Mason 2015). The "lack of compromise and consensus" is also evident in research on public responses to compromise (Harbridge, Malhotra, and Harrison 2014) and legislative strategy (Anderson, Butler, and Harbridge-Yong 2020). And, the "experience of particular people" – potentially bringing politics into nonpolitical contexts – is also something one can find evidence for in the research (Iyengar et al. 2019). Even the *New York Magazine* story "Donald Trump Is Destroying My Marriage" (Langmuir 2018) has some roots in empirical patterns: People are more likely to select partners who agree with them politically (Huber and Malhotra 2017).

Although the research on polarization has a connection to the images of political partisanship seen in the media,[6] the scholarship is, of course, much more nuanced. There is variance in how Americans feel about political parties and why they feel this way. Put another way, media coverage offers a simplified version of a complex and large research agenda. When NPR headlines a news story with "Republicans and Democrats Don't Agree, Or Like Each Other – And It's Worse Than Ever," it is a headline that can undoubtedly be supported by empirical research (Taylor 2017). On the other hand, it is also a headline that narrows a set of complicated, sometimes conflicting, findings to one statement. It is, of course, a headline's job to do just that – but when placed in the wider context of media coverage (e.g., Klar and Krupnikov 2016; Levendusky and Malhotra 2016), the type of broad statement in the NPR headline masks a nuanced body of empirical work.

---

[6] Indeed, 16 percent of the articles in our sample of polarization papers included comments from scholars – two of these articles were written by scholars.

In this section, we analyze affective polarization in three steps. First, we turn to over-time survey data to consider the two components of affective polarization: Animosity for the out-party and affinity for the in-party. Then, we turn to the foundations of affective polarization, tracking the relationship between partisan identities and issue positions. Continuing to explore the research on affective polarization, our next step is to consider its downstream political consequences. Finally, we turn to a study of partisan divides during a contentious political event – Donald Trump's 2020 impeachment. Taken together, this section will paint a more complex portrait of affective polarization. There is certainly plenty of evidence of strong animosity toward the out-party. On the other hand, there is also some evidence that people are repelled by political rhetoric that focuses on partisan affect and view the motivations of *both* parties with cynicism.

2.3.1 Levels of Affective Polarization

Affective polarization is the idea that people harbor simultaneously a deep sense of animosity for the other side and a strong affinity for their own side (Iyengar and Westwood 2015). Since affective polarization focuses on people's *feelings* toward the other side (rather than perspectives on the issue positions of the other side), the main measures used to capture affective polarization are feeling thermometers that ask people to place both parties on a scale from 0 (very cold) to 100 (very warm) (Iyengar et al. 2019). In addition to these thermometers, there are other measures that focus on social distance or perceptions of the other party that can also be used to capture affect (Klar, Krupnikov, and Ryan 2018; Druckman and Levendusky 2019; Druckman et al. 2021b). We begin with the thermometer measures, though in later sections of this chapter – and in other chapters of this book – we will return to the social distance measures.

The benefit of relying on the thermometer score is it allows us to consider affective polarization over time, as many scholars have done (e.g., Iyengar and Krupenkin 2018; Groenendyk 2019). The ANES has included feeling thermometer ratings for the Democratic and Republican parties since 1978, which means we can observe changing levels in affective polarization using each year of the survey as the comparative baseline. We use the ANES thermometers to consider two patterns: The overall pattern of affective polarization and the feelings that people have about their own party versus the feelings they have about the opposing party.

2.3.1.1 *What Are We Measuring?*

Before we turn to over-time patterns in affective polarization, we want to pause and consider measurement. Thermometer scores translate into measures of affective polarization because they allow scholars to track the difference in ratings that respondents give to one party versus the other. While the difference in their ratings reflects affective polarization, responses to the question about the out-party reflect the level of out-group animosity. Since 1978, ANES respondents have been asked to rate the "Democratic Party" and "Republican Party."[7] It is up to the respondents to give meaning to these abstract terms.

Who, exactly, the respondent imagines when they are told to rate the "[Democratic/Republican] Party," is a question with broad measurement implications (Druckman and Levendusky 2019). Is this question about Nancy Pelosi or Mitch McConnell? Is this question about someone with a yard sign? These distinctions, as Druckman and Levendusky (2019) explain, are important: "[I]f someone says Republicans are untrustworthy, is that their Republican neighbor, or is that an assessment of President Trump?" (116). In an experiment where some people were randomly assigned to rate "Democratic/ Republican Party candidates and elected officials," "Democratic/Republican Party voters," or the "Democratic/Republican Party," they find that these descriptors significantly affected rates of animosity toward the out-party. People, they show, give significantly higher ratings to party voters than to party elites, and importantly, when asked to rate the "Democratic/Republican Party," people assume they are rating elites, rather than voters.

In April 2019, Kingzette (2020) replicated these patterns with a different sample and a within-subjects design. Again, he finds significant differences in how people feel about elites and how they feel about ordinary voters, and yet again, he found that asking people to rate "the party" produced evaluations of elites rather than ordinary voters. Republicans, for example, give thermometer scores to ordinary Democrats that are 49 percent higher than the scores they give to Democratic politicians and 43 percent higher than the scores they give to the Democratic Party. As Druckman and Levendusky (2019) conclude, "part of what scholars have called affective polarization, then, is not simply dislike of the opposing party, but is dislike of the opposing party's elites" (120).

All of this is to say that the patterns we are about to present in the next section likely capture people's ratings of the *elites* of the opposing party – rather than of ordinary voters from the opposing party. To this extent, then, we are capturing levels of affective polarization as they relate to partisan elites, which is not precisely the intention in research on affective polarization (Iyengar et al. 2019). That being said, the over-time changes are, nonetheless, instructive.

2.3.1.2 *Levels of Affective Polarization*

Conceptually, affective *polarization* means rating the parties on the opposite ends of the thermometer. The first step toward tracking these patterns, then, is the absolute value of the difference in ratings given to the two parties. We take the absolute value of the difference – rather than the difference between the in-party

---

[7] Prior to 1978, the ANES asked respondents to rate "Democrats" and "Republicans." In 1980 and 1982, they asked both versions, and people rated the parties in the "Party" version a little lower on average.

and out-party – because we want to include independents in our analysis, since independents often have clear partisan preferences (Klar and Krupnikov 2016).

In Figure 2.1a we see that, as much of the research suggests, the level of affective polarization has increased starkly. The absolute difference in party ratings in 1980 was about 25, but by 2020, it had doubled to about 50; this is a sharp increase even from 2016, when this difference was 34. The pattern in Figure 2.1a is stark but leads to a related question: *Why* has this difference in ratings increased? Is it because people are lowering their evaluations of the out-party, or is it because they are raising their evaluations of the in-party? Or, is this a function of both effects?

In Figure 2.1b, we plot three sets of mean thermometer ratings. Again, we do not want to drop independents from this analysis; therefore, we do not use partisan identity to split the sample. Instead, we split respondents based on which party they rated higher on the feeling thermometer. The solid line plots the mean rating for the party that respondents favor. The dashed line plots the mean rating of the party that respondents like less. The dotted line plots the mean evaluation for respondents who give both parties the same rating.

In this panel, we see a pattern: Americans have grown to dislike one party to a much greater extent than they favor the other party. In the 1980s, the mean rating for one's less preferred party was about 42 degrees, what the ANES identifies as "a bit cold." In 2016, it was a chillier 24 degrees – well below

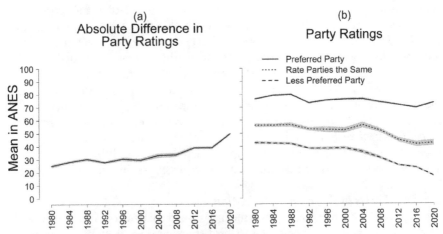

FIGURE 2.1 Changes in feeling thermometer ratings of parties among ANES respondents in presidential election years (1980–2020)
Source: Data from American National Election Study cumulative file and the 2020 preliminary release. In panel b "Preferred Party" is the party that respondents give a higher feeling thermometer rating to, and "Less Preferred Party" is the party that respondents give a lower feeling thermometer rating to. Shaded areas represent 95 percent confidence intervals.

what the ANES describes as the "fairly cold" threshold. Just four years later, in 2020, the mean out-party rating is a freezing 17 degrees.

Another declining line is the mean ratings given by people who rate the two parties the same way. What this means is that people who feel the same way about the two parties feel *worse* about both parties. Much like the other two lines, this pattern reflects a generalized sense of negativity about both political parties.[8]

Rounding out the results are mean thermometer ratings for the preferred party. Here the mean rating was almost 80 degrees in 1984 and 1988. By 2008, the rating fell to 73 degrees and went slightly lower in 2016; in 2020, the rating was again at 73 – right around what the ANES defines as the "fairly warm" threshold. This over-time decline, of course, pales in comparison to the decline in less preferred party ratings over the same time period, but the size of the decline is less important than the fact that it is a *decline* in people's ratings of their preferred party.

2.3.1.3 *Partisan Animosity*

We are certainly not the first to note that the most pronounced pattern in thermometer ratings of parties is animosity for the other side. Iyengar and Krupenkin (2018), for example, note the same pattern. An increase in out-party animosity, they note, is the most important factor of the growing affective polarization. It is animosity toward the out-party, rather than affinity toward your own party, they argue, that motivates political behavior. Druckman et al. (2021a) find some evidence for this point when studying opinion and behavior during the COVID-19 pandemic: It is animosity, not affinity that predicts political outcomes.

Identifying a similar pattern in feeling thermometers, however, Groenendyk (2018) argues that the over-time changes in thermometer scores "cannot be accounted for by affective polarization alone" (170). Rather, he suggests, the patterns reflect a "lesser of two evils" scenario: Because people have grown to like their party less, they compensate by downgrading the opposing party that much more. The result is what he terms a "surplus of partisan animosity," but not a greater attachment to one's own party. "Partisans have clearly divided against one another, but not necessarily into more cohesive teams," he writes (170).

Groenendyk's (2018) point is an important one. Some people are certainly, highly affectively polarized. They dislike the other party and they like their own party. But many people who dislike the other party do not harbor as much affinity for their own party. Certainly, they like their party better than the other party, but their feelings about their own party do not seem to reflect the type of attachment one would expect of affective polarization. To return to Lippmann's idea that politics is how we envision it, just because the "pictures in our heads" of the other party are terrible does not mean that the images of our own party are all that rosy.

---

[8] In 1980, 4.5 percent of respondents rated both parties the same way. In 2020, the percentage has increased to 12 percent.

There is another important question lurking within these patterns. Given the research on question-wording effects in partisan ratings (Druckman and Levendusky 2019), what have we actually captured in Figure 2.1? Is this figure reflecting how people feel about *anyone* associated with a particular partisan group, or is it reflecting people's views of the other party's elites? Given existing research (Druckman and Levendusky 2019; Kingzette 2020), we suspect that Figure 2.1 captures ratings of political elites. We will address this measurement confound – and how it affects perceptions of the scope of affective polarization in America – in Section 2.4.

2.3.2   The Role of Partisan Identities and Issue Positions

What differentiates research on affective polarization from research on polarization more generally is that affective polarization speaks to a more generalized animosity (Iyengar et al. 2019), a growing social, rather than ideological, distance between the two parties (Garrett and Bankert 2020).[9] As evidence of this, scholars point to the idea that increases in animosity toward the other side have been more extreme than the increases in issue polarization (Mason 2015, 2018). Although some scholars do see shifts in mass ideological positions (e.g., Abramowitz and Saunders 2008), in their review of affective polarization research to date, Iyengar et al. (2019) write, "we argue that affective polarization is largely distinct from the ideological divide, and that extremity in issue opinions is not a necessary condition for affective polarization" (130).

In short, affective polarization is separate from ideological polarization: A person can harbor animosity for the other side without holding extreme ideological positions. Importantly, however, this conceptual distinction does not mean that affective polarization must be devoid of all issue-based reasoning. There is evidence, for example, of individual-level correlations between issues and affective polarization. People whose positions are largely aligned with their own party across numerous issues, for example, are more likely to be affectively polarized (Bougher 2017). Similarly, positions on domestic issues correlate with feelings toward the other party (a measure of affective polarization) (Webster and Abramowitz 2017).

Importantly, these correlations do not suggest that issue positions, rather than identity, are the primary determinant of affective polarization. Clarifying the relationship between issues, partisan identity, and affect comes with notable empirical challenges. It is difficult to randomly assign levels of either affective polarization, issue positions, or partisan identity (Druckman et al. 2021a, West and Iyengar 2020, though see Broockman, Kalla, and Westwood 2021). As

---

[9] Mason (2015) writes that affective polarization is a subset of a concept she defines as "social polarization," differentiating affective and social polarization via the inclusion of behavior. The two concepts, however, speak to the same type of political division in the American public (Garrett and Bankert 2020). Therefore, we rely on the term *affective polarization*.

a result, it is difficult to measure the causal effects of changes in these individual characteristics. When we observe relationships between partisan identity, issue positions, and affective polarization, then, we cannot be certain which of these factors is the originating (or even the primary) driving force (Bougher 2017; Druckman et al. 2021a).

The inability to randomly assign central factors is a key limitation in determining *why* people are affectively polarized. Evidence may point to the idea that identity can influence affective polarization but that does not mean that attachment to one partisan group over another is the originating source of the animosity (Orr and Huber 2020). Rather,

The finding that individuals report liking a hypothetical member of their own political party more than an out-party member could originate in several sources. Moreover, over-time changes in measured partisan animosity could originate in multiple sources beyond partisanship per se, such as changes in the nonpartisan inferences one makes on the basis of partisanship (e.g., increasingly believing Republicans are conservative) or changes in the importance of these inferences (e.g., increasingly disliking conservatives) (Orr and Huber 2020, 571).

Relying on an experiment that randomly assigns the types of cues that people receive about a hypothetical person, Orr and Huber (2020) consider the effect of partisan cues versus cues about policy positions. Although, as one may expect, partisan cues do have a significant effect on individual judgment, the effect drops significantly when policy information is introduced. Moreover, they also find that the effect of sharing a policy position is larger than the effect of partisanship on how participants feel about this hypothetical person in the treatment. "In a horse race between partisanship and policy," Orr and Huber write, "policy appears to dominate, calling into question the argument that partisanship as a group orientation dominates policy positions as an explanation for partisan animosity" (579).

Orr and Huber's (2020) study, we note, is not an outlier. Rogowski and Sutherland (2016), for example, show that ideological differences between candidates increase affective polarization. Boudreau and MacKenzie (2014) find that policy information can overwhelm partisan cues, suggesting that people are responsive to policy positions rather than relying solely on party. Yet, revisiting the Orr and Huber (2020) finding, Dias and Lelkes (2021) suggest that understanding affective polarization is more complicated than party or policy. Rather, Dias and Lelkes argue that both partisan identities and policy positions are pivotal – though policy positions are pivotal in large part because they signal partisan identities.

Jointly, Orr and Huber (2020) and Dias and Lelkes (2021) complicate the relationship between partisan identities, issues, and affective polarization. Partisan identities certainly matter, but policy positions *also* matter; though the effect of policy is more limited than that of partisanship, it is still present (Dias and Lelkes 2021). We can extrapolate these results to a still broader point. The possibility that policy positions matter because they signal partisan identities (as Dias and Lelkes [2021] conclude) suggests that policy disagreement increases affective polarization because in the "pictures in our heads" (Lippmann 1922) extreme positions and vocal partisans are often linked.

2.3.3 Downstream Effects of Affective Polarization for Evaluations of Elites

It is not a stretch to expect that an electorate that harbors deep animosity toward the opposing party should affect the very process of governance. If people are guided by affect – rather than ideological predispositions – then the way they evaluate their representatives may also be a function of nonpolicy factors. "When citizens' support for a candidate stems primarily from their strong dislike for the opposing candidate," write Iyengar and Krupenkin (2018), "they are less subject to the logic of accountability" (212). The outcome, they suggest, is politicians who have an incentive to "inflame partisan negativity, further entrenching affective polarization" (212).

There are several implications of the argument Iyengar and Krupnekin (2018) make. The first, foreshadowed by Levendusky and Malhotra's (2016) study of media coverage, is that affective polarization could lead to a declining preference for compromise and bipartisanship (Wolak 2020a). If partisan affect governs most political preferences, and if affect toward the other side is largely negative, Wolak (2020a) explains, then compromising may seem like giving up. Comments from members of Congress reflect this concern. "There's so much pressure on [members of Congress] from the outside to be partisan and to fight, not do the things that we're supposed to, such as compromising and working together," Representative John Dingell noted in a 2013 interview (Wolak 2020a, 3). The connection between compromise and affective polarization is intuitive. If people harbor deep animosity toward the other side and if we assume that this animosity is driven largely by partisan identities, then compromising with the opposing party may seem untenable. Indeed, there is reason to believe that some people do view their party's decision to engage in compromise as giving up (Hibbing and Theiss-Morse 2002).

It may be surprising, then, that, in this age of unprecedently high affective polarization, Wolak (2020a) finds that Americans are not averse to compromise. Far from it, she argues, support for compromise is a value that is "outside" of partisan politics. Using data from the 2016 ANES, Wolak finds that affective polarization does not shape beliefs about compromise. Rather, the main result in Wolak's analysis is tied to *ideology*: Moderates are much more likely to prefer compromise relative to people who hold strong ideological positions.

Other research reinforces Wolak's finding. In an experiment that manipulates affective polarization to track its causal effects, Broockman, Kalla, and Westwood (2021) find that increasing affective polarization does not lead people to oppose bipartisanship among members of Congress. In other words, higher levels of affective polarization do not lead to a desire for more overtly partisan behavior. Even more importantly, using data collected around the same time as the 2020 ANES, Broockman, Kalla, and Westwood (2021) demonstrate that increases in affective polarization do not seem to affect support for various democratic norms. Notably, Broockman, Kalla, and Westwood (2021) clearly capture affective polarization as animosity toward ordinary voters from the opposing party, rather than toward elites – which may what the ANES data is capturing at least in part.

It is possible, of course, that people may reject breaks in democratic norms in the abstract but be more supportive of rhetoric that promises them a politician who will, as Representative Dingell noted, "be partisan and to fight" for them. In a series of studies conducted in 2018 and 2019, Costa (2021) considers this possibility by varying whether legislator statements focus on pure partisanship (e.g., either criticizing the opposing party or supporting one's own party) or focus on policy. Costa (2021) consistently finds that it is policy that matters. In fact, she shows that people reacted negatively to partisan criticisms (e.g., "I am disgusted at today's [Democrats/Republicans]. They are dishonest, dangerous, and bad for America" (Costa 2021, 9)), even when those statements came from politicians of their own party. And, in another striking result, she finds that statements like "We should do everything it takes to make sure [Democrats/Republicans] lose the next election" do not have any statistical significance on people's evaluations of legislators.

Costa concludes that "concerns about affective polarization, in terms of what it means for perceptions of representation, may be overblown" (2). This is not to argue, as Costa notes, that politicians do not behave in the very ways that lead to negative responses in her experimental studies. Yet, the fact that politicians behave in a certain way is not, in and of itself, evidence that this behavior is effective. Costa's research suggests that people may be voting for candidates in spite of their rhetoric – not because of it. As she notes, a fruitful question may be *why* politicians continue to believe that purely partisan rhetoric will remain effective.

The reason the type of rhetoric Costa considers in her study may *seem* effective during a campaign is that in a two-party system, people may view their options through a "lesser of two evils" perspective and may feel like they have no choice but to cast a vote for the candidate who seems "less bad" (Groenendyk 2013). In the absence of the types of ideological cues that Costa includes in her study, perhaps her participants would have supported candidates whose rhetoric they dislike. The same may be the case in surveys that ask people broad questions about partisan political events. The most likely outcome is that people express support for the elites of their own party, but this does not necessarily mean that they especially like what the elites are doing. This is not to suggest that people who support party elites who make harmful choices are secretly politically virtuous, but rather that in some cases, what is interpreted as active partisan approval is actually passive acceptance.

Building on this idea, we consider the perceptions of the opposing party in the context of a contentious political event: President Donald Trump's 2020 impeachment. Our goal is not to make an argument either about the role of ideology or about people's willingness to hold the elites of their own party responsible for political outcomes. We also do not make an argument about the extent to which these patterns co-occur with affective polarization. Rather, our goal is to build on research that considers how people evaluate overtly negative affective cues from elites (e.g. Costa 2021) and explore whether responses that may initially suggest unwavering partisan support hide some ambivalence and cynicism about the behaviors of partisan elites.

2.3.4 Evaluating Elites: Trump's 2020 Impeachment

Research on affective polarization suggests a series of seemingly conflicting patterns. Animosity toward the other party has increased sharply, but affinity for one's own party has not grown stronger. Some people have strong partisan identities, but others do not perceive their partisanship to be as important as their other identities. Partisan identities do drive affective polarization, but policy may also matter. Affective polarization is at a historic high, but people still value compromise and do not like political rhetoric that preys on partisan affect. In this section, we consider how these different dynamics may intersect during a contentious, partisan political event through a study focusing on President Donald Trump's 2020 impeachment trial.

Trump was impeached on two accounts following a whistleblower report in the summer of 2019 that he withheld military aid from Ukraine in exchange for help in his 2020 reelection (Fandos 2020). The impeachment and eventual acquittal were, as one may expect, heavily partisan. On December 18, 2019, when the House of Representatives took a formal vote on both of the Articles of Impeachment, 229 House Democrats (98.2 percent of all elected Democratic House members) voted in favor of the first article and 228 Democrats (97.8 percent of all elected members) voted in favor of the second article.[10] On the Republican side, 97.4 percent of the members voted against the resolution, and none voted in support.[11]

After a trial in the Senate, Trump's ultimate fate was decided by a similarly partisan split. All forty-five Democratic senators voted that Trump was "guilty" on both Articles of Impeachment. One Republican senator – Mitt Romney – voted "guilty" on Article 1, Abuse of Power, but "not guilty" on Article 2, Obstruction of Congress.[12] The remaining fifty-two Republican senators voted

---

[10] Those who voted against either of the two articles were Collin Peterson, Jeff Van Drew, and Jared Golden. Peterson was a representative from a largely conservative Minnesota district. Voting against the impeachment did not seem to help Peterson in 2020 when he lost the seat to a Republican. Van Drew switched parties following the vote and won reelection that fall. Golden won reelection in his district in Maine. One Democratic House member voted present, and another did not vote.

[11] Five Republican House members did not vote.

[12] Romney's vote to remove a sitting president of his own party was the first time this had happened in an impeachment trial. We will return to partisans' complicated relationship with Romney in

"not guilty" on both of the two articles. In the end, these partisan splits suggest a simple story: Trump was impeached because the House had a Democratic majority, but he was acquitted because the Senate was held by Republicans.

Just as members of Congress fell along partisan lines when it came to impeachment, so did the American electorate. In a YouGov/Huffington Post survey of 1,000 Americans conducted just days before the final vote in the Senate (January 31–February 2, 2020), 82 percent of Democrats believed that Trump should be removed from office, while 85 percent of Republicans believed that he should not be removed from office. The independents, who formed a plurality of the sample, were more evenly split: 35 percent believed that Trump should be removed from office, 39 percent believed that he should not be removed from office, and 26 percent were unsure.

Although public opinion patterns may show a clear partisan story, the issue with public opinion on matters such as Trump's impeachment is that we only observe the public's desired votes on the outcome of the case. These binary choices, however, may not reflect people's reasons for their ultimate decisions. Put another way, when Republicans report that Trump should not be removed from office, they may genuinely believe that Trump is not guilty. On the other hand, they may also believe that Trump is guilty of the acts of which he is accused but that these acts do not warrant removal from office. On the Democratic side, voters may believe that Trump is guilty and should be removed from office. Some, however, may believe that the specific crimes in question do not constitute removal but that Trump has surely committed other crimes that are *certainly* worthy of removal.

Furthermore, people's responses to questions about the impeachment may also be driven by a general dissatisfaction with politics. Republicans may believe that Trump is guilty and that Trump's actions do warrant removal, but that the Democratic Congress members who support removal from office would not make the same case if the president was a Democrat. Democrats may believe that Trump's actions do not necessarily warrant removal but that Republican leaders would work to remove a Democratic president for lesser transgressions.

Put another way, people's opinions on impeachment may reflect a deeply divided electorate and two different political realities. Indeed, this is likely the case for a certain portion of the electorate. But binary choices in questions about impeachment may also reflect a more passive acceptance of elite behavior: Americans who are choosing sides not because they fully trust their elites but rather because of the cynicism with which they view elites in both parties.

We consider the role of partisanship in people's opinions on impeachment through a study fielded during the Senate impeachment trial in January 2020 (study Q20). In this study, we first asked participants whether they believed that Trump should be removed from office. Among Democrats, 83 percent thought

---

Chapter 4. One year and eight days later, during Trump's second impeachment trial, six other Republicans joined Romney in finding Trump guilty this time of an inciting insurrection.

that Trump should be removed, and another 10 percent were not sure. On the Republican side, 81 percent thought that Trump should not be removed, and another 5 percent were not sure. This is in line with the YouGov data cited previously, which suggests that our sample is not unusual with respect to the ultimate question of removal.

What differentiates our study from the many polls measuring people's positions on impeachment, however, is that we asked four follow-up questions. The first two questions were designed to challenge Republicans by focusing on the behavior of Republicans in Congress; the second set focused on Democrats. In each of these questions, participants were asked if they agreed or disagreed with a statement about the impeachment. The statements were as follows:

Statement 1: *Republicans would vote to impeach a Democratic president who did the same things President Trump has done.* The Republican elites' position on impeachment was that it was unreasonable (Cornwell, Morgan, and Cowen 2020), therefore, the partisan response to this statement for Republican study participants would be to disagree with this statement.

Statement 2: *Republican senators who will not vote to remove President Trump from office love their political party more than their country.* As this statement suggests that the impeachment/removal votes are a function of partisanship – rather than the goal of best representing Americans – the partisan response to this statement is for Republican study participants to disagree.

Statement 3: *The main reason Democrats impeached President Trump is that they hate him and his policies.* Democratic elites' position on impeachment was that it was due to Trump's actions with regard to Ukraine and resulting threats to national security, rather than any of his particular policy positions (MacKinnon and Gramer 2019). The partisan response for Democratic participants in this case, then, would be to disagree with the statement.

Statement 4: *Democrats were looking for reasons to impeach President Trump even before he officially took office.* The Democratic position was that Trump's actions with regard to Ukraine gave the Democrats, as House Speaker Nancy Pelosi said, "no choice" but to proceed with impeachment (MacKinnon and Gramer 2019). Therefore, the partisan response to this statement for Democratic participants is to disagree.

In considering the partisan patterns in the responses to these statements, we focus on the proportion of the survey participants who *disagree* – either strongly or somewhat – as it is disagreement that indicates a response in line with the elite, partisan position. We note, however, that our measure also included a "neither agree nor disagree" option, meaning that the proportion of participants who did not fall in to the "disagree" category did not necessarily agree with the statement. There is some reason to believe that people who select the "neither agree nor disagree" category may also be avoiding a party-line response or, potentially, obfuscating their position in some way (Berinsky 2004). Still, the result that allows us the most clarity on partisan responding without making assumptions about why people may have selected a certain option is the proportion of people who disagree.

We first turn to Statements 1 and 2 (at the top of Figure 2.2), which focused on the positions of Republican elites. When we asked participants if they agreed that Republican members of Congress would vote to impeach a Democratic President who did the same thing Trump had done, we see that only 6 percent of Democrats disagreed with that statement – it is, of course, not surprising that few Democrats do not believe that if roles were reversed Republicans would forego impeachment. More surprising, however, are the patterns among Republicans: Only 51 percent of Republicans disagreed, meaning only half of the Republicans in our sample followed the elite party position on this aspect of impeachment.

Statement 2 focused on whether Republican senators who would vote to acquit the President love their party more than their country. Again, 7 percent of Democrats disagreed with that statement – an expected result. Meanwhile, again half of Republicans disagreed, meaning that only half were willing to respond in the way Republican Party elites would have likely responded. In total, only 37 percent of Republicans disagreed with *both* of those statements. That is, the majority of Republicans were unwilling to say that their party was acting purely out of principle, rather than out of partisanship.

Our second set of statements (bottom bars of Figure 2.2) was designed to put the Democrats on the spot by focusing on Democratic members of Congress. In Statement 3, participants were asked if they agreed that Democrats pursued impeachment because they do not like Trump. Among Republicans, 11 percent disagreed with the statement – a small minority – which was, again, not a surprise. Yet, only 56 percent of Democrats followed

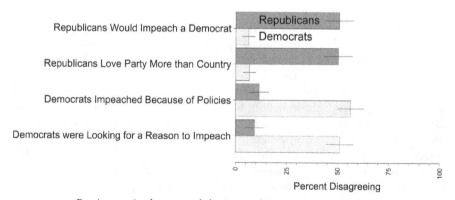

FIGURE 2.2 Partisan attitudes toward the impeachment process in 2020
Source: Data from Q20. Error bars represent 95 percent confidence intervals.

the position of Democratic Party elites and disagreed with the statement. This, of course, is the majority of Democratic participants, but this proportion was not nearly as high as the 83 percent who thought the President should be removed.

Finally, in Statement 4, participants were asked if they agreed that Democrats were looking for reasons to impeach President Trump even before he officially took office. Here, 9 percent of Republicans disagreed with the statement, again a response in line with partisan predispositions. At the same time, only 51 percent of Democrats followed party elites and disagreed. In total, 57 percent of Democrats failed to disagree with at least one of those two statements – meaning that more than half of our Democratic participants seemed to have some skepticism about the actions of their party elites.

Of course, the answers to these questions may hide some more complicated motivations. At the same time, the patterns here are somewhat unexpected in a political context that appears not only partisan but also affectively polarized. Despite the fact that over half of survey participants fell into their partisan camps on the ultimate question about Trump's removal, asking follow-up questions suggests that many were cynical about the motivations of their *own party*. When asked questions that focused on their party's motivations, they expressed skepticism. These results suggest that some of the partisan answers on the ultimate question of removal had more to do with beliefs about out-party actions than actual belief in the in-party's position. Some people will support their party – or their candidate – no matter what. But others may have more doubts about the motivations of their own party.

2.3.5 The Scope of Animosity

Research leaves little doubt that some people are affectively polarized. At the same time, however, scholarship also suggests important nuance to these levels of affective polarization. It is this nuance that may be most likely to be lost as political science research is translated to media coverage. The headline "Republicans and Democrats Don't Agree, Or Like Each Other – And It's Worse Than Ever" is, without a doubt, true and accurate, but more interesting is the broad base of research that complicates the role of affective polarization in American politics.

Our goal in these sections, then, was to take stock of the shape and implications of this phenomenon for American politics. First, over time, affective polarization has clearly, sharply increased – but this is due to animosity toward the opposing party. These patterns, however, are complicated by questions of measurement; the thermometer scores that track these over-time changes may be reflecting people's feelings about elites, rather than ordinary voters (Druckman and Levendusky 2019). Moreover, although animosity has increased, many people still feel relatively lukewarm toward *both* parties; shifts in animosity do not necessarily produce more unified, partisan groups (Groenendyk 2018; Groenendyk, Sances, and Zhirkov 2020).

Although the core of affective polarization is a focus on nonideological factors, there is research to suggest that issue positions do factor into the equation. Some people dislike the opposing side largely as a function of identity; others dislike the other side for the issue positions they hold (Orr and Huber 2020) – or at least because of some interaction between policy and party (Dias and Lelkes 2021). Moreover, although the implications of a growing animosity toward the other side would imply that people should be most supportive of politicians who invoke negative partisanship, people seem to prefer political candidates who focus on issues (Costa 2021). Some partisans may support their party no matter what, but others – as our impeachment study suggests – are cynical about the political elites who, ostensibly, represent them. It is clear that there is affective polarization in America, but the research on this phenomenon is more complicated, nuanced, and sometimes surprising than the headlines may suggest.

2.4 ALL THE POLARIZED PEOPLE

The results in Figure 2.1 should not have surprised anyone who follows American politics. Other research we discussed in this chapter on the other hand, may be more unexpected. It may surprise people that many Americans value compromise (Wolak 2020a) and dislike appeals to negative partisanship (Costa 2021). Equally, if not more, unexpected, is the idea that affective polarization does not have broad political consequences (Broockman, Kalla, and Westwood 2021). It may also be surprising to see, as we do in the impeachment study, that many people question the motivations of their own political elites. Especially unexpected, however, may be the conclusion in a study by Groenendyk, Sances, and Zhirkov (2020): The modal partisan is actually not all that polarized. Reconciling the results in Figure 2.1 and the other patterns in this chapter may suggest that people's affective ratings of parties in surveys may not always speak to their other, potentially more important, political beliefs.

Of course, for some people survey ratings of parties may be directly reflective of political outcomes. Some people may give very low ratings to the out-party, very high ratings to the in-party, dislike compromise (when it comes at a cost to their party), prefer politicians who rely on rhetoric that uses negative partisanship, and engage in antidemocratic behaviors (Broockman, Kalla, and Westwood 2021). In fact, as Druckman et al. (2021a) find, there are some people who harbor so much animosity toward the other party that their behaviors *during a pandemic* reflected partisan cues. There are, however, other people who – as the research we describe suggests – may report animosity toward the opposing party on surveys, but for whom this animosity is less reflective of broader political behaviors (Broockman, Kalla, and

Westwood 2021). Key to distinguishing between these different types of people, however, is an idea that we have already addressed (albeit briefly) in this chapter: Measurement.

2.4.1 A Dislike of Party, a Dislike of Elites, or a Dislike of Partisanship

In Figure 2.1, we show several important patterns for American affective polarization. First, polarization, when measured as the difference in partisan thermometer ratings, has been steadily increasing since 1980. Second, key to this increase in polarization is animosity toward the opposing party, *not* affinity for one's preferred party. In theory, affective polarization is the component of both of these evaluations – animosity and affinity; in practice, however, scholarship has often focused on the animosity component alone as it seems to be more important (Iyengar and Krupenkin 2018).

Before presenting the thermometer scores in Figure 2.1, however, we highlighted an important measurement issue: Because the measure asks about the party generally, it is likely that these thermometer ratings capture people's feelings about party elites, rather than ordinary voters (Druckman and Levendusky 2019). Although both of these types of ratings speak to someone's feelings about the parties, disliking elites is not the same as disliking ordinary partisans. A dislike of elites may, as Druckman and Levendusky (2019) note, reflect unhappiness with the political system or even concerns about representation (see Fiorina 2017). Affective polarization, for example, correlates with lower trust in government (Hetherington and Rudolph 2015) – which may reflect that this measure often captures feelings about elites (Druckman and Levendusky 2019). A dislike of rank-and-file members of the opposing party, however, may suggest a deeper dissatisfaction with the opposing side and a stronger role of partisan identity.

Even a measure that is more explicit about who the partisan label is referencing – for example, "[Democratic/Republican] voters" – still suffers from potential confounds. In this question, the respondent again has to make many inferences about this hypothetical voter. Consider, for example, a social distance measure of affective polarization: How happy or unhappy would you be if your child married a [Democrat/Republican]? Since the question only mentions this hypothetical in-law's partisanship, some respondents may infer that partisanship is an important identity for that person. This type of inference may bring with it judgments about the voter's political positions and, potentially, the frequency with which they will discuss politics. If people are unhappy about a future in-law from the opposing party, then, is it because they dislike that party – or because they worry that they will have to suffer through that person's political discussions at family dinners? Of course, many studies suffer from potentially undetected confounds (Dafoe, Zhang, and Caughey 2018), but in the case of affective polarization measures, these confounds could lead to an over estimation of the relative rates of affective polarization.

If ratings of parties depend on whether people believe they are rating elites or ordinary partisans, they may also depend on the *types* of ordinary partisans that people imagine. In turn, accounting for who people imagine they are rating offers a better portrait of affective polarization in America. It is one thing to harbor animosity toward the elites of the opposing party, but it is another to dislike ordinary people who belong to a different party but may not actually care about politics all that much.

We consider this possibility in a study conducted with Jamie Druckman, Samara Klar, and Matthew Levendusky (2021b). In this study, we analyze what happens when we offer survey respondents more information about the behaviors and ideology of the partisan that they are rating. Respondents were randomly assigned to one of twelve conditions in a two-factor experiment with a 4 × 3 design. The first factor was the frequency of discussion, and the respondent was randomly assigned to rate partisans who (1) rarely, (2) occasionally, or (3) frequently talked about politics; those assigned to (4) the control received no information about discussion frequency. The second factor focused on ideology: Here, the respondent was randomly assigned to rate either (1) moderate Democrats and moderate Republicans or (2) liberal Democrats and conservative Republicans; those randomly assigned to (3) the control again received no ideological information. Across all conditions, we repeatedly specified that the respondents were rating ordinary partisans – *not* political elites.

These conditions reflect different types of partisans. Someone who frequently talks about politics and is an ideologue is likely to be a more active, vocal partisan. Someone who doesn't talk about politics all that frequently and is more moderate, however, is likely less invested in politics. Our study captures, then, who people are evaluating when they answer questions designed to measure affective polarization.

Our study was conducted in 2019 in three waves. In the first wave, our participants ($N = 5,191$) answered a series of questions about their political attitudes; in our second wave, the same participants ($N = 4,076$) were randomly assigned to one of the partisan rating conditions described earlier. In our third wave ($N = 4,048$), participants answered an additional set of questions about their ideological positions. Our participants – who were a nationally representative sample – rated the parties on thirteen different measures, which included thermometers, social distance measures, and traits. The social distance measures asked participants how they would feel about their child marrying someone from the other party and also asked about friends and neighbors. In the traits battery, participants were asked questions such as "How well does 'patriotic' describe [target group]?" We rely on these different measures because we want to ensure that our patterns are not unique to one particular way of capturing affective polarization. Across all the measures, participants saw the same type of partisan. If someone was randomly assigned to a moderate partisan who rarely discusses politics, this is the type of partisan they rated in every measure. We combined all the measures into one 0 to 1 scale, which produced measures for the out-party and the in-party ($\alpha = 0.88$ for the out-party and $\alpha = 0.87$ for the in-party). Details are available in Online Appendix V4.

In our previous work with this data (Druckman et al. 2021b), we have focused on the out-party animus measure alone, finding that changes in the descriptions of partisans had a significant effect on out-party animosity. In this section, however, we will use both the in-party and out-party measures, which allows us to look more directly at affective polarization. We do, however, follow Druckman et al. (2021b) and eliminate pure independents from this analysis, as the main goal is not to look for population levels but to consider treatment effects.

To capture polarization with our index, we use four different thresholds. In Figure 2.3a, respondents are polarized if their in-party score is greater than or equal to 0.9 and their out-party score is less than or equal to 0.1. From there, we lower the in-party threshold by 0.1 and raise the out-party threshold by 0.1 until the in-party threshold is 0.6 and the out-party threshold is 0.4 in Figure 2.3d. In each panel of Figure 2.3, we plot the expected proportion of respondents who are polarized in each of the "frequency of discussion" treatments. Here we do not include the ideology treatment for the ease of presentation, but, as we report in Druckman et al. (2021b), the ideology treatment had substantively small effects compared to the effects of the frequency of discussion treatment.[13]

In every panel in Figure 2.3, we see a similar pattern. Regardless of the polarization threshold, the "rarely talks about politics" treatment has the lowest proportion of respondents who are polarized. Also, regardless of polarization threshold, the "frequently talks about politics" treatment is statistically indistinguishable from the control group. What this suggests is that when people answer questions that ask them to consider how they feel about someone from the opposing party without any additional context, people answer these questions while imagining someone who frequently discusses politics.

Although our analyses focus on the index measure of affective polarization, we can consider the thermometer scales alone as a comparison to the results in Figure 2.1. Figure 2.1 relied on the ANES thermometer, which likely captured feelings toward elites; in the 2020 ANES, the absolute difference in ratings between the two parties was 50 degrees, signaling a high level of affective polarization. In the control group of our study, which specified that people were rating ordinary voters but gave no other information about these voters, the absolute difference on the thermometer scale is 40. Although it is lower than the 2020 result in Figure 2.1, it is still markedly high; the slightly lower rating is also in line with the types of shifts Druckman and Levendusky (2019) find when they shift between ratings of elites and ordinary voters – which is the case here as well.

---

[13] We calculated these proportions using logit models where we controlled for the ideology treatment and nothing else (see Online Appendix M2.1).

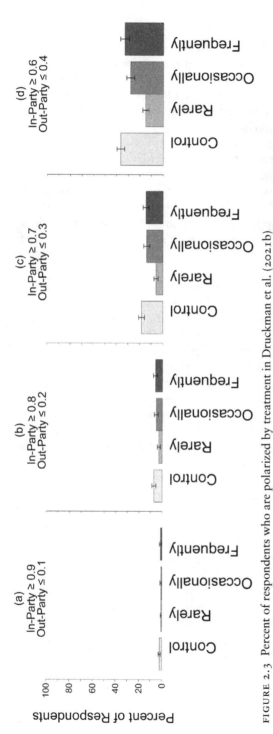

FIGURE 2.3 Percent of respondents who are polarized by treatment in Druckman et al. (2021b)

Source: Data from Druckman et al. (2021b). Error bars represent 95 percent confidence intervals. Predicted percentages are based on models available in Online Appendix M.2.1.

When we specify, however, that the opposing partisan will rarely discuss politics, the absolute difference between thermometer ratings drops to 11 degrees. In fact, even when people are told that the partisan will occasionally talk about politics, the difference in ratings is 21 degrees – nearly half as low as the 40-degree difference in the control condition. Once people are told that this is an ordinary partisan who is not focused on being vocal about politics, we see much lower levels of affective polarization.

The patterns we find are similar to those we found in our previous work with Klar (Klar, Krupnikov, and Ryan 2018). There, we focused only on one measure of affective polarization – the question about a child's marriage – but again randomized whether participants were told that the child-in-law would talk rarely or frequently about politics. We find that most respondents do not care what party their child-in-law supports. It does not make them happy if the child-in-law supports the same party as the respondent, and it does not make them unhappy if the child-in-law supports the other party. Second, relative to both, a control condition without any additional description and a condition in which the child-in-law was described as frequently discussing politics, people felt happier about the child-in-law in the "rarely talks about politics" condition. In contrast, they become less happy about their potential child-in-law when they were described as someone who "frequently talks about politics." Notably, people rated both out-partisans *and* in-partisans lower when they were described as people who frequently talk about politics.

We do not take these shifts in feelings about parties due to measurement as evidence that people are not affectively polarized – some people *certainly* are. Indeed, even when these people are told that another person will never speak to them about politics, some people still do not want to have anything to do with this person; they are *unconditionally* polarized. But this is not uniformly the case. When given an abstract entity to rate – "The Democratic/Republican Party" – people may assume that they are rating elites. The patterns in Figure 2.1 may reflect declining support for out-party elites, as much as they reflect affective polarization. Even when measures specify the ratings of ordinary voters, if partisanship is the only descriptor, people believe that the party is the most important characteristic of a person (or people) they are evaluating. As a result, the negative evaluations of the opposing party may be a function of the perceived intrusion of politics. If one is going to be around someone who frequently talks about politics, then it is much preferable when that person is from the same political side (Settle and Carlson 2019).

More broadly, then, the inferences people make about who they are rating in measures of affective polarization affect the extent to which America appears polarized. We conclude as follows in Druckman et al. (2021b):

What is the scope of affective polarization in America? We argue that when people are asked to evaluate the other party, they draw on stereotypes and bring to mind an unrepresentative member of it: An ideologue who is extremely engaged in politics. As a result, they express considerable animus toward the other party. But when asked to evaluate someone who actually looks like the modal member of the other party – someone more moderate, who is largely indifferent to politics – animus falls markedly. Americans dislike the ideologues from the other party who appear on television and those that they see on social media, but they are more indifferent than hateful of the modal member of the other party (22).

How people imagine the other side, then, is critical to understanding the scope of affective polarization in American politics. In Druckman et al. (2021b), we focus on specifying frequency of discussion and ideology of the partisan. Yair (2020) suggests another important measurement issue: "In a media environment that regularly depicts partisan polarization and fights between ever-warring political rivals," he writes, "it is perhaps not unreasonable for partisans to be wary of outpartisans even if they harbor no animosity toward the opposition" (7–8). There is evidence for Yair's argument; in a series of studies, Moore-Berg et al. (2020) find that partisans commonly "dramatically overestimate" how much members of the other dehumanize them (14870). In Chapter 8, we will show a similar overestimation on measures of ideological extremity and frequency of political discussion.

These types of arguments bring us back to Lippmann's (1922) idea of "pictures in our heads." Measures of affective polarization capture how people imagine partisans; whether they then reflect animosity toward a certain partisan, or as Yair (2020) suggests, wariness, the fact that remains that the imagined partisan can change the measured level of polarization. We can adjust measures of affective polarization – indeed, this is what we will do in certain chapters of this book – but perhaps a more important investigation should explore why people imagine a partisan as an "ideologue who is extremely engaged in politics" (Druckman et al. 2021b). Although much of the book hints at the answer to this question, we will turn to it most directly in Chapters 7 and 8.

2.5 THE NATURE OF AFFECTIVE POLARIZATION

Research on affective polarization in American politics leads to three, seemingly contradictory, conclusions. The first conclusion is, simply, affective polarization in American politics has dramatically increased over time (Figure 2.1). Although scholars have argued that this dislike for the opposing side often appears to be driven by highly salient partisan identities, there is evidence to suggest that ideological predispositions may also be at least somewhat at the root of certain divides (e.g. Orr and Huber 2020).

The second conclusion, however, is that the translation of affective polarization into downstream political consequences is more complicated than one may initially assume (Broockman, Kalla, and Westwood 2021). Groenendyk, Sances, and Zhirkov (2020), for example, argue that those who are affectively polarized increase the spread of the distribution of attitudes toward parties, but they are not the modal partisans (Groenendyk, Sances, and Zhirkov 2020). The modal partisan is more ambivalent toward both parties, which may also explain why appealing to negative partisanship is a less effective political strategy when compared to issue appeals (Costa 2021).

The third conclusion is that when people are asked to think about partisans, they are most likely to think of the most ideological and engaged partisans. People's dislike for the opposing party is driven by a focus on the partisans who *frequently* discuss politics (Druckman et al. 2021b; Klar, Krupnikov, and Ryan 2018). What people dislike, then, is not simply the opposing party but behavior that brings partisanship and politics to the forefront of their lives. Although previous research suggested that independents especially dislike the discord that comes with politics (Klar and Krupnikov 2016), there is now evidence that some partisans may also dislike politics.

These three conclusions lead to two possibilities, both of which we have hinted at throughout this chapter. The first possibility is that there are two groups of people – and that these groups cut across party lines. What separates these two groups may not be the *type* of partisan identification (e.g. Democrat or Republican) but the *salience* of that identification. We can translate this to a broader idea: Perhaps what separates the two groups of people is the importance they place on politics – that is, their level of political involvement. For one group of people, the deeply involved, politics holds an important place in their lives. The importance they place on politics is also intertwined with the salience of their partisan identities and their high levels of affective polarization. These people are *unconditionally* polarized: Even if they are told that the member of the opposing party will never discuss politics with them or that this person is not all that politically extreme and harbors no ill-will toward them (e.g. Moore-Berg et al. 2020), they will report an intense animosity for that person. But more than just animosity, this group may also have an affinity for their own side; they are unconditionally polarized not only because they dislike the other side but also because they very much like their own side.

Another group of people may behave differently. The members of this group may sometimes report high levels of animosity for the other side, but this animosity may be much more conditional. For this group, much of the animosity will be directed at elites; their ratings of the opposing party change depending on how much an out-party member discusses politics and where they stand on issues. Some members of this group may harbor lukewarm feelings toward their own side, and other members of this group may even hold a disdain for politics, which in surveys may be confused with a disdain for the out-party (Klar, Krupnikov, and Ryan 2018).

These two groups lead to the second possibility: The first group, which is likely made up of people who are deeply involved, receives the most attention from journalists and other political actors, which, in turn, shapes the portrait of American politics. If the second group is worried about political conversation and has the type of wariness that Yair (2020) suggests, it is likely because the deeply involved have become, to use Ahler's (2014) words, "easily accessible archetypes" of what it means to be an active partisan in America.

We address these two possibilities in the remainder of this book. We begin in Chapter 3 by investigating why involvement forms a critical divide in the American electorate. People who are deeply involved have a focus on politics that is beyond political interest; rather, it is a focus on politics that guides how they spend their day, how often they seek out political information, and, ultimately, their need for expression and feelings for the opposing party. As we demonstrate in the chapters that follow, it is those who are deeply involved who are most likely to be unconditionally affectively polarized, harboring an animosity toward the opposing party that cannot be explained by measurement issues or general wariness alone. This is not to argue that those with lower levels of involvement are politically neutral, consistently virtuous, and immune to cues from political demagogues. Rather, it is to suggest that the deeply involved are more likely to imbue their political positions with an additional sense of certainty, more likely to give politics a primary place in their lives, and more likely to express their positions publicly. In turn, these involvement differences have consequences for partisan politics in America.

Pivotal to the role of involvement, as we have already suggested and as we show in Chapter 7, is political expression. Compared to those who are less involved, people who are deeply involved are more likely to publicly express their political preferences and they are more likely to believe that political expression on social media is beneficial and informative. Because the deeply involved are more likely to express their political views publicly and because these views are often the most extreme and partisan, the political exemplars people observe are most likely to be those with highest levels of involvement. The "pictures in our heads" of partisans are images of those who are deeply involved in politics. Ultimately, we suggest that the affective polarization that divides American politics can only be understood in the context of the involvement divide – the other divide.

3

Beyond Political Interest

I want a world in which jazz ... is treated with dignity and esteemed by people who have been educated in our schools or at home to appreciate good music when they hear it. But this will not happen ... because, hey, jazz is hard to understand; it requires effort to appreciate; and, as a result, nobody likes it.

Morris B. Holbrook, Professor Emeritus of Business, Columbia University

It is often said that jazz is the only true American art form. It is also probably the least consumed genre of music in America.[1]

Of course, some people do like jazz. They will tap their feet and snap their fingers when they hear Duke Ellington. They may note, with fondness, how much they love Dizzy Gillespie. They may even read a think piece on how Norah Jones brought a mixture of jazz and pop into the mainstream of American music.

Morris B. Holbrook is not one of these people.

Sure, Morris B. Holbrook is interested in jazz, but to describe his feelings about jazz as mere interest would likely be an insult to him. Morris B. Holbrook knows even the most obscure of jazz performers; he finds something important in a Chet Baker performance that, he admits, others would characterize as "feeble" and "clumsy" (Holbrook 1987). Jazz records fill nearly every corner of his home, and he has a "backup collection of portable radios and tape players" (Holbrook 1987). He spends a good deal of time looking for new developments and recordings in the jazz world.

---

[1] According to a 2018 CBS news poll, only 7 percent of Americans stated that jazz was their favorite genre of music. Moreover, Nielsen ratings consistently show that jazz is one of the least consumed music genres. The idea that jazz is unpopular is what Holbrook was alluding to in the quote that opens this chapter, which was part of Holbrook's 2012 interview with Alan Bradshaw for the Sage *Legends in Marketing* interview series.

But even more importantly, Morris B. Holbrook believes that *other people* should listen to jazz and love the same type of music that he does. In August 1987, Morris B. Holbrook changed his answering machine greeting to jazz recordings so that people who called him could listen to his favorite music. To make sure people called his home, he made his number public by including it in an academic essay. "I want the reader to feel the depth of my commitment to jazz," Morris B. Holbrook wrote, " ... I despair of adequately conveying that deep involvement through words alone" (Holbrook 1987).

Jazz music may be different than politics, but the idea of interest remains the same. Some people are interested in politics, but other people – a minority – are like Morris B. Holbrook.

To capture contemporary American political culture is to understand the difference between political interest and the type of "deep involvement" that is analogous to Morris B. Holbrook's feelings about jazz. While previous research offers a rich portrait of what makes people interested in politics, in this chapter, we move a step further and consider what defines a *significantly deeper* focus on the political.

Feeling about politics the way that Morris B. Holbrook feels about jazz, we argue, is different than being interested or even engaged in politics. People who are interested and engaged may believe that politics is important, and they likely believe that political participation is an important civic duty and have beliefs (perhaps even strong beliefs) about a preferred set of political outcomes. But the type of "deep involvement" in politics that we define in this chapter – and demonstrate in the remainder of the book – leads to political goals that are broader, more urgent, and more all-encompassing than interest and engagement alone. Morris B. Holbrook made his phone number public on the mere chance that somebody might call it and listen to his beloved jazz recordings. Similar motivations lead people who are deeply involved in politics to share their political opinions (often with large groups of strangers) in the hope of increasing the ranks of their political side. It is this intersection between private focus and public expression, we argue, that has been so profoundly consequential for American politics.

Ultimately, Morris B. Holbrook publishing his phone number has little impact on the world (who reads academic journals, anyway?). But the fact that a vocal minority of people constantly and loudly express their political feelings is important for American politics.

3.1 POLITICAL INTEREST

3.1.1 Defining What It Means to Be Interested

The task of defining political interest may initially seem deceptively simple – an "I know it when I see it" phenomenon. Yet, interest is a more nuanced state of being, an intersection between people's emotions and their cognitive processes

(Renninger and Hidi 2011; Prior 2019). A person could be interested in politics because political events lead them to have an almost visceral, emotional response (Silvia 2005). A person can also be interested in politics because they have thought through a political event and have determined that they should be interested – a more cognitive process (Prior 2019).[2]

In perhaps the most thorough definition, Prior (2019) considers two facets of political interest: the situational and the dispositional. *Situational* interest, he argues, is interest that stems from an emotional jolt: Something we encounter in our day-to-day lives can suddenly make us feel the emotion of interest. Consider, for example, a person who does not necessarily follow jazz. If one day they happen to see an article with an intriguing headline about a jazz musician, they may suddenly feel an emotional jolt that leads them to read the article. This jolt is likely a sense of curiosity – a desire to explore something about which one is uncertain (Kashdan and Silvia 2009). The sudden curiosity may even lead the person to spend the next couple of hours searching out more information about the jazz musician, and they may even spend some time listening to the music. But this level of interest is often passing. If you spend a slow Saturday afternoon searching for information on a jazz musician, it does not mean that the musician's greatest hits will become the soundtrack to your life.

We can say the same about a situational interest in politics. Political events can certainly produce curiosity: It is likely that, on September 4, 2019, many people were curious about why Sharpie markers had suddenly become a topic of national discussion. Eventually, this curiosity may have translated into an interest about President Donald Trump's motivations to misrepresent the path of Hurricane Dorian using the aforementioned marker (Watson 2019). But for many, this interest was likely passing – it was a function of a desire to know more about the particular incident with the Sharpie rather than of a *general* interest in politics as a domain.

The distinction between being interested in a *particular* political incident versus being interested in *politics* underscores the difference between situational interest and what Prior (2019) terms *dispositional* interest. A dispositional interest is a "sustained" – nearly constant – level of interest in a phenomenon. Prior describes a dispositional interest as a sort of "cognitive appreciation" of an area. In other words, one not only feels the emotion of interest but also holds a belief that something *should* be interesting. A person who carefully follows jazz – someone like Morris B. Holbrook – would reason that an article about a jazz musician *should* and *will* be interesting to them, even before the headline sparks any sort of emotional response. A person who has a dispositional interest in politics will continue to read about the latest political events long after everyone has forgotten about the Sharpie incident.

---

[2] Notably, these two processes need not go hand in hand. People may have a cognitive response without any emotional responses (Gawronski and Bodenhausen 2006).

Beyond the distinction of situational interest as context specific and dispositional interest as more constant is the threshold of curiosity. Although curiosity can be considered a trait or a personality characteristic (Kashdan and Silvia 2009; Prior 2019), whether people experience curiosity is also related to context: People differ in the extent to which certain situations can make them feel curious (Litman and Spielberger 2003). People with a dispositional interest, Prior suggests, have a lower threshold for the type of curiosity that sends them on a quest for more and more information.

A person who has a sustained interest in politics does not need something entirely unexpected – like a president using a Sharpie to alter a government map – to become curious. A person whose political interest is dispositional may become curious even about the most mundane of political events or perceive an intrinsic value in getting information about those events.

3.1.2 Capturing Political Interest

Much of what political scientists know about those with a situational political interest and those with a dispositional political interest hinges – like most other research on political behavior – on survey questions. We can identify people who (we assume) are interested in politics because, in surveys, they select response options like "very interested [in politics]" or "extremely interested [in politics]." They may also report that they are "very much interested" in political campaigns.[3] We have already explored the patterns in these self-identification questions in Chapter 1.

Although the survey questions differ, Prior (2019) finds that, regardless of question wording, most survey measures do capture the extent to which people are interested in politics – or at least they perceive themselves to be interested in politics. A person's response to the political interest question remains relatively stable over time, reinforcing the idea that interest is often dispositional (Prior 2010; Russo and Stattin 2017). What is more, political interest consistently predicts a person's willingness to follow political news, political knowledge, and willingness to engage in political discussion (Leighley 1991; Bekkers 2005; Boulianne 2011; Strömbäck, Djerf-Pierre, and Shehata 2013). Although we show in Chapter 1 that there is notable variation in these forms of political engagement among respondents who place themselves in the highest interest categories, the variance across interest categories nonetheless reinforces that people who have a dispositional interest in politics are different from those who may have a passing situational interest or no interest at all (Prior 2019).

But having a dispositional interest in politics is not the same as being the Morris B. Holbrook of politics.

When asked a survey question about one's level of interest in jazz, for example, a person who generally likes jazz may report that they are "very

---

[3] These are the response options for the standard ANES questions on political interest.

interested." Faced with the same question, Morris B. Holbrook would also report that he is "very interested." And yet, this response option would come nowhere near explaining the nature of his deep involvement with jazz.

We can say the same for politics. Because surveys cannot distinguish between these two groups, the category of "very interested" people includes those for whom politics is just that – an interest – along with those for whom politics is a much deeper focus. To understand contemporary American political culture, however, one must understand the divide between those who are deeply involved and those who are not. Relying on a theoretical approach that intersects research on group formation, individual psychology, consumption, and the emergence of political norms, we next explain what it means to be *deeply involved* in politics, why the deeply involved have so much voice in politics, and why the political preferences of this minority may drown out other political voices.

3.2   DEEP INVOLVEMENT IN POLITICS

It is probably not difficult to imagine someone who seems almost "obsessed" with politics. Maybe it is someone who seems to follow nearly *everything* that happens in political news. It could be a person who constantly tries to talk about politics, even as their conversation partners send strong signals that they want the conversation to stop. Perhaps it is someone who posts on social media about politics more than five times on any average day – what Settle (2018) considers to be the high end of social media use. Or, it may even be someone who can explain why any mundane political event could have extensive downstream consequences.

There is a challenge in describing this type of person. The word "obsessed" – which we used earlier – carries with it negative connotations, suggesting a process that is beyond a person's control (Japutra, Ekinci, and Simkin 2017). Other research that focuses on voracious fans of sports teams and entertainment programs refers to these people as "fanatical" (Holbrook 1987; Hill and Robinson 1991; Thorne and Bruner 2006). While this term may be appropriate for someone who is focused on sports and television, it is more difficult to translate the term to the political perspective. Furthermore, as Holbrook (1987) notes, the term "fanatical" has "pejorative implications" and implies that someone is "uncritical" in their approach to their "fandom." This is, of course, not the case with politics. Someone who follows politics on an hourly basis can be remarkably critical of *everyone* associated with many political events.

In what follows, then, we will use the term *deep involvement* to describe a person whose focus on politics transcends interest and becomes something much more important in their lives. This term is appropriate for a variety of reasons. Holbrook (1987) uses "deep involvement," for example, to describe his own consumption of jazz. The term implies a focus that is more profound than interest without suggesting that a person is uncritical or not in control of their engagement.

Even more importantly, the term *involvement* has roots in political science (Riesman and Glazer 1950; Berelson, Lazarsfeld, and McPhee 1954; Eulau and Schneider 1956; Campbell et al. 1960; Converse 1962).[4] Indeed, we begin the very first chapter of this book with a quote from Berelson, Lazarsfeld, and McPhee (1954), who wonder about the role those who are deeply involved in politics should play in the broader political process. This early work defined involvement as a combination of interest, a sense of "affect" toward politics, and a sense of responsibility to be part of politics (Eulau and Schneider 1956). People who were more involved, Eulau and Schneider (1956) suggest in one of the earlier definitions of the concept, had "internalized" a "commitment to the political process." Similarly, the authors of *The American Voter* perceived involvement in politics as a sort of psychological predisposition that brought together a number of characteristics of political engagement. Building on this definition, scholars have suggested that involvement may also include political knowledge, political learning (Prior 2007), political discussion with others, and active attempts at persuasion (Jennings and Markus 1988). Putting these ideas together, Federico and Hunt (2013) define involvement as the "investment of self in politics" (90) – a definition developed by two political psychologists, which is very much in line with Holbrook (1987).[5]

If we consider involvement as "the investment of self," then *deep involvement* is an investment that is especially high and has the potential to be all-consuming. What differentiates deep involvement, we argue, is the presence of three characteristics. The first two characteristics focus on how people relate to political information. People who are deeply involved: (1) *spend time on politics* at a cost to other activities and (2) perceive many *political events as profoundly (and sometimes equivalently) important*. The third characteristic turns to more social components: People who are deeply involved are more likely to *express thoughts and opinions to others* –through discourse, public statements, or even consumption.

There is also a final characteristic that often co-occurs with (and could be a consequence of) deep involvement, though it need not necessarily be a definitional part of deep involvement: an *intense dislike* of people whose political preferences differ from their own. To foreshadow our empirical approach to capturing deep involvement, because this final characteristic is

---

[4] We could also make a connection to even earlier work by Mead (1934); though Mead was writing of concepts that are inherently political, he was, however, not a political scientist.
[5] There is some research that uses the term "political involvement" to mean purely participatory acts (Mettler and Welch 2004), though most of the research view involvement as a concept that is causally prior to participation (e.g. Huddy and Khatib 2007).

a co-occurrence, it will not form part of our involvement measure; rather, we will use traditional measures of affective polarization (discussed in Chapter 2) to capture this animosity *separately* from involvement.

Before we turn to a discussion of these various characteristics, we want to note that it is important not to equate deep involvement with specific types of political action. Certainly, people who are involved in politics would be more likely to participate in politics than those who have little political interest (indeed, this is a key argument in *The American Voter*). Being deeply involved, however, does not necessarily mean taking part in what Hersh (2020) terms "deep" political engagement: attempts to mobilize or persuade through community organizing. Indeed, some deeply involved people may be more likely to donate to a campaign in a different state or purchase a political T-shirt from a candidate they cannot vote for than engage in the type of local politics, as Hersh (2020) discusses. There are many people who are deeply involved in politics who will never take part in a protest to end a political injustice – and many people who are *not* deeply involved in politics who will, without hesitation, do so.

As we will explore in this chapter, the deeply involved will spend large parts of their day reading and watching the news. They will know the minute details about the political events of the day – which should not be confused with more general political knowledge. Their days will be filled with anxiety, anger, frustration, and at times, exuberance about politics. The deeply involved will make their political views public and are often likely to voice their opinions to large groups of anonymous strangers over social media. Put another way, definitionally, these people are deeply involved in *the topic* of politics, rather than in politics itself.[6]

If deep involvement does not always directly translate to extensive political action, then the deeply involved may, at first, seem inconsequential. After all, why would people who spend most of their time worrying about politics have any capacity to affect change? Yet, we suggest that deep involvement has created a deep divide in American politics. Without engaging in traditional forms of community organizing or sustained political action, the deeply involved, we argue, have still produced irreversible shifts in American politics.

3.2.1 The Characteristics of Deep Involvement

As a next step, we delve into the characteristics of deep involvement. We begin with the two characteristics that focus on how people interact with political information around them. Then we turn to the more social and expressive components of deep involvement. Finally, we discuss the dislike of the other side – a characteristic we treat as an important co-occurring outcome with deep involvement rather than a definitional component.

---

[6] We thank Hersh for suggesting this differentiation.

We discuss these characteristics of deep involvement separately, but we see deep involvement as the interaction of the first three: spending time on politics, believing in the importance of political events, and engaging in expression related to politics. Here, we follow research on the sociology of involvement, which suggests that these three components intersect to create a more consequential form of involvement – deep involvement (Thorne and Bruner 2006).[7]

3.2.1.1 *Spending Time on Politics*

One cannot be considered deeply involved in the topic of politics if one does not spend any time following politics. Indeed, a key factor in deep involvement is the extent to which a person devotes their time, as well as energy, to one's area of focus (Thorne and Bruner 2006). Sometimes, deep involvement may even mean making lifestyle changes (Belk, Ger, and Askegaard 2003). A person deeply involved with politics, for example, may cancel meetings at work to make sure that they could watch a congressional hearing live.

People who are deeply involved make these accommodations for two reasons. First, they derive an inherent pleasure from spending time on their topic of focus (Dickerson and Gentry 1983; Thorne and Burner 2006). Second, and perhaps even more importantly, deeply involved people alter their lives because they feel a sense of irritation and anxiety when something prevents them from fully engaging with their chosen topic (Hill and Robinson 1991).[8]

Consider two people who are taking a four-hour flight on an airplane with broken Wi-Fi. A person who is just interested in politics may give a passing thought that something may happen in the news while they are in flight. A person *deeply involved* with politics, on the other hand, would be anxious about this very same possibility.

This is precisely what writer Nick Stockton (2017) experienced. "Where were you when covfefe happened?" writes Stockton, referencing President Donald Trump's 2017 tweet, which included the typo in question. "I was deep in the middle-seat torpor on a red-eye to New York City." While in flight, Stockton missed Trump's original tweet; by the time he landed, covfefe was everywhere, and Stockton had to catch up. "After the catch-up came the letdown – a mixture of regret (I missed it), shame (Why do I care that I missed it), and anxiety (Wait, what else did I miss?) – and it all felt too familiar." In other words, Stockton experienced one of the emotional aspects of deep involvement with politics – a sense of anxiety when he was physically unable to spend time keeping up with political news.

This emotional reaction may extend beyond a deeply involved person's own experience to how they perceive the experiences of others. A deeply

---

[7] We thank a reviewer of this manuscript for suggesting this language to clarify the interaction between these characteristics.

[8] This is an area that has also been called "positive addiction" in athletes (Glasser 1976).

involved person may feel a sense of sadness when they hear that others do not spend any time following political news. Writing about "politicized fandom," Dean (2017) argues that people whose "fandom" is political – that is, those who are deeply involved in politics – are more likely than fans of other things to be focused on the behaviors of nonfans. This is because, as Dean (2017) writes, "politicized fandom" is often "outwardly oriented" (413); a person deeply involved in music may be focused on the music community, but a person deeply involved in politics is thinking of the broader society. Therefore, if people feel a sense of anxiety when they cannot follow the news, they may feel a similar sense of worry or even sadness and frustration when they think of *others* who are not regularly following politics.

3.2.1.1.1 A MEDIA ENVIRONMENT RIPE FOR SPENDING TIME ON POLITICS Pivotal to this first characteristic of deep involvement is the contemporary media environment. In 1922, writing about the nature of news, Walter Lippmann noted that it is impossible for the news to cover "all the happenings in the world" (214). For Lippmann, news was doled out at specific, daily intervals by newspapers. The news, Lippmann argued, "does not tell you how the seed is germinating in the ground, but it may tell you when the first sprout breaks through the surface" (216). To be deeply involved in politics in Lippmann's world, then, would be to be a voracious reader of newspapers – perhaps subscribing to more than one. There was a regimentation to this approach: People knew exactly when they would get their next jolt of information.

The contemporary media environment looks very different from Lippmann's world. Rather than receiving news at regimented, expected times each day, people can now receive news at almost any point in their day (Rosenberg and Feldman 2008). The rise of twenty-four-hour news channels has introduced an almost continuous news cycle, which has been exacerbated by the Internet and, even more recently, social media (Kreiss 2014). While, in Lippmann's world, print newspapers were limited by the number of printed pages they could fill, the contemporary media environment offers an almost infinite space for news (Lewis and Cushion 2009). News is everywhere, all the time – there is now room not only for news about "when the first sprout breaks through the surface" but also for how "the seed is germinating in the ground" (Lippmann 1922).

In Lippmann's world, receiving news updates every hour was impossible, but, in contemporary America, a person can receive news updates continuously (Lewis and Cushion 2009; Rosenberg and Feldman 2008). "The internet is doing exactly what it's supposed to: give me all the information, all the time," writes Nick Stockton. "And I want to hold that fire hose of information right up to my face and gulp down as much as I can."

3.2.1.2 *Importance of All Political Events*

If a person deeply involved with politics devotes a tremendous amount of time to following political events, how do they interpret what they see in the news? Although all people attempt to find meaning in the events that happen to and around them (Baumeister 1991; Holt 1995; Park 2010), people who are deeply involved with politics are not just searching for meaning, they are searching for the *significance* of the event.

When people search for the meaning of an event, they are searching for "possible relationships among things" and "a meaning [that] connects things" (Baumeister 1991, 15). To search for the meaning of an event is to "make sense" of something that occurred (Janoff-Bulman and Frantz 1997; Park 2010). To search for *significance*, on the other hand, is to consider the "value or worth" of an event (Janoff-Bulman and Frantz 1997). Searching for meaning comes before searching for significance (Park 2010), and the more people know about a certain topic generally, the easier it will be for them to find its meaning (Holt 1995). While people who are not especially interested in the topic may stop once they determine the meaning of an event, the people who are deeply involved will be much more likely to search for the event's *significance*.

To search for significance is to look for the broadest possible implication of an event (Holt 1995). For someone who is a deeply involved baseball fan, for example, this may mean explaining why their team's acquisition of a certain pitcher foretells that a World Series win is now a sure thing (see Holt 1995 for more baseball examples). Deliberately combing through details, a person could explain even the most minute event as a first step toward a broadly consequential outcome (Davis and McGinnis 2016).

While scholars have long outlined sports fans' ability to interpret the most minor interactions between players as important clues about a team's future (Davis and McGinnis 2016), politics is an area that is especially susceptible to a search for significance. In the political world, everything could – with enough interpretation – become highly urgent (Vázquez-Arroyo 2013). From a negative perspective, politics easily lends itself to the narrative of "catastrophization," or the idea that there is a "shadowy presence of catastrophe" looming behind every political event (Vázquez-Arroyo 2013, 745). From a more positive perspective, any small event can be perceived as a first step in a path to victory for one side over the other.

People who are deeply involved have a much greater *capacity* to find significance; after all, they know much more information about the topic than someone with a more passing interest (Thorne and Bruner 2006). People who have a lot of political knowledge have a greater capacity to explain why a political argument is unconvincing (Taber and Lodge 2006), and in the same way, people who know more about politics can more easily conceive of the steps that could connect a relatively minor political event to a political catastrophe.

This search for significance, of course, also intersects with the very media environment that has made spending a good deal of time on politics possible. Filling more and more hours with news means more and more news programming. This means more and more commentary and dissection of news events. In this type of format, Berry and Sobieraj (2013) argue, program hosts work to create a sense of camaraderie with viewers – as if they are welcoming viewers into a special community. Within this community, hosts share what appears to be private "insider" information, feeding viewers' beliefs that every political event could have important consequences (Berry and Sobieraj 2013). For the sake of programming, even small political events could become a means of filling hours.

Let us return for a moment to Nick Stockton, the writer who missed President Trump's "covfefe" tweet while in flight. Part of his anxiety about missing the tweet, Stockton notes, was due to his concern about the tweet's significance. This tweet, Stockton writes, could be part of the "cable news countdown clock hurtling toward . . . impeachment."

3.2.1.2.1 SEARCHING FOR SIGNIFICANCE VERSUS CONSPIRACISM Searching for the political significance of events in the way that the deeply involved are likely to do is different from relying on conspiracy theories to explain political outcomes (Oliver and Wood 2014). When people seek out conspiracy theories, people engage in "conspiracism," a tendency which stems from a person's perception that there are unseen "malevolent forces" controlling politics (Oliver and Wood 2014, 953). Conspiracism, Oliver and Wood (2014) demonstrate, aligns with tendencies to believe in the supernatural and the paranormal. The search for political significance, on the other hand, relies on political knowledge that is grounded in real-world politics, although it may require a very particular chain of events that has a low probability of occurrence.

Moreover, the search for significance is often forward-looking. Someone searching for significance could, for example, propose the following chain of events (based on a change in the Vice President's 2019 calendar):

Vice-President Mike Pence has canceled a number of events, his favorability is consistently higher than President Donald Trump's, so these cancelations may signal that he could be resigning as Vice President to run against Trump in the Republican Primary.

In this chain connecting Pence's cancellations to the GOP primary, each event is grounded in real-world, observable politics – though the entire chain of events coming together is unlikely.

Conspiracism, however, often seeks to explain events after they have occurred, relying on many facts that are unobservable (which likely could never be empirically demonstrated). Consider this example from Oliver and Wood (2014; table 1): "The United States government mandat[ed] the switch to fluorescent light bulbs because [they] make people more obedient and easier to control" (956).

These examples illustrate another important difference. The search for significance requires attention to political news (e.g. learning that Pence has canceled events) and political knowledge (e.g. knowing the steps Pence would need take to start his own campaign). In contrast, buying in to the idea that the government is trying to control people through light bulbs requires little attention to the news, little political knowledge, and little political interest. Indeed, a person may use conspiratorial thinking ("the secret organization controls everything anyway") to disassociate from following politics entirely. Perhaps for these reasons, there is little relationship between conspiracism and political interest (Oliver and Wood 2014).[9]

This is not to argue that a person who is deeply involved will not engage in conspiratorial thinking. It is, of course, possible that a person who is deeply involved can search for significance but may also believe in certain conspiracy theories. In other words, just because someone engages in the search for significance in some cases does not preclude them from also falling prey to conspiracism in other cases. Rather, the point is that the search for significance mechanism we describe here is different from conspiracism.

3.2.1.3 *Different Forms of Political Expression*
A person with a deep involvement in politics may spend a tremendous amount of time following political news and find significance in even the most mundane of political events. But what good is predicting that Mike Pence's event cancellations will lead to his resignation if other people are not alerted to this possibility? Moreover, a person who spends a tremendous amount of time doing something will crave conversation about that topic with others. A key characteristic of deep involvement in a topic is the desire for various forms of expression (Kozinets 2001).[10] This form of expression may mean sharing one's thoughts and opinions with others but also may take the shape of literally costly consumerist commitment (Thorne and Bruner 2006). We begin with expression as sharing opinions and turn to consumption later in this section.

Research on fans suggests these people are most interested in discussions with others who can share "the same level of intensity" (Dimmock and Grove 2005; Thorne and Bruner 2006). So too people who are deeply involved with politics most enjoy political discussions with other politically focused people. Deep involvement, then, means seeking out political conversations, either in

---

[9] Miller, Saunders, and Farhart (2016) find that liberals who have high political knowledge – that is, the level of political knowledge associated with someone who spends a good deal of time on politics – are *less likely* to believe in conspiracy theories. They do not find the same for conservatives.

[10] This tendency will be conditional; Kozinets (2001) argues that public self-expression is often moderated by the possibility of social stigma associated with one's interest.

person or via social media. These conversations can further cement a person's existing deep involvement (Seregina and Schouten 2017).

In addition to discussions with other fans, there is also the desire to *publicly* express one's involvement (Thorne and Bruner 2006; Guschwan 2011; Pegoraro 2013). These displays become a shorthand for an expression of allegiance and identity (Kozinets 2001; Guschwan 2011; Pegoraro 2013). In much the same way, public expression can be a part of deep involvement with politics, where it may take the form of writing a letter to the editor (which is then published in a newspaper) or, perhaps more commonly, sharing one's political opinion or a political story publicly via social media.

The need for public expression may also intersect with the previous characteristic of deep involvement – the search for significance. If the deeply involved are more likely to search for and perceive significance in even the most minor political events, then every political event signals the potential for some even larger political catastrophe or victory (Vázquez-Arroyo 2013). If, returning to Dean's argument (2017), deep involvement also means an "outward" concern, then public expression may also be driven by a desire to inform others and correct misperceptions about the seeming meaninglessness of some piece of political news: This event that may seem small actually has tremendous consequences.

Consider Connie Sherman, who in 2018 was a manager of a dental practice in San Diego, California. Since the 2016 election, Sherman told a reporter that she has not been sleeping well, instead staying up late into the night checking news headlines. "When [special counsel] Robert Mueller's indictments news dropped, I wound up staying up in the middle of the night when I should have been sleeping, just thinking about it, just worried for our country," she told a reporter (Kwong 2018). Sherman's anxiety is likely fueled by her higher-than-average involvement in politics (she was, after all, staying up late to follow political news). For the sake of comparison, in a CNN poll conducted around the time of Sherman's interview, fewer than half of Americans reported that they were following news about Mueller's first indictment – Paul Manafort – very closely or even somewhat closely.[11]

For people like Connie Sherman, public expressions of politics can help alleviate the tension of knowing too much. First, being public about politics can help the deeply involved feel like they are providing a service by informing others about a looming political problem. This is especially likely to happen on social media where a public post is likely to receive an almost immediate reply, a gratification of one's efforts (Hart et al. 2015). Second, public expression can help those deeply involved with politics feel better *emotionally*. Constantly seeing the potential of a catastrophe can make one politically anxious. Indeed,

---

[11] Cable News Network (CNN). CNN Poll: August 2018 – Poll 7, August 2018 [survey question]. 31115414.00010. SSRS [producer]. Cornell University, Ithaca, NY: Roper Center for Public Opinion Research, iPOLL [distributor], accessed September 17, 2019.

some clinical psychologists have even argued that there are specific anxiety disorders tied directly to worries about escalating political events (Panning 2017). If this anxiety is overwhelming, there is a benefit to sharing it publicly. Research suggests writing out one's emotional state – a process called affect labeling – can relieve the intensity of an emotion (Torre and Lieberman 2018). Publicly posting about one's emotional state on social media can mimic affect labeling and, in turn, make people feel better (Fan et al. 2018) – even if only until the next headline appears.

3.2.1.3.1 DISTINGUISHING TYPES OF EXPRESSION It is important to distinguish between the types of expressive sharing we consider in this book – identity signaling and political emoting – from efforts toward increasing activism. We will delve more deeply into this distinction in Chapter 7, but, for now, we note that there are important differences between posting on social media with the goal of activism (e.g. Freelon, McIlwain, and Clark 2018; Jackson, Bailey, and Foucault Welles 2020) and the type of opinion sharing we discussed in the previous section. For groups that have been institutionally excluded from the political process, public expression, especially on social media, can take on the form of community organizing; through social media engagement, these groups can spread their messages, reach larger groups of people, and affect the media agenda (Auger 2013; Freelon, McIlwain, and Clark 2018; Edrington and Lee 2018). This is public expression designed to increase the chance of some particular action, often presenting a clear means by which to engage and act in order to enact important social change.

In contrast, the opinion sharing we consider here lacks any sort of cohesive calls to action. Although the deeply involved may believe that they are, broadly, increasing awareness and thereby ameliorating some political outcome, their public expressions are often likely to appear more as individualized opinions than planned parts of a broader, organized movement (see, for example, Edrington and Lee 2018 on the use of social media in the Black Lives Matter movement). Hersh (2020) terms this form of public expression as "political hobbyism" – a behavior he distinguishes from actual community organizing or proactive efforts at political change.

3.2.1.3.2 EXPRESSION AS COSTLY CONSUMPTION To this point, we have focused on expression as sharing one's opinion either via a discussion or publicly. One can also express one's involvement through more literally costly consumption. Consumption is such a key component of deep involvement that a good deal of literature on involvement focuses on *consumer* involvement – people whose focus on a topic is channeled toward costly consumption of items related to that topic (Kozinets 2001). Indeed, scholars of involvement may criticize this section of our chapter because we have not discussed consumption as a separate characteristic of involvement.

We include costly consumption as part of the expressive characteristic because, in a political context, consumption may often be inextricably linked with expression (e.g. Dean 2017). Clothes with political slogans, bumper stickers, and even "selfies" with candidates (Dean 2017) may all be categorized as consumptive behaviors because they likely require some financial costs. Yet, these consumer behaviors are also highly expressive: A shirt with a political slogan expresses an allegiance to a particular political idea, and a selfie with a candidate posted on social media can express a political identity. If we think of displays of allegiance as "inescapably based on a constructed ideology intended to promote a shared vision of history, identity, and heritage" (Thompson 2002, 38), then political consumer goods are inherently politically expressive.

We do acknowledge that other forms of political consumption may be less openly and clearly expressive *on their own*. Opting to engage in a "buycott" of a particular company that supports your preferred political cause by spending money on their products is costly (Kam and Deichert 2020), but it does not have an inherent expressive component unless the "buycotter" then publicly chooses to share why they have purchased a particular item. Donations to political causes are another form of "political consumption" that do not result in the obtainment of a physical item but are a clearly costly – a type of act associated with involvement (Galuszka 2015). Again, however, donations are not immediately expressive unless a person chooses to publicly state that they have donated money.

We classify these more "consumerist" and costly behaviors under the general heading of expression because they signal an allegiance to a particular topic of involvement. At the same time, however, we acknowledge that these are different forms of expression, driven, potentially, by different mechanisms – indeed, when we measure involvement, we will treat these costly behaviors differently. Our goal here, then, is not to suggest that donating money to a political cause is the same as making a social media post stating one's opinion or sharing a news story. Rather, because people who are deeply involved in other topics are likely to spend their money in ways that signal a costly commitment (Galuszka 2015), we believe that political donations – even if not necessarily public expression – are a different form of expression associated with deep involvement.

3.2.1.4 *Intense Dislike for Different Approaches to Involvement*
People who are deeply involved spend time following politics, they interpret political importance in even small political events, and they are drawn to social interactions and public expressions of politics. We now turn to a fourth characteristic that is somewhat different, in that we argue it *co-occurs* with deep involvement but is not necessarily a definitional aspect: a dislike of those who have different approaches to involvement. Throughout the book, we will measure this fourth characteristic separately from our measure of involvement.

Looking in from the outside, all people who are deeply involved may seem similar in their zeal for the topic. Imagine a person who is a fan of the television show *Doctor Who* – the sci-fi fixture airing hundreds of episodes since 1963 with 13 separate actors taking on the role of "The Doctor."[12] To those who have never seen the show, it may seem that all *Doctor Who* superfans are, basically, one and the same. Yet, there is a deep debate within the community of the deeply involved "Whovians" (Booth and Booth 2014). There is disagreement about which seasons of *Doctor Who* are most important and which Doctors deserve the most reverence. At its core, this is a debate about the right and wrong ways to be a *Doctor Who* fan (Booth and Booth 2014).

While a fight about the most authentic *Doctor Who* season may seem trivial, the idea of "appropriateness" signals an important component of deep involvement. People who are deeply involved, be it with *Doctor Who*, sports, or jazz, may have a frustration with those who are not at all involved, but they reserve their strongest resentment for those who, they believe, are not involved in the correct way (Hills 2002; Booth and Booth 2014). In much the same way, a person with a deep involvement in politics may feel frustrated with and concerned about someone who does not follow political news at all, but they may harbor the most animosity for someone who expresses their deep political involvement by championing the "wrong" side.

This sense of animosity is, in some ways, to be expected. A person who is deeply involved spends countless hours researching, following, and otherwise engaging in a particular topic. They have considered why even small events can become profoundly significant. They are also engaging in numerous discussions, making their involvement very public, and may even spend their money in ways related to their topic of involvement. What may emerge, then, is a clear set of beliefs about the right and wrong ways of involvement. If politics is at its core "who gets what, when and how" (Lasswell 1936), deep involvement is likely to lead someone to very specific preferences about the who, the what, and the how.

In this context, people who are deeply involved may perceive their preferences in an almost moral manner (Hills 2002; Gray 2003; Williams 2013). In turn, even small deviations from what they believe to be an appropriate form of involvement can become not just incorrect but potentially insulting and even immoral (Williams 2013). Hills (2002), for example, discusses how people who have a deep involvement with art may view someone with different taste as morally repugnant. If divides within deeply involved groups are, ultimately, about what are the most appropriate preferences, then politics lends itself to divides that are especially profound.

People's allegiances to parties are remarkably stable and constant over their lifetimes (Green, Palmquist, and Shickler 2002). Moreover, there is evidence to

---

[12] Deeply involved *Doctor Who* fans would note that while thirteen actors have played "The Doctor" as a lead role, other actors have played versions of The Doctor in smaller roles.

suggest that, for some people, these identities have only grown stronger in recent decades (Iyengar et al. 2019). Even if we set identities aside, the Democratic and Republican Parties have different positions on a variety of political issues that are critical to the way people live their day-to-day lives. For people who are deeply involved, who believe that even the most minute political event can have a myriad of significant consequences, a divergence in preferences can seem much more important than supporting the wrong team – it can seem like supporting the wrong future for America.

These beliefs about the appropriate way to be involved need not cross partisan lines but can also occur within party. People who are deeply involved have the capacity to magnify even the smallest of differences (Hills 2002; Booth and Booth 2014). In politics, this may mean ideas not only about which party it is appropriate to support but also about the most appropriate way to be a Republican or a Democrat. While political scientists have typically conceived of this as the difference between strong and weak partisans (Greene 1999), when this co-occurs with political involvement, this may take the form of differentiating between the most appropriate way of being a strong partisan. Although, throughout this book, we will focus on the animosity across parties as this provides the greatest clarity in measurement, we do note that a deeply involved person may also possibly direct their animosity even at those who hold a similar partisan position. Moreover, this animosity need not mean that someone has to identify with a political party – one can refer to themselves as an independent, believe that there are appropriate ways to be involved, and dislike those who are differently involved.[13]

The ultimate outcome here is a perspective that is clear (Williams 2013) and a resentment toward people who are getting their involvement "wrong" (Booth and Booth 2014). Alongside the three previous characteristics of involvement co-occurs a clarity about what constitutes appropriate political preferences, and any preference outside of these bounds is considered wrong, immoral, and maybe even dangerous. Indeed, research in cognitive psychology suggests that there is a certain sense of cognitive rigidity associated with a deep involvement and attachment to political positions (Zmigrod, Rentfrow, and Robbins 2019).[14]

---

[13] Pivotal here is the reason why someone describes themselves as "independent." If these are people who identify as independent because, as Klar and Krupnikov (2016) suggest, they are avoiding politics, then these people are probably not deeply involved. However, someone who meets the characteristics of deep involvement may identify as an independent because they perceive both parties as being incorrect and therefore harbor animosity for both political sides.

[14] Previous research associated cognitive rigidity with people who espoused conservative viewpoints – an idea termed "rigidity-of-the-right" (Jost et al. 2003). More recent work, however, has demonstrated that this cognitive rigidity is not limited to those on the right of the ideological spectrum and manifests itself in a similar manner among both liberals and conservatives (Zmigrod, Rentfrow, and Robbins 2019).

It is important here to underscore two points. First, the certainty that the deeply involved may feel in their political beliefs should not be conflated with the normative implications of those beliefs. In other words, just because the deeply involved, as we argue above, have a certainty in their beliefs that is verging on morality does not mean that these beliefs are in actuality moral or just. What we mean here is that some deeply involved people have beliefs that would clearly promote more justice and improve society; when they dislike the opposing side, then their animosity is geared at people who hold unjust, harmful beliefs. But some deeply involved may perceive their beliefs as moral even if those beliefs are unjust and harmful. Because this group too is certain in their beliefs, they direct their animosity at people whose political ideas are clearly normatively better. One should not conflate certainty with the normative components of beliefs, and it is the certainty that leads to animosity.

The second point is that, throughout this section, we have deliberately used the term "co-occurrence" to describe the relationship between animosity and the three other characteristics. Research on involvement suggests that the type of dislike for different ways of involvement we discuss in this section usually emerges after a person meets all the previously discussed characteristics of involvement (Booth and Booth 2014). At the same time, randomly assigning the characteristics of involvement would be quite challenging, which means we cannot with causal certainty say that the definitional characteristics of deep involvement cause the animosity toward those who are differently involved. Indeed, it is possible that this animosity emerges in parallel to the other characteristics or that harboring some animosity toward the other political side actually increases involvement (which leads to even more animosity). Therefore, in the chapters that follow, we treat this animosity as a co-occurrence rather than suggesting a causal relationship: People who are deeply involved are also more likely to harbor animosity for those with different political views.

3.2.2 Deep Involvement in Summary

Interest in politics is the motivation and desire to learn more about political events either most of the time or only on occasion (Prior 2019). A deep involvement in politics is a state of focusing on the political. The characteristics we discussed, then, do not only differentiate people who are merely interested and people who are deeply involved, but also suggest that the deeply involved are unique in how they relate to politics. Bringing all the characteristics together, the following portrait emerges of a deeply involved person.

First, a person who is deeply involved in politics likely spends a tremendous amount of time following politics. While a person who is generally interested in politics would feel an emotional reaction when presented with political information and even seek out more information about politics (Prior 2019), a person who is deeply involved is more likely to feel a sense of emotional discomfort when there is something preventing them from following political updates. Furthermore, a deeply involved person may also feel a similar sense of worry and concern when they believe that *other people* are not sufficiently following politics – an outward focus driven by politics (Dean 2017).

The deeply involved also see significance in political events in a way that a person who is merely interested may not. This may involve catastrophizing, seeing the profound downstream consequences in small political outcomes or overinterpreting mundane events. If deep involvement in politics is about looking outward (Dean 2017), however, a deeply involved person who sees how a small political event can have tremendous consequences may feel a particular frustration when other people around them do not see the same gravity in political events.

Another key characteristic of deep involvement is expression. This expression includes both opinion-based forms (e.g. social media posts) and consumerist forms (e.g. purchased political items and campaign donations). The deeply involved person is also likely to perceive posting on social media as an important way to inform others about the consequences of various political events. Furthermore, a deeply involved person may also signal their allegiance through costly signals like donations.

Co-occurring with the three definitional characteristics of deep involvement is a sense of frustration with those who do not engage in deep involvement. This frustration is also likely accompanied by a strong animosity toward those who are deeply involved but in an "incorrect" way. To foreshadow the findings in the remainder of the book, the greatest levels of polarization and animosity are among people we can identify as deeply involved.

3.3   MOST OTHER PEOPLE

The number of pages we have devoted to those who are deeply involved with politics may give a reader the impression that these people form a large percentage of the American electorate. This, as many surveys suggest, and as we will demonstrate in greater detail in this book, is not the case. More than half of Americans are at least somewhat disengaged from politics: In 2018, 68 percent reported that they had "news fatigue."[15] In 2019, only 15 percent of people told Pew that they actually *liked* seeing political posts and discussions on social media.[16] Yet, even the people who would be classified as engaged based on their survey responses fall far short of the behaviors associated with deep political involvement.

---

[15] Pew Research Center Survey, fielded February 22–March 4, 2018: www.pewresearch.org/fact-tank/2020/02/26/almost-seven-in-ten-americans-have-news-fatigue-more-among-republicans/
[16] Pew Research Center Survey, conducted June, 2019: www.pewresearch.org/fact-tank/2020/08/19/55-of-u-s-social-media-users-say-they-are-worn-out-by-political-posts-and-discussions/

The deeply politically involved form a minority of Americans. What makes the deeply involved consequential is not their proportion within the public but their willingness to be much more vocal than the majority of Americans who are *not* deeply involved in politics. Furthermore, because the political media often focus on partisan conflict, the types of people featured in the news are likely to give the impression that most of America is deeply involved. As comedian John Mulaney quipped, "I don't know if you've been following the news, but I've been keeping my ears open and it seems like everyone everywhere is supermad about everything all the time."[17]

3.3.1 Encountering the Deeply Involved

Before we consider the relationship between those who are and are not deeply involved, we want to pause and consider how people who have less involvement in politics encounter those who have much higher involvement levels.

As we will show in Chapter 5, most people are in core networks with those who have similar levels of political involvement. Nonetheless, it is quite likely that even a person who does not have any close friends who are deeply involved will still encounter someone with high levels of involvement. Some will encounter those who are heavily focused on politics through their own broader social networks. Since those with deep involvement are more likely to post publicly on social media, having this kind of person anywhere in one's network increases the likelihood of seeing this person's political posts. Even those who do not have friends (or tangential acquaintances) who are deeply involved, however, have likely seen the political thoughts and opinions of this small group. This is related to expressiveness – a characteristic of deep involvement – and we return to this point in Chapter 7.

Another reason why the deeply involved are important, however, is because, as we will demonstrate in greater depth in Chapter 8, the contemporary media environment has indirectly offered this minority a disproportionately large platform. In turn, the deeply involved become our political comparisons because they are most likely to emerge from news coverage as symbols for whichever political events are deemed important on a given day (e.g. Edelman 1988). In the next sections, then, we consider what comparisons to the deeply involved mean for those who are less involved.

3.3.2 Redefining Political Engagement as Deep Involvement

One characteristic of deep involvement, as we discussed previously, is a desire to share one's views publicly. When someone is deeply involved, be it in politics, sports, or jazz, the people around them will usually hear about it. It is reasonable to expect that people who are not deeply involved in the topic may

---

[17] From his 2018 Netflix special, *Kid Gorgeous at Radio City.*

find conversations with someone who *is* deeply involved, at best, boring. Imagine discussing *Doctor Who* with someone who has a "My Other Car is a TARDIS" bumper sticker when you are not 100 percent certain that a TARDIS isn't from *Battlestar Galactica*. Or imagine discussing jazz with Morris B. Holbrook when you've only ever listened to Kenny G. Much of this conversation would probably involve you dutifully nodding your head while listening to an explanation of some detail that you have never thought about before and may not find especially important. Aside from boring you, however, this type of conversation may have broader consequences. Talking to someone who is deeply involved may give you a cue about what it takes to engage with a particular topic.

People use the social cues around them to determine the boundaries of groups (Ellemers, Spears, and Doosje 2002; Miller, Brewer, and Arbuckle 2009). When interacting with others, people begin to form perceptions about the norms that govern the group to which those others belong (Turner and Reynolds 2012). Hearing Morris B. Holbrook discuss his jazz preferences, for example, can serve as a signal to someone about what it means to be a true fan of jazz. In much the same way, encountering a person deeply involved with politics may serve as a signal about what it means to be political in America. Even more broadly, interactions with the deeply involved help people form the political "pictures inside our heads" (Lippmann 1922), to return to an idea from Chapter 2.

3.3.3 Comparisons to the Deeply Involved

If political participation and political knowledge are both considered normatively good (Rosenstone and Hansen 1993), then ordinary people may believe that the deeply politically involved are perceived as (or at least perceive themselves to be) superior. We suggest, however, that the comparison process that arises when people encounter those who are deeply involved in politics – either on their social media feeds, in person, or through the news – may work somewhat differently. To consider these comparisons, then, we can think of different types of people who are deeply involved.

One possibility may be that some of those who are deeply involved produce a "self-improvement motive" upon comparison (Suls, Martin, and Weaver 2002). When someone perceives a deeply involved person as superior, a comparison may lead a less involved person to want to become more like them – which, in the context of politics, may mean becoming more deeply involved. This may be especially likely to happen when a person perceives someone who is deeply involved as objectively more successful (Suls, Martin, and Weaver 2002) and when they believe that becoming like the deeply involved person could increase their own social status (Lockwood and Kunda 1997). This type of outcome, however, is unlikely unless someone believes higher levels of involvement will give them more status and unless they are already somewhat involved in politics. Engaging with other involved individuals is more likely to increase involvement if someone already wants to be much more heavily engaged in a topic (Seregina and Schouten 2017). In other words, this sort of comparative process is likely to make someone who is already highly involved more deeply involved.

Research on self-comparisons suggests that another possibility may be more likely when a person with low or average levels of involvement compares themselves to someone who is highly involved: They may compare themselves negatively to someone who is deeply involved – that is, that they have less knowledge or have not done enough. Being "less than" someone else is not enjoyable for most people (Spears, Doosje, and Ellemers 1997; Ellemers, Spears, and Doosje 2002). Facing a comparison that could potentially place them into a lower status motivates people to develop strategies to make this type of comparison less legitimate (Ellemers and Van Rijswijk 1997; Doosje et al. 1999). One such strategy is developing a preemptive dislike for members of the group who could be perceived as superior (Alicke 2000; Minson and Monin 2012). People are especially likely to turn to this strategy when they imagine that someone who considers themselves superior may judge them negatively (Monin, Sawyer, and Marquez 2008; Minson and Monin 2012).

Being judged – especially by someone who believes that they have the moral higher ground – "stings" even if "the actual morality of their choice is debatable" (Minson and Monin 2012, 201–202). Preemptively dismissing a person who could view us negatively, then, is a natural human reaction to decrease the sting (Minson and Monin 2012). This dismissal can take on different forms. It may mean ridiculing the person, finding them annoying, deliberately avoiding them, or generally evaluating them negatively (Monin, Sawyer and Marquez 2008; Minson and Monin 2012).

Distancing oneself from the politically involved could be a natural reaction. In 2012, for example, Cristina Kalpa decided not to vote for president. "Two friends from college tore me apart," she told *New York Times* reporters (Tavernise and Cohn 2019). These friends, Kalpa said, sent her texts "saying 'something had to be wrong with me'." Kalpa never spoke to these friends again. The former friends' judgment, however, had deeper consequences. Kalpa told *The New York Times* that she feels that too many people her age "started to have this all-or-nothing view about people's opinion." What began as a dismissal of two friends who judged her (harshly) has translated into a general dislike of people who have a certain type of political engagement.

This form of negative comparison may have an even broader effect. People compare themselves to others on a variety of dimensions (Spears, Doosje, and Ellemers 1997; Ellemers, Spears, and Doosje 2002). On some dimensions of a comparison, a person may fare better; on others, the same person may fall short. The key to these comparisons, then, is to ensure that the dimensions on which you may fall short are considered trivial (Ellemers, Spears, and Doosje 2002; Turner and Reynolds 2012). Discussing politics with someone who is deeply involved may leave you feeling ignorant about current affairs. On the other hand, if you decide that politics and the news are largely irrelevant and unimportant, then you are no longer inferior to your deeply involved conversation partner.

"It's just not part of my everyday thinking," Shannon Cavalier told a *New York Times* reporter. Although Cavalier works with someone who "gets really worked up" about politics, this does not bother her because she decided that politics is simply something she does not follow. Kalpa – whose friends "tore [her] apart" politically – used to be more politically engaged and active, making political posts on social media and following the news. The interaction with her former friends, however, caused a breaking point; *The New York Times* implies that after the 2012 election, Kalpa disengaged from politics entirely.

There is, however, another possibility. Encountering a deeply involved person may take the form of a downward comparison: a comparison to someone who is worse on some characteristic. Downward comparisons need not always be negative – sometimes a comparison to someone less fortunate may lead people to become aware of their own comforts and privileges (Suls, Martin, and Wheeler 2002). Yet, exposure to a deeply involved person whose beliefs are not just extreme but also objectively harmful for society or democracy may have potentially negative consequences. Downward comparisons help people when their positive self-evaluations are threatened (Muller and Butera 2007) and, in the context of politics, may give a person an "at least I'm not as bad as . . ." justification. Seeing a deeply involved exemplar sharing harmful political positions in a news article, for example, gives a less involved person a way to justify their own slightly less harmful beliefs. "I may have voted for a candidate with harmful positions," a person may think to themselves, "but at least I do not spend a good deal of time expressing these positions on social media."

3.3.4   Involvement in Perspective

The types of behaviors that define deep involvement, especially their tendency to express their opinions, mean that even those who do not have close friends who are deeply involved are likely to encounter the voices of the deeply involved. Whether through social media feeds or the news, the deeply involved are likely to emerge as the "pictures in our heads" of politics (Lippmann 1922). If the deeply involved come to define what it means to be political, then they may also serve as a basis of political comparison. The result is a set of possible comparisons that shape not only how people see their own role in politics but also politics more generally. These comparisons may lead those who are less involved to begin to ignore those who are deeply involved, or they may lead them to ignore politics more generally. Sometimes, these comparisons may also allow those who are less involved to justify harmful beliefs and ideas. Overall, however, these types of comparisons, regardless of motivation, are more likely to lead a negative evaluation of a deeply involved person.

3.4 DEEP INVOLVEMENT AND THE DEMOCRATIC PROCESS

We began this chapter with Morris B. Holbrook, a man focused on jazz. Holbrook's attention to jazz fits the psychological profile of deep involvement: He follows jazz closely, considers the significance of various events in the jazz world, and wants everyone to know how much he loves jazz to the point of making his home telephone number public. He also dislikes people who like jazz the "wrong" way, referring to Kenny G as an "abomination" and arguing that "the very existence of iTunes caters to the appallingly short attention spans of mass-market listeners" (Holbrook 2008, 122).

Of course, jazz and politics are different. Morris B. Holbrook may want everyone to love jazz and desperately wish that people stopped listening to what he calls "smoothjazz" (Holbrook 2008). But Morris B. Holbrook cannot, with any sense of credibility, argue that the fate of America depends on people loving jazz. If he said that listening to Kenny G could destroy America, people would deem him foolish and unreasonable.

Those deeply involved in politics, however, have a stronger case because the stakes of politics are so much greater. In explaining why Republicans stuck with the scandal-plagued President Trump, Senator Mitt Romney noted, "[B]oth parties feel very deeply that if the other party were in charge, that terrible things would happen for the country, for the people, and that it's critical for them to hold onto their leadership so that those awful things ... won't come to pass."[18] Politics is important; it is plausible that even small political events *could* have profound consequences.

Compounding the importance of politics is the idea that political participation has long been considered something that is, ultimately, good for society (Almond and Verba 1965). Political scientists have often worried about people's ideological inconsistencies and seeming political apathy (Converse 1964). Similarly, journalists seem alarmed with Americans who show little knowledge about and interest in politics. "Political scientists have been studying what voters know and how they think for well over 65 years," wrote Jason Brennan (2016) in *Foreign Policy* in the wake of 2016 presidential

---

[18] The somber coda to Romney's comment is that on January 6, 2021, a group of insurrectionists stormed the US Capitol as Congress was certifying President-Elect Joe Biden's victory – they were incited to do so by the losing candidate, Donald Trump, while some Republican senators objected to the vote backing Trump's lies about a stolen election. As the Senate was being evacuated, Romney told his fellow Republicans, "This is what you've gotten, guys" (Fandos, Schaff, and Cochrane 2021).

election. "The results are frightening. Voters generally know who the president is but not much else."

In this context, the deeply involved could emerge as ideal citizens. They are attentive and knowledgeable, and their very public political discussions suggest genuine engagement. They may appear to behave just how the founders envision a participatory citizenry. As Zink (2009) writes, the founders had "a vision of America in which civic duty and the secure enjoyment of individual rights are mutually compatible and, indeed, are necessary companions" (453). Moreover, one could infer from decades of political science arguments that the deeply involved form the foundation of a functioning representative democracy.

But these arguments about the importance of the involved ignore the idea that the deeply involved are not "reference librarians" (Ahn, Huckfeldt, and Ryan 2015). They do not simply gather information, synthesize it, and help the citizenry better understand the world. Instead, with their deep involvement comes a strong certainty that their perception of politics is the appropriate, correct worldview. Society needs some people like that. But, as Berelson, Lazarsfeld, and McPhee (1954) note, if more and more people behave like the deeply involved, then the system crumbles, and we end up in a dystopia.

There may have been a point in time when the deeply involved were just people who were more knowledgeable and engaged than the average citizen. At that time, these deeply involved citizens were likely useful for the democratic process if only by passing the information they learned from the news onto others (Katz and Lazarsfeld 1955). Changes in the media environment and the entrenchment of political partisanship, however, have altered what it means to be deeply involved. They are no longer just knowledgeable, engaged citizens. Rather, they are fixated on politics, anxious, and stressed by political events. Alongside these behaviors is a deep animosity for anyone with different political beliefs. Moreover, although the deeply involved are certain that their beliefs are correct and in the interest of larger public, it is important not to conflate the certainty that co-occurs with deep involvement with normative implications of the beliefs the deeply involved hold. In sum, people who are interested, knowledgeable, and willing to discuss politics are without a doubt necessary for democratic outcomes, but there is no guarantee that all those who are deeply involved will behave like the people we want for this job.

4

The Deeply Involved Are Different

The times that I've spent to get a little bit more educated, all the options suck. I don't feel like one is great so I'm not going to vote at all.
Focus Group Participant, Milwaukee, WI, as quoted in the Knight Foundation's 100 Million Project

In 2019, the Knight Foundation surveyed 4,000 "persistent nonvoters" – people who had stayed home for the majority of the previous six national elections.[1] These people are, as the survey data suggest, not deeply involved in politics. In fact, they are unusual for the *total* lack of involvement: Voter turnout in America is not as high as it could be, but most people vote at least in presidential elections if they are eligible.[2] From one perspective, the nonvoters in both, Knight's survey and, later, their focus groups, serve as a contrast to the deeply involved people in Chapter 3 – people who stayed up late at night reading the news and felt anxious when they could not follow the news. But from another perspective, many of the nonvoters were acutely aware of politics: The focus group participant we quote earlier reports that their voting options "suck," another participant worried about voting for the "lesser of two evils," and still another questioned whether people in government can actually represent them.

The nonvoters in Knight's study may not be deeply involved but at least some of them are probably in agreement with those who *are* deeply involved that,

---

[1] The Knight Foundation report describes these people as follows: "The group was made up of a combination of those who are eligible but not registered to vote, as well as those who are registered to vote but participated in zero or one of the last six national (presidential and midterm) elections between November 2008 and November 2018" (5).

[2] The US Election Project reports 60.1 percent voter turnout in 2016 among the Voter Eligible Population and turnout was higher in 2020. This rate is, of course, lower during midterm elections where the majority of people typically do not vote.

politically, things are not going well.[3] But agreeing that politics is broken is not the same as agreeing on how to fix it. Indeed, as we will show in this chapter, there are involvement differences in people's perceptions of the most important issues facing America and what it would take to resolve these issues. In other words, a person's level of involvement may not affect whether they believe the system is dysfunctional, but it is their level of involvement that shapes what they believe makes the government especially broken – and whether what is broken can, actually, be "fixed." Involvement, we argue in this book, marks a divide in American politics not only because it shapes how much time people spend following politics but also because it produces variation in how people perceive the role of politics in American society. As we will show in this chapter, there are involvement divides in what people believe are the important issues of the day, how people view politicians, and importantly, how certain they are that they know the correct way to address the important problems of the day.

In order to begin tracking involvement divides, however, the first step is a measure of involvement. Therefore, we begin this chapter by describing the measure we created to place people on a continuum of involvement, in order to distinguish those who are deeply involved from the rest of the public. We then demonstrate that this measure captures a unique concept that is related to other concepts it should theoretically be related to – thereby, demonstrating its validity. We also track this measure across three differently recruited samples.

In the second half of the chapter, we shift focus to a series of analyses that consider the relationship between our measure of involvement and a variety of political outcomes. We first turn to studies on the role of deep involvement in political preferences and subsequently consider an exploratory analysis of involvement and issue positions. Here we see how involvement cuts through a variety of political outcomes like evaluations of the opposing party, evaluations of politicians, and perceptions of the most important issues facing America.

As a final step, we analyze the relationship between the certainty of political beliefs and involvement. In Chapter 3, we theorized that certainty in one's political beliefs should co-occur with deep involvement. We test this idea using an issue where the correct course of action was, *at the time of the study,* uncertain: whether schools should hold in-person instruction and restaurants should be open during the COVID-19 pandemic. We find the types of involvement gaps we theorized in Chapter 3: Those who are deeply involved are much more certain that they know what policies should be put in place.

---

[3] In the Knight Foundation survey, 54 percent of persistent nonvoters and 61 percent of voters reported that America is on the "wrong track." Of course, as we will suggest in the remainder of the chapter, most of the people in the voter sample are probably not deeply involved. Nonetheless, the survey data do point to the idea that the nonvoters do not have a particularly positive view of politics.

People may agree that politics is broken, but we see involvement divides in people's beliefs about how to fix it.

4.1 HOW DO WE MEASURE INVOLVEMENT IN POLITICS?

To measure involvement, we need to separate the *indicators* of involvement from factors that may co-occur with or be consequences of deep involvement. The indicators of deep involvement relate to the characteristics we discuss in Chapter 3: time spent following politics and concerns about missing new information, expression (both public and costly), and a belief in the importance of political events. As we discuss in Chapter 3, given the context of politics, these characteristics also turn "outward" (Dean 2017), which means that the deeply involved may be concerned about the extent to which others follow politics and perceive outcomes to be important.

In developing our measure, we will deliberately separate these indicators from what we describe in Chapter 3 as co-occurrences of deep involvement: certainty in one's beliefs and animosity for those who hold different beliefs. Although certainty and animosity are likely to appear alongside deep involvement, they are not a definitional part of deep involvement. This means that spending a large part of one's day following political news would be an indicator of deep involvement, but having a strong dislike for people who do not share one's political views would be a likely co-occurrence. Feeling sad and anxious that other people are not following politics would be an indicator of deep involvement, but feeling certain that one's views are correct would, again, be a co-occurrence. The goal in developing the scale, then, is focusing on indicators. We can then measure the co-occurrences separately and track the relationship between the two.

4.1.1 Scale Foundations

To develop a scale of deep involvement, we began with fifteen questions attempting to capture the indicators of involvement. All fifteen questions asked a respondent whether they agreed or disagreed with a statement. Our eventual scale is present in Table 4.1 with the excluded set of questions shown in Table 4.2. The statements discuss spending time on politics, viewing political events as important, and expressing political views (in costly ways as well). Since the characteristics we describe in Chapter 3 are abstract, we translate them into measurable ideas by presenting individuals with concrete examples of deeply involved behaviors. These statements include both personal and outward-looking ideas – for example, how people feel about politics and how they feel about others' relationships to politics.

We conducted a pre-test that included all fifteen measures (listed in Tables 4.1 and 4.2). As the goal of this study was to produce a scale – *not* identify nationally representative patterns in deep involvement – we rely, for

TABLE 4.1 *Items that form the involvement scale*

Variable	All Respondents		Democrat	Republican
	Factor 1	Factor 2	Factor 1	Factor 1
It is important to share your political opinions with others.	0.835	0.075	0.813	0.844
It is important to share political news stories with other people.	0.804	0.124	0.769	0.785
It is important to encourage others to be more involved in politics.	0.662	0.453	0.689	0.572
When people tell me that they do not follow politics, it upsets me.	0.622	0.220	0.523	0.802
It is important to spend at least 30 minutes a day learning about the latest events in politics.	0.586	0.311	0.524	0.791
It is important to correct people's misperceptions about politics even if they do not want to hear these corrections.	0.579	0.275	0.586	0.545
It is important to donate money to political campaigns.	0.544	0.145	0.505	0.612

Factor analysis relies on varimax rotation. All items were coded in the same direction. Eigenvalue for factor 1 = 5.04, factor 2 = 1.01, and factor 3 = 0.57.

now, on a convenience sample ($N = 299$) recruited via the online labor market Amazon's Mechanical Turk (MTurk). At a later point in this chapter, we will rely on national samples that allow us to track the *prevalence* of deep involvement in the public.

Using the initial data we collected, we ran a factor analysis to determine which questions respondents answer in similar ways. The factor analysis could have suggested that all of our fifteen statements fell onto different dimensions – for example, it is possible that some statements were part of a time-spent dimension while others were part of an expression dimension. This would suggest that involvement, as we consider it, is not a single unique characteristic but actually two (or more) separate characteristics. The factor analysis could have also said that none of these statements work together because respondents do not agree or disagree with these statements in any clear pattern. This would suggest that either political involvement is not a real characteristic or we just did a terrible job of measuring it.

In the end, the results suggested that the items loaded primarily onto a single dimension (which we have called involvement). Of course, not all

TABLE 4.2 *Items included in the original pretest that do not form part of the final scale*

Variable	All Respondents		Democrat	Republican
	Factor 1	Factor 2	Factor 1	Factor 1
People should regularly contact their elected officials.	0.496	0.393	0.477	0.417
It is important to think about how your actions affect political outcomes.	0.490	0.443	0.588	0.290
People who think politics doesn't affect them are naïve.	0.266	0.584	0.236	0.309
It is every citizen's duty to vote in elections.	0.248	0.557	0.221	0.111
People should not talk about politics at family events.	0.246	0.029	0.370	0.094
People should be able to ignore all political news if it does not interest them.	0.232	0.293	0.280	0.106
Hearing about certain types of political events or political situations can ruin my day.	0.222	0.270	0.082	0.408
I believe it is rare for people to feel anxious about the outcome of an election.	−0.290	0.244	−0.094	−0.497

items were equally good at capturing that single dimension, which is the benefit of conducting a factor analysis. As a result, the seven items that were identified as being a clear single factor form our involvement scale (see factor loadings in Tables 4.1 and 4.2). In Online Appendix V5, we include the scree plots used to develop the scale, as well as the results of an alternative rotation approach.

In the original pre-test, all seven items that were identified as forming the involvement scale were in the same direction, that is, agreement always indicated higher involvement. Given respondent tendencies to engage in survey satisficing (Krosnick 1991; Krosnick, Narayan, and Smith 1996), however, we randomly selected two measures to serve as reverse-coded items. In practice, this means that we reversed two of the items – adding "not" before "important" – to avoid accidentally measuring someone as highly involved or highly uninvolved because they were responding in a rhythm to all the questions.

The seven items that emerged from the factor analysis reflect the various characteristics that we discuss in Chapter 3. Statements about "spend[ing] at least 30 minutes a day learning about the latest events in politics," "when people tell me that they do not follow politics, it upsets me," and that "it is important to encourage others to be involved in politics" reflect the characteristic of spending time on politics.[4] The latter two statements are about other people, which speak of outward components inherent in a political deep involvement (e.g. Dean 2017): Deep involvement is marked by emotional reactions when either you or others are unable or unwilling to follow politics. Next, a set of statements reflect the expression characteristic: These are statements about sharing opinions, sharing news stories, and donating money – which, we argue in Chapter 3, speaks to a costly signal. Finally, a statement also addresses the importance of politics, again through an outward-facing lens. Capturing this perception that even small events may be important is one of the more difficult ideas to measure; therefore, we try to capture it here through the intersection between expression and the importance of political perceptions.

We use this seven-item measure in the studies that form the foundation of our book – although we will make a modification to the measure in Chapter 7 when we focus more directly on involvement and social media use. The list of all of the studies we use is at the end of the book in Appendix A.1. All of the main studies were fielded using survey companies that work to produce samples that approximate national representativeness. Nonetheless, because the survey companies used here – Dynata, Qualtrics, and YouGov – are not survey companies that rely on probability sampling, it is possible that each of the surveys were nonrepresentative in different ways. Hence, observing slight differences in the distribution of the involvement variable could be the result of these differences in sampling procedures.

In all of the studies used in this book, the involvement measure was always asked early on in the survey, after basic demographics. We did this because, both in this and later chapters, the involvement scale will be used as a moderator in experimental analyses and we wanted to make sure that this moderator was always measured pre-treatment (Montgomery, Nyhan, and Torres 2018). To ensure that responses to this involvement scale did not affect any of our experiments (Klar, Leeper, and Robison 2020), the questions that form the involvement scale were usually asked in a separate survey wave from our experimental treatments. Finally, the order of the seven items was always randomized to avoid any bias that could be caused by having a particular item first.

We will use all three surveys throughout the chapter. As we discuss in Chapter 1, we will also return to these samples throughout the book.

---

[4] The statement uses "involved" in a colloquial sense – not in the sense theorized in Chapter 3 and the remainder of this book.

Therefore, we abbreviate the samples to D19 (Dynata 2019; $N = 1,564$), Q20 (Qualtrics 2020; $N = 1,586$), and YG20 (YouGov 2020; $N = 1,500$).

4.1.2 Scale Distribution

As a first step, we begin with the mean and the distribution of political involvement across our different samples. We recoded the variable on a 0 to 1 scale so that higher values indicate deeper involvement. Figure 4.1 displays the mean respondent answer to all seven items in each of the three main samples, with the overall scale score at the bottom of the figure. The bottom of the figure also includes the Cronbach's alpha for the involvement questions for each of the studies, with higher values suggesting better scale reliability. First, we see that no item has a mean response that reflects either strong agreement or strong disagreement. Across the three studies, we note that the Q20 sample consistently leads to slightly lower responses to the items than the other two studies.

Since we combine our seven measures into one involvement scale, in Figure 4.2, we display the distribution of the involvement scale for each of our samples. In all three samples, we see a curve that reflects a normal distribution – very few respondents are totally deeply involved, and very few respondents are totally uninvolved.

This largely normal distribution is to be expected. Deep involvement, as we described in Chapter 3, means making politics a central part of one's life. Most people are not going to do that and will instead prioritize other activities and hobbies (Galais, Blais, and Bowler 2014). On the other hand, few people will absolutely reject that politics is important. Anyone who has ever received government benefits, paid taxes, gotten a driver's license, or waited for a pothole to be fixed on their road understands that government impacts lives and that politics shapes what that government looks like. Hence, it is no surprise that our measure suggests that there are few people who are deeply involved and few people are very uninvolved, while most people lie somewhere in between.

4.1.3 Is Involvement Different from Other Forms of Political Attachment?

To argue that involvement in politics – and deep involvement in particular – is a dividing factor in American politics means suggesting that involvement is its own separate characteristic. Put another way, it means that the idea of involvement is a concept that cannot be captured with another commonly used measure. For example, we commonly measure partisan strength with a follow-up question asking whether someone is a strong or not strong Democrat/Republican after the respondent answers an initial question asking if they are a Democrat or a Republican. An alternative measure of strength of partisanship, however, is the speed with which the respondent answers that initial partisanship question (e.g. Huckfeldt et al. 1999). There could be

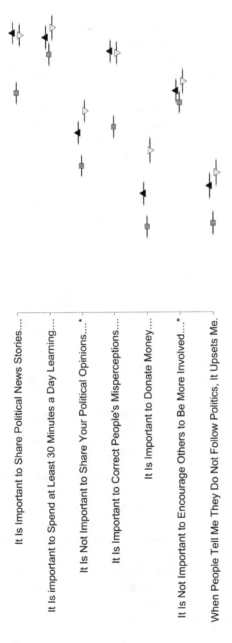

Overall Scale

▲D19: α = 0.79, ■Q20: α = 0.82, ▽YG20: α = 0.76

0.3   0.4   0.5   0.6   0.7

Mean Respondent Answer

FIGURE 4.1 Mean respondent answer to each involvement question in the three main studies
Source: Data from D19, Q20, and YG20. Error bars represent 95 percent confidence intervals. Items marked with * were reverse coded.

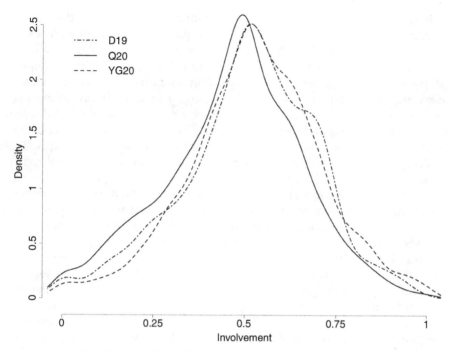

FIGURE 4.2 Distributions of the full involvement scales for each of the three main studies.
Source: Data from D19, Q20, and YG20.

advantages to this alternative measure (e.g. it is continuous and allows for greater variance), but there are disadvantages as well (without a correction for baseline response time, it conflates a weak partisan attachment and slow reading). Regardless of the alternative measure's strengths and weaknesses, however, the alternative measure does not require new theories about the associations between strength of partisanship and vote choice or political activism because the concepts of partisan strength are the same regardless of the measure chosen.

In the case at hand, however, we are asserting that deep involvement is a concept heretofore not captured by common measures included in political science surveys. Certainly, involvement is related to other concepts, but we believe it captures certain aspects of political interest and engagement that previous measures have missed. To determine whether involvement is it is own concept – or simply another way to capture a variety of other characteristics that connect people to politics – we consider the correlation between involvement and a number of other political measures. Here, we focus on measures of partisan strength, ideological extremity, and interest, all factors that capture facets of people's attachment to politics (Mason 2018).

Relying on correlations requires looking for nuanced results. If there is no correlation between involvement and interest, partisan strength, or ideological extremity, for example, then that means we have not created a valid measure of our concept. Involvement *should* be related to these measures; for example, people who are deeply involved will, by definition, be more interested. Indeed, as we argued in Chapter 1, some of the important variation in involvement is likely happening at the highest levels of interest measures. But the correlation between our measure and these other items should not be perfect, or else, the scale we have created is simply a substitute for one of these other concepts.

These additional measures – interest, partisan strength, and ideological strength – are included on the studies run by Q20 and YG20. Notably, in YG20, these additional measures are captured by the YouGov panel, rather than measured as part of our survey, which means that responses to our involvement measure could not have affected responses to these questions and vice versa. In both studies, involvement is most strongly related to interest ($r = 0.45$ in Q20 and $r = 0.44$ in YG20). It is also related, albeit more weakly, to partisan strength ($r = 0.22$ in Q20 and $r = 0.25$ in YG20) and ideological extremity ($r = 0.17$ in Q20 and $r = 0.23$ in YG20).[5] Using Cohen's correlation thresholds, none of these meet the threshold for a high correlation; the correlations with partisan strength and ideological extremity fall below the medium correlation threshold (Cohen 1988). These weaker – but present – correlations suggest that involvement is its own concept but it is most closely related to political interest.

Perhaps, however, involvement is just the combination of these three factors, that is, a person who is deeply involved is simply a strong partisan who is ideologically extreme and very interested. We can test out this possibility by running an OLS regression predicting involvement using these three variables (see Online Appendix M4.1). If the variables can explain most of the variance in involvement, then it would mean that involvement is the combined occurrence (or lack thereof) of these three concepts. In both Q20 and YG20, however, the R^2 of the models is only about 0.22, suggesting that there is a good deal of variance left unexplained by a combination of interest, partisan strength, and extremity.

4.1.4 Capturing Involvement

In sum, as we consider our seven-item scale of involvement, we see patterns suggesting that this scale is capturing the hoped-for variation among Americans. The shape of the distribution suggests that most people are in the middle of the scale, with few people being deeply involved or totally uninvolved.

---

[5] As the measurement details in Online Appendices V2 and V3 explain, the measure of ideological extremity in Q20 has 4 points and only 3 points in YG20, which could explain the slight discrepancy.

This is consistent with our theoretic argument that deep involvement is an approach to politics that is costly and consuming. That the measure correlates – albeit relatively weakly – with ideas like interest, partisan strength, and extremity is also suggestive of an important outcome. People who are deeply involved are likely more interested, more partisan, and more ideological, but the combination of these factors, as we will continue to demonstrate throughout this book, is not enough to explain involvement.

Throughout this chapter and the remainder of the book, we will use the full involvement scale created by our set of seven questions (but we do make a modification to the scale in Chapter 7). This means that, with few exceptions, we will not create involvement categories. Where we do create categories for the ease of presentation (e.g. we do so when we consider voter turnout rates), we specify the thresholds. Still, in many of the results we present here, we see particularly notable changes in the upper third of our involvement scale – which means that a person offered at least somewhat involved responses to each of the seven questions on average. In our discussion of our results, then, the references to the deeply involved and deep involvement refer to these people at the highest points on our scale.

4.2 CHARACTERIZING INVOLVEMENT

With this scale in hand, our next step is to consider if there are certain types of people who are more likely to be deeply involved (i.e., be higher on our involvement scale). This set of analyses is exploratory; we estimate a series of models for each of our three main studies predicting involvement. The models include partisan strength and ideological extremity but exclude interest because we do not have an interest measure in study D19. We note that when we estimate the models for the other two samples including interest, our results remain unchanged (see Online Appendix M4.2). In addition to partisan strength and ideological extremity, we also control for a number of demographic indicators in the model. Probably of greatest interest among this set of demographic variables are education and income since they are associated with what Hersh (2020) terms "political hobbyism," an idea that may be reflected in some of the expressive components of involvement. Furthermore, Hersh (2020) also argues that hobbyism is more likely among liberal Democrats than conservative Republicans. Therefore, we also include variables indicating whether the respondent is a Democrat or a Republican (with pure independents used as the reference category).

The coefficients from the three models are plotted in Figure 4.3a. In Figures 4.3b and 4.3c, we re-estimated the models splitting the data between Democrats and Republicans as a check. We see across all of the models that partisan strength consistently predicts higher levels of involvement. Ideological extremity is also associated with higher levels of involvement, although more consistently among Democrats. Moreover, we also see across all three data sets

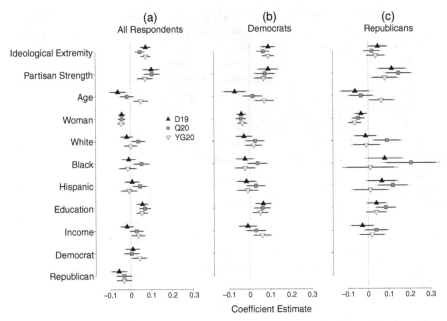

FIGURE 4.3 Coefficients for models with respondent involvement as the dependent variable
Source: Data from D19, Q20, and YG20. Error bars represent 95 percent confidence intervals; where the intervals do not cross the 0 line, the results meet levels of statistical significance. The constants are left off the plot. The constants are 0.472 (D19), 0.345 (Q20), and 0.407 (YG20).

that Republicans are somewhat less likely to be involved than Democrats and independents. One should be cautious about this result for independents, however, as partisan strength is related to involvement and pure independents have no partisan strength by definition. As a result, we would still expect a strong Republican to have higher levels of involvement than a pure independent, but our results suggest that a strong Republican would be somewhat less involved than a strong Democrat.

Also, in line with Hersh (2020), the models show a relationship between education and involvement, but unlike Hersh (2020), we do not see a relationship between income and involvement. When we look at the models for each party, the education variable is only consistently statistically significant in the Democratic model. The size of the coefficient, however, is similar in the Republican models that suggests that the lack of significance may be due to relatively fewer Republicans in the samples (reflecting that there are fewer Republicans at this time in America). This connection between education and involvement is reasonable. From the civic voluntarism perspective (Verba, Schlozman, and Brady 1995), for example, education provides resources and skills that allow individuals to participate in more forms of political activity. Since involvement is associated with costly engagement in politics, education should open the door for this type of behavior.

We see no consistent patterns with regards to age or race. When it comes to gender, however, women are less likely to be deeply involved across all models. There are several possible reasons for this. First, there is research to suggest that women generally have had lower levels of engagement with politics (Bennett and Bennett 1989; Burns, Schlozman, and Verba 2001; Lawless and Fox 2010). Moreover, women are often less confident in their political opinions and have lower political self-efficacy (Preece 2016). It is also possible that, by asking whether respondents would want to correct someone "even if they do not want to hear [it]," the involvement measure implies an aggression in conversations that women often reject (Wolak 2020b). That being said, we do not see especially large gender gaps in this component of the measure, suggesting that the gender differences in involvement speak to patterns beyond measurement issues.

These analyses, then, begin to paint a picture of the deeply involved. These people are more extreme in their partisan attachments and their ideological perspective. They are more educated. They are more likely to be men. And, of course, the deeply involved are interested in politics. But this demographic portrait is not enough to characterize just how different the deeply involved are from other people. In the coming sections, we will delve more deeply into the divide in political preferences between those who are and are not deeply involved.

4.2.1 The Involved Are (Somewhat) More Knowledgeable

A characteristic of deep involvement is spending a good deal of time on politics. To this end, one of the questions that makes up our measure of involvement is whether one should spend time learning about politics daily. This may suggest that people who have higher levels of involvement should be more knowledgeable. On the other hand, people who are *not* deeply involved may pay attention to political news during campaigns and other salient political events; indeed, many people pick and choose when to increase their attention to politics (Bolsen and Leeper 2013). In turn, these individuals may be somewhat knowledgeable but not necessarily deeply involved.

Furthermore, as the very knowledgeable political scientist Arthur Lupia writes in his book on civic competence, in politics, there are so many laws, rules, and regulations that he knows "next to nothing about [their] content" (Lupia 2016, 2). Politics is not like following a television show. People can quote *Seinfeld* by heart because there are only 180 episodes typically lasting only 22 minutes. To be an expert on all things, *Seinfeld* takes dedication, but it is possible. It is impossible to be completely knowledgeable about politics because, as Lupia (2016) notes, the amount of politically relevant information is infinite. You need to know the relevant actors, the institutions, and historical contexts that they operate in; moreover, understanding the effects of public policy may require knowledge of state and local conditions, as well as additional expertise in the physical and social sciences. This means, then, that, unlike a person who is deeply involved in something like *Seinfeld* or *Star Wars*, those who are deeply involved in politics will not (and cannot) know nearly everything about politics. They are likely to know more than the average person, but the relationship between involvement and knowledge is unlikely to be perfect.

In Q20, we included a four-question knowledge battery containing a series of common political knowledge questions (who are Mike Pence and Mitch McConnell? Which of these spending categories does the federal government spend the least on? How long is a senator's term?). The score on this battery correlates with involvement at $r = 0.14$.[6] Figure 4.4 presents a scatter plot with knowledge score on the y-axis and involvement on the x-axis. We added some random noise to make it easier to see where each respondent falls. We have also added a line that represents a LOWESS smoother, which indicates the nonlinear relationship between involvement and knowledge. The figure shows that the average number of correct answers increases as involvement increases. At the

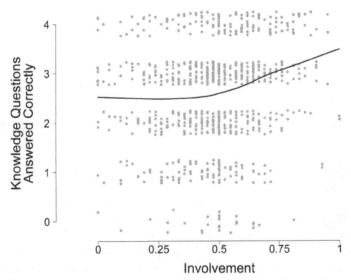

FIGURE 4.4 The relationship between involvement and political knowledge
Source: Data from Q20. Line represents a LOWESS smoother.

---

[6] The scores were distributed as follows: 0 = 4%, 1 = 13%, 2 = 29%, 3 = 36%, and 4 = 19%.

same time, a lot of respondents with perfect scores on the knowledge battery have relatively average involvement scores, while some of the people high on involvement have demonstrated blind spots in their knowledge.

To better understand the relationship between knowledge and involvement, we ran a series of logit models – one for each of the four knowledge questions. The models included controls for party, partisan strength, ideological extremity, and standard demographics (full models are in Online Appendix M4.3). Figure 4.5 plots the predicted probability that a respondent got a particular question correct. The *p*-values in the figures are two-tailed for the coefficient on the involvement variable.

Involvement has no effect on the knowledge of the vice president, as the majority of respondents at all levels of involvement know who the vice president is. On the other hand, involvement has a strong relationship with the ability to identify Mitch McConnell as the senate majority leader (at the time the question was asked). Indeed, if we were to apply a Bonferroni correction to account for the multiple comparisons in this analysis, this is the lone result that would pass the significance threshold. Study participants who have higher levels of involvement are also more likely to know the length of a senator's term, but the relationship falls short of statistical significance. Involvement does have a statistically significant relationship with knowledge that America spends less on foreign aid than Medicare, national defense, or Social Security. At the same

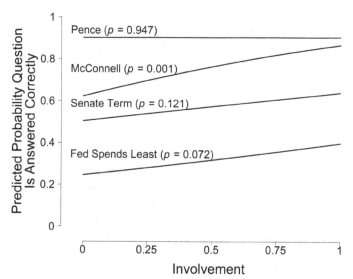

FIGURE 4.5 The relationship between involvement and the probability that each of the knowledge questions is answered correctly
Source: Data from Q20; *p*-values represent the two-tailed *p*-value for the involvement variable in the logit model that can be found in Online Appendix M4.3.

time, many of the 15 percent of respondents who had the highest involvement scores were incorrect about the particular patterns of government spending. While America spends sixteen times as much on Medicare and twenty-five times as much on Social Security as it does on foreign aid, this group of respondents was more likely to pick Medicare (28 percent) or Social Security (22 percent) as the area where the federal government spends the least. Although the modal respondent among the most highly involved chose the correct answer (43 percent), most respondents in this group got it wrong.

The deeply involved are, on average, more knowledgeable than the less involved, but the relationship between involvement and knowledge is far from perfect. Part of the reason for this imperfect relationship is the structure of the knowledge measure that we include in our study. Measures that attempt to capture political knowledge can differ in what they are measuring; some may focus on more general political knowledge, while others may be specific to particular political topics (Barabas et al. 2014; Lupia 2016). The questions asked in our study are somewhat "static" – a senator's term has been fixed since the eighteenth century; the vice president and majority leader had been in their positions for years; and these are the typical knowledge measures included in many political science surveys (Lupia 2016). These types of questions may mute the advantage of the deeply involved: Someone who spends a good deal of time following news on a daily basis is likely significantly more knowledgeable about the day's political events. In other words, the deeply involved would likely dominate knowledge questions that focus on the details of specific news events but appear only slightly more knowledgeable than occasional news watchers on measures that rely on "static" questions of political knowledge.

4.2.2   The Deeply Involved Vote (So Do the Less Involved)

As a next step, we consider the relationship between involvement and voter turnout. We should expect that this relationship is likely positive – indeed, our measure includes an indicator of costly engagement. Our goal here, then, is not to theorize a causal relationship between involvement and voter turnout but rather to consider a correlation. In Figure 4.6, we present the self-reported turnout rates for different levels of involvement in YG20. The turnout measures are from the 2016 primary and general election, as well as the 2018 general election; these were provided by YouGov as part of their panel measures and therefore were captured at a different point of time than our involvement measure. For ease of presentation, the involvement measure is broken into three categories: low (the 13 percent of respondents who scored less than 0.333), high (the 22 percent of respondents who scored above 0.6666), and medium (the 65 percent of respondents who scored somewhere in between). In Online Appendix M4.4, we include results that treat the involvement measure as continuous.

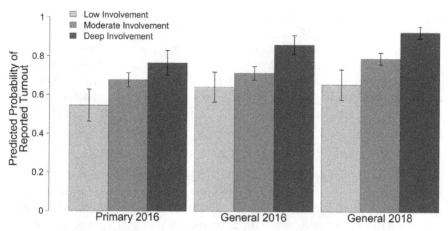

FIGURE 4.6 Mean self-report turnout by various levels of involvement in three elections
Source: Data from YG20. Error bars represent 95 percent confidence intervals.

As the voter turnout measure is self-reported, the patterns in Figure 4.6 almost certainly overstate the amount of turnout within each of the different groups, but it is not clear what this means for the cross-group patterns. Those at the highest levels of involvement would likely feel the most pressure to say they have voted, but they may also have voted in the greatest numbers. Moreover, people with moderate involvement may also feel social pressure to vote. Therefore, it is possible that not only is the turnout rate in every group is biased upward but also the results underestimate the role of involvement.

Regardless, the overall patterns in Figure 4.6 suggest that the deeply involved turn out at higher rates than the rest of the general public. But we note that the majority of people who do not score high on involvement also reported high levels of turnout. For example, 71.4 percent of people in the "medium involvement" category reported turning out in 2016. Although lower than the 86.1 percent of those in the high involvement group who reported turning out in 2016, this is still a notable level of turnout. Of course, this may be due to some over-reporting, but, even if this is the case, the results suggest that involvement does not necessarily shape the perceived responsibility to vote. This same pattern holds if we model turnout behavior controlling for standard predictors of turnout. As an additional robustness check, we adjust our involvement measure by removing the donation question – as this question may be too closely related to other forms of participation, such as turnout. We find identical patterns in the relationship between turnout and involvement as those shown in Figure 4.6. We present the results in Online Appendix M4.5.

What emerges from these turnout patterns, then, is that the deeply involved are more likely to turn out, but turnout rates are not necessarily dramatically higher among this group. The less involved also want to have a say in politics.

Put another way, it would be incorrect to say that the deeply involved are the only ones engaged in politics and fulfilling their civic duties. Those with the highest involvement levels are spending more time on politics and expressing more political opinions, and they are very likely to vote. But lower levels of involvement should not be associated with a lack of turnout – a person need not check the news hourly nor do they need to post about politics on social media in order to turn out and vote.

4.3   INVOLVEMENT AND POLITICAL PREFERENCES

Thus far, the deeply involved differ on some demographic characteristics: They are more educated and more likely to be men; they are also more likely to be strong, ideological partisans. The deeply involved are more knowledgeable about politics on average, though the relationship between involvement and knowledge is not perfect. The deeply involved are more likely to (say that they) vote, but the less involved also reported relatively high levels of turnout. Still, these differences do not necessarily mean that the political preferences of the deeply involved are substantially different from those who are less involved. In what follows, we shift focus from the characteristics of the deeply involved to their political preferences. We begin by considering the relationship between deep involvement and the way people view others: Do the deeply involved, as we suggest in Chapter 3, have less tolerance for those with different political opinions? We then consider differences in political attitudes: Do the deeply involved differ on which types of political issues they believe are most important?

4.3.1   Involvement and Affective Polarization

In Chapter 3, we suggest that co-occurring with high levels of involvement is belief in the benefits of one's position; the outcome of this belief, we suggest, is not just a commitment to one's own position but an animosity toward those who hold different positions. In a political context, one measure that could reflect this is affective polarization, which is defined as a simultaneous affinity for one's own side and animosity toward the opposing side (Iyengar, Sood, and Lelkes 2012). Therefore, as a next step, we consider the relationship between involvement and affective polarization, captured in various forms. We begin with measures that rely on thermometer scores and then turn to social distance measures.

4.3.1.1   *Affective Polarization: Thermometer Measures of Parties and Partisans*

We present a number of measures of affective polarization in Chapter 2, but one commonly used measure is the feeling thermometer rating of the two parties that asks individuals to rate Democrats and Republicans on a scale from 0 (or very cold feelings) to 100 (or very warm feelings). In Chapter 2, we explain that this measure has a potential confound – if a survey asks a respondent to rate "Republicans" or the "Republican Party," respondents may picture party elites (Druckman and Levendusky 2019; Kingzette 2020). Since people generally harbor significantly more animosity toward political elites than ordinary voters, these measures may overstate the level of affective polarization toward ordinary rank-and-file members of a party (Druckman and Levendusky 2019; Kingzette 2020).

We included feeling thermometer measures in the second wave of study D19 and in study Q20. In D19, the question asked about "Republicans" and "Democrats" (which may lead to the confound that Druckman and Levendusky [2019] describe); in Q20, then, we adjusted the measure by specifying that respondents are being asked to rate Democratic and Republican *voters*. To capture affective polarization, we consider the absolute value of the difference between the ratings given to the two parties; higher values mean greater levels of affective polarization. We consider the relationship between involvement using LOWESS smoothers and present these results in Figure 4.7.

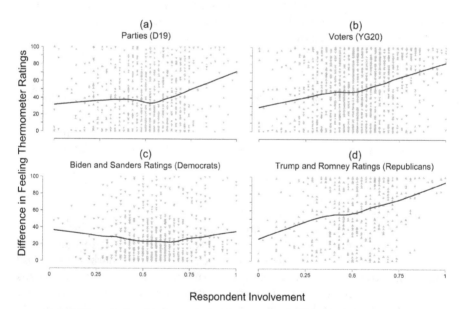

FIGURE 4.7 The relationship between involvement and affect toward parties, partisans, and elites
Source: Data from D19 and YG20. Y-axis reflects the difference in ratings toward one party versus the other (a and b) and differences in evaluations of politicians of one's own party (c and d). For example, the Republicans panel shows that differences in ratings of Trump and Romney increase with involvement.

Beginning with Figures 4.7a and b, which present the relationship between involvement and ratings of the two parties (either generally or party voters), we note two patterns. First, there are gaps in these thermometer ratings of parties even among the uninvolved. In other words, even people who are very low on our measure do not give identical ratings to the Democrats and Republicans. Second, those partisan gaps increase as involvement increases – and they increase nonlinearly. In the D19 data, for example, the line is fairly flat until we get to above-average levels of involvement, and then the line sharply bends upward. Those who are deeply involved – respondents who score above 0.6 on our scale, which means that they indicated some involvement on each question – have distinctly more extreme levels of affective polarization. We see a similar pattern with the Q20 data: Affective polarization increases with involvement, but the slope is steepest after the point we would treat as deep involvement.

Underlying these shifts in slope at the highest levels of deep involvement is another pattern. Among those with average and low levels of involvement, animosity toward the out-party *is greater* than the affection they have for the in-party. This is consistent with the over-time patterns we saw in Chapter 2: Over time, Americans have expressed more animus than partisan love. The deeply involved appear more affectively polarized, however, because they have both high levels of warmth toward their party and the highest animosity toward the other party; this is a pattern in line with our theoretic discussion in Chapter 3. Clearly, there is affective polarization among the less involved, but it seems to lack the intensity of the polarization among the deeply involved.

4.3.1.2 *Affective Polarization: Thermometer Measures of Political Elites*

Thus far, these patterns speak to the theoretic points in Chapter 3: Strong affinity for your own side and animosity toward the other side – measured here as affective polarization – are likely to co-occur with deep involvement. That these patterns are captured through a measure that compares ratings for the two parties is also to be expected. As we write in Chapter 3, partisanship is fundamental to the structure of American politics. If people who are deeply involved harbor the most animosity toward those who get it "wrong" when they engage in politics, one of the more consequential ways to be "incorrect" is to support the opposing party. But, as we argue in Chapter 3, this animosity need not cross party lines. Those who are deeply involved harbor an intense dislike for those who have a different approach to involvement, which means that they may even have some animosity toward members of their own party. This is the "true fans know there is only one best *Doctor Who* Doctor" possibility – but in the case of partisanship. If part of deep involvement is a clear belief that there is only one appropriate way to be a part of something, then we should also observe intraparty differences (which, we note, have been increasing in recent years; see Groenendyk, Sances, and Zhirkov 2020). For example, a deeply involved Republican could harbor resentment not only toward a Democrat but also toward a fellow Republican who just happens to support the "wrong" Republican politician.

Therefore, we turn to these intraparty differences in Figures 4.7c and d by focusing on differences in ratings of politicians within both parties; here, we use data from study YG20. In this study, we asked participants to rate the following politicians on a thermometer scale: Democratic nominee for president, Joe Biden; Republican nominee for president, Donald Trump; Democratic Senator Bernie Sanders; and Republican Senator Mitt Romney. We asked for ratings of Biden and Trump as they were the presidential nominees of the two major party; we asked for ratings of Sanders and Romney as they are more divisive figures within each party. The results Figures 4.7c and d take differences in the ratings of same-party politicians among respondents of that party: The figures presents differences in Democrats' ratings of Biden and Sanders (Figure 4.7c) and Republicans' ratings of Trump and Romney (Figure 4.7d).

The results suggest some intraparty differences, and interestingly, the phenomenon is prevalent at *both* ends of the involvement spectrum. Among Democrats, the results suggest that those who are uninvolved tend to prefer Sanders, and those who are deeply involved tend to prefer Biden. However, it should be noted that the average ratings for *both* men increase among Democrats as involvement increases. It is important to note that this survey took place after the primaries and in the midst of the COVID-19 pandemic. It is possible, then, that had we taken the survey a couple of months earlier, with the Democratic primary front and center, the intraparty differences would have mattered more to the involved.

The pattern is much clearer among the Republicans: The difference in ratings for Trump and Romney grows with involvement. Republicans like President Trump as much as they like Republican voters generally, and those ratings increase with involvement at a similar level. The ratings for Romney, who became the first Senator in history to vote to remove a sitting president from his own party with his vote in Trump's first impeachment trial, are different.[7] Republican ratings for Romney *decrease* as involvement increases. Among Republicans we classify as deeply involved (those who score higher than 0.667 on our scale), Trump has an average rating of 85 degrees; Romney, in contrast, has an average rating of 24.4. Those who are not deeply involved rate Trump at 75.7 and Romney at 32.1 degrees. At the time of this survey, deeply involved Republicans believed that there is an appropriate way to be part of politics, and they were especially certain it is not to remove the Republican president from office.

We should also note that Romney's ratings among out-partisans (i.e. in his case, Democrats) are different from those of the other three politicians. Biden and Sanders both have a mean feeling thermometer rating among Republicans of approximately 18 degrees. Trump's mean feeling thermometer rating among

---

[7] He was also the Republican nominee for president in 2012.

Democrats is 12 degrees. In contrast, out-partisans are very ambivalent toward Romney, which leads to more positive ratings than those out-partisan politicians generally receive.[8] In fact, Romney does better with Democrats than with his fellow Republicans. Romney's mean rating among Democrats is 42 degrees, but it is 30 degrees among Republicans. Furthermore, Republicans are twice as likely as Democrats to rate Romney at 10 degrees or below. This cross-party comparison is especially striking when we focus on the deeply involved. As we already mentioned above, deeply involved Republicans rated Trump at 85 degrees and Romney at 24.4 degrees; deeply involved Democrats, however, rated Trump at 6.9 degrees and Romney at 43.8.[9]

Overall, the emerging pattern in these results is that the deeply involved are more affectively polarized than other people and that they may also perceive more intraparty differences. This is consistent with our argument in Chapter 3 – co-occurring with deep involvement is a narrow perception of what constitute "correct" political beliefs and behaviors. This manifests itself not only in animosity toward the out-party but also in support for the in-party.

4.3.1.3   *Affective Polarization: Social Distance Measures*

In the preceding sections, we rely on thermometer measures of polarization; in this section, we turn to a measure of social distance. Since affective polarization is often considered a social phenomenon (e.g. Garrett and Bankert 2020; Broockman, Kalla, and Westwood 2021), measures of social distance are especially well suited to capturing how people feel about those who are different from them. Here, we return to the same measure we already introduced in Chapter 2: a question that asks respondents how they would feel if their child married a Democrat and one that asks how they would feel if their child married a Republican (Iyengar, Sood, and Lelkes 2012).

In Chapter 2, we delve into the potential confounds in this measure: Since the only thing people know about this future in-law is their partisanship, they may assume that party is especially important to this person. As a result, when people report that they would be unhappy if their child married someone of the opposing party, they may be unhappy about the presence of politics rather than the party itself (Klar, Krupnikov, and Ryan 2018). Therefore, in the measure we use here, we follow Klar, Krupnikov, and Ryan (2018) and modify the question slightly to indicate that the potential in-law *rarely* talks about politics. This allows us to rule out the possibility that a respondent would be unhappy with their child marrying someone from the other party simply because they worry that they are going to have to talk about politics all the time. Specifying that conversation is rare suggests to the respondent that partisanship

---

[8] Independents rate all four below the 50-degree mark. Trump's mean is 31 degrees. Romney's mean is 32 degrees. Biden's mean is 35 degrees. Sanders' mean is 42 degrees.

[9] Among Democrats who are not deeply involved the average ratings are 13.5 degrees for Trump and 40.6 degrees for Romney.

is not all that important to the new in-law, or that, at the very least, they will never have to discuss politics with this new family member (Klar, Krupnikov, and Ryan 2018). On the other hand, if a person is unhappy with an out-party in-law even if they are promised that politics will never come up, then their polarization is more clearly *unconditional* – they dislike the partisan identity, rather than any particular behaviors that may be related to that identity.

In study D19, we asked respondents about their child marrying a Republican or a Democrat who rarely talks about politics. These questions rely on a five-point response scale, and we will focus on the absolute difference between the answers to the Democrat and Republican questions. We present two sets of results in Figure 4.8. In Figure 4.8a, we present the results for the full sample; in Figure 4.8b we replicate the analysis in Klar, Krupnikov, and Ryan (2018) and break the sample into strong and weak partisans.

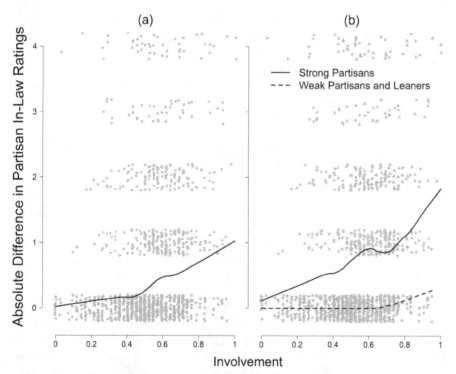

FIGURE 4.8 Relationship between involvement and affective polarization using the measure from Klar, Krupnikov, and Ryan (2018)
Source: Data from D19. Higher values on *y*-axis reflect more affective polarization. The dashed line in panel b includes respondents who report that they are weak partisans, as well as those who report that they are independent but lean toward a party. In the scatterplot in panel b, down triangles are Democrats; up triangles are Republicans.

First, consistent with Klar, Krupnikov, and Ryan (2018), most people in our study give similar answers to the Democratic and Republican questions – more than 60 percent of respondents have a score of 0, giving equivalent ratings to the possibility of having an in-law of either party in their closest family circles. In fact, the answer most people give is that they would be neither happy nor unhappy – indicating that partisanship is *not* what they are most concerned about when thinking about who their hypothetical child might marry. Of those who do have a preference for one party over the other, the difference is typically only one place on the scale.

As the previous set of results in this chapter suggests, we see higher levels of affective polarization as involvement increases (Figure 4.8a). People who are deeply involved are more likely to be happy with a child who marries someone of their own party and unhappy with an in-law from the opposing party.

In Figure 4.8b, we see that these patterns are reinforced by partisan strength. People who are strong partisans who are also deeply involved are especially displeased at the thought of welcoming someone from the other party into their family circle. In contrast, weak and leaning partisans almost always have a score near 0 *regardless* of their level of involvement – though deep involvement does increase affective polarization slightly even here.

The patterns in Figure 4.8 underscore the relationship between affective polarization and deep involvement; these results also point to a potentially broader idea. Buttice, Huckfeldt, and Ryan (2009) argue that polarization is not simply measured by "the location of preferences on some underlying scale, but rather the frequency with which citizens on one side of the political continuum communicate with citizens at the opposite side of the political continuum" (46). What our results hint is that the deeply involved prefer social interactions with people on their own side of the continuum. This is, of course, to be expected. As we discuss in Chapter 3, a person who is deeply involved prefers to discuss their topic of involvement with those who have similar beliefs and preferences. The implication, however, is that there may be a correlation between deep involvement and specific types of social contexts and networks. This is an idea we will explore in greater depth in Chapter 5.

4.3.1.4   *Implications of Involvement for Affective Polarization*

People who are deeply involved, we suggest in Chapter 3, may take a view of their preferences that verges on moral (Hills 2002; Gray 2003; Williams 2013). Ultimately, the outcome may be a strong affinity for their own positions and an animosity for those who hold different views. In the preceding sections, we have considered this affinity/animosity through two perspectives: a cross-partisan lens and an intraparty lens. We find that deep involvement co-occurs with higher levels of affective polarization, captured using both thermometers and social distance measures. We note that *both* animosity and affinity underlie this affective polarization for those who are deeply involved. We also find that deep involvement produces intraparty divides: These divides are especially clear on the Republican side.

The results in the three preceding sections, however, underscore variance in affective polarization: There are some people who are very affectively polarized, but there are other people who are more ambivalent about the parties. There are some people who have affinity for their own side and animosity toward the other side, but there are other people whose animosity is mostly directed at the other party's elites. We find that these differences correlate with deep involvement. Those who are deeply involved also happen to be more affectively polarized. Those at lower levels of involvement are more likely to get along with anyone as long as partisanship is not that individual's defining characteristic. The deeply involved, on the other hand, are much less forgiving not only of allegiance to another party but also when someone of their *own* party is politically involved in a way they perceive to be "incorrect."

4.3.2 The Most Important Problems

In March 2010, Democratic President Barack Obama signed into law the most significant piece of legislation of his administration, the Affordable Care Act (ACA), also known as Obamacare. Four and a half years later, the future leader of the Senate Democrats, New York Senator Chuck Schumer, said that, by passing the landmark legislation, "Democrats blew the opportunity the American people gave them" (Mimms 2014). Schumer argued that prioritizing a lack of health insurance was a mistake because the vast majority of registered voters were already insured even prior to the passage of the ACA. "When Democrats focused on health care," he continued, "the average middle-class person thought, 'The Democrats aren't paying enough attention to me'." At the time of ACA's passage, about forty-six million nonelderly people in America lacked health insurance.[10] Seven years later, the number of uninsured Americans was reduced by twenty million, that is, of course, a lot of people. But Schumer's argument was that ten times as many people saw no direct benefit from the ACA, and both groups of Americans included Democrats.

The case of the ACA is instructive. It is often easy to see differences in perceptions about what issues should be prioritized as partisan divides: Democrats want to prioritize one set of issues, and Republicans want to prioritize a different set of issues. But Schumer's comments about the most important piece of legislation his party passed in decades demonstrate that there are important intraparty considerations as well. These intraparty divisions are not just about what should be the party's third or fourth priority but also about what should be the *top* priority. In the previous sections, we found that involvement affects how partisans felt about different politicians within their

---

[10] Data from the Kaiser Family Foundation American Community Survey.

own party. In this next section, then, we conduct an exploratory analysis to consider whether and how involvement fits into these intrapartisan debates over issue importance. Do people who are deeply involved, we investigate, care about different issues than those with lower levels of involvement?

To track issue priorities in the second wave of Q20, we gave respondents a set of twenty-five issues and asked them to choose the two issues that they believed were the most important issues facing the country. The list was compiled based on the open-ended responses Gallup had recently received to a similar "most important issues" question. Using the Gallup list as a foundation, we then clarified each issue in order to obtain a more precise view of what aspect of the issue people believed was a problem. For example, in our study "abortion" on its own is not a possible choice for the most important issue. Rather, the respondent can choose either the number of abortions performed or threats to abortion rights. The goal is to make it clearer to respondents what *exactly* they are saying is a problem.

An important note is that this survey took place in early 2020 prior to the COVID-19 pandemic reaching America and prior to the murder of George Floyd by a Minneapolis police officer, but during President Trump's *first* impeachment. So, this is a snapshot of what people believed were important issues at a time period that already seems historical. The goal, however, is not to track the universal set of important issues; rather, the goal is to consider whether there are involvement divides in issue importance within parties.

To examine partisan gaps and potential involvement gaps, we ran twenty-five separate logit models. Each of the models includes only two variables: partisanship (pure independents are excluded) and involvement. We then calculate the probability that a respondent will name an issue as one of the two most important in four scenarios: (1) Democrats with an involvement score of 0 (i.e. not at all involved), (2) Republicans with an involvement score of 0, (3) Democrats with an involvement score of 1 (i.e. most deeply involved), and (4) Republicans with an involvement score of 1. These predicted probabilities are shown in Figure 4.9.[11] The issues in the figure are listed in the order in which all respondents said that the issue was important, with the most commonly chosen issues at the top.

First, we notice that one issue stands out. Among all types of respondents, a high percentage report that the cost of health care costs is an important issue facing the country. For other issues that are commonly rated as important, however, we see subgroup gaps in perceived importance. For example, climate change is the third most commonly chosen issue. However, this is largely driven by one subgroup, deeply involved Democrats. Deeply involved Democrats have a 38 percent chance of choosing climate change. This compares to less than

---

[11] Because we were attempting to describe importance within the population, we used sample weights for these models. The weighting procedures are described in Online Appendix V6. The twenty-five logit models are in Online Appendix M4.6.

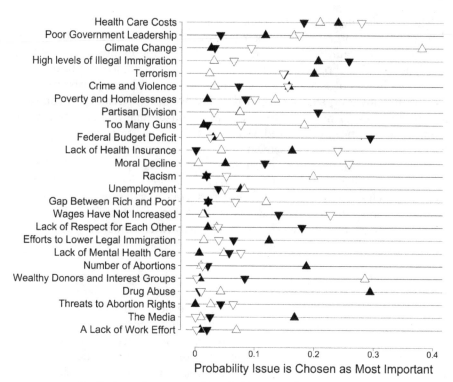

FIGURE 4.9 Predicting what respondents believe are the most important issues by involvement and party

Source: Data from Study Q20. Black triangles = Republicans; white triangles = Democrats; triangles pointing up = involved; triangles pointing down = uninvolved. X-axis is the predicted level of importance; higher levels mean more perceived importance. Models are available in Online Appendix M4.6.

a 10 percent probability for uninvolved Democrats and around a 3 percent probability for all Republicans, regardless of involvement. So, while there is a large partisan gap in seeing climate change as one of the most important issues facing America, this gap is larger once we account for involvement within the Democratic Party.

We see a similar phenomenon with the issue of the budget deficit. Here, the lack of concern among all Democrats and deeply involved Republicans is even more pronounced – they all have a 4 percent chance or less of rating the budget deficit as major problem. On the other hand, uninvolved Republicans have an almost 30 percent chance of choosing it as one of the most important issues. And with regard to the issues of low wages, the divide is greater between the deeply involved and the uninvolved than between Democrats and Republicans.

These results suggest a larger point. If politicians want to prioritize the issues that are most important to their voters, the question they have to ask is, "which voters?" In our data, climate change and wealthy donors are the issues that deeply involved Democrats believed were important in addition to health care costs. The importance of those issues (other than health care costs) to other Democrats, however, sharply declined as involvement decreased. In contrast, low wages, lack of health insurance, and moral decline in the nation were unimportant to deeply involved Democrats, but their importance to other Democrats increased as involvement decreased.

While the within-party differences were less pronounced among Republicans, paying attention only to the deeply involved would cause Republican elites to miss some of their voters' concerns. For example, division between Democrats and Republicans is the fourth most commonly chosen problem by Republican respondents, but it was rarely chosen by the deeply involved Republicans (who, as we suggest in the previous section, are polarized themselves).

In sum, our data suggest that involvement cuts across parties, creating gaps that may have representational effects. If politics, as Lasswell (1936) suggested, is about "who gets what, when and how," then the patterns we present in this section add a complication to "who" and "what." As we write in Chapter 3, a component of deep involvement is the need for expression – indeed, this is part of our involvement measure. When there are many issues that require attention, what distinguishes issues that are addressed by the government from those that remain unaddressed is, often, the loudness of the voices calling for action on a particular issue (Verba, Schlozman, and Brady 1995). Not only do the deeply involved care about different issues but also their voices are likely louder.

4.4 INVOLVEMENT AS A CONFIDENCE GAP

Deeply involved people harbor more animosity toward those who have different political positions; they also believe that different issues are important. The next potential involvement gap we analyze does not consider differences in actual political preferences and positions but differences in how people *feel* about these positions. Chapter 3 hints at a relationship between involvement and certainty; those who are deeply involved, we suggest, are more certain that they are holding the correct position. Although we will test this idea of certainty, in this section we also extrapolate to a broader conception of confidence. If involvement co-occurs with certainty that one knows the best policy course, then it is possible that involvement also co-occurs with a sense of political efficacy. In other words, people who are deeply involved may generally feel more confident in their ability to influence politics.

In this chapter, we consider certainty and confidence using an experiment and a series of survey questions included in YG20. We begin with the experiment, which addresses certainty, and then turn to survey questions that track a broader confidence in one's ability to influence politics.

4.4.1 Certainty in the Best Policy

As a first step, we turn to an experiment to examine whether involvement has a relationship with certainty in one's beliefs. In this study, we operationalize certainty as one's belief that they know what policies are best for the public. This follows from Edelman's (1988) argument that certainty in one's position often translates into the belief that this position is in best interests of the public.

The experiment was part of YG20 and was fielded in late June, 2020. Therefore, the field dates occurred at a point that could be described as either the resumption of the first wave or the beginning of second wave of the COVID-19 pandemic in America. The study, then, focuses on policies related to COVID-19. All respondents were asked two questions, but the precise formulation of those questions was randomly assigned. One group was asked, "Please tell us if you think the following policies would be a *good idea* in terms of the nation's public health and economic security" (emphasis added). The other group was asked, "Please tell us if you think the following policies are *going to take place* in the majority of U.S. states" (emphasis added). The key difference is that the first version of the question asks what the policy *should* be ("good idea" treatment), and the second asks what the respondent believes the policy is going to be in actuality ("prediction" treatment). Respondents were given five options: (1) I am very confident this [is a good idea/will happen], (2) I am confident this [is a good idea/will happen], (3) I am confident this [is a bad idea/will not happen], (4) I am very confident this [is a bad idea/will not happen], and (5) I do not know if this [is a good idea/will happen]. Hence, people who are confident in their assessments of the first formulation have strong normative beliefs, while individuals who are confident in the second formulations have confidence in their ability to predict political outcomes.

Respondents were asked about two COVID-related policies: schools opening in the fall of 2020 and restaurants operating at full capacity in July 2020. These particular questions provide a useful context for addressing confidence. During the summer of 2020, there was tremendous uncertainty about the progression of COVID-19 and, in particular, the role children (and schools) play in the spread of the virus (e.g. Saleem et al. 2020). Therefore, reporting confidence in this case would be a strong signal about an overall predisposition toward one's place in politics.

In analyzing our experiment, our focus is not on what people thought about these policies.[12] Instead, we are interested in how *certain* and *confident* people

---

[12] The distributional results by party are as follows. For whether it is a good idea to open schools: all respondents – 36% good idea, 41% bad idea, and 23% don't know; Democrats – 16% good idea, 58% bad idea, and 25% don't know; independents: 31% good idea, 41% bad idea, and

are in their beliefs and predictions. Hence, we coded our dependent variable as 1 if the respondent was very confident, 0.5 if the respondent was confident, and 0 if the respondent said they did not know. In Figure 4.10, we plot the predicted values from a model in which we interact treatment assignment with involvement.

As the figure demonstrates, for the "prediction" treatment, regardless of whether the question is about schools or restaurants, involvement has no effect on confidence about what will happen. Put another way, people at all levels of involvement are equally uncertain about which policies will actually be

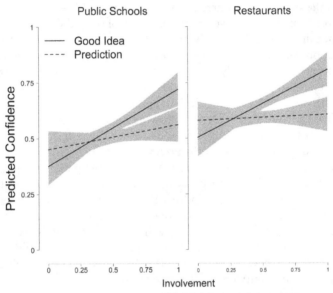

FIGURE 4.10 How involvement shapes beliefs about COVID-19 policies
Source: Data from Study YG20. Shaded areas represent 95 percent confidence intervals. Models are available in Online Appendix M4.7.

28% don't know; and Republicans – 65% good idea, 19% bad idea, and 16% don't know. For whether schools will open: all respondents – 53% yes, 26% no, and 21% don't know; Democrats – 39% yes, 31% no, and 30% don't know; independents – 50% yes, 31% no, and 19% don't know; and Republicans – 73% yes, 17% no, and 10% don't know. For whether it is a good idea for restaurants to open at full capacity: all respondents – 26% good idea, 59% bad idea, and 16% don't know; Democrats – 9% good idea, 78% bad idea, and 13% don't know; independents – 22% good idea, 59% bad idea, and 21% don't know; and Republicans – 50% good idea, 33% bad idea, and 17% don't know. For whether restaurants will open at full capacity: all respondents – 31% yes, 53% no, and 16% don't know; Democrats – 21% yes, 62% no, and 17% don't know; independents – 23% yes, 54% no, and 23% don't know; and Republicans – 49% yes, 41% no, and 10% don't know.

implemented. The patterns, however, are different in the "good idea" treatment. Here, confidence increases with involvement. First, the deeply involved are significantly more certain that their beliefs represent the correct course of action than those who are uninvolved. Across treatments, the deeply involved are also significantly more certain and confident about what *should* happen than what will happen. In contrast, those at lower levels of involvement are equally uncertain about what should happen and what will happen.

The results suggest that most of our respondents have a belief about what should happen and what will happen, but they will not go as far as to say that they are "very confident" in either case. On the other hand, the minority at the highest levels of involvement – the deeply involved – are much more likely to say that they are "very confident" about what *should happen* but are not as confident about what *will actually happen*.

One possibility is that the involved are more confident because they have more information, which provides them with a better understanding of what the best policies would be. Although this may be reasonable when it comes to certain political issues, that does not make as much sense in the case of COVID-19, where research was – and still is – evolving. Furthermore, if underlying knowledge was the mechanism driving the increased confidence, we would expect more educated study participants to have similarly higher confidence. We do not see this pattern: Education has no effect on what people believe the best policy should be. Furthermore, people who are more educated are actually *less confident* about what they believe should happen. Indeed, these patterns imply that following more information on COVID-19 may have the effect of making people less confident about the appropriate course of action.

Yet, the deeply involved are certain about what is the best COVID-19 policy. When faced with a widespread pandemic caused by a novel virus that scientists are trying to learn about on the fly, the deeply involved are still confident that they know what we are supposed to do.

4.4.2 Confidence in the Ability to Influence Elections

People who are at higher levels of involvement have more certainty and confidence that they know the best policy approach. Next, we consider this confidence more broadly through a series of questions measuring internal efficacy adapted from Niemi, Craig, and Mattei (1991), asking respondents whether they agreed or disagreed with the following statements:

1. I think that I am as well-informed about politics and government as most people.
2. I consider myself well-qualified to participate in politics.
3. I do not understand many of the important political issues facing our country.
4. I feel that I could do as good a job in public office as most other people.

These questions measure the extent to which the respondents believe that they have the knowledge and ability to participate in politics. Internal efficacy is a key component in translating responses to world events into participatory action. For example, if an individual encounters political information that makes them anxious, then they are more likely to participate in politics as a way of dealing with that anxiety only if they are highly efficacious – that is, they believe that their actions will make a difference (Rudolph, Gangl, and Stevens 2000). Furthermore, not only can internal efficacy spur individuals to action but also participation can cause individuals to be more efficacious (Valentino, Gregorowicz, and Groenendyk 2009). Hence, those rich in internal efficacy often become richer.

To analyze the relationship between involvement and efficacy, we ran four separate models for each of the four statements. The dependent variable was coded 1 if the respondent gave the efficacious statement (agree to statements 1, 2, and 4 and disagree to statement 3) and 0 if the respondent gave any answer lacking in internal efficacy (disagree to statements 1, 2, and 4 and agree to statement 3, or neither agree nor disagree to any of the statements). Besides involvement, the other variables in the model were partisan strength, education, gender, age, income, and partisanship.

In the results in Figure 4.11, we concentrate on three variables: partisan strength, education, and of course, involvement. We look at partisan strength because strong attachment to a party is associated with potentially higher internal efficacy (Huddy, Mason, and Aarøe 2015). Higher levels of formal education should also result in higher feelings of internal efficacy as education provides individuals with the skills necessary to participate in politics – though there are other routes to gain the knowledge necessary for both participatory skills (Brady, Verba, and Scholzman 1995) and feelings of efficacy (Beaumont 2011). Our goal is to consider whether involvement has a larger association with internal efficacy than these other variables.

The answer, according to the results in Figure 4.11, is yes. Partisan strength is weakly correlated with beliefs about whether the respondent believes they are well informed but not the other three measures. There is a statistically significant relationship between education and three of the internal efficacy measures. Involvement is positively associated with all four questions, and the size of that relationship is much larger than any other variable. These results are similar to Morrell (2003), who found that education was moderately associated with internal efficacy in the ANES, but interest, discussion frequency, and watching the news were *jointly* responsible for the largest association with internal efficacy. The intersection of these three variables likely correlates with our involvement measure.

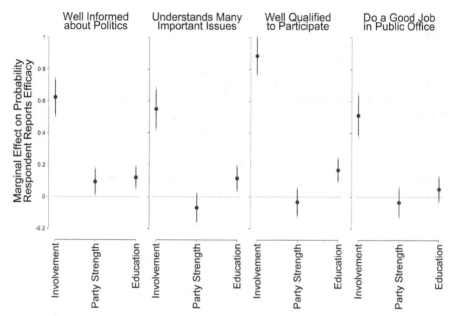

FIGURE 4.11 Comparing the associations between involvement, partisan strength, and education with measures of internal efficacy
Source: Data from Study YG20. Thin error bars represent 95 percent confidence intervals, while thicker bars represent 90 percent confidence intervals. Models are available in Online Appendix M4.8.

4.5 CONCLUSION

In this chapter, we developed a measure of involvement that allowed us to describe how differences in involvement shape American politics. The involved are more interested in politics, more extreme in their views, and more attached to their party. They have more affectively polarized attitudes toward voters and elites alike. The deeply involved prioritize different issues than less involved individuals in their own party. And, perhaps most consequentially, the deeply involved are certain in their viewpoints and confident in their ability to participate in politics.

Is deep involvement in politics a substitute for other forms of nonpolitical involvement? Indeed, some pundits have argued that for people who are especially engaged with partisanship, politics has come to replace religion (e.g. Green 2018; Gerson 2019). In YG20, we do find that people who identify as atheist or have higher mean values of involvement than the rest of the population (0.58 vs. 0.52; p = 0.00). However, we also included a religious battery in Q20 and did not find a similar difference (0.47 vs. 0.48; p = 0.26). Therefore, while it is possible that some people have replaced religion with politics, it is equally plausible that some religious people have found a second religion in politics.

Although this chapter suggests involvement divides in a variety of important political variables, this chapter also leaves a question – how does a person come to be deeply involved? In the next chapter, we turn to one explanation: socialization. Deep involvement, we will show, is socialized – though, perhaps not always intentionally – in childhood homes. Then, it is reinforced through social contexts, such as which college one attends. Then, in adulthood people eventually find themselves in "homophilous bubbles of involvement" – they are most likely to discuss (or avoid) politics with people who are just as (un) involved as they are. Involvement in politics, indeed much like involvement in other topics, is a self-reinforcing social cycle.

5

Bubbles of Involvement

A lot of times when I talk to people about Star Trek, they think I am a fanatic. It feels good to talk to someone that is really interested in what you are interested in.
                                    Randy, Star Trek fan in Thorne and Bruner (2006)

Bobby once owned twenty-two cars. In fact, he had so many cars that he had to store them "everywhere, in my garages, friends' and relative's garages" (Bloch, Commuri, and Arnold 2009, 54). Bobby, as his twenty-two cars might suggest, is deeply involved in cars and auto-repair. He attributes his deep involvement to his childhood interactions with his father, who, Bobby recalls, also loved cars. When he owned the twenty-two cars, Bobby says, "My two sons were old enough to enjoy cars as well and they too were hooked" (Bloch, Commuri, and Arnold 2009, 54).

John is deeply involved in jazz (though, perhaps, slightly less so than Morris B. Holbrook). He was not always deeply involved in jazz, though. In fact, as he describes it, "I don't think I was truly hooked on jazz until college." He attributes his involvement in jazz to his freshman-year college roommate; that roommate's music collection, John recalls, "was almost entirely jazz" (Bloch, Commuri, and Arnold 2009, 55).[1]

Stephanie recalls spending a large portion of her life hiding her deep involvement in *Star Trek*. Then, she attended a *Star Trek* convention and discovered many other people with the same interest: "[S]ome of these people have become very close friends. We have a lot in common and have had some of the same experiences" (Kozinets 2001, 74). Kozinets (2001) explains that

---

[1] The "John" referenced here is not the co-author of the book. The co-author's freshman-year roommate (who was not into jazz) agreed to get him a ticket to a Blur concert the roommate was attending and then forgot; this troubling experience in his college social context is not the main reason the co-author prefers Oasis.

Stephanie found her own community of people who were equally deeply involved in *Star Trek*. She found "others of her own kind" – people who validate her love of the show (Kozinets 2001, 74).

Deep involvement is, inherently, social. Bobby loves cars because his father talked about cars; Bobby's sons love cars because Bobby introduced them to cars. John became deeply involved in jazz because his college roommate was deeply involved in jazz. Stephanie found her own social community of people who are as deeply involved in *Star Trek* as she is. Deep involvement is often socialized, and it is maintained in social contexts.

The stories Bobby, John, and Stephanie tell are about cars, jazz, and *Star Trek*, but they could easily be about politics. Politics is also, inherently, social. Where Bobby tells of his dad's influence on his love of cars, someone can tell a story of how their parents' interest in politics led them to also have a high level of political interest (e.g. Prior 2019). John recalls how his freshman-year roommate taught him about jazz, but another person may recall how their freshman-year roommate encouraged them to become politically engaged (e.g. Minozzi et al. 2020; Strother et al. 2021). Stephanie felt alone in her love of *Star Trek* until she found a community of like-minded people. So too someone may find themselves in a social context where they do not feel comfortable discussing their politics and deliberately seek out and cultivate a more politically supportive social environment (Rainie and Wellman 2012; Van Duyn 2018).

This parallel between the role social interactions play in shaping deep involvement and the role they play in shaping political preferences suggests an important possibility: social factors may allow us to trace the "origin story" of deep involvement. In Chapter 4, we already saw that people who are deeply involved are politically different from those who have lower levels of involvement – to the point that they do not want members of the other party in their family even if they know the other person will not want to talk about politics. In this chapter, we consider social experiences like Bobby's and John's to track the antecedents of this deep involvement in politics. Then, we analyze social networks to see whether deeply involved people gravitate, like Stephanie, toward others who are deeply involved in politics.

We find patterns that reflect the three stories that begin this chapter. People who are deeply involved in politics recall political conversations with their parents; they also seem to have similar college experiences. In Chapter 4, we found that people who are deeply involved in politics were most likely to report that they would be unhappy if their son or daughter married someone of the opposing party – they were most likely to reject those who were politically different. In this chapter, analyses of social networks reflect that the deeply involved "practice what they preach": People who are deeply involved are in networks with people who are just like them.

5.1 DEEP INVOLVEMENT IN A SOCIAL CONTEXT

Before we turn to analyses of the relationship between social contexts and involvement, we must begin with a caveat. Providing definitive causal evidence about how social interactions either shape or maintain involvement is beyond any particular research team at this point. At a minimum, such an explanation would require following individuals from childhood through at least early adulthood, meaning results would not be available for about thirty years from now (e.g. Jennings and Niemi's Youth and Socialization Study). Even then, however, the analysis would still be largely correlational – after all, we cannot randomly assign people to the myriad different choices and events that shape the social components of people's lives.

Past research, however, does allow for a path forward by suggesting a number of social factors that are especially likely to be important to the development and maintenance of involvement. These social factors – parental socialization, early-life experiences, and network formation – are deliberately reflected in the three stories that start this chapter. Each story may be simple but each reflects large foundations of research about the way social experiences affect our ultimate preferences. As we turn to each of the social factors we consider in this chapter, we will return to the body of work underlying our empirical tests.

5.2 SOCIALIZATION AND DEEP INVOLVEMENT

Studies suggest that parents are often "important initial triggers" of involvement (Bloch, Commuri, and Arnold 2009, 54). Bobby, the man who is so deeply involved in cars that he at one point owned twenty-two of them, attributed his own deep involvement to his father's deep involvement in cars. In interviews with deeply involved people, Bobby's story was common: "the transfer of interest from a parent to the child," Bloch, Commuri, and Arnold (2009) concluded, "was deliberate, persistent, and began early."

The development of political interests may, for some, also begin with parents. Children learn about both politics and political engagement by observing their parents: The more the parents engage with politics, the more likely are the children to engage with politics later on (Wolak 2009; Dinas 2014). Even if (as adults) children reject their parents' particular political views (Hatemi and Ojeda 2021), parents are still often their first sources of political experiences.

Key to the relationship between children and politics is the extent to which the parents discuss political topics at home – something that politicized parents are more likely to do (Wolak 2009; Dinas 2013). It is these discussions, then, that give children information about their parents' political preferences and views of the political world (Jennings, Stoker, and Bowers 2009). Notably, while Bloch, Commuri, and Arnold (2009) assume deliberateness in parental transmission of preferences, political scientists are more agnostic. Wolak (2009), for example, notes that children may simply *overhear* their parents discuss politics with others. We set the idea of deliberate versus accidental socialization aside for now, but we will return to it in Chapter 6 when we use parenting decisions to analyze the relationship between involvement and the value of politics.

Although research connects parents' political discussions with the transmission of *partisanship* to children (Wolak 2009), consistent with research in other domains, these discussions may also increase children's levels of involvement. People who have clear signals about which party is better are unlikely to possess the underlying ambivalence that dampens political interest (Huckfeldt, Mendez, and Osborn 2004). We can extrapolate this idea to socialization: If children receive clear partisan signals from their parents (either deliberately or accidentally) about which party is better, then they may have a greater engagement with politics. Furthermore, if children see their parents openly expressing opinions about politics, they may be more likely to believe that they too can express opinions about politics. This domain-specific self-confidence might relate to a more general feeling of self-confidence that is associated with early development of a partisan identity (Wolak and Stapleton 2020).

This is not to argue that parents are the lone factor in political socialization. Although the role of parents is pivotal, political socialization also occurs in schools (Holbein and Hillygus 2020; Neundorf, Niemi, and Smets 2016), especially in high school, where both civics classes and interactions with peers can help adolescents develop political identities (McDevitt 2018). In addition to social interactions with peers, research suggests that a student's participation in activities such as student government (Verba, Schlozman, and Brady 1995; Galston 2004), clubs, and competitive sports (Fox and Lawless 2014) could also affect their future relationships with politics.[2]

Given the different early-life factors that may influence political engagement, we turn to a survey in which we measured a variety of socialization factors. Specifically, we asked respondents about what their home was like when they were a child, as well as what their high school experience was like both in and out of the classroom. These measures were included in study Q20, and we turn to the relationship between deep involvement and these various measures in the next section.

---

[2] The connection between engagement and sports is somewhat less empirically clear than the connection between student government and political engagement. Verba, Schlozman and Brady (1995) do not find that participation in sports increases engagement. On the other hand, Fox and Lawless (2014) suggest that participation in sports may affect political ambition, rather than political engagement. Since our focus is on involvement – a perception of the importance to politics, rather than participation directly – we do consider the role of sports as a potentially relevant factor.

5.2.1 Different Forms of Socialization

In Figure 5.1, we present the results of an OLS model, which treated involvement as the dependent variable and socialization measures as the main independent variables. These variables capture the role of politics in the family home, political interactions in schools, other school activities, and school type. In this model, we include the same set of demographic variables that were used in the previous chapter to predict involvement (results in Figure 4.3) but this time as control variables. These variables are ideological extremity, partisan strength, age, gender, race, ethnicity, income, and partisanship.

For comparison, we present estimates for the models with and without the socialization measures. In Figure 5.1, we first present the coefficient estimates for variables that were included in the demographics-only model (Figure 4.3a in the previous chapter). While the effects of most variables are largely unchanged due to the addition of the socialization measures, we do see some differences. Most notably, we find that including measures of socialization means that education is no longer significant. We will deal more directly with the role of education in a coming section of this chapter but for now note that this result would suggest that education *itself* is not providing a means by which people

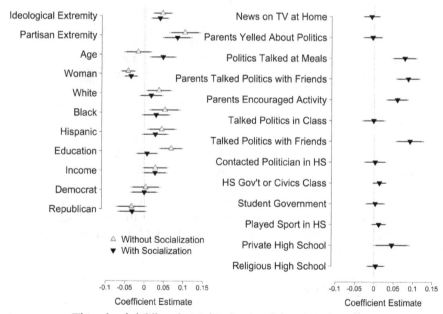

FIGURE 5.1 The role of childhood socialization in adult political involvement
Source: Data from Q20. The thick lines represent 90% confidence intervals, while the thin lines represent 95% confidence intervals. The up-pointing triangles and intervals in the left panel reflect a model without additional socialization measures.

become deeply involved. Rather, it may be that some home environments encourage both education and political involvement; hence, the *home* is the primary factor, and educational attainment is simply a proxy for the home environment (see also Kam and Palmer 2008; Weinschenk and Dawes 2021).

When we look at the additional socialization variables (Figure 5.1), a clear pattern emerges. The socialization variables that consistently have a relationship with involvement are those measures that indicate political discussion: talking about politics with your school friends, watching your parents talk about politics with their friends, and talking about politics with your family. Moreover, people who remember their parents encouraging them to be active in politics are also more likely to report being deeply involved. Put another way, the factors that are most likely to be associated with involvement are most directly social.

Furthermore, we see that none of the measures of school activities are significant predictors of involvement: taking a civics class, playing a sport, or participating in student government do not affect involvement. The lack of a correlation between involvement and civics class or sports should not come as a surprise. In their review of the data on the effects of civics classes on future turnout, Holbein and Hillygus (2020) find only small effects. Moreover, Verba, Schlozman, and Brady (1995) find that participation in sports has limited effects on the civic skills necessary for participation. The lack of a correlation between student government and involvement may be more surprising, given the patterns in Verba, Scholzman, and Brady (1995). Still, it is possible that student government could be an important way in which students learn civic skills necessary for participation (Verba, Scholzman, and Brady 1995), without having any relationship to the importance people place on politics (i.e. involvement).

Although the socialization experiences we measure preceded the present-day measurement of involvement, we note that our results are still correlational. It is plausible, for example, that people's present-day deep involvement leads them to remember more social political experiences in their childhoods than do those who have lower levels of political involvement. Still, even if present-day involvement is correlated with *perceptions* of childhood experiences, it is notable that these perceptions are more social. People who are deeply involved, our results suggest, either have childhoods with more social political interactions or, like Bobby who remembers talking about cars with his dad, remember their childhoods as full of political discussion.

5.2.2 An Additional Check

Our data suggest that people's memories of a childhood full of political conversation correlate with present-day involvement more so than other socialization factors that have been associated with increased political engagement (e.g. participation in student government). Since our sample is designed to represent the general population, however, there is variance in how long ago a person in our sample was living in their parents' home. Therefore, we conduct an additional check using a survey that focused specifically on younger people. The survey was completed in 2013 as part of a multicountry "Civic Network" study designed to analyze young people's use of social media to engage in civic behaviors (Vromen, Xenos, and Loder 2013). The study includes three separate surveys conducted in three different countries, and here we use the American survey.

The American component of the Civic Network study (N = 1,228) included interviews with respondents aged 16–29. Importantly, the survey was based on quota sampling to produce relatively equivalent subgroups of three age groups ((1) 16–19, (2) 20–24, and (3) 25–29), which means the resulting data is not a representative sample of Americans aged 16–29. Therefore, we use the data to consider the relationships between measures, rather than estimates of population-level dynamics. Importantly, for our purposes, the Civic Network survey included measures of the extent to which politics was discussed in the respondents' home as they were growing up as well as measures of their present-day levels of political engagement. The survey does *not* include our measure of involvement (after all, it is a new measure we developed), and therefore, we use a variety of characteristics associated with involvement as proxies.

Since the Civic Network survey included many questions about political behavior, there are a variety of measures that offer helpful proxies. A number of these questions, we note, are quite close to the measures that make up our involvement scale. First, we proxy the perceived importance of participatory activities with questions about campaign involvement and donation behaviors. We proxy the importance of learning about politics, another involvement measure, via a question on the Civic Network study that asks about the importance of "knowing how to vote on major issues," as well as a question about attention to news. Another involvement measure asks about the importance of expressing opinions, and we proxy this with a Civic Network measure that asks about the importance of discussing social and political issues with others and posting on social media.

In Figure 5.2, we consider participants in three categories: (1) people who report that they "never" or "hardly ever" discussed politics with their parents and families, (2) people who report that they "sometimes" did so, and (3) people who report that they discussed politics with parents and families "frequently" or "all the time." We find that, in this survey of young respondents, frequency of family discussion correlates with various behaviors related to involvement. The group reporting that their parents discussed politics "frequently" or "all the time" is significantly higher on each involvement proxy than either the "never"/ "hardly ever" group or the "sometimes" group. Especially notable are the patterns for sharing political thoughts on social media, where respondents in families with frequent political discussion are

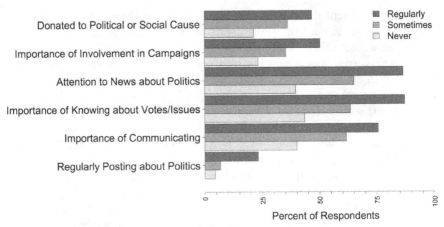

FIGURE 5.2 Political discussion with parents and political behaviors
Source: Data from the American component of the Civic Network study. Bar shading corresponds to how frequently the respondent reports talking about politics with their parents.

nearly 19 percentage points more likely to post regularly than those whose families rarely discuss politics.[3]

Jointly, the results from this check using the Civic Network study and the results from our study measuring involvement directly reinforce the co-occurrence between conversations with parents and indicators of involvement. People whose parents talked about politics are then more likely to become deeply involved in politics. Much as experiences with parents are antecedents of involvement in other areas, so too do parents seem to play some role in people's later relationship to politics.

5.3   COLLEGE CHARACTERISTICS AND INVOLVEMENT

In the second story that begins this chapter, John (not the co-author) recalls being introduced to different forms of jazz through interactions with his college roommate (Bloch, Commuri, and Arnold 2009). John's experience is not unique. The earliest adult socialization for many Americans takes place in

---

[3] We combine measures about Facebook and Twitter to obtain a general social media variable. We note, however, that the two measures are slightly different. The Facebook measure asks how people how often they "post [their] own thoughts or comments on politics or social issues," while the Twitter measure asks about sharing "information about news and politics (through tweets or retweets)." If we split these measures, we obtain similar results: There is a 17-percentage-point difference separating the rarely and frequently categories in the Facebook measure and a nearly 20-percentage-point difference separating these two groups on the Twitter measure. If we were to use a different Twitter measure, this time asking whether people "discuss politics or issues in the news (through replying to others' tweets)," we would see a difference of 18.3 percentage points.

college; in fact, there is research to suggest that college environments may be more important to the development of political preferences and identities than the family home (Stoker and Bass 2011). Moreover, the college environment can take the place of familial socialization for children who do not discuss politics with their parents (Raychaudhuri 2018). Indeed, the importance of college has led some conservatives to fear that political socialization in college is too powerful, often taking the form of "liberalization" of college students (Mendelberg, McCabe, and Thal 2017).

This fear of liberalization originates with Newcomb's (1943) pre–World War II study of women at Bennington College, which showed that students generally shifted from conservative attitudes when they arrived to more liberal attitudes when they left. The women tended to keep those more liberal attitudes after they graduated and as they aged (Newcomb et al. 1967). Since Newcomb's work, research has shown that the liberalization hypothesis is not unconditional and not uniform. As Mendelberg, McCabe, and Thal (2017) demonstrate, some college environments can liberalize students, but other college environments can conservatize students. Even more recently, Strother et al. (2021) also find no evidence of overall liberalization but do find college students moving politically closer to their college roommates. What is important for our purposes is not the ideological direction of any potential socialization that occurs in college but simply that the college environment exerts a role in shaping political preferences (Newcomb et al. 1967; Mendelberg, McCabe, and Thal 2017; Mendelberg et al. 2020; Strother et al. 2021).

As a next step, then, we turn to the relationship between college attendance and involvement. We note that our analyses here are more limited – especially in comparison with other studies of the college environment (Mendelberg, McCabe, and Thal 2017; Minozzi et al. 2020; Strother et al. 2021). That being said, however, our goal is not to determine how college interactions shape ideology, partisanship, or even specific issue positions. Rather, the data we present will allow us to consider whether the *type* of institution – a proxy for the broader social environment in which a person attended college – correlates with involvement. As a result, this analysis can help us move beyond educational attainment as a general measure and closer to socialization in context.

In study Q20, 731 respondents said they attended (but did not necessarily graduate from) a four-year college, and 485 provided information about the college they attended, which allows us to get information not only about the participant's education level but also about their college or university.[4] There

---

[4] We conduct a check to ensure that involvement does not predict a willingness to share where a participant went to college and find that there is no relationship between these two variables. Other demographic variables are similarly not predictive of willingness to name one's college, with the lone exception of income that comes closest to, though ultimately does not meet, conventional levels of statistical significance.

are, of course, selection effects both in terms of who attends college and which colleges they attend (see Hillygus 2005; Berinsky and Lenz 2011). Also, because our sample is designed to approximate the general American population, some of the participants in our study were recently in college, while others attended decades ago. This means that other factors could have affected their attitudes and priorities in the intervening years between college and the survey, and this is more likely for those who have been out of college for longer. We do control for these differences in time from graduation with our age variable.

Our focus is on college-level factors; the first set is based on the colleges' US News and World Report rankings. First, US News breaks the college type into three basic categories: (1) national universities that "offer a full range of undergraduate majors, plus master's and doctoral programs, and emphasize faculty research or award professional practice doctorates"; (2) national liberal arts colleges that "focus almost exclusively on undergraduate education and award at least 50% of their degrees in the arts and sciences"; and (3) regional universities or colleges that focus on undergraduate and some master's degree programs.[5] This final category is split into eight different sets of rankings based on whether the school has graduate degrees and the particular region – though, we combine them for our analysis. Second, we also consider the college's ranking within these different categories. Although many of our participants graduated from college in the past, we use present-day rankings, since there is relatively little movement in these rankings (Bowman and Bastedo 2011; Gnolek, Falciano, and Kuncl 2014; see also Hillygus (2005) for a similar approach to the use of rankings).

An additional set of college-level characteristics is related to the economic factors associated with the college experience. Here, we use what Mendelberg et al. (2020) term the "affluence" of the college: the income levels of the student body. Specifically, here we include the proportion of the institution's student body that is in the first percentile of the income distribution and the proportion of the student body in the lower 60% of the national income distribution.[6] We include these economic characteristics as Mendelberg et al. (2020) demonstrate that campuses that are "majority affluent" are more likely to increase participation levels among students. Again, we note that the affluence data we have is from 2017, which may be many years after some of our respondents attended college. That being said, we expect that over-time changes would be more likely to affect the lower 60 percent proportions than the 1 percent proportions. Studies suggest that over the previous twenty years, the proportion of college students who come from the bottom 60 percent of the income distribution has increased – though this increase is not equally distributed across all institutions (Fry and Cilluffo 2019). In contrast, the proportion of

[5] Among the top-ranked national universities attended by respondents are Harvard and Princeton. Among the top-ranked national liberal arts colleges were Swarthmore and Wellesley. Among the top-ranked regional college and universities were James Madison and Cal Poly.
[6] Data collected via *The New York Times*.

undergraduates at the highest ends of the income distribution has remained the same (Fry and Cilluffo 2019).

A third set of college-level characteristics will be used as controls in some of our analyses – for example, the cost of tuition at the college. Again, we use present-day tuition; although the actual cost of tuition changes over time, the relative order of universities (i.e. most expensive, less expensive) stays relatively constant. Indeed, checks on tuition data from previous decades show that the most expensive institutions in our data set were similarly the most expensive institutions in the past as well. Finally, we also collect information on the size of the study body, which we also treat as a control.

We rely on two analytic approaches. First, we use LOWESS smoothers to track how various college-level characteristics coincide with levels of involvement. This approach makes no assumption about the particulars of the relationship but rather explores the patterns that may emerge. In addition to the LOWESS smoothers, however, we also estimate a model that allows us to control for individual-level characteristics that may also influence involvement, and age that accounts for time to degree.

In this model, we include self-reported variables related to the college experience. The first is a dummy variable indicating whether the individual was in the college Republicans or the college Democrats. Following Hillygus (2005), who finds that coursework is a key determinant of future political participation, we also consider the role of the participant's college major. Like Hillygus (2005), we split the majors into categories: arts/humanities, economics/business, and hard sciences. Unlike Hillygus, however, we also distinguish political science majors from other social science majors. In addition, the models also include the standard demographic controls (as we did in the previous analyses).

Although all the variables included in these analyses were factors that previous research had suggested were important to determining a link between the college experience and politics, we note that our analyses are still largely exploratory. In other words, there is reason to believe that college rank, student body affluence, college tuition, and individual-level college experiences have a downstream effect on political engagement, but we have no expectations that one particular variable should be more important. Rather, our goal is to consider whether and how variables that speak to campus – institution type, ranking, affluence, and tuition – correlate with involvement.

5.3.1 College Characteristics: Results

As a first step, we use LOWESS smoothers to track the relationship between involvement and college-level characteristics. In Figure 5.3a we show the relationship between university type, ranking, and involvement. In Figure 5.3b we present the relationship between student body affluence (using the one percent proportion) and involvement. Jointly, the figure suggests two patterns. First, we see higher levels of involvement not only among those study participants who reported attending liberal arts colleges than other types of institutions but only among schools ranked about fifty or higher (about the top fifth of those schools). Second, we see higher levels of involvement among participants who attended institutions with a more affluent student body. In sum, these results point to the idea that involvement is correlated with well-ranked liberal arts colleges and an affluent student body.

As a second step, we estimate a model in which we include all of the college-level characteristics, as well as measures that speak to individual-level college experiences (full model in Online Appendix M5.1). In this model, not surprisingly, people who were members of their college Democrats or college Republicans club score 0.15 higher on average on the 0 to 1 involvement scale. There are no statistically significant effects of college major.

The model also reinforces the results we show in Figure 5.3. The relationship between college type and ranking has a significant role in involvement. Even

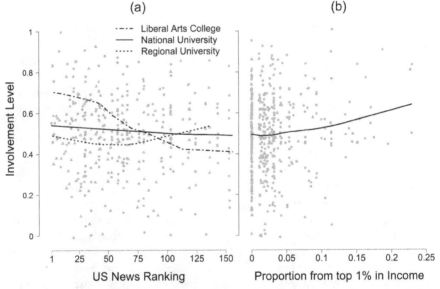

FIGURE 5.3 Attributes of four-year colleges and the political involvement of their alumni

Source: Involvement data from Q20. In panel a, ranking data are from the US News and World Report college rankings. In panel b, data on income cohorts are from opportunityinsights.org as reported in *The New York Times*. In scatter plots, circles represent national universities; squares represent national liberal arts colleges; and triangles represent regional colleges and universities. Random jitter is added to the scatterplots to make the different respondents easier to see. In panel a, the rankings plot is truncated on the x-axis. The highest possible ranking for national universities is 388, for liberal arts colleges is 223, and for regional colleges and universities is 176.

after including a series of controls, we see highest levels of involvement among those who attended well-ranked liberal arts colleges. The affluence measures are also both significant, though the larger effect is from the one percent measure. We note that college tuition does not have a significant effect in this model. Although there is a positive correlation between tuition and involvement, the effect disappears once we include other measures. If there is an economic component to this effect, then it is most likely the affluence of the student body, rather than tuition that affects involvement. This result is in line with Mendelberg et al. (2020) who find that campus affluence leads to more participatory behaviors among college students.

Research suggests that there are a number of reasons why we may have observed these patterns. Campuses with opportunities for community and civic engagement (Benenson and Bergom 2019), higher levels of "social cohesion," and opportunities for students to have a role in institutional governance may be more likely to encourage future political engagement (Thomas and Brower 2017). And these types of out-of-the-classroom experiences may be more likely in a liberal arts college (Hersh 1999). Furthermore, as Benenson and Bergom (2019) note, selective four-year institutions (such as highly ranked liberal arts colleges) spend more per student. In turn, these types of environments may lead to the small, in-depth political discussions that increase the likelihood of student engagement with politics (Thomas and Brower 2017). By the same logic, then, these types of environments would also increase involvement.

The relationship between student body affluence and involvement is a more expected outcome given the patterns in Mendelberg et al. (2020). Affluent individuals, they argue, are more likely to participate in politics, which may encourage everyone around them to do the same. They also make an argument similar to the one we make above about liberal arts colleges: Institutions that have a higher percentage of affluent students "may offer more opportunities for academic or extra-curricular activities that promote civic engagement or political awareness" (Mendelberg et al. 2020). In turn, they argue that these types of campuses may also create "campus norms" of political engagement. These norms of engagement can have some effect on actual participatory behaviors (Shulman and Levine 2012).

The above-mentioned college-level explanations get to the same point: there are certain types of college campuses that are more likely to facilitate political engagement. This may be for a variety of reasons: perhaps these campuses are better equipped to create opportunities for engagement, or they may be campuses that produce more close-knit communities, or perhaps these are campuses where the norm of political engagement is very strong. It is this norm of political engagement that may suggest a self-reinforcing pattern for certain types of institutions: Students who are already socialized to be more politically involved are drawn to certain campuses because they perceive the institution to have a certain set of political norms. In turn, the presence of these politically involved students further entrenches the political norms of the campus, which leads others to increase their levels of involvement.

5.3.2   The College Environment: An Over-Time Analysis

To this point, our results suggest that some college environments are more likely to correlate with higher levels of involvement in politics. As we note, however, it is important to acknowledge the limitations of these results. In our sample, people vary in age – meaning that some people completed college many years ago and others more recently. We also cannot distinguish between a decision to attend a certain type of school (i.e., selection effects) and the actual effect of that campus environment on individual behavior. The self-reinforcing pattern we note in the previous section is inherently difficult to track. Therefore, just as we did in the previous section, we turn to an additional source of data.

Starting in 1999, the National Longitudinal Study of Freshmen (NLSF) interviewed a group (N = 3,924) of students just as they were starting their fall semester in college.[7] The survey then followed these students through their college experience, up until graduation. We note that much like the Civic Network study we use in the previous section, the NLSF is not a random sample of freshmen: The survey was deliberately designed to have equivalent samples of Asian, Black, Latino, and White students. This means that just as with the Civic Network study, we do not consider our analyses as estimates of population-level patterns – rather, we consider the relationships between several different variables.

The NLSF does not have our involvement measure – in fact, it does not have many measures related to political engagement – therefore, we rely on an imperfect proxy. In the wave of the study coinciding with a student's junior year of college, participants were asked to name two campus organizations to which they belonged. We use these questions to create two versions of our dependent variable: whether a student named a group that the NLSF coded as "political/social awareness, including environmental" as the first group that came to mind or whether a student named such a group as at all. In both cases, naming a political group is coded as 1 and all other groups as 0. Participants who said they were not involved in any groups at all were also coded as 0.

Our independent variables are all taken from the first two waves of the survey, collected some three years prior to our dependent measure. Here we proxy pre-college political engagement with a measure that asks students how true the characteristic "politically active" was for them in their last year of high

---

[7] This research is based on data from the National Longitudinal Survey of Freshmen, a project designed by Douglas S. Massey and Camille Z. Charles and funded by the Mellon Foundation and the Atlantic Philanthropies. The sample included students from nine liberal arts colleges, fourteen private research universities, four public research universities, and one historically Black college.

school: We code students who reported that it was "not true at all" as 0 and those who reported that it was either "somewhat true" or "very true" are coded as 1. The results we present are robust to a change in this coding where only those who reply "very true" are coded as 1. Our second key independent variable is the classification by the NLSF of the student's college as liberal arts, private research, or public research. All the liberal arts colleges in the NLSF sample were highly ranked, with all but one ranked in the top fifty by US News.

We also control for individual characteristics such as the participant's gender, race, and ethnicity; whether the student was born outside the USA; whether they had sought out financial aid when applying to college; whether they had participated in student government in high school; whether they had taken any government classes in high school; and whether they said they read the newspaper while in high school. We account for a variety of family characteristics, including their parents' income and education, how often the parents talked to the students (generally, not about politics), and whether their parents read the newspaper. Finally, we also control for the student's major once in college (an indicator for political science), and in an attempt to control for the decision processes that lead people to certain schools (i.e. how much did the student want to attend this particular college), we also rely on a question (asked in the students' sophomore year) about whether the school they were attending was one of their most preferred schools while they were applying to college. As checks, we also estimate models where we proxy the high school environment through measures that asked participants whether their high schools had certain types of facilities but note that our results do not change based on the exclusion or inclusion of these variables.

Relying on these measures, we estimate a model that predicts involvement in a political group junior year as a function of the variables measured at the start of freshman year (and one measure from sophomore year). We include two interactions: one between liberal arts colleges and high school political engagement and the second between private research colleges and high school political engagement, leaving public research colleges as the reference category. We include the interactions because these allow us to discern the effect of a priori interest and that of the college experience.[8] We note that there is attrition in the survey over the years and participants do skip questions, leaving us with $N = 2,347$; when we estimate a model with no controls ($N = 2,966$), we obtain very similar results.

---

[8] In this model, we include only students who remained at the same college for their entire college experience. This is done because our college-level measures are from a student's freshman year, and if they changed colleges, the college-level measure no longer reflects their college experience. This means that we exclude 140 students who, by the time of the junior year, were no longer enrolled at their freshman year college.

As a first step, we estimate a model where attending a liberal arts college is the dependent variable and find that high school political engagement does not predict that a student will attend a liberal arts college (full model in Online Appendix M5.2A). We want to emphasize that we do not see this as evidence that involvement does not lead people to select certain colleges; rather, this is just a note that within this particular sample and measure, we do not observe that a proxy of high school political engagement leads someone to enroll in a liberal arts college. With this in mind, we turn to our main analysis in which we use freshman-year measures to predict junior-year political behavior (full model in Online Appendix M5.2B). Given that our key independent variables are included as an interaction, we focus on the marginal effect of attending a liberal arts college and the marginal effect of attending a private research university on involvement – as proxied by participation in a political group.

Here, we use the "first group mentioned" measure – although the patterns are similar when we consider both groups mentioned. We first find that, relative to attending a public research university, attending a private research university increases the likelihood of belonging to a political group equivalently for both students who were and were not politically engaged in high school. For students who were *not* politically engaged, the marginal effect of a private university is 0.034 ($p = 0.004$), and for those who *were* politically engaged, the marginal effect is 0.045 ($p = 0.003$). The effects are somewhat different for those who attend liberal arts colleges. Here we find that attending a liberal arts college has a marginal effect of 0.064 ($p = 0.026$) for those who were not politically engaged in high school and an effect of 0.024 ($p = 0.381$) for those who were. In short, these results suggest that the private university has a similar, relatively small, effect on belonging to a political group for all students, but the liberal arts college experience is especially important for those who were previously *not* engaged in politics.

Jointly, the results in this check underscore the patterns in our main analysis: There is something particular to the liberal arts environment, but, generally, more affluent places (like the private colleges in this sample) also increase people's relationship to politics. Even with this additional check, however, we again want to be cautious. There are theoretically relevant reasons to think that there is something about a certain type of college environment that increases levels of political involvement. Even with this additional over-time data, we cannot exclude the possibility of self-selection into a particular college environment. After all, family income correlates with both family political discussion (Neundorf, Niemi, and Smets 2016) and attending certain types of affluent, well-ranked colleges (Benenson and Bergom 2019). Keeping these caveats in mind, our results still lead to important implications: College does not uniformly correlate with deep involvement, just as it does not uniformly correlate with other political outcomes (Mendelberg, McCabe, and Thal 2017; Benenson and Bergom 2019; Mendelberg et al. 2020). Rather, if there is a relationship between the college experience and high levels of political involvement, it is specific to certain types of more affluent, selective college environments.

5.4 THE SOCIAL NETWORKS OF THE INVOLVED

To this point, we have considered involvement through two social lenses. First, we have shown that involvement (or lack of involvement) is associated with childhood socialization: For example, "I am deeply involved in cars, because my dad was deeply involved in and constantly talked about cars." Second, our results show a correlation between the college environment and deep involvement: For example, "I became deeply involved in jazz because of my college roommate." In this section, we continue our focus on the social but now consider the relationship between deep involvement and social networks. Specifically, we consider whether people who are deeply involved in politics have networks like Stephanie – the woman from the start of this chapter who is deeply involved in *Star Trek*. Many of Stephanie's closest friends are people who are also deeply involved in *Star Trek*; because Stephanie is in a network of "others of her own kind," her love of *Star Trek* is not unusual (Kozinets 2001, 74).

Stephanie found her network of other deeply involved *Star Trek* fans; she felt like she could not discuss her love of the show with her family so she deliberately sought out others with whom she felt more comfortable talking about *Star Trek* (Kozinets 2001). Yet, this does not always have to be the case. It is possible, for example, that Stephanie may have begun as a casual fan of the show, found herself working in an office full of deeply involved fans, and eventually grew to be a deeply involved fan herself. In fact, that is the story John tells about his deep involvement in jazz: He did like jazz before college, but it was the random assignment to a roommate who was deeply involved in jazz that deepened John's attachment (Bloch, Commuri, and Arnold 2009).

When it comes to politics, we expect that people who are deeply involved in politics will be in social networks with other people who are equally as deeply involved. Indeed, as we describe in Chapter 3, discussion and expression are pivotal to deep involvement, much like Stephanie wanted to have discussions with actual *Star Trek* fans, so too people deeply involved in politics will want to talk to others who are similarly involved. As we write in Chapter 3, people who are deeply involved want to talk to others who have "the same level of intensity" (Dimmock and Grove 2005; Thorne and Bruner 2006).

We are, however, agnostic about the *mechanisms* that produce these networks. We believe that agnosticism on this point is beneficial as, likely, there are many mechanisms working – often in tandem – to produce networks that are similar not only in political preferences but also in involvement. It is possible, for example, that a version of Sunstein's (2002) "law of group polarization" occurs in terms of political interest as well. Sunstein argues that in a small group discussion where all discussants have similar political preferences, the discussants will not conform to the group's average position but rather will move to a more extreme position because there is no disagreement to pull them toward the middle. The same could occur in the context of involvement. In a social group, people may not retain the average level of involvement in a group but rather shift to extreme ends – some becoming deeply involved and others becoming much less involved because there is no disagreement about the importance of politics.

Another possible mechanism is repeated interactions. If a group of individuals who are above average on involvement form a tight social network, it would not surprise anyone if the individuals in the group become *more* involved after interacting with one another for a while. Because they share above-average levels of involvement, the group may spend more time talking about politics than they would if they had members who were less involved. As other topics are removed from the agenda, the group may experience an involvement cascade. We would expect a similar dynamic to occur in the opposite direction if a social clique was composed of people with lower levels of involvement.

These two previous mechanisms speak to involvement similarities developing in already existing networks (i.e., networks that could have originated based on nonpolitical interactions): Another mechanism is one we have already mentioned – like Stephanie, people who are deeply involved may seek out other people who are similarly involved (Thorne and Bruner 2006). For someone who has a deep level of involvement, "discussion of the area of interest with friends, family, and casual acquaintances who are not fans often proves unfulfilling," which would suggest that the deeply involved are likely to engage in a more deliberate search for networks of people with similar interests (Thorne and Bruner 2006, 55). Even if this search produces a network that is digital, the outcome is still a product of someone's motivated search for similar people.

Regardless of whether it is a function of group dynamics, intentional choices, coincidences, or some combination of all these factors, the outcome is that people will find themselves in social networks with similarly involved people. This homophily in levels of involvement, in turn, may affect how people view others who have different perspectives about the importance of politics. How people perceive those who are more or less involved than they are is an idea we will explore in greater depth in Chapters 7 and 8. For now, we focus on the levels of involvement within a person's network.

When we discuss a respondent's social network, we do not mean their whole network. Individuals are embedded in multiple networks of associates in their neighborhoods, at their jobs, in their extended families, and on social media. To capture and characterize these full networks is beyond the scope of what one can do with a standard survey (but we will return to social media in Chapter 7).[9] Instead we use the approach common in studies of social influence on political attitudes (e.g. Huckfeldt and Sprague 1995; Huckfeldt 2001) and look only at

[9] For an example of combing survey data with other records to show effects from less proximate members of a network, see Pietryka and DeBats (2017).

core networks, that is, we look at the friends and family who are closest to the individual and are the most likely to influence their political preferences (Sokhey and Djupe 2011).

In the second wave of study Q20, we included a "name generator": a question that asks the respondent to name the members of their core network and then subsequent questions about those people. There are two commonly used name generators. One asks explicitly about political discussion, while the other asks the respondent to name people with whom they discuss "important matters." It may not make too much of a difference which name generator one uses (Klofstad, McClurg, and Rolfe 2009), but here we used the "important matters" form because our goal was to ask respondents to consider who they speak with generally, beyond just politics, to determine if the involved have core networks that are especially interested in politics.

As with previous versions of this measure, respondents could name up to three members of their core networks.[10] For each member of the core network, we ask respondents about their frequency of discussion and the member's political preferences. Research suggests that people are generally quite capable of guessing the political preferences of those in their networks (even if they do not know these preferences directly), and when perception differs from reality the *perceived,* values are actually better predictors of social influence (Huckfeldt 2007; Ryan 2011).

Before turning to the results, we again note a caveat about causality. We cannot determine whether it is involvement that causes a particular type of network or if it is the network that causes involvement – indeed, this is the type of agnosticism about mechanisms we discussed earlier. It is possible that one's friends and family (i.e. their core network) can cause future involvement. It is also possible, however, that people who are deeply involved are more likely to seek out friendship with certain types of similar people. This is a common concern in studies of social influence; it may seem like the network caused an individual's behavior in a specified statistical model, but what actually happened is that the individual decided to engage in that behavior and created a network that enabled this course of action. For example, someone might take up smoking due to peer pressure. Or alternatively, a smoker might seek out other smokers. Or perhaps, nonsmokers do not want to spend time with smokers and so what looks like peer pressure or people seeking out similar individuals is actually the result of "unfriending" (Noel and Nyhan 2011).

In the case at hand, it is possible that if a deeply involved individual becomes close friends with people who are not involved, then that individual could cause everyone else in the network to become involved as well – or the others could convince the involved person to calm down about politics. In both these situations, the network causes involvement level. But it is also possible that the deeply involved have particular preferences and interests that make them

[10] See, for example, the 2008–2009 American National Election Study panel.

seek out people who have the same preferences and interests. Or, there is a third alternative: Someone seeks out friends who are involved in politics, and repeated discussions deepen their levels of involvement. Indeed, all three types of patterns would be consistent with the development and maintenance of involvement generally (Thorne and Bruner 2006).

It is also possible that people who are not involved cannot handle being associated with the involved and distance themselves from their involved friends. Relatively, few people have actually blocked someone on social media because of politics (Bode 2016; Duggan and Smith 2016),[11] but differences in political preferences and political interest make for unstable romantic relationships (see Huber and Malhotra 2017) and likely affect other core network relationships. Yet, because we measure involvement and the network around the same time, we cannot observe the dynamic of network ties forming or breaking to know the causal pattern.

The goal of this analysis, therefore, is descriptive rather than causal: We jointly consider the networks of the involved and uninvolved. We also do not want to assume a linear relationship between involvement and our network measures. For this reason, in Figure 5.4, we use LOWESS smoothers to present these relationships. The smoothers draw a line that shows the best relationship between the two variables allowing for the size and even direction of the relationship to change as the values of the variables increase. This analysis is done for descriptive purposes with limited statistical assumptions.

We present our results in Figure 5.4. The y-axes in Figures 5.4a and b present the mean interest and frequency of political discussion in the network; panels c and d present two measures of partisan network homogeneity. In the first measure of network homogeneity (Figure 5.4c), we simply took the absolute difference between the respondent's partisan identity and the perceived partisan identities of each of their network members; we recoded the variables so that larger values indicated greater homogeneity. The second measure (Figure 5.4d) excluded pure independents. The second measure is simply the count of individuals in the core network who the respondent believes are supporters of their party – the score, therefore, ranges from 0 (the respondent supports a different party than those in their core network) to 3 (every member of the core network supports the same party as the respondent).[12]

Turning first to political interest and discussion, we see a near-perfect linear relationship between the network averages and involvement. Not surprisingly, whether by direct choice or by social influence, the uninvolved do not talk about politics with their friends; the deeply involved talk about politics constantly; and most people are somewhere in between. Similarly, as involvement increases,

---

[11] According to a Pew Report, 27 percent report blocking people on social media due to politics, although 31 percent report that they have changed settings to simply see less politics.
[12] If the respondent believes a member of the core network is a pure independent, then that is counted as disagreement in this coding scheme.

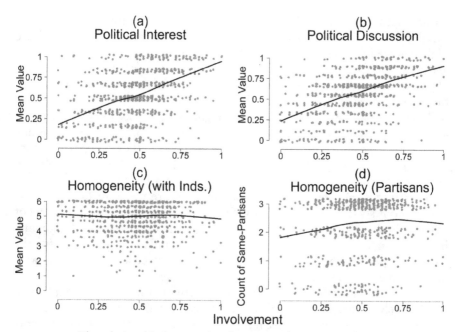

FIGURE 5.4 The relationship between involvement and core-network structure
Source: Data from Q20. Lines represent LOWESS smoothers. Higher levels on *x*-axis represent more involvement; a score of 1 would mean the highest level of involvement. Higher levels on *y*-axis reflect higher mean interest among core network members (panel a), higher mean levels of political discussion (panel b), greater homogeneity (panel c), or strict homogeneity in terms of partisanship (panel d).

the level of political interest within the individual's core network also increases. In short, people are in their own social "involvement bubbles."

Network homogeneity, however, suggests something else. For the first measure of homogeneity, we see absolutely no relationship between involvement and homogeneity. To understand why this is the case, consider how this measure captures homogeneity. The homogeneity measure in Figure 5.4c combines not only the partisan direction of homogeneity but also factors in partisan strength. So, people with little partisan attachment who reach across party lines to other people with little partisan attachment look the same as people with strong partisan attachments who have friends who have weak partisan attachments to the same party.[13] Deep involvement has no effect

---

[13] An example might demonstrate why this is. Consider a strong Democrat and an independent who leans Democratic. The previous results suggest that these individuals would have different levels of involvement with the former being more involved than the latter. Let's assume the strong Democrat only wants to associate with other Democrats. Their three friends are another strong Democrat, a weak Democrat, and a leaning Democrat – this will lead to a homogeneity

on homogeneity here, likely because this measure is capturing homogenous social groups in terms of both partisan strength *and* partisanship. In the case of the people low on involvement, they have low levels of partisan attachment and are associating with other people with low partisan attachment, regardless of party. The deeply involved are associating with the other strong partisans in their party.

The second measure of homogeneity (Figure 5.4d) looks strictly at whether an individual *exclusively* has members in their core network who are in the same party – this type of network cannot include members of the other party or pure independents. With this measure, we again see that most networks are fairly homogeneous but that the homogeneity increases a bit as involvement increases. In other words, people who are deeply involved are the most likely to have homogenous social networks. Jointly, then, these results suggest a great deal of homophily in social networks. They demonstrate not only partisan homophily but also homophily in terms of engagement. The uninvolved are in networks with other people who are uninvolved, and the involved are in networks with other people who are involved.

It is popular to argue that amateur party activists (the types of people who would likely be deeply involved on our measure) fail to understand the real world because they live in partisan bubbles – hence, the idea that they support politicians and policies that are only popular on Twitter (Cohn and Quealy 2019). But here we suggest another bubble: the "involvement bubble." Some people are in a bubble of the deeply involved. To them, it appears that politics is of great importance to everyone they know – probably because it is. On the other hand, people who sometimes pay attention to politics and have weak partisan attachments are also in a "bubble" – this "low-involvement" bubble, however, is just much larger than the other one. It also avoids politics and is often ignored in discussions of mass politics as a result.

5.5   THE SOCIAL SIDE OF POLITICS

In their study of deeply involved fans, Thorne and Bruner (2006) found that many of the fans were motivated by a desire for social interaction with others. In their long qualitative interviews, they found that many of fans they spoke to estimated that "pretty much all" their friends were equally involved fans (Thorne and Bruner 2006, 64). Involvement, as we argued in Chapter 3, may

score of 5 (6 + 5 + 4 = 5; remember, 6 is the highest homogeneity score due to our recoding of the difference variable). Now, let's imagine the leaning Democrat who is not involved does not care as much about the partisanship of their friends; they just do not want to spend all their time talking about politics. Obviously, this rules out having strong Republicans as friends, but it probably also rules out having strong Democrats as friends. So, let's imagine this individual's three core network members are a leaning Democrat, a pure independent, and a leaning Republican. This again leads to a homogeneity score of 5, even though this network includes a member of the other party.

mean long hours spent following information about the topic of your interest, but involvement is also social. Randy, a forty-eight-year-old *Star Trek* fan, explains this idea succinctly to Thorne and Bruner (2006): "Because a lot of times when I talk to people about *Star Trek*, they think I am a fanatic. It feels good to talk to someone that is really interested in what you are interested in" (63).

From start to finish, involvement is social. Bobby, the one-time owner of twenty-two cars, is deeply involved in cars because cars were also important to his father. We see evidence of this type of socialization in political involvement as well. People who are deeply involved are more likely to report that their parents discussed politics. Involvement correlates first with conversations with one's family – be those conversations about cars or politics.

John, who is deeply involved in jazz, ties his involvement to college experiences. College experiences shape people's relationships with politics (Raychaudhuri 2018; Mendelberg et al. 2020), and we too find evidence that the college context shapes involvement. We see a relationship between well-ranked liberal arts colleges, student body affluence, and deep involvement. Well-resourced campuses and students, our results suggest, are more likely to produce deeply involved people.

Stephanie, perhaps, is the best example of Thorne and Bruner's (2006) connection between deep involvement and social interaction. Faced with a network that did not understand her involvement in *Star Trek*, Stephanie created her own network of fans. Although not all networks are as deliberately created as Stephanie's – some are more accidental developments – we do show that people are often in "involvement bubbles." In other words, people mostly interact with others who are equally as (un)involved as they are. To someone who is deeply involved, everyone else may also seem to have a similar relationship to politics, and that is likely because many of the people to whom they talk are, actually, also deeply involved.

The patterns we find in this chapter reinforce the importance of social context to involvement, but they raise the possibility of still broader implications. First, we saw that childhood experiences correlate with levels of involvement in adulthood. This outcome suggests the possibility that it is deeply involved parents who raise deeply involved children. If parenting, at its core, is about imparting to children the values we believe are most important for a well-functioning society (e.g. Gutmann 1995), then do deeply involved people have a different set of values? And, if deep involvement is social, do involvement differences manifest themselves in people's perceptions of public political expression? Finally, if people's networks are homogenous when it comes to involvement, does this mean that people may misjudge how others feel about politics?

In the remainder of this book, we address each of these questions. In Chapter 6, we turn to the relationship between involvement and parenting. The studies in the chapter speak to involvement differences not only in parenting but also in how people perceive what is valuable for a functional society. In Chapter 7, we consider how involvement not only shapes people's willingness to express themselves on social media but also affects perceptions of those who engage in public expression. Chapter 8, then, brings many of these ideas together, investigating what happens when the involvement gaps in expression, homogenous networks, and affective polarization collide in the public sphere.

6

Perceptions of the Most Sacred Duty
(Co-authored with Michael Yontz)

All I know is we're not Republicans.
              Judith, 10 years old, July 1957, in an interview with Fred Greenstein

The night of the 2016 presidential election, eight-year-old Miriam was, according to her father, "inconsolable." Miriam, as her father Eli Shearn told *The Washington Post* some four years later, had become very engaged in the 2016 presidential campaign – something that Shearn had encouraged (Rubin 2020). Miriam's parents were strong supporters of then-Democratic nominee, Hillary Clinton, setting up Miriam with red and blue crayons to watch the votes come in on election night. When Clinton lost the election to Republican Donald Trump, Miriam went to bed crying. Shearn told *The Post* he remembered thinking: "Why did I get her so invested in this?"

Catherine Glenn Foster, the head of Americans United for Life, has also been working to engage her children in politics; she is, at this point, less regretful than Shearn. Foster had "taken her three children (ages 13, 7, and 5) to anti-abortion marches from the time they were in strollers." Although she had discussed abortion policies with her oldest daughter, Foster told *The Post* the marches were especially important: "We can all sit behind our computers and raise awareness on social media all day. But there's something about seeing all those people and feeding off all that energy that is hard to duplicate. I want my kids to experience that" (Rubin 2020).

On a different platform, Kirsty Woudstra expressed more uncertainty. Although she initially wanted to take her eleven-year-old daughter to a political rally, she found that she could not bring herself to do it. "What I am afraid of," Woudstra wrote, "is forcing my politics on her before she has the time and experience to form her own. I'm afraid of this because it happened to me" (Woudstra 2017). Her mother's decision to take her to antiabortion rallies as a child, Woudstra wrote, "deeply affected" their relationship.

Woudstra feels a sense of resentment toward her mother because as an adult, she now has very different beliefs about abortion; she feels "shame" about having attended the antiabortion rallies. Although her own kids know Woudstra is politically engaged, she hesitates asking children to "physically participate in [her] politics."

Shearn, Foster, and Woudstra all reflect a delicate balance: How does one introduce their children to political ideas without actively imposing certain political worldviews? This question reflects the broader push and pull of parenting. On the one hand, parents *do* have a good deal of authority over their children's lives. On the other hand, this authority must also be balanced against the child's autonomy (Gutmann 1980, 1995). Parenting, then, is allowing a child to make their own decisions and constraining these decisions if they are likely to lead the child in a direction that will have poor outcomes for the child, society, or both (Gutmann 1980). In a political context, this idea of a "poor outcome" is sometimes objectively clear but other times heavily dependent on the parents' own political positions and beliefs.

Although there are certainly many sources of political socialization (see Sapiro 2004), parents and other family members are the important starting point in the formation of people's political worldviews (see e.g. Pye 1959; Greenstein 1965). Indeed, in Chapter 5, we see some evidence that involvement is correlated with different political experiences in the family home: The deeply involved are more likely to recall political conversations during family dinners, and they are more likely to report that their parents encouraged them to be politically active. As a next step, then, we turn the lens of involvement more directly toward the family. In this chapter, we investigate whether there are involvement differences in the way people perceive the balance of parental authority and children's autonomy in the context of politics.

Although on the surface our studies focus on parenting, how people choose to raise their kids is indicative of their broader values. If guardians' goals are to transmit to their children a set of values, then the (large and small) decisions they make are reflective of these goals (Grusec, Goodnow, and Kuczynzki 2000). As a result, parenting decisions are revealed preferences of what people perceive to be most important for their families and, even more broadly, a functional society. What, if anything, people tell their children about politics is a reflection of the value they place on politics itself. People who are deeply involved believe that politics holds an important place in society, and tracking parenting allows us to consider the scope of this importance better than any other political or social context.

When considered as revealed preferences about the role politics should play in society, the results we present in this chapter suggest a nuanced pattern: We find that most people, *regardless of involvement*, feel somewhat uncomfortable with parents who push their children toward politics. People's beliefs in the value of children's autonomy (Rudy and Grusec 2001), our results suggest, are stronger than their beliefs in the value of politics. Yet, the people who are deeply involved *are* more supportive of parents who try to engage their children in partisan politics and ideological debates. Moreover, involvement also plays a role in people's beliefs about the parental decisions *they* would make, and people who are deeply involved are more likely to report that they would encourage their children to engage in politics. Still, the involvement differences we demonstrate in this chapter are somewhat smaller than those we observe in other chapters. This result, perhaps, speaks not only to the involvement differences in people's views of the role politics should play in society but also to the complex tradeoffs in values that parenting represents.

6.1 WON'T SOMEBODY PLEASE THINK OF THE CHILDREN?

Long before parenting magazines, parenting blogs, parenting columns, and parenting podcasts, there was John Stuart Mill. Mill did not have any advice on toddler tantrums or the amount of homework reasonable for an average eight-year-old. What Mill did have were strong ideas about parental responsibility. "It is one of the most sacred duties of parents," Mill wrote in his 1859 treatise *On Liberty*, "after summoning a human being into the world, to give to that being an education fitting to perform his part well in life toward others and toward himself" (Mill 1956, 132).[1] For Mill, "to bring a child into existence without a fair prospect of being able, not only to provide food for its body, but instruction and training for its mind, is a moral crime, both against the unfortunate offspring and against society" (132).

Parents are, of course, no strangers to being judged for their (small and large) parenting decisions. Indeed, as of this writing, there are numerous places on the Internet that one can visit to either judge the parenting of a stranger or vent one's frustration about strangers judging their parenting. Mill's perspective, however, is much broader. In a democratic society, parents' responsibilities take on an added dimension: One of Mill's educational goals is that a child becomes a citizen who is capable of engaging in the responsibilities of a representative democracy (see Gutmann 1980, 338, for a discussion). In other words, the reason parenting matters so much is because parenting is the transmission of values.

Mill's beliefs about the role of children and parents in perpetuating a functional society were prescient. At the heart of contemporary worries about the health of American democracy are worries about the political engagement of young people (Niemi and Junn 1998; Galston 2004; Holbein and Hillygus 2020). Schools can offer students the skills and knowledge necessary for participation (Niemi and Junn 1998; Holbein and Hillygus 2020), but it is parents who are often the first to instill in their children an early curiosity about politics, reinforcing the belief that political and civic participation are actually *important* (Beck and Jennings 1982; Jennings,

---

[1] Mill acknowledges that "as law and usage now stand," the parent in question here is the father.

Stoker, and Bowers 2009; Dinas 2014; Neundorf, Niemi, and Smets 2016). Indeed, Weinschenk and Dawes (2021) find that it is family factors, not civic education, that play the largest role in determining future political engagement. Put another way, empirical studies of families suggest that Mill was right to focus on the role of the parents.

Certainly, parents are not the lone socializing agents that have an effect on people's political development (Sapiro 2004; Neundorf, Niemi, and Smets 2016; Mendelberg et al. 2020; Minozzi et al. 2020). Our goal in this chapter, however, is not to parse the effects of parenting on political socialization from the effects of these other socializing agents. Rather, our approach here differs from much of the literature on socialization in that it is not on the *outcomes* of socialization (this was our focus in the previous chapter). The focus of this chapter is on parenting *decisions* – do parents deliberately introduce politics into their children's lives? It is these parenting decisions, rather than the eventual outcomes of socialization, that more clearly speak to people's values. We use "values" in this chapter in the same manner as Gutmann (1995): Broad ideas about what parents find important, rather than a predetermined set of specific political worldviews (see Connors 2020 for a discussion).[2]

Although the idea that parents hold some responsibility for producing the next generation of good citizens may seem both normatively good and largely uncontroversial, what this means for actual on-the-ground parenting is more difficult to parse. It is one thing to agree that parents have a responsibility to mold their children into good citizens; it is quite another to agree on *how* parents should go about doing so. Much like with a lot of "good in the abstract" parenting advice ("raise curious kids!"), parents are left to their own devices to figure out what, exactly, they need to do on a daily basis to perpetuate a functioning democracy. It is important, for example, that young people learn about the process of voting (Holbein and Hillygus 2020), but does this mean that parents should also deliberately attempt to direct their children toward other forms of political participation?

Does producing a good citizen, for example, mean teaching a child that it is important to vote or does it mean teaching a child that it is important to *vote for a specific party*? Should parents explicitly tell their children about the "'goodies' and 'baddies' of the political world" (Dinas 2014), or are political sides something that a child should figure out for themselves as they grow up? Some parents, for example, may perceive that it is impossible to raise a good citizen without mentioning to their children that some political sides are wrong, bad, and dangerous. Meanwhile, others may disagree that one should discuss politics with their children at all. The inherent ambiguity in the most

---

[2] These values may include partisan predispositions, though we note that – as Connors (2020) finds – positions on the predetermined set of political values are also heavily susceptible to partisan cues.

appropriate way to handle politics within the family underscores the role of parenting as a revealed value preference.

6.2 INTRODUCING CHILDREN TO POLITICS

In one of the earliest studies of political socialization, Greenstein opened his 1965 book, *Children and Politics,* with an extended passage from Alexis de Tocqueville's *Democracy in America.* "A man has come into the world," the passage began, "his early years are spent without notice in the pleasures and activities of childhood." Although de Tocqueville implied that childhood was a time for things other than politics, Greenstein (1965) found at least some evidence to the contrary: Elementary school children had thoughts and opinions about political leaders.

Revisiting politics and childhood in 2017–2018, Oxley et al. (2020) found – much like Greenstein – that young children are aware of political leaders. And, just like the children in Greenstein's study, children in 2017–2018 also had largely positive views of the *presidency as an office* (Oxley et al. 2020). Unlike Greenstein's young survey respondents in the late 1950s, however, Oxley et al. (2020) see a greater willingness among children to criticize the elected president. "We suspect that this divergence in assessments occurs because the sites of children's learning regarding the president and the presidency differ," Oxley et al. write. "Messages about the president as a person are communicated via parents, community members, and (directly or indirectly) the mass media, whereas the primary agent of socialization regarding the presidency is the school" (152).

The shifts Oxley et al. find among children likely reflect shifts among parents. Parents in 2017–2018 viewed the president more negatively than parents in 1957–1958. In 1957–1958, when Greenstein was conducting his surveys, 60.5 percent of people approved of then-President Dwight D. Eisenhower; comparatively, in 2017–2018, when Oxley et al. conducted their research, 41 percent of people on average approved of President Donald Trump.[3] What children in 2017–2018 had heard about the president, in part from their parents (though, undoubtedly, also from the media), was probably more negative than what they had heard about the president in the late 1950s. As both sets of authors suggest, then, the changes from the late 1950s to the late 2010s reflect that children's political perspectives are, at least in part, products of their parents' politics. Whether the transmission of these politics is deliberate, however, is a different question.

---

[3] Statistics are based on Gallup: https://news.gallup.com/poll/203198/presidential-approval-ratings-donald-trump.aspx; https://news.gallup.com/poll/116677/presidential-approval-ratings-gallup-historical-statistics-trends.aspx

6.2.1 Parenting and Politics

The family home is often the first place where children are exposed to politics (Dalton 1980; Jennings and Niemi 1968, 1981; Neundorf and Smets 2017). Within the home, parents are role models and sources of political cues for their children (Kudrnáč and Lyons 2017); the more engaged the parents are in politics, the more political cues children are likely to receive(Jennings, Stoker, and Bowers 2009; Dinas 2014; Neundorf and Smets 2017). In turn, the more cues children receive, the more likely their political preferences are to match those of their parents (Jennings, Stoker, and Bowers 2009; Wolak 2009). Beyond partisanship and issue positions, seeing how parents engage with politics offers children a clue about the role politics should play in day-to-day lives (Dinas 2014). Even if children, ultimately, reject their parents' political positions or perceive these positions differently than the parents had intended (Hatemi and Ojeda 2021), parental behavior serves as an important initial input.

If parents are models of political participation for their children (Kudrnáč and Lyons 2017), this political modeling may not always be free of partisan sides and political conflict. As parents head out to vote – and may even bring their children along to the voting booth – some may tell their children for which candidate (or party) they will be voting. Even parents who hope to avoid discussing political sides with their very young children may, without thinking, describe a politician as "the bad guy" when their three-year-old points at the television screen and asks, "Who is that?"[4] While a *Good Housekeeping* guide to discussing politics with children suggests that parents should "check [their] own snide comments and eyerolls" (Cornwall 2020), parents may not always be conscious of their own political behaviors.

Indeed, Greenstein (1965) highlights this very tension between parents' best intentions and their actual behaviors. Parents, Greenstein notes, are clearly "agents of political socialization" in that they represent a source from which children learn about politics. At the same time, socialization differs between the "conscious and intentional" – or the merely accidental (Greenstein 1965, 13). Some of what children learn about politics from their parents, Greenstein suggests, is overheard and "informal" (45). "Party identifications," he writes, "probably develop without much explicit teaching on the part of the parents" (73). When ten-year-old Judith – quoted the start of this chapter – told Greenstein that what she knows about her family is that they are not Republicans, she may have done so without any deliberate efforts by her parents.

Other forms of socialization, however, are more deliberate. Children who come from politicized family homes are more likely to be generally interested in

---

[4] Parenting blogs may suggest that the real problem with this story may not be the description of a politician as "the bad guy" but the fact that a three-year-old was watching television. That being said, an article in *Good Housekeeping* titled "The Right Way to Talk about Politics with Your Kids, According to Experts" (Cornwall 2020) suggests that parents should "talk about bad and good ideas, not good and bad people."

politics (Dinas 2014). In fact, as Dinas (2014) shows, these children from politicized homes are actually more likely to eventually diverge politically from their parents *because* they are socialized to be interested in political discussions and activities; over time, in new political networks, they learn more about politics and may eventually differ from their parents. Politicized parents, Dinas (2014) argues, do not just have strong attachments to a party, but they have a strong level of engagement in politics and they "facili[tate] political discussions at home" (848) – they talk to their children about politics.

Focusing on these "conscious and intentional" parenting decisions more directly, McDevitt and Kiousis (2015) consider the possibility of "active political parenting," a concept they define as "intentional effort to encourage youth development based on recognition of the child's interest in politics and potential for further growth" (20). Operationally, active political parenting involves encouraging children to talk about politics and campaigns, as well as paying attention to news stories – behaviors that the authors view as intentional efforts to introduce politics. This form of parenting, McDevitt and Kiousis (2015) argue, can come from two motivations: the parents' own focus on politics or the parents' desire to be responsive to their children's interest in politics.

Of course, one may wonder how children become interested in politics to begin with. Prior (2019), for example, finds a relationship between parents' political interest and those of their children. Although children can certainly gain an interest in politics outside of the home (McDevitt and Kiousis 2015), for some people politics is a part of childhood from an early age due to the "politicization" of family (Dinas 2014). Put another way, in households like the ones we introduced at the beginning of the chapter – ones in which children are coloring election maps and attending political rallies – children do not just overhear offhand mentions about politics and are then exposed to politics fully in classroom discussions. Rather, they learn about their parents' political worldviews because their parents have had explicit conversations about political topics and issues well before the children themselves express any interest in politics. Moreover, these parents may have also facilitated other forms of political engagement – for example, rally attendance – before their children were old enough to have their own agency to seek out political information. In short, as Greenstein suggests, sometimes children pick up their parents' political views and behaviors because of something they overhear or see by accident, but sometimes, they pick up their parents' politics because the parents have consciously worked to make sure this would happen.

It is not our goal to make an argument that some parenting approaches to politics are better – or more valuable for society – than others.[5] Some people may believe that teaching children about political conflicts and political sides is not only valuable but necessary. Others may agree that parents carry

---

[5] Indeed, the authors of this book are not qualified to offer parenting advice – see footnote about a three-year-old watching television.

a responsibility to mold their children into good citizens but may believe that
doing so requires being nonpolitical, or at least nonpartisan. Even if children do
pick up political or partisan ideas, these people may prefer that it be, as
Greenstein (1965) suggests, largely accidental. Again, it is not our intent to
adjudicate between the two varying perspectives – such adjudication would be
impossible. Rather, we treat these differences in parenting decisions as
indications of what values people hope to impart to their children most
clearly. Our goal, then, is to explore whether political involvement cuts across
parenting decisions in the way it cuts across other political indicators.

6.3   INVOLVEMENT AND PARENTING

Ultimately, parents transmit to their children a set of values, where values are
the ideas that parents find most important (Gutmann 1995). As we discussed in
the previous sections, sometimes this transmission is accidental and almost
unconscious; other times, this transmission is clear, deliberate, and effortful.
In a 2017 article about children at political rallies, for example, one father
explained his reasoning like this: "[T]he girls don't get to choose what we do on
vacation. We go and show them art and architecture. And they always give us
a hard time about it, but we say, 'No, these are our values. And when you're
with us, this is what you're going to do'" (Francis 2017). In what follows we
consider how involvement could intersect with people's perceptions of the role
parents should play in their children's political lives.

There are a number of reasons that we may expect that involvement may
shape beliefs about parenting in the context of politics. As we explain in
Chapter 3, people who are deeply involved have a different relationship with
politics than those who are less involved. The deeply involved spend more time
following political information and are more likely to see even mundane
political events as consequential. Co-occurring with this focus on politics, we
show in Chapter 4, comes a clear perception of the "the 'goodies' and 'baddies'
of the political world" (Dinas 2014, 827).

The importance the deeply involved place on politics, as well as a dislike for
those who are on the opposing political side, may manifest themselves through
parenting. People who are deeply involved may believe that parents should
work deliberately to impart to their children the importance of politics; they
may be more likely than those with lower levels of involvement to support
parenting that actively brings politics into children's lives. On the other hand,
those who are deeply involved are also more likely to harbor animosity for those
who have different political positions. In turn, the deeply involved may be more
likely to support deliberately political parenting – but *only* when that parenting
promotes appropriate political positions. To return to an idea from the
beginning of this chapter, how people make and perceive different parenting
decisions is indicative of their revealed preference of what are ideas that are
most important for a functioning society. Seeing involvement differences in

people's perceptions of parenting would signal differences in people's fundamental views about the value of politics for American society.

6.3.1 Involved Parenting in Practice

People who are deeply involved, as we have shown in Chapter 5, recall a childhood filled with politics. From this perspective, the idea that parents are politicized and actively engage children in politics may be natural for those who are deeply involved. We will consider these ideas more directly through a series of experiments, but we begin with a preliminary, correlational approach to involvement and parenting. To consider the relationship between children and parents, McDevitt and Kiousis (2015) rely on a data set of parent/child dyads; their results are part of a broader data set collected by McDevitt. The families were recruited from Arizona, Colorado, and Florida, and were interviewed at various points in time between 2002 and 2004.[6] We can use this data set to begin considering the possibility of a co-occurrence between a parent's political involvement and their parenting decisions when it comes to politics. For ease of discussion, we will refer to McDevitt's data set as the Civic Cohort Survey.

As comprehensive as the Civic Cohort Survey is, the study does not capture our measure of political involvement. It does, however, include measures such as the level of attention to politics and frequency of political discussion that will allow us to proxy political involvement. Specifically, we code parents who report paying a great deal of attention to politics *and* who report frequently talking about politics (with peers, not their children) as "deeply involved." There are two ways to do this. As McDevitt and Kiousis (2015) report, their three-wave survey has a good deal of attrition from each wave. This means that using responses from Wave 1 (2002) gives us the highest number of survey participants. On the other hand, however, it is their Wave 2 (2003) attention measure that is the closer proxy to our involvement measure: The Wave 1 attention question asks about the 2002 campaign, but the 2003 question asks about attention to *politics generally*.

Regardless of whether we use the Wave 1 or Wave 2 attention question, however, our proxy produces approximately similar rates of deep involvement: 13.9 percent of parents can be considered deeply involved when we use the Wave 1 measure and 12.7 percent when we use the Wave 2 measure – which are both similar (if slightly lower) to the percentage of people we find to be deeply

---

[6] McDevitt began recruitment with high school students in Maricopa County, Arizona, El Paso County, Colorado, and Palm Beach/Broward counties, Florida. The surveys relied on "a combination of interviews modes – mail back, telephone, and web-based surveys – and provided small incentives ($5 phone cards). There is substantial attrition from year to year, as we needed to gain cooperation from both a parent and an adolescent to complete a dyad, while keeping up with youth respondents during a mobile phase of their lives" (23).

involved in Chapter 4 using our actual involvement scale. Therefore, we use the measure that allows us the highest number of participants (Wave 1 measure), and include the results using the Wave 2 measure in Online Appendix M6.1. Using our involvement proxy, we next track how parents describe their political interactions with their children. We present these patterns in Table 6.1.

The patterns in Table 6.1 are, on one level, suggestive. Parents who we would consider deeply involved (at least using the proxy measure) are more likely to discuss the election with their children and are more likely to discuss politics *in general* with their children even in an off-election year (Wave 2 of the Civic Cohort Survey is in 2003). These involved parents are also more likely to encourage their children to follow politics in the news and think about political ideas. As we might expect, parents who themselves are more engaged in politics are more likely to have political interactions with their children.

TABLE 6.1 *Patterns of parents' behavior by level of parents' involvement (proxy measure)*

	Deeply Involved Parent (Proxy)	Less Involved Parent (Proxy)	*p*-value (Two-Tailed)
Frequently encouraged child to pay attention to a news story (*N* = 540)	66.67%	39.57%	0.000
Strongly agree: Easy to talk to child about politics (*N* = 535)	36.00%	31.96%	0.489
Frequently discuss *the election* with child (*N* = 540)	50.00%	15.88%	0.000
Frequently encourage child to think about politics, even if you two might disagree (*N* = 538)	60.81%	39.44%	0.000
Frequently encourage child not to argue about politics with adults (*N* = 536)	5.41%	6.49%	0.722
Frequently express political opinions to challenge your child (Wave 2, *N* = 250)	42.86%	7.91%	0.000
Frequently discuss *politics* with child (Wave 2, *N* = 249)	25.71%	6.54%	0.000
It is important that political opinions are compatible with those of child (Wave 2, *N* = 250)	20.00%	5.58%	0.003

Source: Data from Civic Cohort Study. Measures with a lower N were asked only in Wave 2.

On the other hand, there is variance in these political behaviors even among the parents whom we code as deeply involved using a proxy measure. Although the difference in political discussion between the deeply involved and less involved parents is about 19.2 percentage points, only 25.7 percent of deeply involved parents report discussing politics with their children during a year with no campaign. While 66.7 percent of deeply involved parents encouraged their children to consider political news, another third did not. What this suggests is that parents' political involvement does seem to co-occur with more attempts to socialize their children, but we cannot argue that there is uniformity in political behavior among deeply involved parents.

Of course, this first set of correlational results has a number of limitations. First, we are relying on a proxy for political involvement. Second, the questions were never designed to track a full range of parenting decisions. Moreover, since the Civic Cohort Survey began with high school juniors and seniors, these measures – especially in the second wave – may be about parenting people who are, demographically, nearly adults. We also want to emphasize that the results carry another uncertainty: Parents who are more involved may report more political interactions because they believe that this is the correct answer to the question, not because they engage in more political interactions with their children. In fact, only 17.9 percent of high school students whose parents report frequently discussing the election with their child report frequently discussing the election with their parents.[7] In short, the patterns in Table 6.1 suggest that involvement may affect parenting, but it is difficult to categorize the breadth and extent of this effect without turning to another source of data. In the next section, then, we turn to a series of experiments.

6.4 FOUR STUDIES ON PARENTING

Studying parenting, as the previous section suggests, is challenging. For starters, asking parents about their parenting decisions in surveys may not necessarily offer the most accurate representation of day-to-day behaviors. As we found using the Civic Cohort Survey in the previous section, children and parents living in the same households reported different experiences. Only 50 percent of children (or, in this case, high school students) whose parents strongly agreed that it was easy to discuss politics with their child strongly agreed that it was easy to discuss politics with their parents. Among children whose parents strongly agreed that they encourage their children to discuss political opinions even when their opinions differed, only 39.2 percent recalled their parents doing so. In short, how parents remember their parenting and how children experienced this parenting may differ. This is

---

[7] Obviously, socially desirable responding on the part of the parents is not the only explanation for this discrepancy. Anyone who has interacted with or been a teenager understands that the parents could have been talking about politics, but the teenager was not listening.

likely an inevitable part of growing up, but it may also be the result of measurement.

Parents – and mothers especially – are often used to having their behaviors heavily judged by others, which may lead parents to answer survey questions in ways that they believe are more socially desirable (Morsbach and Prinz 2006). As a result, surveys of parents may not only reflect actual parenting choices but also parents' perceptions of what they believe these choices *should have been*. There is certainly something instructive in measuring people's beliefs about what is desirable to others: If the results in Table 6.1, for example, reflect parents' beliefs about what parenting should look like, then the involvement differences are still important evidence of different worldviews. Nonetheless, given that tendencies to misrepresent behaviors are not randomly distributed among parents (Morsbach and Prinz 2006), it would be difficult to draw clear conclusions from the data.

Second, although we begin with parents, we can use parenting to capture a broader set of views. Considering how *others* view parenting choices, for example, is also indicative of the value people place on politics. Moreover, since, as we suggested previously, questions of parental responsibility are inherently abstract, we must focus on responses to specific cases rather than abstract questions of what parents *should* do. To this end, we turn to four different experiments on politics in the family, which were embedded in studies D19, Q20, and YG20.

Our approach relies on previous methods in the study of parenting (e.g. Ishizuka 2019). Specifically, we randomly assign people to descriptions of decisions made by other parents and ask them to evaluate these parents; we also ask whether they would have made a similar parenting choice. This experimental design allows us to address potential social desirability concerns by placing the focus on a different set of parents (rather than on the respondent, if the respondent happens to be a parent) and also allows us to measure beliefs about parenting without relying on abstractions. Furthermore, this means we do not need to restrict our sample to parents only.

6.4.1 Study Approach

Parenting often involves making costly choices about a child's time. It is these costly choices, however, that are the clearest forms of revealed preferences about what people believe is most valuable for a child. If a child had an infinite amount of time, parents would need to make few decisions about what activity is especially important because a child could do everything. In reality, however, encouraging a child to do one activity means that they are going to do less of something else. Therefore, key to understanding how people feel about parents who deliberately encourage political behavior is to factor in costs: Are people supportive of parents who encourage their child to engage in politics *rather than some other activity*? To address this idea of costs directly, in our studies parents always face a choice. We subsequently track how our participants evaluate the particular choice the parents make in a trade-off situation and how political involvement affects people's perceptions of this trade-off.

In our first three studies, there is either a partisan behavior or a conflictual issue at stake. Although Study 4 relies on a structure similar to the first three studies, the treatments focus on parents who encourage civic behaviors that are explicitly nonpartisan. Across the four studies, we also vary the age of the child. Studies 1 and 2 focus on parents who have a nine-year-old child. The age of the child is specifically selected given research on the role of parental political socialization and childhood development (van Deth, Abendschön, and Vollmar 2011). Indeed, in the example that opened this chapter, a father described an eight-year-old who had been encouraged by her parents to become very engaged in the 2016 election, and a mother mentioned taking a five-year-old to an antiabortion rally. Still, although research suggests that children as young as six may already know political concepts (Oxley et al. 2020), Greenstein (1965) specifically noted that a nine-year-old may be too young to understand anything about politics. The benefit of our multistudy approach, however, is an ability to consider a variety of contexts. Therefore, Studies 3 and 4 present participants with older children: a seventeen-year-old (Study 3) and a fourteen-year-old (Study 4).

As we will discuss when we consider the details of each study, all treatments were pretested with a different set of participants to ensure the exclusion of confounds that could influence people's evaluations of the parents in question.

6.4.2 Measures

Although the treatments differed, we rely on the same set of measures in each of the four studies. Political involvement is our main covariate. In all studies, political involvement was measured prior to treatment. In Studies 1, 2, and 3, involvement was measured in the first wave of a two-wave study. In Study 4, involvement was measured in the same wave but prior to treatment. In every analysis, we interact involvement with the experimental treatments to test whether involvement conditions the effects of the treatments – that is, it tests whether the deeply involved see the treatment differently from the rest of the public.

All studies rely on two outcome measures. The first outcome measure asked participants how favorably or unfavorably they felt about each of the parents. The second outcome measure asked participants whether they would make the same choice as the parents in the treatment. Both are asked on a seven-point scale. Details about the measures are available in Online Appendix V1 (Studies 1 and 2), V2 (Study 3), or V3 (Study 4).

Our four studies track different types of political scenarios. Study 1 considers parents who encourage their children to donate money to a political cause, and Study 2 turns to attendance at political rallies. Study 3 replicates the political scenario of the first study but now with an adolescent rather than a younger child. Finally, Study 4 focuses on nonpartisan civic participation. The goal across these studies is to consider a variety of different political contexts: Some focus on partisan politics (Studies 1 and 3); some focus on ideological issues (Study 2); and some focus on civic engagement without partisanship (Study 4). Our consideration of these scenarios is largely exploratory: Although we anticipate that we will see involvement differences in responses to our treatments, we do not have any a priori expectations about the way these differences may vary across studies.

6.5   STUDY 1: A NINE-YEAR-OLD MAKES A DONATION

In our first study, the participants read about a nine-year-old child who donates part of their birthday money. The idea that a parent would suggest that a child donate some money is often something that is noted as a part of general civic socialization (Ottoni-Wilhel, Estell, and Perdue 2014). In this case, we will vary whether the donation is to a political (and, in particular, partisan) or nonpolitical organization. This first study was part of Wave 2 in D19.

6.5.1   Study 1: Treatment

We begin with a scenario in which a nine-year-old child donates part of their birthday money. Since, as we noted previously, people's responses to parental efforts may differ by the party these efforts benefit, the first factor in this two-factor experiment is the recipient of the donation: (1) the national committee of the participant's in-party, (2) the national committee of the participant's out-party, or (3) a nonpartisan charity (Make-A-Wish Foundation). We pretested the nonpartisan charity to ensure that people had no unexpected associations between the charity and a political party. We present the results of this pretest – in which the selected charity is compared against other nonpolitical organizations – in Online Appendix M6.2.

The second factor is the decision process: (1) the child selected the donation recipient or (2) the parents suggested the donation recipient. The experiment produces a 3 × 2 factorial design, for a total of six experimental conditions. In all conditions, the child was never referred to by a gendered pronoun. The full wording of the treatments is available in the appendix at the end of this book.

Since this study randomizes the partisanship of the parents relative to the participant (i.e., in-party vs. out-party), we conduct the analyses in two ways. First, we restrict the analysis to the 731 participants who identify with or lean toward a party (this follows from Druckman and Levendusky 2019). Second, we also analyze the full sample, independents included (shown in Online

Appendix M6.3). Both sets of results lead to substantively similar conclusions about perceptions of parents who encourage children to participate in politics.

6.5.2 Study 1: Results

We begin with our first dependent variable – the participants' evaluation of the parents. Although our outcome variables were asked on a seven-point scale, we dichotomize the variables here for ease of interpretation (we show the results without the dichotomization in Online Appendix M6.4 – they are substantively similar). We begin by looking at treatment effects generally, and then we will look at how involvement shapes these evaluations.

First, we see that *regardless of condition*, only a minority of participants are supportive of the parents' decision to suggest that the child donate the birthday money (Figure 6.1a). In fact, in the condition where we see the highest levels of favorability for a partisan donation – an in-party donation where the child selected the recipient – only 42 percent of participants have a favorable view of the parents. As we would expect, out-party donations have lower support than in-party donations, but the differences are not statistically significant. We do observe increases in favorability in the Make-A-Wish condition (relative to the partisan conditions): Here, we see that 52 percent of participants support the parents when the child selects the recipient on their own and 49 percent when the donation recipient is suggested by the parents. Although the parents fare marginally better when the child selects the recipient on their own – especially in the political conditions – these shifts are not significant.

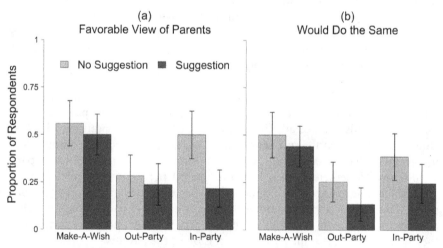

FIGURE 6.1 Evaluations of parents in Study 1 (nine-year-old who donates birthday money)
Source: Data from D19. Error bars represent 95 percent confidence intervals.

In Figure 6.1b, we see similar patterns for our second outcome variable: "Would you make the same decision as the parents?" Again, there are slight increases in support for the parents in the Make-A-Wish condition: 49 percent of people report they would do the same thing when the donation recipient is not suggested by the parents and 41 percent when it is. Nonetheless, the majority of our participants report that they would *not* make similar decisions as the parents in the treatment – especially when the "same decision" means asking a child to donate money to a political party.

Next, however, we consider whether the respondents' political involvement shifts their perceptions of the parents. In Figure 6.2, we plot predicted probabilities for each of the dependent variables from a model that conditions the treatment effects on involvement. The top panels (Figures 6.2a, b, and c) are for the favorability dependent variable, while the bottom panels (Figures 6.2d, e, and f) are for the dependent variable about whether the respondent would make the same decision.

First, we see that involvement is most closely related to positive views of the parents when the donation is going to the nonpartisan charity, rather than to a party. In the Make-A-Wish conditions, we see that involvement significantly ($p < 0.001$) predicts parental favorability. Participants at the highest end of the involvement scale are about 75 percent likely to view the parents favorably, compared to a 21 percent likelihood at the very bottom of the involvement scale. Whether the parent suggested the donation recipient has no effect on the favorability at any level of involvement.

In the political partisan treatments, positive views of the parents *do* increase with involvement but only in the no-suggestion treatments, and the effect does not reach clear levels of significance ($p = 0.06$). Furthermore, the feelings are generally lukewarm. In the treatment that produces the highest levels of support for the parents – the condition in which the donation is in-party and not at the parents' suggestion – 60 percent of participants on the highest end of the involvement scale view the parents favorably, but only 22 percent of the participants on the lowest point of the involvement scale feel the same way.

That being said, involvement more closely predicts the likelihood of reporting that one would make the same decision as the parents in the experiment. This is especially likely to be the case in the conditions where the child selects the donation recipient without a suggestion from the parents. Here, involvement has a significant effect in both the out-party and in-party conditions. Nonetheless, even here the overall perception is still lukewarm when the parents suggest the political donation or if the donation is to the out-party. The highest support among the deeply involved comes when the child chooses on their own to donate to the in-party with 67 percent reporting that they would make the same parenting decision as the parents.

In sum, the first study suggests that people have complicated feelings about parents' encouragement of a child's political donation – especially when the donation recipient is chosen at the behest of the parents. Involvement, as

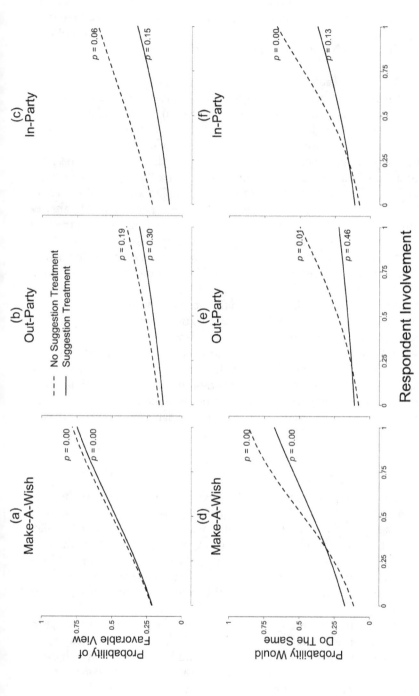

FIGURE 6.2 Does involvement moderate treatment effects in Study 1 (nine-year-old who donates birthday money)?
Source: Data from D19. The *p*-values listed in the figure show the significance of the effect of involvement on the dependent variable for each treatment.

Figure 6.2 demonstrates, does condition people's response to the parents in the study, but even among those who are deeply involved, there is some hesitation about supporting parents who encourage their child to make a political donation. Still, as involvement decreases, support for the parents plummets.

6.5.2.1   *Additional Checks*

As this is the first of our four studies, we want to address two additional checks on the results. These checks also apply to the remaining three studies. First, an alternative explanation underlying these results may be that people believe that a child's autonomy is more socially desirable, which may lead them to understate their support for the parents. To consider this possibility, we conducted a study with a separate sample relying on a "fake good–fake bad" manipulation (Holbrook, Green, and Krosnick 2003; Claassen and Ryan 2016; Klar and Krupnikov 2016). In this design, people are either assigned to answer two questions about political parenting as if they are trying to make the best impression possible ("fake good") or the worst impression possible ("fake bad"). A difference between treatments signals the potential for social desirability, and the patterns in the "fake good" condition signal the direction of socially desirable responding. We present the results in Online Appendix M6.5. We find no evidence that it is socially desirable to report that parents should not engage in deliberate political socialization; if anything, we see very weak evidence of social desirability in the other direction.

As a second check, we also considered our results for people in our studies who do and do not have children. People who have not made parenting decisions, for example, may respond to our treatments differently from those who have. We find no evidence of such a pattern (Online Appendix M6.6). In other words, in all four studies, people respond in the same manner regardless of whether or not they have children of their own.

6.6   STUDY 2: A NINE-YEAR-OLD ATTENDS A POLITICAL RALLY

It is notable, of course, that even in the Make-A-Wish condition where the child does not make an overtly political contribution, only about half of our participants support the parents. This outcome may suggest that people's concern is not just donations to a political party but also the fact that the parents are asking a child to donate their birthday money at all. Perhaps asking the child to part with something that others had given them as a gift was just a bridge too far. With this possibility in mind, we turn to a different scenario in Study 2.

In Study 2, participants were again presented with the parents of a nine-year-old child, but we consider a different type of political behavior. In Study 2, the parents were faced with two conflicting events and had to decide which event the family would attend. One of these events was always held constant: the child's soccer game. The manipulation of the second event is the first experimental factor, and participants were assigned to treatments in which the soccer game conflicted with either: (1) a grandparent's 73rd birthday party, (2) a political rally (likely) *congruent* with the participant's political beliefs, or (3) a political rally (likely) *incongruent* with the participant's beliefs. The second experimental factor is the parents' decision; participants were randomly assigned to a treatment in which the parents had (1) decided the family would attend the soccer game or (2) decided the family would attend the other event. In total, this experiment had a 3 × 2 factorial design, forming six experimental groups. The full wording of the treatments is available in the appendix at the end of the book.

The political event in question was a rally about abortion policy: either a pro-life or pro-choice rally. We deliberately selected a rally that focused on an ideological issue, as our first study focused on partisanship. In our analyses, we assume that Republicans would view the pro-life rally as party politically congruent and Democrats would view the pro-choice rally as politically congruent.[8] In Online Appendix M6.7, we reanalyze the data dividing subjects on the basis of ideology rather than partisanship; the main conclusions are unchanged. For ease of discussion, however, we refer to the "in-party rally" treatment and the "out-party rally" treatment.

We also deliberately selected a conflictual political issue following McDevitt's (2018) argument that there is an important benefit to introducing children to the inherent conflict in politics. The idea of bringing children to a rally follows from examples of parents who actively work to politically engage their children – some younger than nine years old (Rubin 2020). Indeed, this chapter opens with just such examples: Catherine Glenn Foster who has brought her own children (one at an age younger than the child in our treatment) to pro-life rallies and Kristy Woudstra who recalls attending these types of rallies as a young child.

Prior to fielding the experiment, we again conducted a set of pretests with a different sample of subjects. We pretested a variety of sports the child could be playing to check for possible confounds; we also pretested the nonpolitical event to make it equally important to the soccer game (see Online Appendix M6.2 for details on the pretesting process). Since the birthday party and soccer game were evaluated as equally important in pretests, we can treat the conditions in which the participants are assigned to the birthday party as a baseline for comparison to the political groups. Finally, in the treatments we also clarified for the participants that the soccer game was *not* highly important; specifically, the participants were told that "the [child's] team is expected to lose the game; the child is not a star on the team."

---

[8] There are some overlooked nuances in abortion opinion. For example, in the 2018 CCES, nearly half of Democrats supported a ban on abortions after the 20th week of pregnancy. Further, the clear majority of Republicans (72 percent) opposed making abortion illegal in all circumstances. However, the basic partisan gap is clear: 81 percent of Democrats say women should be allowed to get an abortion as a matter of personal choice, and only 28 percent of Republicans agree.

6.6.1   Study 2: Results

Just as we did in the first study, we consider evaluations of the parents and whether the participants would make the same decision. Figure 6.3 displays the bivariate results. In Figure 6.3a, as we expected following our deliberate pretesting, we see that in the soccer game/birthday party conditions, our participants are split, making this comparison a useful baseline. Next, we see that the majority of participants (along both outcome variables) are more supportive of the parents when they attend the game rather than the rally. Relative to our baseline comparison of the game versus the birthday, we see that participants are significantly more favorable toward the parents when the parents pick the soccer game over the rally (*regardless* of the political side of the issue). When the parents opt to skip the game, only 21 percent of respondents view the parents favorably in the out-party rally treatment, and 26 percent of respondents view the parents favorably in the in-party rally treatment. On the other hand, when the parents select the game, around 70 percent of respondents view the parents favorably in regardless of the political side of the rally.

We see similar patterns in Figure 6.3b, when we turn to our second outcome measure – would you make the same choice as the parents? Here, only 17 percent of respondents say they would, just like the parents, skip the game to attend the rally; this is true in both in-party and out-party treatments. In the out-party rally treatment, 84 percent of respondents say they would do the same as the parents in the treatment and skip the rally, and 76 percent of respondents say they would skip the rally in the in-party rally treatment.

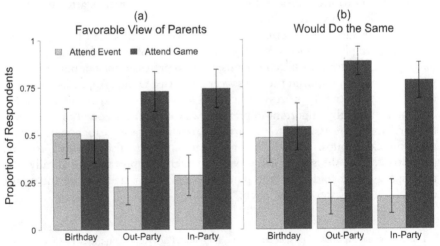

FIGURE 6.3 Evaluations of parents in Study 2 (nine-year-old has a soccer game that conflicts with another event)
Source: Data from D19. Error bars represent 95 percent confidence intervals.

Notably, we again see that the participant's likely position on the issue does not have much of an effect. Although participants are slightly more favorable toward the parents when they pick the congruent rally over the soccer game than when they select the incongruent rally, this difference does not reach conventional levels of significance (difference of 6.1 percentage points, two-tailed $p = 0.25$). We see very similar patterns in our second outcome variable.

Thus far, the results are similar to those in Study 1: People are not supportive of parents who deliberately engage their children in political participation. As a next step, then, we again consider how political involvement affects these perceptions. In Figure 6.4, we display the results of the model in which we condition the treatment effects on involvement – just as we did in Study 1. In these plots, the line represents the marginal effect of the parents choosing to attend the game rather than the other randomly assigned event (i.e. birthday party or one of the rallies). Notably, we see the lowest marginal effects for the treatments in which the parents are deciding between the game and the birthday party – again reinforcing our reliance on this set of conditions as a baseline. Turning to the political conditions, however, we see that *regardless* of level of involvement, selecting the game always has a large, positive marginal effect. In other words, at all levels of involvement our participants seem to be more supportive of parents who pick the soccer game over a political rally.

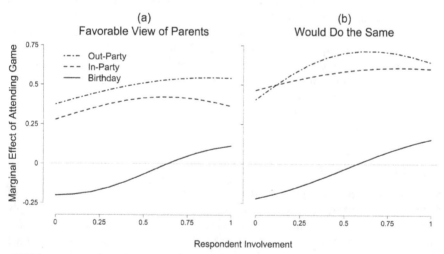

FIGURE 6.4 Does involvement moderate treatment effects in Study 2 (nine-year-old has a soccer game that conflicts with another event)?
Source: Data from D19. Lines represent the marginal effect of attending the child's soccer game versus attending the event. When the line is above the vertical line at 0 on the y-axis, then respondents on average evaluate the parents better when the family attends the soccer game; when the line is below the vertical line at 0 on the y-axis, then respondents on average evaluate the parents better when the family attends the event.

Moreover, the lines in Figure 6.4 are quite flat, suggesting few differences by level of involvement.

The consistent preference for the parents who opt to attend the game, rather than a political rally, is notable given what the game is. Our treatments specify a soccer game for a nine-year-old whose team is *expected to lose*. This is not an opportunity to win a World Cup or a state championship. Still, the majority of study participants believe it is more important for the child to experience the game than have a political experience. Indeed, even among participants who are at the highest end of the involvement scale – the deeply involved – 87 percent support the parents when they pick the soccer game compared to 50 percent who support the parents when they pick the in-party rally.

The first two studies, then, point in the same direction: People are not supportive of parents who, when faced with a choice, direct their child's time toward political ends. Even when we consider political involvement, support for parents who engage in deliberately political parenting is, at best, lukewarm even among those who are deeply involved. That these results hold across both donation behaviors and rally attendance suggests that this is not simply a function of a certain type of political behavior (e.g., donation) being especially undesirable for children. These studies may suggest that few people perceive that politics requires direct and deliberate parenting efforts.

Yet, perhaps there are alternative explanations for these results. As Greenstein (1965) wrote, "the nine-year-old is a small child ... his world is one of toys, games and fantasy." People, then, may be supportive of parents who encourage political action but believe that the child in our treatments is just too young. This is especially possible given the low levels of support for these decisions among the deeply involved. In other words, the first two studies may be missing an important involvement divides in perceptions of parenting due to the age of the child in the treatments. To address this possibility, we turn to Study 3, which will present a new sample of participants with a seventeen-year-old – a teenager nearly old enough to vote but still under their parents' watch.

6.7   STUDY 3: A SEVENTEEN-YEAR-OLD MAKES A DONATION

Our first two studies suggest that most people are not all that supportive of parents who engage in deliberate political socialization. Even the deeply involved, a group for whom politics plays a central role in their lives, were not overwhelmingly supportive of parents who suggested their children donate money to the parties or who decided that their child should attend a rally instead of a soccer match. It is possible, however, that these results are age-dependent; people, for example, may be uncomfortable with these types of parenting choices when the child is nine years old but may be more supportive of this approach for an older child.

Our next step, then, is to consider what happens when the child in question is a seventeen-year-old adolescent. There is research to suggest that seventeen-year-olds can engage in active political discussion with their parents (McDevitt 2018) – some even influencing *their parents'* political beliefs, rather than the other way around (McDevitt and Kiousis 2015). Even more importantly, there is evidence to suggest that it is normatively beneficial for adolescents to become politically active (Kahne, Lee, and Feezell 2012). If our participants were dissatisfied with the parents in the first two studies because a nine-year-old child is just too young, then age is much less likely to be an issue in this next study.

Study 3 (part of Q20) follows a design similar to the first study: Parents encourage the adolescent to give a donation. Given that the child in question is now seventeen years old, we focus on money that they have earned from a part-time job, rather than money that they were given as a birthday gift.[9] Importantly, unlike in the first study, the parents do *not* suggest a recipient in any of the conditions; in all the conditions, the recipient of the donation is selected by the seventeen-year-old. This means that the donation recipient represents the adolescent's political preference. The parents in this study, then, are encouraging participation and engagement but do not seem to be actively pushing the adolescent toward a *particular political position*. Once again, the donation recipients are: (1) the national committee of the study participant's in-party, (2) the national committee of the study participant's out-party, or (3) nonpartisan charity (Make-A-Wish again). We again measure the same outcomes as in the previous two studies.

6.7.1 Study 3: Results

The bivariate results of the third study are displayed in Figure 6.5. In Figure 6.5a, we first see that, unlike in Study 1, now a majority of participants view the parents favorably when the adolescent donates to Make-A-Wish. This pattern suggests that the participants do seem to view the seventeen-year-old differently than the nine-year-old, now approving of the parents' decision to encourage the adolescent to donate their money. This is notable, as this result suggests that people are not *unconditionally* opposed to parental efforts to socialize their children toward donating earned money. What our participants do seem opposed to is when the parental encouragement results in *political* donations. Even though the child in question is now seventeen-year-old, the patterns for the political condition reflect those for the nine-year-old in Study 1: The majority of participants have unfavorable views of parents and report that they would not make the same parenting decisions when the adolescent donates to a partisan organization. In other words, although the parents just encourage the donation and do not suggest a recipient, participants evaluate the parents more negatively when the adolescent donates money to a partisan outlet.

---

[9] We also randomize the gender of the teenager in this study; we find that the gender of seventeen-year-old does not condition the treatment effect nor does it have an independent effect on its own.

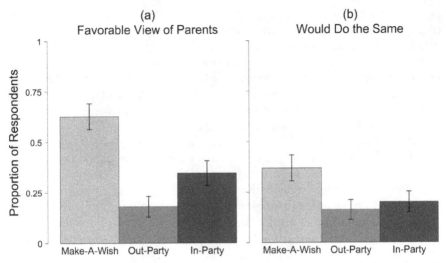

FIGURE 6.5 Evaluations of parents in Study 3 (seventeen-year-old donates work money)

Source: Data from Q20. Error bars represent 95 percent confidence intervals.

In Study 3, we also find more consistent *partisan* differences. Participants were twice as likely to view the parents favorably if the seventeen-year-old donated to the in-party instead of the out-party. Yet, even when the donation went to the same party as the participant, only 35 percent of participants viewed the parents favorably, a proportion that is almost 28 percentage points lower than when the seventeen-year-old donated to Make-A-Wish, where 63 percent view the parents favorably. Again, despite the fact that the parents only suggested making a donation – and did not suggest the recipient – the adolescent's donation decision reflected on the parents.

The patterns shift, somewhat, when participants are asked if they would have done the same thing as the parents (Figure 6.5b). Here, we do not see a difference between the in-party and out-party treatments, with fewer than 20 percent of participants reporting they would do the same thing as the parents and encourage a seventeen-year-old to donate their money. Although more participants are more positive in the condition where the adolescent makes a donation to Make-A-Wish, even in this condition, only 37 percent report they would make the same choice as the parents.

As a next step, we again consider the role of political involvement; Figure 6.6 displays the predicted views of the parents now conditional on the respondent's level of involvement. First, in Figure 6.6a, we do not see any involvement differences when the donation is to Make-A-Wish – people at both ends of the involvement scale feel generally favorable toward the parents, and the effect of involvement is not statistically significant. The patterns in the political treatments are different. Here, we see that the involved *do* view the parents

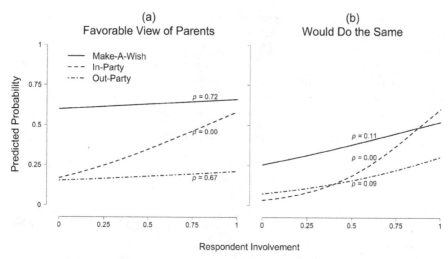

FIGURE 6.6 Does involvement moderate treatment effects in Study 3 (seventeen-year-old donates work money)?
Source: Data from Q20. The *p*-values in the figure are the (two-tailed) *p*-values of the effect of involvement on the dependent variable in each treatment.

more positively than those at the low end of the involvement scale when the donation is to the in-party, meaning that involvement strongly conditions how people think about teenagers engaging in partisan activities. Those at the top end of the involvement scale, the deeply involved, have about a 60 percent probability of reporting that they view the parents favorably, compared to 17 percent for those at the low end of the involvement scale. Not surprisingly, however, the favorability toward the parents does not extend to parents whose seventeen-year-old donates money to the out-party.

We see similar patterns on our second outcome measure, in Figure 6.6b: Would a participant behave in the same way as the parents? In the in-party treatment, we see that participants who are on the low end of the involvement scale have a 3 percent probability of reporting that they would behave the same as the parents in the treatment – compared to 60 percent probability among those on the high end of the involvement scale. Notably, the probability of behaving the same way is considerably lower in the out-party condition, even among people who are deeply involved (30 percent).

In sum, the results of the third study suggest that the age of the child does matter. We may have begun the chapter with an eight-year-old who became very engaged in the 2016 election, but many participants in our studies much preferred the parents of a civically engaged seventeen-year-old to a similarly engaged nine-year-old. Once our focus is on an adolescent, we do see emerging differences between those who are deeply involved and those with less involvement: The deeply involved are much more supportive of the parents who encourage political action and more likely to report that they would make similar choices. This is not to argue that the deeply involved uniformly support the parents but to suggest that if the parents in our treatment are going to find support among any group, it will be among the deeply involved.

6.8   STUDY 4: A FOURTEEN-YEAR-OLD PARTICIPATES IN CIVIC ENGAGEMENT ACTIVITIES

To this point, participants in Studies 1 and 2 were mostly critical of parents who encouraged their nine-year-old to engage in political participation, and a majority of participants in Study 3 were also critical of parents whose seventeen-year-old opted to donate money to a political party. Although we saw few involvement differences in the studies with the nine-year-old child, once our treatment included an adolescent, involvement did condition the results. People who are deeply involved, as the third study shows, were more supportive of parents in the in-party conditions than those on the lower end of the involvement scale. Taken together, our results suggest that, first and foremost, age matters. Once the child is older, the now-familiar involvement differences emerge.

The studies, however, leave an open question. All three studies present parenting that encourages political engagement, but the resulting engagement is partisan and ideological. Even in Study 3, where the parents encourage the donation, but the seventeen-year-old makes the ultimate decision on the recipient, there is an indirect connection between parental efforts and partisanship. There are, of course, other ways that parents can include politics in their children's lives. For example, we can return to Kristy Woudstra – the parent who hesitates to bring her daughter to an openly political rally. Even as Woudstra avoids having her children "physically participate in [her] politics," she notes that "they come with me when I vote. I have a giant chalkboard in the kitchen the kids know not to touch. It's solely for my often-political quotes . . . .." In other words, Woudstra sends her children political signals, but these are signals of more general *civic* engagement.

Woustra's behavior may be appealing to many people. Indeed, there are often parental and community requests that schools teach civics without engaging in discussion of ideas that are deemed controversial (Galston 2004). It is possible, then, that what people – regardless of involvement – want to see is this type of civically minded socialization. If parenting and perceptions of parenting are revealed preferences about what is beneficial for society, then perhaps what people believe is most beneficial is nonpartisan political socialization. This is the idea we turn to in our final study.

6.8.1   Study 4: Design

Study 4 follows a similar approach to Study 2: The parents are deciding whether the family will attend a soccer game or another event that happens to conflict with the game. Just as in Study 2, the participants are told that the child is not a star on the soccer team and that the child's team is expected to lose the game. Furthermore, just as in Study 2, the condition in which the parents are choosing between the soccer game and 73rd birthday party forms the base of comparison. The first difference between this study and Study 2 is that in the remaining conditions, the soccer game conflicts with civic – but not overtly *partisan or ideological* – events. In these conditions, participants were randomly assigned to the soccer game conflicting with either: (1) a voter registration drive, (2) a local candidate forum, or (3) a food bank event. The second difference is that in all study conditions, the parents decided that the family would attend the other event (i.e. not the soccer game). Although this means we will not be able to compare parents who opted to attend the soccer game to parents who chose a different activity, we will still be able to compare all conditions to the pretested birthday party baseline. A final difference between Studies 2 and 4 is that now, the child is older: In Study 2, the child was nine; here, the child is fourteen. This is done, again, to ensure that the patterns we observe are not a function of a child's age.

   Unlike the previous three studies, this study was conducted in a single wave. Finally, because there is no assignment in this study that relies on the relationship between the parents and participants' political party, there is no need to exclude independents. Still, to ensure that our results are comparable across studies, we present analyses of Study 4 that exclude independents in Online Appendix M6.8. We find that even if we do exclude pure independents, our results remain substantively unchanged.

6.8.2   Study 4: Results

Much as we did in the first three studies, we first consider the condition in which the parents opt to attend the birthday party over the soccer game. In Figure 6.7a, we see that 45.5 percent of participants across the entire sample evaluate the parents favorably and 52.5 percent report that they would make the same decision. This is slightly lower than in Study 2, in which 56 percent viewed the parents favorably and 55 percent reported they would make the same decision as the parents when the parents chose the birthday party rather than the game. The shift may be due to the age of the child: People may believe that a nine-year-old should attend family events, but fourteen-year-olds should honor commitments that they made.[10] Nonetheless, that

---

[10]   We thank Jessica T. Feezell for suggesting this explanation.

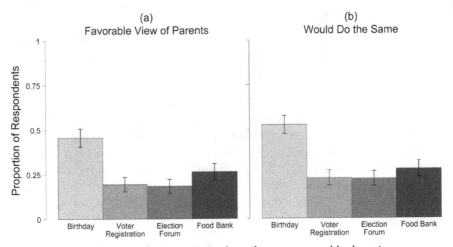

FIGURE 6.7 Evaluations of parents in Study 4 (fourteen-year-old who misses a soccer game)
Source: Data from YG20. Error bars represent 95 percent confidence intervals

nearly half the participants evaluate the parents positively again suggests that this condition is a useful baseline condition.

Relative to this baseline condition, however, our remaining three conditions show significantly lower support for the parents. Among the three civic behaviors, attending the food bank event rather than the soccer game earns the highest level of support: 26.3 percent evaluate the parents positively, and 27.6 percent report that they would make the same decision as the parents. Still, this is a statistically significant and substantively large decline in support relative to the baseline condition ($p < 0.001$).

Participants give still lower evaluations to parents who select either the voter registration drive or the candidate forum – the civic behaviors that are closer to politics. Here, evaluations are not only significantly lower than the evaluations of the parents who opt to go to the birthday party ($p < 0.001$) but also significantly lower than the evaluations of the parents who opt to go to the food bank.[11] We also see significant differences between choosing the more politically oriented civic behaviors and the birthday party on the measure that asks participants whether they would make the same choice as the parents (Figure 6.7b). In sum, even when the activities in question were nonpartisan and nonconflictual, our participants

---

[11] The comparison between the food bank and voter registration drive conditions is $p = 0.009$; the comparison between the food bank and the election forum is $p = 0.025$. There is no significant difference between the evaluations of parents who chose the voter registration drive and the election forum.

still had negative reactions to parents who chose these civic activities over the soccer game.[12]

As a next step, we consider our results by involvement (Figure 6.8). First, as we would expect, we find that involvement does not at all condition responses in the birthday party treatment (Figure 6.8a). This is, of course, to be expected given that this treatment has no political implications. We again, however, see that involvement moderates effects in treatments where the parents choose to attend more civic events. Across all three events, people at the highest end of the involvement scale are significantly more likely to support the parents than those on the low end. The highest level of support is in the voter registration drive condition, where 58 percent of people at the high end of the involvement scale report viewing the parents in a favorable way. We see similar patterns when we track our second outcome variable – would you make the same decision (Figure 6.8b). Again, people who are deeply involved are significantly more likely to report that they would make the same decision relative to those who are less involved.

The patterns we see in Study 4, then, fit in with those of the previous three studies. People generally are not all that supportive of parents who pick a political activity over a more "fun" activity, even when this political activity is more civic, as it was in Study 4. People who are deeply involved are certainly more supportive of the parents who do encourage civic participation. Again, however, this support is not uniform even among people at the highest levels of involvement.

6.9 (DEEPLY INVOLVED) PARENTS, CHILDREN, AND POLITICS

Across four studies, we vary the political activities and the ages of the child. Regardless of these design changes, our studies show similar patterns. First, when it comes to young children, most participants are not supportive of parents who choose to expose their children to politics. This outcome may not be unexpected among those who are less deeply involved, but it is notable that even our most involved participants seem to have some qualms about a nine-year-old participating in overtly partisan and ideological activities.

The patterns are clearer when we consider treatments that include older children. Although many of our participants are not pleased with the parents who encourage a seventeen-year-old and a fourteen-year-old to engage in

---

[12] It is, of course, possible that our participants inferred partisan leanings to these civic activities. For this reason, we consider whether our results differ by participants' partisanship (see Online Appendix M6.8 for full results). We find no evidence that this is the case. Democrats and Republicans respond to our treatments in largely identical ways, suggesting that our results are not a function of participants inferring an underlying partisan leaning.

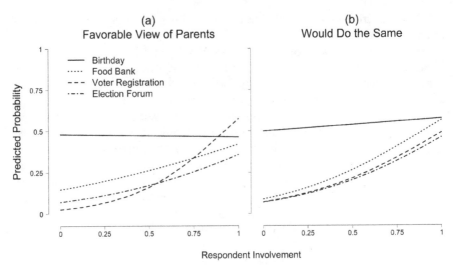

FIGURE 6.8 Does involvement moderate treatment effects in Study 4 (fourteen-year-old who misses a soccer game)?
Source: Data from YG20. For the parent's favorability (panel a) the (two-tailed) *p*-values of the effect of involvement on the dependent variable in each treatment are as follows: birthday = 0.910, food bank = 0.048, voter registration = 0.000, and election forum = 0.013. In panel b, – whether the respondent would have done the same – the (two-tailed) *p*-values of the effect of involvement on the dependent variable in each treatment are as follows: birthday = 0.619, food bank = 0.000, voter registration = 0.001, and election forum = 0.001.

political action, those who are deeply involved are now much more supportive. Still, even among those who are deeply involved, the support for political parenting is not as high as one may expect given the importance this group places on politics.

How do we reconcile these findings with the way the deeply involved remember their own childhoods in Chapter 5? In other words, if the deeply involved recall family dinners filled with political discussion and parents who encouraged political action, why isn't their support for the parents in our study more uniform? We suspect the explanation lies in an intersection of several ideas. The first has its roots in McDevitt and Kiousis (2015). As McDevitt and Kiousis (2015) argue, political interactions "trickle-up," meaning that parents engage with children because they want to be part of the child's political interests, not just because they want to socialize the child into politics. It is possible that when those who are deeply involved look back on their childhoods, they perceive that their political conversations with their families were more on equal footing: Their parents talked to them about politics because they wanted to engage in the *child's* interests. The parents in our experiments, however, may seem less attractive – it is more difficult to justify their political actions as purely the child's idea.

Second, our studies suggest that people may have little interest in political socialization that comes at a cost. When people consider parental responsibility, it is unlikely that they consider parents' encouragement of political behavior as costly activities in the sense that it means that a child does not get to do something else. When people who are deeply involved recall their childhoods as full of political engagement, it is unlikely that they consider all the other things that they could have done instead. It is possible that if our studies included a child whose whole day was empty, at least the civic activities would garner more support. Yet, the costly nature of the choice is important: It is one thing to be supportive of a totally costless action, but it sends a clearer message about preferences when the choice involves a tradeoff.

Still, even keeping these limitations in mind, there is little question that people who are deeply involved are more likely to support overt political socialization. This support is not uniform, and in some cases, this support is not overwhelming. Still, if there is a group of people who would support a nine-year-old donating their birthday money to a political party, that group of people is more likely to be the deeply involved.

People who are deeply involved are more supportive of parents who actively socialize their children into politics. They are more supportive of parents who encourage partisan action, ideological action, and civic action. This support takes on a broader meaning when we return to John Stuart Mill: "[I]t is one of the most sacred duties of parents, after summoning a human being into the world, to give to that being an education fitting to perform his part well in life toward others and toward himself." People who are deeply involved have different political preferences (Chapter 4), and they have different social networks (Chapter 5). As we will see in the next chapter, the deeply involved are also much more likely to have a (literal) political voice. What this chapter suggests is that deep involvement may cut across something even more fundamental to American life: How do people perceive the "most sacred duties of parents"?

Parenting is, in itself, a series of important decisions. But parenting is also a form of revealed preferences: It is one thing to report on a survey that one believes some idea is beneficial for society, but it is another thing to believe that parents should deliberately shape their children's lives to transmit that idea. Survey responses about political values are often signals about the type of person one hopes to be, rather than genuine political values (Connors 2020), but the stakes are higher when we consider parenting. From this perspective, our results suggest that involvement cuts across fundamental beliefs about the value of political socialization for producing the next generation of citizen and, by extension, of the value of politics for society.

Although pretests do not point to clear evidence of social desirability biases, the deeply involved may be more likely to believe that they should support the political socialization in our treatments. The patterns we see in our studies, then, may reflect the type of norms signaling Connors (2020) finds in studies of political values, but may not reflect how the deeply involved parent their own children. This sort of outcome, however, would still be meaningful. Perceptions that something is necessary and desirable depend on people's beliefs about the norms of a given society. If the deeply involved are more likely to believe that the socially desirable response to our experiment is to support the parents engaged in deliberate political socialization, these beliefs speak to another possible involvement divide: a divide in whether people believe active political participation is an important norm in American society.

7

A New Form of Self-Expression

You sort of participate hoping that it ends up in something or that it creates some value somewhere. But sometimes you can question it and you don't trust that it's really worthwhile to tweet that ... you hope that it is.

Beverly, a Twitter user, in Penney (2016)

In *Back to the Future*, one of the few things that Marty McFly takes with him from 1985 to 1955 is a camcorder. Marveling over the video camera, Doc Brown exclaims, "This is truly amazing; a portable television studio. No wonder your president has to be an actor." The camcorder is an amazing invention, but it is a limited one. Although it has one aspect of a television studio, it lacks its most important component: a true broadcasting antenna. Only people who are physically in the same area as the camcorder can see the recording.

Both the political and media contexts were different as we wrote this book in 2019 and 2020 than they were in 1985. In 1985, the president was Republican Ronald Reagan; a former actor whose film, *Cattle Queen of Montana*, was playing in Doc Brown's fictional hometown in 1955 (a full year after its release). In 2020, the president was also a Republican who had appeared in 11 movies (almost always playing himself). Donald Trump's rise to power, some have suggested, is in part a product of the shifts in the media environment that have occurred in the decades that followed 1985 (Wells et al. 2020). In these new media environments, people have access to a device that is both the portable television studio *and* the broadcasting antenna. Pairing smartphones with social media, people can broadcast pictures, videos, and their thoughts to the world (de Zúñiga, Molyneux, and Zhang 2014).

Social media, along with the rise of digital platforms more generally, have broadened the scope of information available to the individual. Ordinary people can now be active participants in the dissemination and even the production of news (Boczkowski, Mitchelstein, and Walter 2011; Wallace 2018). Although professional journalists are still the main sources of news gatekeeping (Soroka 2012), social media now give people a direct means of engaging with those who hold the keys to the gate (Xu and Feng 2014; Diehl, Ardèvol-Abreu, and de Zúñiga 2019).[1] All you need is a smartphone (which 81 percent of Americans reported owning in 2019)[2], a social media account, and the willingness to tell the world whatever is on your mind.

How willing someone is to share their thoughts and opinions with the world – especially on political topics – however, is likely to depend on their general relationship with politics. As we theorize in Chapter 3, a desire to express one's political views to others in a variety of ways is a component of deep involvement. Indeed, the deep involvement measure we introduce in Chapter 4 uses indicators about the importance of expression to capture levels of involvement. Expression also lurks in the background as we track the role of political socialization in involvement in Chapter 5. In this chapter, then, we turn to a more direct analysis of expression, primarily through a focus on one particular platform: social media. Given our argument in Chapter 3, we anticipate that those who are deeply involved will be much more likely to express their politics on social media. Our goals in this chapter, however, are broader; we are interested not simply in differences in levels of expression but the implications of these differences. How do people at lower levels of involvement feel about those who constantly and loudly express their political opinions on social media?

The willingness to express one's political opinion on social media may carry broad political potential. People who are not deeply involved – the majority of Americans – may not spend large parts of the day keeping up with the news, but many may still pay attention to the major news stories and many vote in national elections. This group has clear political preferences, and these preferences, as we argue in Chapter 4, may diverge from those of the deeply involved. Yet, if the deeply involved minority are more willing to express their political opinions on public social media platforms, then this group has a louder political voice.

We will delve into the implications of this louder political voice more directly in the next chapter. For now, our goal is to explore the relationship between involvement and expression on social media. First, we use an adjusted measure of involvement to demonstrate that involvement does in fact correlate with

---

[1] Notably, however, research suggests that, at least on Twitter, journalists largely ignore members of the public whom they do not know and do not reply to their tweets (Molyneux and Mourão 2019). We will turn to journalists in Chapter 8.

[2] Pew Research Center on Internet and Technology, June 2019. The largest disparities in smartphone ownership are between age groups: older people are less likely to own smartphones. Aside from those over 65, research suggests that the main inequalities are in smartphone reliance (e.g. the extent to which people use smartphones exclusively to access the internet), rather than ownership (Dunaway et al. 2018).

willingness to publicly express political opinions on social media, as we theorized in Chapter 3. Here, we find evidence that the deeply involved are much more likely to share their opinions about politics. Then, we turn to the main results of this chapter and analyze how people perceive those who post about politics. First, we consider how people perceive the motivations of those who post about politics on social media. Second, we turn to perceptions of their knowledge and extremity. Finally, we consider affective responses to people who post about politics. In these studies, our goal is to consider how involvement colors these perceptions. Those who are deeply involved, for example, are much more likely to perceive that people who post on social media about politics have civic goals; they are also more likely to have more positive affect toward those who post. The less involved, we find, are much more cynical about political posts. We conclude by considering the implications of this relationship between involvement and perceptions of political expression.

7.1 EXPRESSING POLITICS

In 1985 (or, really, any period prior to about 2005), a person who very much wanted to discuss politics (or, really, any topic for that matter) was at the mercy of their friends and family. In order to discuss politics, a person would have to find some willing group of people they knew, arrange a point in time in which they could be in the same place, or, at least, at which they could both be by the telephone, and only then could they have the conversation. Of course, one's family could provide a readily available audience. A person could wander into the kitchen and immediately engage an unsuspecting family member in a conversation about something that Reagan had said that day.

The problem for the deeply involved citizens of 1985, however, was that there was no guarantee that other proximate people would be equally interested in politics. If your most politically interested friend happened to be at the movies or away on vacation, you might have to wait three hours or even a couple of weeks to discuss politics. And, since in 1985 there were no smartphones, you could not even text this friend your political thoughts in real time – unlike today when you can text your friend as long as you have convinced yourself that your texts are not actually disturbing their vacation time. Relying on your family for political conversation was also difficult. If your family members were not actually all that interested in politics, then the resulting conversation would probably be unsatisfying (see e.g., Thorne and Bruner 2006). It is, likely, unfulfilling to express a set of thoughts you had been formulating for several hours in your head, only to be met with a weak "that's interesting."

The world looks very different in 2020. A person who wants to discuss politics need not do so with their families and need not call a friend. Certainly, they may still prefer to have political conversations with people they consider friends, and they may engage in political discussions with their families. Indeed, research suggests that most political conversations are incidental, rather than deliberately arranged (Minozzi et al. 2020) – and for many people, this occasional talk of politics is more than enough. But if these occasional chats about especially unexpected or salient political events prove unsatisfying, a politically engaged person can turn to social media. Your family may not appreciate hearing a steady stream of your political opinions, but there is a chance that someone on some social media platform might. Posting your political thoughts to social media may mean that someone will disagree with your opinion, but it also opens the possibility of finding people who agree.

Yet, expressing political thoughts on social media is not always as simple as posting and hoping for the best (although it can be). Rather, as we will suggest below, social media posts may reflect a more complicated interaction between a person's motivation for posting, their perceptions of their audience, and the audience response. We consider these different ideas in two steps. First, we define the types of social media posts that we will discuss in this chapter. Second, we turn to the types of motivations that may lead people to post on social media about politics.

7.1.1 A Particular Type of Expression

When we discuss sharing political opinions on social media, it is first important to separate the type of expressiveness we will consider in this chapter from social movements and mobilization efforts that also rely on social media posts. Social media, as research suggests, can serve as a medium for protest and activism (Freelon, McIlwain, and Clark 2018; Jackson, Bailey, and Foucault Welles 2020). Because social media can bring together groups of people who are physically located in different geographic locations, these platforms can overcome the constraints of physical space and unite people in a common goal (Housley et al. 2018). Within this context, other affordances of social media can further the development and organization of a social movement (Housley et al. 2018). The use of hashtags, for example, can help "those without access to traditional forms of power to create compelling, unignorable narratives" (Jackson, Bailey, and Foucault Welles 2020, 185). Focusing on the Black Lives Matter movement, Freelon, McIlwain, and Clark (2018) demonstrate a "social media power": "[S]ocial media movements can attract elite attention via social media as their concerns are broadcast through news outlets" (1005). Critical to this power is what they term "commitment" – the idea that people who are part of a social movement will continue sharing information about that movement over time. Commitment means that "movements and their interactants will not disperse (digitally speaking) when the next trending topic emerges," as they write (Freelon, McIlwain, and Clark 2018, 995).

The expression that we consider in this chapter, however, is different from posts that form part of a social movement. Our focus is not on social movements but rather on posts made by people sharing opinions and news stories however they feel the need to do so. The stories and opinions shared may be unified by a common topic, but that topic may be as broad as, simply, "politics." Although these posts are likely to promote a political side or candidate and may even, on occasion, include hashtags associated with social movements, these posts need not have the *commitment* to a movement in the sense that Freelon, McIlwain, and Clark (2018) describe.

The posts we focus on can take on a variety of forms. Some may be purely or largely informational, like sharing an article from a news source (e.g. Kraft et al. 2020). Others may be opinion-based – even though the opinion is, ostensibly, tethered to a news article or piece of objective information. In expressing these opinions, the individual may choose to engage directly with others or simply treat their post as a "monologue" (e.g. Freelon 2015). Sometimes, these forms of expression may also include a call to political action, where that action may range from clear ("call your congressperson!") to vague ("we have to do something") (Segesten and Bossetta 2017). Within this context, it is possible that some individuals do have a unifying element to their posts: One person, for example, may be more likely to post about national politics; another may be more likely to post about local government; a third person may be more focused on economic issues. It is also entirely possible, however, that the lone unifying element to a person's posts is an ideological position.

If the posts we are describing here are not tethered to the goals of a social movement, then what motivates people to publicly express themselves on the topic of politics? We can broadly fit these motivations into two umbrella categories: opinion leadership motivations and social motivations (following Ahn, Huckfeldt, and Ryan 2015 and de Zúñiga, Valenzuela, and Weeks 2016). Opinion leadership motivations focus on the informational content of what people share; social motivations focus on an intersection of people's perceptions of themselves, their social network, and their own role within that network. Despite the fact that people are probably more willing to acknowledge their opinion leadership motivations, these two umbrella groups of motivations work jointly – it is unlikely that someone is governed purely by opinion leadership or social motivations. For ease of discussion, however, we will consider the two categories separately below.

As we consider these motivations, we intersect research on embodied discussion with research on social media posting. Although in this chapter our data will focus largely on expression through social media, research on discussion outside of social media environments can still inform how we think about political expression. Where the social media context changes how people think about expression, we discuss why this may be the case. Throughout our analyses, our definition of a "political post" remains broad – we are interested in posts that share news stories and opinions regardless of whether these include any tangible call to action. This definition is central to our goal of understanding the motivations for political expression broadly construed, rather than the implications of political expression within a specific context.

7.1.2 Opinion Leadership Motivations for Political Expression

Not all people are going to follow the news regularly. Although this raises the concern that some people may have little to no information, scholars suggest that the electorate can still be relatively informed so long as some people do follow the news. Through a process called the "two-step flow," information flows from the media to the whole public through a subset of the public (Katz 1957). This means that people who follow the news regularly can act as *leaders*, transmitting news to their less engaged networks (Ahn, Huckfeldt, and Ryan 2015; Carlson 2018). This process is, in some way, made easier via the affordances of social media. A person who follows the news sees a story and can almost immediately share this story with a broad network (Kraft et al. 2020).

Whether we can count on the two-step flow to address informational gaps within the electorate, however, "depends on whether we view political communication among citizens as a civic exercise or as a political process" (Ahn, Huckfeldt, and Ryan 2015, 255). Following Ahn, Huckfeldt, and Ryan (2015), we can consider *civic* and *political* as two types of opinion leadership motivations for political expression.

7.1.2.1 *Civic Motivations*

At baseline, civic motivations can be considered as purely informational. Here, a person may engage others in a discussion of politics because they are hoping to share facts or receive information (Yoo, Kim, and de Zúñiga 2017).[3] Sharing an article from a newspaper with no comment or sharing a list of polling locations, for example, may come close to purely civic motivations. Although these types of motivations may be best suited for a two-step-flow structure of information sharing, purely civic motivations set a standard that may be impossible to meet.

Even if a person posts only news stories and shares no political opinions, people who post about politics on social media (or discuss politics with others) are not simply aggregating the most important stories of the day, and they are not providing a random sampling of a day's news. Even when they eschew sharing their opinions, people are selective in both the types of stories they share (Hasell 2020; Kraft et al. 2020) and how they share information with others (Carlson 2019). Research on Twitter sharing suggests, for example, that people are more likely to share partisan news (Hasell 2020). Moreover, even if the initial goal is to summarize a news event, the summaries are likely to have less

---

[3] Yoo, Kim, and de Zúñiga (2017) term this the receptive motivation and call political motivations "expressive." Here, we follow Ahn, Huckfeldt, and Ryan (2015) in using the term "civic motivations."

factual information and present a skewed view of the articles' factual content (Carlson 2019). As Ahn, Huckfeldt, and Ryan (2015) write, people who choose to share political information are not reference librarians.

One can argue, of course, that a purely informational standard is not the most appropriate form of civic motivation when it comes to politics. Rather, a civic motivation may be better perceived as posting for a largely altruistic goal. From this perspective, a person may post on social media because they believe that whatever they share will be helpful to someone else (Ma and Chan 2014; Munar and Jacobsen 2014). These posts need not necessarily be limited to news or factual information and may often include opinions – so long as the poster perceives that these opinions could be informative to another person or broader community (Munar and Jacobsen 2014). From this perspective, civically motivated sharing is less about the content of the information shared but becomes more about the *perceived* goal for sharing that information.

7.1.2.2 *Political Motivations*

While civic motivations imply purely informational or altruistic goals, political motivations mean expressing an opinion and sharing information with the goal of persuading others (Hoffman, Jones, and Young 2013; Thorson 2014; Yoo, Kim, and de Zúñiga 2017). These types of motivations are easier to identify in practice and may also be more common. In a study considering both civic and political motivations, for example, Yoo, Kim, and de Zúñiga (2017) find more evidence of political motivations than of civic motivations, and interviews with frequent political posters reinforce this pattern (Bastos and Mercea 2016). Penney (2016), for example, quotes a Twitter user named Kyle, who explains his Twitter strategy as follows: "I've got a pretty good reach on that, so I know if I can get a message out, if it changes one or two people's opinions over the long haul, I feel like I've done a pretty good thing" (79). Another Twitter user, Trevor, is focused on the importance of response: " ... when [Trevor] saw that his election-related posts had been retweeted, he described feeling like 'I'm not just shouting into the wind in the forest, there's someone who's heard it and has passed it along to others'" (Penney 2016, 81).

Ultimately, however, there is a confound inherent in adjudicating between civic and political motivations when people share political information. A person may be motivated to post a political thought because they believe that their perspective may be beneficial to the broader community; this person may even attempt to persuade others because they believe that voting for some candidate or supporting some issue may be the best course of action for the greatest number of people. These motivations may be civic in the sense that the poster perceives them as altruistic – this person is genuinely thinking about a community beyond themselves. Yet, to an observer the posts appear to be attempts at political persuasion or simply sharing one's opinion with no benefit to others. This tension between a poster's actual intent and their perceived intent may be especially complicated in a social media environment where posts are observed by broad networks of people who may not always have personal experiences with the poster (Papacharissi 2012). This role of the broader network, then, leads us to the second set of motivations for political posting: social motivations.

7.1.3 Social Motivations for Political Expression

There are a number of ways to think about the role of social motivations in political posts. The first is as simple as the desire to interact with others; the second may be self-presentational. A person's goal in posting about politics is to present a certain image to their broader social networks. This self-presentational goal is not only likely to influence whether someone posts in the first place but also the type of content one posts and how one presents that content. Although we will discuss each type of social motivation separately, they likely work in tandem.

7.1.3.1 *Seeking Political Discussion*

We began our discussion of political expression with the example of a person who just wanted to talk about politics. This idea is not far removed from the desire for expression and conversation we considered in Chapter 3: When someone is interested in a topic, it is natural for them to gravitate toward topic-focused social experiences (Dionísio, Leal, and Moutinho 2008). From this perspective, people are likely to seek out political discussion because, quite simply, they find it enjoyable (Fiorina 1990; de Zúñiga, Valenzuela, and Weeks 2016).

It is easy to think of political conversations as either contentious (e.g., Klar and Krupnikov 2016) or serving some larger deliberative or persuasive purpose (e.g. Conover, Searing, and Crewe 2002). Yet, political conversation does not always have to be combative, and it is often informal (Walsh 2004; Eveland, Morey, and Hutchens 2011; Minozzi et al. 2020). As Eveland, Morey, and Hutchens (2011) find, for example, most people engage in political conversation because they find it enjoyable or want to "pass the time." People's political conversation partners are often just people who happen to be around, and politics comes up because they happen to be talking about other topics (Minozzi et al. 2020; Ognyanova 2020). Translating these more informal conversational practices to social media, then, may mean that some people post about politics not only because they aim to persuade or inform but also because they want to "pass the time" and, potentially, have an enjoyable interaction with someone.

Social media, however, is not the same as a small interpersonal discussion group. First, during in-person discussion, politics often comes up as part of conversations about other topics (Minozzi et al. 2020). In other words, by the time politics has come up, people have already been engaged in a conversation. Originating a post on social media, however, signals an attempt to begin a conversation. Social media posting is basically sharing something and hoping (not assuming) someone will respond at least in a minimal way.

Second, conversations on social media are also much more public than the types of conversations Walsh (2004), Eveland, Morey, and Hutchens (2011), or Minozzi et al. (2020) have in mind. On the one hand, this may mean that ordinary people can reach broader audiences. On the other hand, it also means that people who post about politics open themselves up to more negativity and vitriol (Guess, Nyhan, and Reifler 2020) – which may be especially vicious and harmful for women and minority social media users (Cisneros and Nakayama 2015; Lawson 2018). These patterns may mean greater "communication apprehension" when posting on social media platforms like Twitter (Rubin, Perse, and Barbato 1988). At the same time, Stromer-Galley (2002) argues that a digital medium "may provide a new context for political conversation for those who would not normally engage in face-to-face political conversations." In short, some people – potentially those who believe they know the shape and scope of their social media networks and who generally do not have high levels of apprehension about communicating – may be motivated to post on social media because they believe that they will have enjoyable interactions or, at the very least, interactions that help them pass the time.

Put practically, sometimes a person may post on social media because they are motivated by a desire to inform others of some political event or outcome, and they may post on social media because they are motivated by a desire to persuade someone to support a certain candidate or to come to a certain opinion (and, as we discuss previously, someone may be motivated by the goals of a social movement – though those are not the types of posts we focus on in this chapter). On the other hand, at other times this very same person will post because they are hoping to have an enjoyable interaction with others. The types of posts these varying motivations produce may be different, but they need not always be. It is possible, for example, that someone could post about President Trump displaying a potentially doctored map of a hurricane's trajectory (Stewart 2019) hoping that someone in their network will comment with a joke about the event *and* as a way to signal their more serious concerns about the state of American politics.

7.1.3.2 *Self-Presentation Motivations for Political Expression*

The affordances of social media, as Papacharissi (2012) writes, "imply that presentations of the self, performed in data, persist and are difficult to erase completely, are easily replicated, are available to large scales of known and unknown audiences and publics, and are easily searchable" (1992). In private conversations people can easily identify their (often small) audience, but on social media, this audience is much larger and, potentially, more difficult to define. This means people are left to rely on their "imagined audience." The imagined audience is a "mental conceptualization of the people with whom we are communicating" (Litt 2012, 331). This mental conceptualization "serves as a guide for what is appropriate and relevant to share" (Litt and Hargittai 2016, 1). The idea that people think about what is appropriate to share given a particular (imagined) audience suggests another overarching motivation for posting on social media: self-presentation. Much as people do in face-to-face interactions, on social media people tend to "mobilize [their] activity so that it will convey an impression to others which it is in [their] interests to convey" (Goffman 1959).

We can consider social media as a form of self-presentation in several ways. First, as we discuss in Chapter 3, an aspect of publicly expressing yourself is communicating to others who you are and who you are not (Kozinets 2001; Guschwan 2011). This expression may take on varying forms: If wearing a particular team's T-shirt is an expression of a socially shared identity (Dionísio, Leal, and Moutinho 2008), so too can be a political post on social media.

This expression of identity, however, is often shaped by people's perceptions of their imagined audience. "The digital space," write White and Laird (2020), "has become a venue in which group norms can also be defined and maintained" (69). Although social media posts may be motivated by an overall desire to share something, the imagined audience of one's broader community underlies the motivation to present oneself in a way that others will find at the very least appropriate but at best positive and impressive (Kim 2015). As Kraft et al. (2020) argue, for example, people opt to share certain news articles not simply because they believe these articles are interesting but because they believe that sharing these articles will reflect well on them. Similarly, Choi (2014) suggests that people share information with others as a means of "getting recognition." At other times, people may grow reluctant to post about certain topics because they may have "a negative effect on social status" (Bright 2016, 248).

The goal of impressing the imagined audience, however, may be more nuanced than offering information that people will perceive as useful and important. Part of the self-presentation goal may be the desire for the audience to perceive the underlying motivations for posting in the best way possible. In other words, people may not only want to be the type of social media user who shares content that others find useful in some way but also want to be perceived as the type of user whose motivations in sharing this content are positive, if not altruistic. As Marwick and boyd (2010) write, people who tweet try to project an "authenticity" (see also Papacharissi 2012). When people tweet, Marwick and boyd (2010) write, there is "an ongoing front-stage identity performance that balances the desire to maintain positive impressions with the need to seem true or authentic to others" (11).

For Twitter users whose goal is to promote a brand (or themselves), these attempts at authenticity may mean that promotional tweets are interspersed with more "personal" tweets (Marwick and boyd 2010; Papacharissi 2012).

Someone who is not an "influencer" tweeting about politics, however, does not necessarily have a similar problem with authenticity – their political tweets are likely to be seen as their actual opinions, rather than some promoted content. Authenticity here, then, is projecting the idea that each political tweet is motivated by a desire for some greater or moral good (Kutlaca, van Zomeren, and Epstude 2020). Even if the tweet is, ultimately, an attempt at persuasion, the goal is to seem like someone who is persuading others in the hope of some greater good.

7.1.4 Should I Post This?

In most cases, it would be difficult to identify with precision the motivations that produced a specific social media post. Rather, what people post is likely an intersection of all the varying motivations coming together – some consciously and others potentially subconsciously. Over the course of a day, a person may read an article, have an experience, or even have a thought that they may initially think they could share with their social media networks. Whether this article, experience, or thought is shared, however, is an intersection of a person's perception of the content and their imagined audience. A person may share content with their networks because they believe the content will be useful, important, or persuasive, *and* they may share because they also happen to think this useful/important/persuasive content will lead their imagined audience to find them more impressive in some way. The same person may think some other piece of information is equally important but be less certain that the imagined audience on social media will respond affirmatively, so instead of posting it to their social media feeds, they might email or text the information to the one friend who they are certain will respond positively (Kraft et al. 2020).

This hoped-for positive response is as much about the content of the post as it is about the motivations producing the post. People not only want to have posted something that others will find useful (defined broadly) (Kim 2015; Kraft et al. 2020) but also want others to believe that their motivations for posting the information were pro-social (also defined broadly) (Marwick and boyd 2010). Put another way, if a person posts a ten-tweet thread about some political event, they want their imagined audience to believe the thread was worth reading. The person also wants their audience to believe that the thread was motivated by a desire to make something better, rather than by a desire to just express an opinion, gain more followers, or promote themselves. To return to Ahn, Huckfeldt, and Ryan's (2015) framework, people may have political motivations, but they want others to perceive their motivations as largely civic.

The problem is that communication on social media is different from communication in other social contexts (boyd 2010; Marwick and boyd 2010; Papacharissi 2012). In face-to-face conversation, there is greater clarity about the speakers' intentions through vocal cues and conversational norms

(Cappella 1985; Krauss, Chen, and Chawla 1996; Hall, Carter, and Horgan 2000). On social media, facial, vocal, and other conversational cues are absent. Communication is through text and, potentially, pictures, which means simultaneously transmitting content and motivation can be difficult. Moreover, face-to-face communication often occurs with smaller networks of people, whereas on social media, the networks are larger and more complex (Papacharissi 2010, 2012). The ultimate outcome is that a person posting on social media may believe that their motivations are authentically civic, but a person reading the post may lack the contextual information to arrive at that conclusion.

This mismatch between the poster and the reader may be especially likely in a political setting. Posts on political topics may immediately cue persuasion as a goal (Lupia and McCubbins 1998), and once persuasion is assumed, it may be difficult for a reader to imagine that a post is motivated by any other goal. A poster may promote a political candidate because they believe that this candidate will benefit the greatest number of people, but a person reading the social media post may believe that this is just more self-interested opinion-sharing and political persuasion. This perceptual divide may be especially likely if most political posting on social media is generally limited to a group of people who are heavily engaged in politics, for example, the deeply involved.

In the following sections, we explore deep involvement and political self-expression on social media. We begin by considering posting patterns, analyzing whether, as we hinted in Chapter 3, deep involvement affects how often people post on social media. Then, we shift our attention to the relationship between the poster and the imagined audience. In our studies, however, the audience is not imagined – rather the audience is rating the posters. Here, we present three sets of ratings. First, we focus on motivations for posting, tracking how people perceive the goals of those who post about politics. Second, we analyze whether people perceive those who post on social media as more knowledgeable, comparing these knowledge levels to perceived levels of extremism. Finally, we consider people's affective responses to those who post on social media. In these studies, we also analyze the role of involvement, finding involvement differences across these perceptions of posting behaviors.

7.2 SOCIAL MEDIA AND POLITICS

Before turning to involvement, it is important to acknowledge two points: First, few people post about politics on social media in any sustained way. Second, the people who do post are politically different from the majority who never post. In 2019, a study by Pew found that 22 percent of Americans use Twitter, and that 39 percent of those Twitter users reported that they had tweeted at least once about politics, "which includes mentions of national politicians, institutions or groups, as well as civic behaviors such as voting" over a year-long period (Pew 2019). When Pew researchers analyzed tweets, they found that tweets about national politics only made up 13 percent of all tweets from American adults with a public Twitter account. Even more importantly, 97 percent of those tweets about politics were created by the most active 10 percent of Twitter users. Put another way, most people are not on Twitter and, for those who are, most of Twitter is not about politics.

We can delve into these behaviors more deeply using a Pew survey from the winter of 2016 ($N = 4,654$). Pew asked social media users, now defined more broadly than Twitter, about a variety of posting behaviors related to politics. The patterns from this survey (Table 7.1) suggest most people are not actively engaging in politics on social media. The most frequent behavior is also the most passive – liking a political post.

When it comes to their broader networks, most people also have few political interactions. In a different Pew survey ($N = 4,579$), completed in the summer of 2016, for example, only a minority of survey respondents said that they would comment if they disagreed with a friend's political post; the majority (84 percent) reported that they would just ignore the post.

7.2.1 Who Has Political Interactions on Social Media?

A minority of people engage in politics on social media, but it is a predictable minority. Those who do engage in political expression, Pew found, are different from Twitter users who avoid the topic. Pew found especially large differences between people who did not tweet about politics and those whom they termed

TABLE 7.1 *Political behavior on social media from a Pew survey in winter 2016*

Do you ever use social media to ...	Yes
Post links to political stories or articles for others to read?	22%
Post your own thoughts or comments on political or social issues?	32%
Encourage other people to take action on a political or social issue that is important to you?	28%
Encourage other people to vote?	36%
Repost content related to political or social issues that was originally posted by someone else?	33%
"Like" or promote material related to political or social issues that others have posted?	45%
Change your profile picture to draw attention to an issue or event?	14%
Contact a politician or public official?	16%

Source: Data from Pew in winter 2016.

"prolific political tweeters." The prolific political tweeters made up 6 percent of all Twitter users but were responsible for 73 percent of all tweets about politics. Among this group, 92 percent reported that they "follow the news closely whether or not something important is happening," compared to 53 percent of people who do not tweet about politics. Moreover, people who tweeted about politics had more negative attitudes toward the opposing party than people who did not tweet about politics.

We can consider this relationship between social media posts and animosity more directly using the 2018 Cooperative Congressional Election Study (CCES). We consider the sample in three groups: people who do not use social media for politics (46 percent of respondents), people who read about politics on social media (30 percent of respondents), and people who have posted and commented about politics on social media (24 percent of respondents). In addition to posting behaviors, this CCES module also included a measure of affective polarization, which was asked of a portion of CCES respondents.

The affective polarization measures focus on social distance, asking respondents how they would feel if their child married someone from the Democratic Party or the Republican Party. The particular version of this question is the adjustment we discussed in Chapter 2: Respondents were told that the hypothetical in-law would *rarely* talk about politics. Using this adjusted measure offers two benefits. First, as we note in Chapter 2, a measure in which people are told the partisan would rarely discuss politics captures a level of *unconditional* animosity for the other side – you dislike this person even if you never have to be confronted with their ideas. Second, this measure allows us to control for potential confounds in the measure of social distance between parties (see discussion in Chapter 2).

To measure polarization, we calculate the absolute difference in how respondents said they would feel about a child-in-law from the Democratic Party and a child-in-law from the Republican Party. Since the respondents answered the questions on a five-point scale ranging from "very unhappy" to "very happy," the final polarization measure ranges from 0 (no difference in the two feelings) to 4 (very happy with one party and very unhappy with the other party). Higher values, then, mean greater levels of polarization. Before we turn to the results, however, we emphasize the goal here is not to make a causal connection between posting and polarization; rather, the results are descriptive.

In Figure 7.1, we plot the average level of the polarization variable by social media behavior. First, we see that those who do not use social media to follow politics and those who only read about politics on social media have a mean polarization score of less than 1 (0.70 for those who do not use social media and 0.58 for those who read about politics on social media). This reflects very low levels of polarization – on average, these groups felt similarly about their child marrying someone of their own party and their child marrying someone from the opposing party. Some of these respondents were polarized: 3 percent have a score of 4, marking the highest possible polarization, and another 8 percent

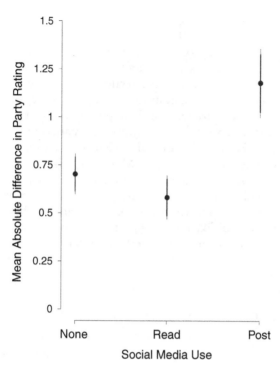

FIGURE 7.1 Social media use and unconditional affective polarization
Source: Data from the Stony Brook University CCES2018. Thick bars represent
90 percent confidence intervals, and thin bars represent 95 percent confidence intervals.

have a score of 3. Overall, however, we see little evidence of widespread
polarization in this group.

Those who *post* about politics on social media have a polarization score that is
about half a point higher than the other respondents (a mean of 1.2). At the same
time, however, we should note that 49 percent of social media posters do have
a polarization score of 0 – meaning that they view both parties in the same
manner. That is certainly a lower percentage than the 67 percent of nonposters
who have a score of 0 but also suggests even among social media posters, many are
not unconditionally affectively polarized. The best conclusion, then, is that among
the affectively polarized, there are more people who post about politics, but those
who post about politics are not necessarily uniformly affectively polarized.[4]

[4] An alternative measure would code a respondent as "polarized" if and only if they were happy
with their child marrying a member of one party and unhappy if they were happy with their child
marrying a member of the other party. Using this measure, 17 percent of Americans are unconditionally affectively polarized but that percentage rises to 29 percent of those who post about
politics on social media.

The patterns we find above speak to research on the relationship between social media and polarization (Bail et al. 2018; Settle 2018). Although that research suggests a specific causal relationship, we do not do so here. Our interest is not in exposure to social media but posting specifically. As a result, we remain agnostic about the causal direction because we are not trying to explain *whether* posting on social media polarizes; rather, our interest is in describing the people who are most likely to post about politics.

Combined with the Pew results, these descriptive patterns are suggestive. The minority of people who post about politics spend a good deal of time following the news and dislike the other party. Moreover, higher levels of affective polarization co-occur with higher levels of social media posting. These are factors that are either a component of our involvement measure (news attention) or, as we have shown in previous chapters, are heavily correlated with deep involvement (dislike for the opposing side and affective polarization). Our next step, then, is to consider the role of involvement more directly: Are people who are deeply involved more expressive about their political positions on social media?

7.3   THE ROLE OF DEEP INVOLVEMENT IN POLITICAL EXPRESSION

In Chapter 3, we suggested that a pivotal factor of deep involvement is the need for expression. In Chapter 4, we include expression as a component of our measure of involvement. To this point, however, our treatment of expression has been more abstract. We know that, both theoretically and by the nature of the measure, perceiving expression to be important is an aspect of involvement. In these sections, however, we turn from abstract conceptions of expression to measures of more concrete expressive behaviors, tracking the relationship between involvement and political posting on social media.

7.3.1   Involvement and Social Media Posting

In May 2019, we sent a survey to 812 people who were registered with the Lucid platform – America's largest marketplace for online samples. Lucid's system allows researchers to get samples that, while not necessarily representative, match desired demographic characteristics (Coppock and McClellan 2019).[5]

---

[5] We note that since the completion of our study, researchers have noted a decline in attentiveness among study participants recruited via Lucid (Aronow et al. 2020), a pattern that could be attributed to increased recruitment from mobile games (Peyton, Huber, and Coppock 2020). In practice, this means that people who participate in the survey via a web application (rather than a browser) or a mobile phone are less attentive. Studies of Lucid samples suggest that the proportion of participants participating in surveys in this way increased in 2020 relative to 2019 when we conducted our study. This is not to suggest that our data are immune to these issues of inattentiveness but rather to note the inattentiveness issues may have been exacerbated in 2020 (Peyton, Huber, and Coppock 2020), after our study was completed.

Still, any sample obtained via Lucid is not going to be representative of the broader public. Our goal, however, was not to get a nationally representative sample. Unlike Pew's efforts, we did not set out to produce a population estimate of how frequently people post about politics. Rather, our goal was to track the relationship between involvement and posting on social media.

In this study, we asked participants how often they post on social media about politics. In addition, however, we asked about their social media posting habits on six other topics: (1) sports, (2) TV/movies/music, (3) community activities and events, (4) day-to-day activities, (5) family and other personal info, and (6) health information. We ask about these additional topics in order to place political posts into a broader context of posting behavior: Are frequent political posters expressive specifically about politics, or are they generally expressive? For each topic, there were five possible response categories: (1) never, (2) less than once a week, (3) once a week, (4) once a day, and (5) more than once a day.

To capture involvement in politics, we return to the involvement scale we validated in Chapter 4 and have used in the previous chapters. In this chapter, however, we modify the scale. As our goal is to consider the relationship between social media posts and involvement, we remove the indicators from our scale that are specifically focused on political expression (sharing opinions and sharing stories). We do so to avoid measurement confounds, and this modified measure allows us to capture characteristics of involvement without including questions that may reflect expression habits within the scale itself. In the analysis that relies on Lucid, however, we use an even shorter version of the scale – validated to adjust for study timing constraints. Just as in the previous chapters, our scale ranges from 0 to 1, where 1 is the highest level of involvement – deep involvement.

Across our entire sample, 44 percent of participants said they never post about politics on social media; for comparison, 49 percent said they never post about sports and 27 percent said they never post about day-to-day activities. Meanwhile, 17 percent said they post at least once a day about politics; 14 percent said the same about sports; and 28 percent said the same about day-to-day activities. In general, then, participants reported posting about politics more than sports and health information but less than the other four categories: TV/movies/music, community activities and events, day-to-day activities and family, and other personal info.[6]

Our main focus, however, is on the relationship between posting patterns and involvement, presented in Figure 7.2. The figure plots seven different LOWESS smoothers – one for each topic category. In Figure 7.2a we see a very nonlinear relationship between involvement in politics and posting

---

[6] We should note that only women post about sports less than politics; men have nearly identical mean posting frequencies for both. So, for men, the only thing they reported posting about less than politics is health information.

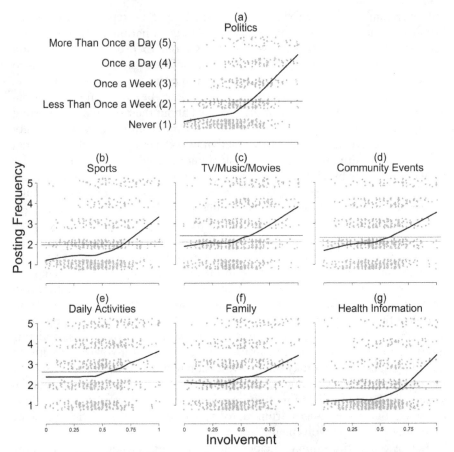

FIGURE 7.2 The relationship between involvement and posting on social media
Source: Data from Lucid. Lines represent LOWESS smoothers with involvement on the
x-axis and frequency on the y-axis.

about politics. Participants below about 0.5 on our adjusted involvement scale –
which is those below a median level – typically report that they never post about
politics. After that point, we see a strong positive relationship between the
adjusted involvement scale and posting frequency. These patterns, then,
suggest a more concrete behavioral outcome to the expressive aspects of
involvement we described in Chapter 3: The deeply involved are more likely
to post about politics on social media.

But when we turn to the other six topical categories, the same pattern
emerges in panels b through g of Figure 7.2. In some cases – for example,
daily activities (panel e) – the slope after the median level of involvement is
less steep, but the basic pattern is the same regardless of the topic. In sum, as

involvement *in politics* increases, people are more likely to post about *everything* on social media.

What accounts for this? As we demonstrated in Chapter 5, childhood political discussion both at home and in school predicted adult political involvement. In contrast, following the news, learning about civics, and being in student government did not predict involvement. What separates the deeply involved from the less involved, then, is that they recall a childhood full of political expression. These socialized experiences may translate to their adult behaviors on social media.

Another possible explanation is that politics is a "gateway." Perhaps people begin by posting about politics – the focus of their involvement – but eventually social media use becomes habitual (Quinn 2016). Once social media use is more habitual, posting may become more automatic, and people may generally post more about everything (LaRose 2010).

7.3.2 Broadening the Range of Expression

To consider whether this relationship between involvement and expression is unique to social media, we turn to study Y20. Here, our study participants are recruited by YouGov, which produces a more nationally representative sample. In this study, we have questions about not only how frequently participants post on social media but also how frequently they talk about politics. This additional measure allows us to track expression more generally, which means we can compare social media expression to face-to-face conversation. We use these measures of expression as dependent variables and estimate four logit models. In the models that focus on talking about politics, one model estimates the probability of rarely talking about politics, and the other estimates the probability of frequently talking about politics. In the models focusing on political posting, one model estimates probability of rarely *posting* about politics on social media, and the other estimates the probability of frequent posting.

In addition to demographic controls, there are two key variables in each of the four models: an adjusted involvement measure and a measure of partisan strength. This is not the full measure of involvement as it is adjusted with the removal of the two indicators that reflect expression.[7] If we follow previous research, strong partisans should discuss politics and post about politics more frequently than independents who may be more inclined to hide their political feelings (Klar and Krupnikov 2016) and are differently engaged in politics (Klar 2014).

We present our results in Figure 7.3; panels a and b show the predicted probabilities of talking about politics frequently or rarely, while panels c and d plot the predicted probabilities for posting about politics frequently or rarely.

---

[7] Cronbach's alpha does not change with the removal of these two questions.

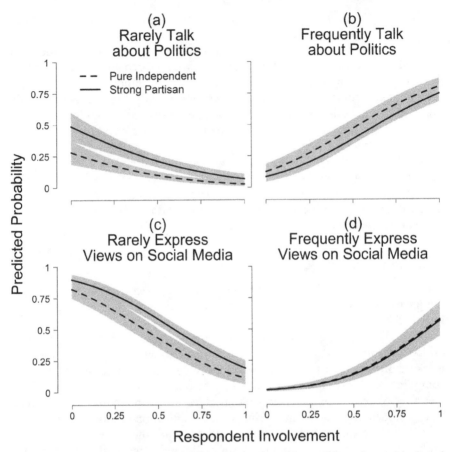

FIGURE 7.3 Involvement is associated with posting on social media and political discussion
Source: Data from YG20. Results based on logit models of either rarely or frequently posting/talking (full models available in Online Appendix M7.1). Shaded area represents 95 percent confidence intervals.

Across all the panels, we present the probabilities by levels of involvement, but we distinguish between strong partisans and independents. We do so to highlight the role of involvement as being distinct from strength of partisanship in political expression. The full coefficient estimates are shown in Online Appendix M7.1.

First, the results in Figure 7.3 suggest that strength of partisanship alone cannot explain either discussion or posting on social media. Although we see some differences between pure independents and strong partisans in the "rarely" figures, the confidence intervals completely overlap in both of the "frequently" figures. Rather, what stands out across all four panels in

Figure 7.3 is the importance of involvement in politics. We see almost a 70-percentage-point increase in the probability of talking about politics frequently, for example, from the lowest level of involvement to the highest level of involvement. When we focus on political posting, we see a 72-percentage-point effect of a shift between the lowest to the highest levels of involvement – this time decreasing the probability the respondent rarely posts. The relationship with frequent posting is less dramatic – it is a 55-percentage-point increase across the full range of the involvement measure.

The patterns in Figure 7.3, then, speak to the theoretic arguments in Chapter 3. Our involvement measure is adjusted to remove indicators that may also capture expression, so these patterns are not a function of "expression predicting expression." Rather, these results reinforce that expression is a critical component of involvement: Being deeply focused on a topic means a continuing desire to engage in discussion and expression related to that topic.

7.3.3 Involvement and Expression

Most people do not post about politics with any regularity. They may be motivated to post about politics during an election, but the political content they produce is likely to be sporadic. Other people post about politics a lot; they post about politics during elections, and they post about politics even when the next election is far away. The same is probably true of other topics as well: Most people are probably not posting on social media about *Star Wars*, but others may post about *Star Wars* with a noticeable frequency. As our data suggest, what predicts one's willingness to post on social media about politics is one's involvement in politics. People who are deeply involved in politics, we show, are significantly more likely to be expressive about politics than those who are less involved. The same is probably true about *Star Wars* – except the measurement of involvement would probably need to focus on the movie.

In some ways, it is much easier to imagine that most people are not posting about *Star Wars* than to imagine that most people are not posting about politics. Yet, as we suggest in Chapter 5, many people are in what we term "involvement bubbles." People who are deeply involved in politics are more likely to interact with others who are as deeply involved, and those who are less involved are in networks with others who have similarly lower levels of involvement. In a 2014 Pew survey, for example, only 15 percent of Twitter users reported that more than half of the posts they see on Twitter are about politics. Although this percentage jumped during the 2016 election, still only a minority of Twitter users – 24 percent – told Pew that "a lot" of the posts they saw were about politics. The networks people observe on social media, then, reflect people's own interests.[8] A person deeply involved in *Star Wars* sees a stream of posts

---

[8] We thank Jessica Feezell for suggesting some of the arguments in this paragraph.

about *The Mandalorian*, with an occasional political post. A person deeply involved in politics will see many political posts with an occasional *Star Wars* post (though, perhaps, that post is about the political preferences of an actress on *The Mandalorian*).

Expression is a critical component of deep involvement. The previous chapters considered this expressiveness in the abstract, and here we considered its more specific behavioral implications. Our interest in this chapter, however, is not merely in the idea that people who are more deeply involved in politics post more about politics on social media – by this point in the book, this was a predictable pattern. Rather, our goal is to move beyond posting behavior to *perceptions* of political posts as well. If people who are deeply involved are more likely to express their political voices, how do people who are less involved perceive these voices? In the next section, then, we begin by exploring how people at different levels of involvement understand the motivations behind political posts on social media.

7.4   PERCEIVED MOTIVATIONS FOR POLITICAL EXPRESSION

Addressing individual motivations for social communication, Ahn, Huckfeldt, and Ryan (2015) conclude that sharing political information "has more to do with the education of preferences than with the transmission of facts" (256). The reason, as we suggest in Section 7.2, is that a pure informational, civic motivation is nearly impossible. People cannot be news aggregators. Given this impossibility, we broadened the definition of a civic motivation. People may not be able to share a random sample of news, but their motivations for what they *do* share may be largely altruistic and informational. Key here is not the content – which, as Ahn, Huckfeldt, and Ryan (2015) suggest, is likely to be communication of opinions rather than facts – but the *motivation itself*.

Given that social media communication is within networks that are much broader than in face-to-face converstions (Papacharissi 2012), the motivation for posting may be more difficult to transmit. A person who shares something about politics may have altruistic motivations, but their post may be perceived as anything but altruistic by others. This gap in perception may be further exacerbated by political involvement. As we argue in Chapter 3, those who are deeply involved may generally see more meaning in political events than those who are less involved. Those who are deeply involved believe that others do not realize the gravity of political events, which means that their goal is to inform others of the potential for a terrible political outcome. If one perceives that a seemingly benign event may have disastrous political consequences, then their motivations for posting about this possibility are, ultimately, civic.

How those who are less involved, however, perceive the motivations of others for sharing political information is an open question. As we suggested in Chapter 3, those who are less involved distinguish themselves from those who are deeply involved in politics. Part of this distinction, we argue, may also mean viewing those who are deeply involved with some negativity and suspicion (Monin, Sawyer, and Marquez 2008; Minson and Monin 2012). Extrapolating this idea would suggest that those who are less involved may not take a positive view of political posts on social media – especially if those posts come frequently from the same, politically engaged person. Moreover, if people perceive political contexts as those of contentious debate (e.g. Klar and Krupnikov 2016), it may be difficult for the less involved to imagine political posts motivated by anything other than the goal of sharing opinion, debating, and seeking the approval of others. Even if a political post is genuinely motivated by civic goals (or, at the very least, if the person posting about politics perceives their motivation as largely civic), those who are less involved in politics may take a more cynical eye toward the motivations producing political posts.

7.4.1 Evaluating the Tension in Perceived Motivations

Identifying what motivates posting about politics is a difficult process largely due to the types of social motivations we discussed previously. People have self-presentational goals not only when they post on social media but also when they answer survey questions (see e.g., Berinsky 2004). This means people want to be perceived in the best possible light even in deidentified, often anonymous surveys (Connors, Krupnikov, and Ryan 2019). Admitting that one's political posts are motivated by goals that are purely political and have no civic components is probably not the best means of achieving these self-presentation goals. Indeed, in studies of people who engage in activism on Twitter, most respondents describe motivations founded in collective goals or emotions, rather than any goals that could be classified as political (Bastos and Mercea 2016).

Although identifying the motivations that produce political posts is both interesting and important, our interests here are not in pinpointing the actual motivations as much as the *perceived* motivations. If, on social media, people are left to judge the motivations of others without the types of contextual information that may be available in embodied conversations, then the way people perceive motivations is potentially more important than the actual motivations that produced a particular post. A poster may have purely civic intentions when posting about politics, but if the person who reads the post perceives the poster's goals as political, or even self-promotional, it is this perception that will guide their response to the post, not the poster's actual motivation. In the next set of analyses, then, we track how people perceive motivations of those who post on social media about politics. We also consider whether these perceptions differ by levels of involvement.

Our data again come from Y20, in which we asked respondents the following question:

People have different reasons why they might post about politics on Twitter and Facebook. Below are six possible reasons why people post about politics on Twitter and Facebook. Please rank them in order from most common to least common.

The six reasons, which were shown to participants in random order, are listed below. These reasons were developed following the research on political discussion and, particularly, social media sharing. Alongside each reason for posting below, we include the weighted percentage of participants across the entire sample who ranked each as the most common motivation:

(1) They are spending time on social media to avoid work: 6%.
(2) They enjoy debating with people: 9%.
(3) They feel good when other people agree with them: 13%.
(4) They believe they will change people's minds on an issue: 14%.
(5) They want to inform other people about what is going on in the world: 23%.
(6) They want to express their opinion: 35%.

Overall, we see that the largest percentage of study participants believe that people are posting about politics on social media to express their opinions – in other words, they assume a motivation that falls under the political umbrella (Ahn, Huckfeldt, and Ryan 2015). At the same time, 23 percent of people rank informing people – a civic motivation – as the second most common reason for posting. As a next step, then, we consider whether these perceptions differ by levels of involvement.

We analyze the relationship between perceived motivations and involvement using six separate regression models – one for each of the six reasons people might post about politics on social media. Since each model is specific to the reason someone might post, each dependent variable ranges from 0 to 5 for all the possible ranks a respondent could have assigned a given reason. For visual clarity in Figure 7.4, we code the dependent variables such that values closer to 0 mean that something was *not* perceived as an important motivation for posting. In contrast, values closer to 5 mean that something was perceived as an important motivation for posting. In each model, we include our involvement scale, and just as it was in other analyses, the involvement measure is adjusted to exclude two questions that may be a confound with expression. We also included a set of demographic controls, including controls for partisan strength (see Online Appendix M7). Figure 7.4 presents the predicted ranking of each reason based on levels of involvement. The reasons are arranged from left to right in order in which they were most commonly named as most important overall. The *p*-value displayed in each of the graphs is the *p*-value for the effect of involvement – that is, whether involvement has a statistically significant effect on the reason's ranking.

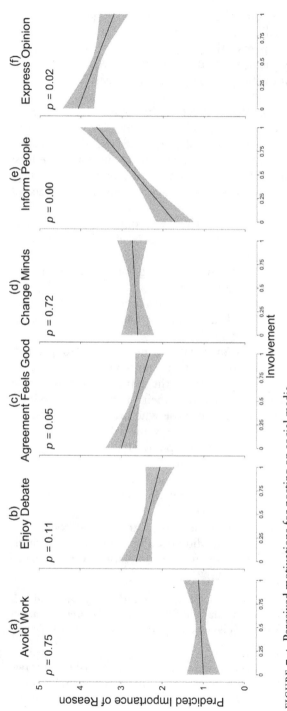

FIGURE 7.4 Perceived motivations for posting on social media

Source: Data from YG20. Results are based on logit models. Shaded area represents 95 percent confidence intervals. Higher values in the dependent variable indicate the respondent is predicted to view the reason as more important. The *p*-values listed are for the effect of involvement for that particular reason.

Starting with Figure 7.4a, it should be clear what everyone agrees upon. People who post on social media are not just trying to avoid work, at least according to our survey participants. Also, we see no statistically significant difference by levels of involvement; for both the least involved and the most involved, it is the posting motivation that is perceived as least important on average.

We also do not see strong involvement effects in Figure 7.4d – whether people's posts are motivated by a desire to change minds. The rankings this political motivation receives are generally middling regardless of involvement levels. Although we see some suggestive evidence in that, those who are least involved are more likely to believe that those who post are doing so because they enjoy debate; the ultimate result does not reach conventional levels of significance (Figure 7.4b).

The largest involvement gaps emerge when we consider a purely civic motivation for posting: whether people post on social media because they want to inform other people about what is going on in the world (Figure 7.4e). For the deeply involved, informing other people is the motivation that is perceived as *most* important (3.6 on the 0 to 5 scale). For the least involved, this motivation has a predicted ranking of 1.7 on the 0 to 5 scale, meaning that is perceived as largely unimportant. Only avoiding work has a lower predicted ranking for the least involved.

In contrast, those who are least involved are more likely to perceive motivations as more political and social, rather than civic. In Figure 7.4f, we see that those who are least involved believe the main reason people post about politics on social media is to express their opinion – a political motivation. In Figure 7.4c, we also see that those who are least involved are somewhat more likely than those who are deeply involved to believe that people who post are doing so because they like political agreement – a social motivation (though we note $p = 0.053$). In sum, there is a pattern across this set of results: The less involved someone is in politics, the less likely they are to perceive that people are guided by civic motivations when they post about politics to social media.

The people who post, however, do believe they are serving some civic function. In a qualitative study of people who post about politics on Twitter, Gabrielle, a 36-year-old from Alaska, explains her motivations for posting to the researcher as follows:

It's stuff that by sharing it, it's possibly educating people on stuff if they even read it. It does have a power to sway. . . . You find something like that, and it's like 'well why aren't people talking about this?' You know this is something we should talk about (Penney 2016, 82).

Gabrielle's reasoning, as Penney (2016) notes, combines two ideas: One is civic ("educating people"), but the other is more political ("power to sway"). Penney (2016) suggests the two motivations can be reconciled as agenda-setting;

Gabrielle is "emphasizing her interest in influencing people as to what to think *about*, rather than what to think" (Penney 2016, 83). Yet, even if Gabrielle is engaging in "networked gate-keeping" (e.g. Meraz and Papacharissi 2013), as Penney (2016) notes, her efforts at persuasion are subtle.

Of course, both Gabrielle's descriptions of her own motivations and the responses of our survey participants may raise the possibility of a confound – self-presentation motivations. People want to describe their motivations in a way that reflects well on them. This may affect the way Gabrielle describes her actions, and it may affect the way our deeply involved study participants rank motivations for posting. If those who are deeply involved are posting about politics, then they may report that others who post about politics are motivated by sharing information because selecting this option reflects well on *them*. We see this possibility less as a confound and more as part and parcel of the link between self-presentation and motivations. If those who are deeply involved perceive that selecting the information motivation reflects better on them in our survey, then they likely believe that this motivation also reflects better on them when they consider their imagined audience.

Another Twitter user, Samantha, a 41-year-old from California, explained this goal of managing the perceptions of motivations more explicitly: "[P]ersonally I'm for Obama in a big way, but I think that you lose credibility if you just sound that way. So I think the most successful way is to present a case and leave it to the reader to decide" (Penney 2016, 83). Indeed, Penney (2016) finds that many of the interviewed active political posters have "educational impulses" (83). This is also in line with our results that the deeply involved – the group who, as we demonstrate previously, are most likely to post about politics – are most likely to perceive posting motivations as informational.

These "educational impulses" of active political posters may also explain why in our study people do not seem to perceive "changing minds" as the most important goal of those who post on social media about politics. If the people who post most about politics are doing so by framing their posts as information, much of what people see may not appear openly persuasive. Alternatively, perhaps the participants in our study – especially those who are low on involvement – do not perceive "changing minds" as something that is plausible via social media posts. In a 2017 survey of African Americans ($N = 1,816$) aged 18–30, for example, fielded by the NORC, 20 percent reported that the best way to "make racial progress in the United States" is "organizing in communities;" 20 percent said the best strategy is voting (both at the national and local levels). Another 10 percent focused on rallies and demonstrations, and 9 percent said "a revolution." In comparison, only 4 percent suggested social media. If social media is perceived as an ineffective persuader, then perhaps people do not see changing minds as a motivation: Why would anyone be motivated by something that, ultimately, won't work?

This possibility of cynicism, however, runs deeper. In our data, people who are less involved do not perceive purely civic motivations for political posts on social media, but they also do not seem to perceive these posts as a function of directly persuasive political motivations. Rather, involvement differences emerge around motivations that are nonpersuasively political and social. Perceiving that people may post either to share their opinions or to obtain agreement from others means perceiving that people are posting at least in part to engage with others within their networks. When those who are less involved report that they believe people post about politics because they want to share their opinions or because "agreement feels good," they are overtly suggesting that the motivation for political posting is self-focused. Those who are less involved are more likely to believe that people post about politics *for themselves* – a perception that is more cynical than imagining that someone is posting because they are trying to persuade others of something.

There is, however, another possibility that these results cannot address. Although those who are less involved may perceive posting motivations as mostly social, rather than civic, their views of the posters themselves may reflect a sort of begrudging respect. In other words, one may assume that the person posting about politics is largely doing so to share their opinion (rather than because they aim to offer some informational value) but ultimately believe that those who post are political experts. Indeed, people often assume that those who spend the most time discussing politics have the most political knowledge, even if they ultimately do not like what these people have to say (Ryan 2011). People who have lower levels of involvement do not believe those who post about politics are motivated by civic goals, but perhaps they do believe that the posts are nonetheless knowledgeable political commentary. We consider this possibility in the next section.

7.5   PERCEPTIONS OF KNOWLEDGE ON SOCIAL MEDIA

On social media, people are routinely faced with large amounts of information. Some of this information is about people's personal lives or their entertainment likes and dislikes, while other information might be political. When faced with new political information from others in a social setting (rather than in a setting with clear hierarchies, such as the news), people are left on their own to determine credibility and knowledge (Huckfeldt 2001; Wagner et al. 2012; Park 2013). Determining who is knowledgeable, however, may be more difficult on social media, where traditional markers of knowledge may be more difficult to convey (Park 2013). A social media platform like Twitter, Park (2013) argues, "provides any user with opportunities to become an opinion leader" so long as that user generates content that attracts attention.

How, then, do people determine who has the knowledge to post about politics? Huckfeldt (2001) offers one part of the answer. In studies of discussion partners, he shows that the people who are perceived to be knowledgeable are people who have the highest levels of political knowledge, education, and interest in politics. Not all of these factors can easily translate to a social media environment. As Park (2013) argues, for example, a key feature of social media is that – especially an environment with broad networks like Twitter – markers of status (like education) are less clear and less important. On the other hand, the possibility that people who are more interested in politics are more likely to be perceived as experts is something that is more likely to replicate in a social media environment as well.

Reconsidering Huckfeldt's (2001) result, Ryan (2011) investigates how indicators of political interest speak to political knowledge. In his analyses, Ryan (2011) shifts focus away from broad measures of political engagement like interest, instead focusing on someone's willingness to talk about politics. He finds that the more someone talks about politics, the more likely they are to be perceived as knowledgeable:

Main respondents are 17 points more likely to perceive a discussant who always talks about politics as an expert than a discussant who never talks about politics. This means the quantity of political information an individual shares is as important to perceptions of knowledge as the quality of the information shared. (Ryan 2011, 344).

Extrapolating Ryan's results to a social media environment suggests that people who post a lot about politics may be more likely to be perceived as political experts than those who rarely bring up political topics. This idea is in line with Park's (2013) argument that on social media, objective credentials may be less important than the posts themselves.

The idea that posting frequency can be correlated with perceived levels of knowledge may suggest that people who are deeply involved, who are most likely to post about politics, may be more likely to be perceived as knowledgeable by others. Since people can distinguish between expertise and motivations (Eiser et al. 2009), it is possible that those with low involvement may be cynical that people post for civic reasons but still believe that the posts reflect expert knowledge. To consider this possibility, we turn to an experiment that tracks the relationship between posting on social media and perceived political expertise.

7.5.1 Effects of Posting on Perceptions of Knowledge

We consider perceptions of posting using an experiment conducted on Amazon's Mechanical Turk (MTurk) in the fall of 2019 (N = 796). This sample, much like the Lucid sample we used, will not provide us population-level estimates of people's perceptions of expertise. Our focus, however, is on comparisons across randomly assigned groups, which makes the use of MTurk more appropriate (Coppock, Leeper, and Mullinix 2018; Krupnikov, Nam, and Style 2021).

In this study, participants were asked to rate a hypothetical individual on two different dependent variables: (1) how much this person knew about politics (a five-point variable from "not much at all" to "a great deal" scaled 0 to 1) and (2) this person's ideology – which we then recoded to capture the perceived ideological extremity of this hypothetical person (a four-point variable from "moderate" to "extremely liberal/conservative" scaled 0 to 1). Although our focus is on perceived knowledge, we include measures of ideological extremity as a comparison.

The experiment had four treatment groups and a control group; in all groups, the participants were told that the person was a forty-year-old white man who followed the news regularly. The goal here was to avoid respondents making assumptions about who this person was based on the characteristics we were varying across the treatments (Dafoe, Zhang, and Coughey 2018). In the control group, participants were simply told about the 40-year-old white man who followed the news. In the treatment groups, we included information about two characteristics: (1) whether the person talked about politics with friends, family, and co-workers and (2) whether the person posted on social media about politics. Information about talking and posting was randomly assigned, forming the four treatment groups.

We note that in this study, we do not measure levels of involvement, which means we cannot capture the involvement differences in perceptions due to posting behaviors as we did when analyzing perceptions of motivations in Section 7.4. Still, the results in this study speak to our broader question about perceptions of posting behavior. Moreover, given that the results in this chapter suggest that it is the deeply involved who are more likely to post on social media, these results likely highlight how the deeply involved are perceived by others. We note, however, that we will demonstrate the role of involvement in perceptions of posting behavior once again in Section 7.5.

The results of the knowledge study are displayed in Figure 7.5. Figure 7.5a shows the means of the perceived knowledge dependent variable by treatment. Figure 7.5b shows the means of the perceived extremity dependent variable by treatment. The clearest result is in Figure 7.5a: If the hypothetical individual does not talk about politics, then people assume this person knows less about politics. This is in line with Ryan (2011). Importantly, however, participants assume a person who does not *talk* about politics is just as ignorant *regardless* of whether or not they post about politics on social media. The combination of posting and talking does lead to the highest average perceived knowledge, but this mean is not statistically distinguishable from control. In short, posting about politics does *not* seem to increase perceptions of knowledge.

Since posting does not affect perceptions of knowledge, we turn to our second dependent variable – ideological extremity – for a comparison. Here, in Figure 7.5b we see that posting about politics increases the perception that someone is more ideologically extreme. We note that the effect of *posting* is unique: When the hypothetical individual is described as talking but not posting about politics on social media, they are perceived as *less extreme*.

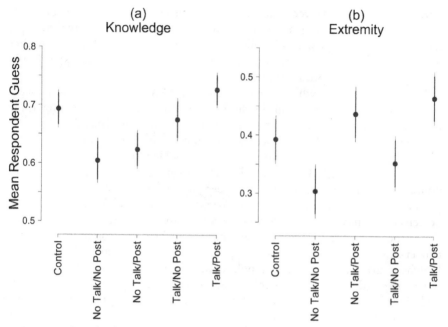

FIGURE 7.5 Results from an experiment on perceptions of knowledge and ideological extremity
Source: Data from MTurk. Higher values mean more knowledgeable (a) and more extreme (b). Thick lines represent 90 percent confidence intervals; thin lines represent 95 percent confidence intervals.

In sum, the results of this study show that people do not perceive someone who posts on social media as an expert just because they post about politics on social media. A person who both talks and posts about politics may be perceived as more of an expert than someone who does neither, but our study suggests this is because people are downgrading the expertise of those who do not talk or post – rather than because they are evaluating the expertise of those who do more positively. The cynicism about the motivations of those who post that we saw in the motivations study (Section 7.4), then, is not hiding increased perceptions of expertise.

What we do see, however, is that those who post are perceived as more extreme. Given the results in this chapter about posting behavior, this is to be expected. As we showed previously, there is a correlation between affective polarization and posting behavior. Moreover, if the people who are most likely to post are a minority who are most deeply involved in politics, it follows that they would seem more fervent in their political preferences to those who observe their posts – which our extremity measure may be reflecting.[9] The more

---

[9] Recall, in Chapter 4, we show that involvement is positively correlated with ideological extremity.

puzzling question, however, is not why the people who post seem more extreme, as the earlier patterns in this chapter foretell this very result, but why the people who talk but do not post about politics do *not* seem more extreme. Put another way, it may be initially puzzling why expression on *social media* specifically leads to greater perceptions of extremity.

We will delve into why posting on social media in particular may factor into perceptions of extremism in the next chapter. For now, we offer three possible explanations. The first brings us back to our previous discussion of differences between face-to-face conversation and interactions on social media. While politics comes up more incidentally during embodied discussion (see e.g., Minozzi et al. 2020; Ognyanova 2020), engaging in politics on social media may be seen as more deliberate. From this perspective, people who initiate conversations on social media may be perceived as having more fervent feelings about politics. Second, since most people engage in these more incidental, organic political conversations (often doing so to pass the time) (Eveland, Morey, and Hutchens 2011), talking about politics may not seem all that extreme or out of the ordinary. Most people, however, are not *posting* about politics, and those who are posting about politics may actually be more extreme (Cohn and Quealy 2019). Finally, these patterns are also in line with Settle's (2018) argument: People observe political conversations on social media that they would never observe in other interpersonal interactions. In other words, these patterns need not be puzzling but rather may reflect people's experiences with politics on and off social media.

To this point, then, the image of the person posting on social media is not especially flattering. Many people perceive their motivations as political and social, rather than civic; they are not perceived as more knowledgeable and they are perceived as being more extreme. As a final step, in the next section we turn to one more analysis and measure affective responses to people who post about politics.

7.6   AFFECTIVE EVALUATIONS OF POLITICAL POSTING

Our final study returns to YG20 data. Rather than focusing on indicators such as motivations, knowledge, and extremity, we turn to a measure that captures affect by asking study participants to rate on a feeling thermometer people who post about politics on Twitter and Facebook. The weighted mean was 42.7 on the 0 to 100 scale. Not surprisingly, this mean varied with the frequency with which the respondent themselves posts about politics on social media. Those who say they rarely post rate those who do post at 34.8. Those who occasionally post rate posters at 47.2. Those who say they frequently post are, not surprisingly, the most favorable – though even this group is hardly enthusiastic about posters universally, rating them at 56.2.

As a next step, then, we analyze how involvement affects how people feel about people who post. In Figure 7.6, we display LOWESS smoothers to demonstrate the relationship between involvement and feelings toward people who post about politics on social media. Figure 7.6a presents the results for all participants, followed by the results for Democratic (Figure 7.6b), Republican (Figure 7.6c), and pure independent participants (Figure 7.6d).

Given the relationship between posting on social media and involvement we found previously in the chapter, the patterns observed in Figure 7.6 are not surprising: There is a fairly linear relationship between involvement and the feeling thermometer rating. Republicans and independents who are less involved hold especially cold feelings toward individuals who post about politics on Twitter and Facebook. Although those who are deeply involved feel more positively about those who post than those with lower levels of involvement, we note that even this group is not particularly warm to posters. The mean rating among the most involved is about 60. Respondents were told a rating of 50 meant that they had no feelings one way or the other. In sum, the deeply involved view social media posters a little more warmly than people they have no feelings about at all.

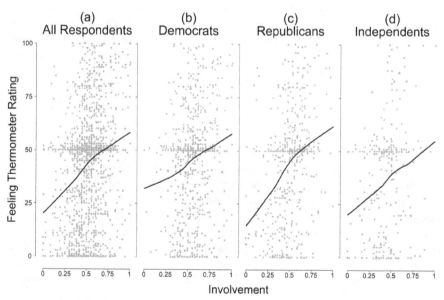

FIGURE 7.6 Affective ratings of people who post on social media by levels of involvement
Source: Data from YG20. Lines represent LOWESS smoothers.

7.7 SIGNS, SIGNS, EVERYWHERE SIGNS

In this chapter, we see a series of patterns suggesting that people who post about politics may not be perceived favorably. They are not perceived as more knowledgeable but are seen as more extreme. On a thermometer scale, people's feelings toward those who post on social media are, at best, lukewarm. People, our results hint, feel better about those who talk about politics than those who post about politics on social media.

Underlying these patterns is a series of involvement differences. The first is in posting behavior: People who are deeply involved are more likely to post on social media. The second is perceptual: Those who are less involved see social media posts motivated by the goal of sharing opinions, rather than by civic motivations. The focus on the sharing opinions, we suggest, hints at a greater cynicism than perceiving social media posts to be about political persuasion. Persuasion is about a larger political cause, but sharing opinions is mostly about the user themselves. A final difference is affective: Those who have higher levels of involvement have warmer feelings about those who post (possibly because they, themselves, are more likely to post).

These patterns may be a function of the medium, but our results are similar to research addressing other forms of political expression. When Makse, Minkoff, and Sokhey (2019) asked people who displayed political signs in their front yards during election season why they did so, one of the most commonly reported motivations was to inform people. Indeed, over 70 percent of people who display signs reported that they perceive signs as informative, and over 80 percent reported that political signs are interesting.[10] On the other hand, people who did not display political signs were significantly less likely to believe that signs were either informative or interesting. Perhaps hinting at affective gaps, people who do not display signs were also significantly more likely than sign displayers to report that they perceive signs to be "an eyesore." These patterns echo our results: Those who are more likely to be drawn to political expression (whether on or off social media) are more likely to perceive something positive from the expressive outputs.

Of course, social media posts and political signs are different (Settle 2018). The idea that a political sign on someone's lawn could have informational value may seem questionable. A sign for a candidate in an obscure local election or ballot initiative may inform others about their electoral choices (or that an election is happening), but how does a sign with a presidential candidate's name offer any information to an undecided voter? The most informational content it provides is that other people in the area like these candidates, but that is something that is already widely known as well (Makse, Minkoff, and Sokhey 2019). But even in an informationally saturated presidential election, a social

---

[10] Results reported in Makse, Minkoff, and Sokhey (2019) Figure 4.1, based on a measure that asks people whether they agree with statements about political signs.

media post can include various facts and ideas beyond a particular candidate. On social media, there is more space for information and, potentially, persuasion. A social media post is also clearly the work of a somewhat identifiable person, while a sign appears on the front lawn of a house – a sign seems more anonymous.

The question, however, is not about the objective value of either yard signs or social media posts – this potential debate is beyond this chapter. Rather, what unites sign displayers and social media posters (and potentially people who express political thoughts in social contexts more generally) is the tension between their actual and perceived motivations for engaging in political expression. Signs that some believe are informative are perceived by others as eyesores. Posts that one hoped would give people vital information are perceived as part of some extreme political agenda. As this chapter suggests, people – especially those who are less involved in politics – are likely to be cynical about political expression.

One reason for this cynicism may be that in contexts like neighborhoods and especially social media platforms, it is much easier to infer political and social, rather than civic, motivations. In neighborhoods, clusters of yard signs may signify solidarity; on social media, posts are often expressed opinions and positive reinforcements from others are public and quantifiable (Burrow and Rainone 2017). For those who are engaged in these forms of political expression, these positive reinforcements may be encouraging, but they may be a cause for cynicism for those looking in from the outside. When we read a post that begins with "a potentially controversial opinion" and then see the hundreds of "likes" and supportive comments, it is easy to roll our eyes at what we may perceive as the poster's "faux modesty." Indeed, the people in our sample who report that most people are motivated to post because "agreement feels good" would probably assume that the poster knew all along that within their network, their post would not be all that controversial.

This potential for cynicism about political expression, however, is what makes involvement differences in how people perceive political expression on social media, especially consequential. The people posting about politics – who are more likely to be deeply involved – are like Beverly who is quoted at the start of this chapter, hoping that their post "creates some value somewhere" (Penney 2016, 80). And, if the post has no broader political value, then at the very least they may have some interactions with others, forming new communities and relationships (de Zúñiga, Molyneux, and Zheng 2014).

People who are less involved, who are not likely to post about politics, cannot observe or understand the motivations of those who *do* post. After all, they are separated not only by posting behavior but also by levels of political involvement. When these less involved people come across political posts, those posts may appear as disparate, unprompted opinions. Sometimes, these opinions are in the contexts of other interactions – either groups of people agreeing with each other or groups of people fighting about politics. When one observes a conversation between other people, especially other people who seem to differ from you, it is difficult to imagine that what motivated the conversation in the first place. Therefore, when those who are less involved see political expression, what they are likely observing are conversations (between the deeply involved) that do not feel like they are for or about them.

Another possible implication of these involvement differences in posting behaviors and perceptions is one that we have yet to address. As both the Pew surveys and our data imply, many of the posts about politics on social media are, likely, produced by those who are deeply involved. The previous chapters of this book have highlighted the numerous ways in which the political preferences and partisan attachments of the deeply involved diverge from those of most Americans. This means that for many less involved people, much of what they see posted on social media about politics reflects a relationship with politics that is quite different than their own. The involvement differences in posts, then, can affect how people perceive both politics and partisanship – something we already hinted at in Chapter 2.

There is still another possibility. People who are deeply involved are more likely to express their political views, which means that their political voices are louder. What if the already louder social media voices of the deeply involved are further amplified by the "true gatekeepers" of news – journalists? Although the possibility that journalists amplify posts that aim to increase the visibility of a social movement has an important benefit (Freelon, McIlwain, and Clark 2018), what happens when journalists amplify posts that have little attachment to any discernable social movement, posts that are essentially opinions (see e.g. McGregor 2019)? We turn to this intersection between journalists, social media, the deeply involved, and "the [political] pictures in our heads" (Lippmann 1922) in the next chapter.

8

The Voice of Which People?

If polarization is not the natural condition of most of the county, then defining our national life by the views of those who are political obsessives is a misrepresentation of American national life and also affects that life, creating a profound weariness that cripples the will to participate in public affairs. Those of us in the press have an obligation to be clear that America is not defined by its most partisan citizens.

CBS News Political Analyst John Dickerson in The Hardest Job in the World:
The American Presidency

In 2018, *New York Magazine* ran an article titled "Donald Trump Is Destroying My Marriage" (Langmuir 2018). The piece featured first-person stories from four individual people and two couples discussing how politics in general – but Trump's 2016 election *in particular* – created tension in their relationships. The people featured in these stories discussed disagreements with their partners over the political issues of the day (though other disagreements could be better classified as arguments over care responsibilities in a marriage). For some of the people featured, these disagreements led to divorce. Donald Trump, wrote author Molly Langmuir in the article's introduction to the personal stories, "sent shockwaves through heterosexual romance."

The *New York Magazine* article offers vivid, powerful examples of what political disagreement means within a relationship. At the same time, it is a story of relatively rare events. Since the 1960s, political agreement within American heterosexual marriages has actually *increased* (Iyengar, Konitzer, and Tedin 2018). Iyengar, Konitzer, and Tedin (2018) show that in 2015, just before the 2016 election, 81.5 percent of people were married to someone of the same political party, and only 5.8 percent were married to someone from a different political party; using voter file data, they demonstrate that 80.5 percent of couples had voted for the same political candidates.[1] Beyond party, Iyengar, Konitzer, and Tedin (2018) find very high levels of political agreement within couples. Indeed, in the story itself Langmuir notes that according to an Ipsos poll, 13 percent of people reported ending relationships (romantic and nonromantic) due to politics. A different poll suggests that about 11 percent had ended a romantic relationship due to politics (Wakefield Research Study 2017).[2]

In a different article, Sue Koren told a reporter from Reuters that she had "unfriended 'maybe about 50' people on Facebook" during and after the 2016 presidential election (Whitesides 2017). But just several lines below, the article reports the results of a recent survey: 17 percent of people had reported cutting ties with someone on social media due to politics, which means that the vast majority had not. Four years later, in the midst of another contentious election, 75 percent of people in an Ipsos poll of 12,648 Americans said that they had not posted anything about the presidential election outcome; only 6 percent reported that they posted "a lot." Some people do "prune" their social media feeds, but it is often due to the volume of political posting rather than content alone (Bode 2016). Moreover, the people who are most likely to engage in "unfriending" are those who themselves are most likely to talk about politics (Bode 2016). Many people, as we show in Chapter 7, are also quite likely to ignore the political posts they do not like.

Addressing the role of partisanship in dating, *The New York Times* introduced readers to Christina Mullins who explained that her father " ... put a clause that [she] would be written out of his trust if [she] married a registered Democrat" (Pajer 2020). Christina's father is an excellent example of the power of political partisanship, but he is part of a minority. As we demonstrated in Chapter 2, most people are actually quite indifferent about the partisanship of their child's future spouse as long as the child-in-law will rarely bring up politics. How people felt about their child marrying someone of the other party relates to their own partisan attachments and, as we show in Chapter 4, political involvement. This seems to be the case with Christina's father; she described him to *The New York Times* as a "strict Republican."

The people featured in these three stories serve as what Levendusky and Malhotra (2016) call "exemplars" of the state of contemporary American politics. These exemplars also provide the vox populi or "vox pops" – the opportunity to hear the opinions of ordinary people who act as stand-ins for the broader state of public opinion (Lewis, Inthorn, and Wahl-Jorgensen 2005;

---

[1] Hersh and Ghitza (2018) show a higher percentage of heterosexual marriages between people from different parties. They do, however, find that most of these marriages are between older people, suggesting the same trend that Iyengar, Konitzer, and Tedin (2018) point to – this type of interparty marriage is on the decline.

[2] Wakefield Research Study. 2017. "The Trump Effect on American Relationships." www.wakefieldresearch.com/blog/2017/05/10/new-wakefield-research-study-trump-effect-american-relationships

Beckers and Harder 2016). But these exemplars are also potentially unusual cases. People who got divorced as a result of politics are an unusual case because most people do not have political disagreements in their relationships.[3] Some people "unfriend" others on social media due to political differences, but many people just ignore the politics they see on their feeds. And, while a journalist can certainly find someone whose father would care about the political preferences of their future spouse, surveys suggest one could also easily find someone whose parents are not all that worried about it.

The three stories we highlight are not unusual. Including vox pops in articles is a common journalistic approach (Beckers 2018; Tworek 2018; McGregor and Molyneux 2020), and this type of exemplification has also frequently appeared in coverage of partisan polarization (Levendusky and Malhotra 2016). But there is another pattern to these stories: The people profiled (i.e., the vox pops) offer hints not only of their partisan preferences but also of their relationships with politics. "Sarah," one of the people profiled in the *New York Magazine* story on marriages, talks of spending time following and engaging with politics. "Elizabeth" explains how she would "sit on couch in living room and obsessively watch *Rachel Maddow*."[4] We are not told much about Christina in the *New York Times* story, but we know that her father cares quite a bit about politics. These are not randomly selected members of the American public – though, to be fair, vox pops rarely are (see e.g., Beckers 2019). Rather, these are people whose experiences exemplify the central thesis of an article that politics has burrowed deep into all facets of daily life: These are people who have strong political positions, but they are also people whose stories hint at deep political involvement.

In coverage of political partisanship and polarization, vox pops are likely to amplify the voices of those who are most politically divided (Levendusky and Malhotra 2016), but as we argue in this chapter, a byproduct of this practice is attention to the voices of the deeply involved. Because the people featured are not only those who reflect the central thesis of the article but also the people who are willing to speak to a journalist, the resulting interviews are not a random sample of Americans. They may not even be a random sample of politically polarized Americans. Yet, even when stories are explicit that these vox pops are not representative of broader public opinion, the voices of these people are influential (Beckers 2019). As Levendusky and Malhotra (2016) argue, "When citizens read media coverage claiming that the electorate is polarized using exemplars, they will think that voters are more divided on the issues."

It is not difficult to imagine why the deeply involved are often represented as vox pops. Who better to personify partisan divisions than someone who harbors

---

[3] In some cases perhaps due to increasing partisan divides in America (Iyengar, Konitzer, and Tedin 2018).

[4] Names from the *New York Magazine* story are in quotation marks as the story notes that these are not real names.

deep animosity for the other side? And who better to speak to this animosity than someone who is readily willing to express the depth of their negative feelings? Indeed, as we show in the previous chapters, the deeply involved are not only likely to have especially high levels of out-party animosity (Chapter 5) but also highly likely to publicly express this animosity (Chapter 7).

But there is, of course, a broader question underlying these patterns: Why are journalists so drawn to polarization coverage in the first place? The coverage of polarization generally and the use of vox pops to illustrate that polarization, we suggest, are inextricably linked to a variety of factors shaping the news. Political polarization has become a prominent news agenda (Klar and Krupnikov 2016; Levendusky and Malhotra 2016), which means that journalists are more likely to search out stories about the topic of political divides (Boydstun 2013). Exacerbating these tendencies is social media, which allows for what McGregor and Molyneux (2020) term a "virtual collocation" of varied forms of information, "which journalists use to construct narratives" (598). Journalists' interactions on social media, both with other journalists (Usher, Holcomb, and Littman 2018) and with members of the public, shape what they bring with them to newsrooms (McGregor and Molyneux 2020), how they perceive the state of public opinion (McGregor 2019), and the consequent selection of vox pops (Tworek 2018).

In this chapter, our goal is to consider why the voices of the deeply involved may be such a prominent part of the news coverage of polarization. We note that this chapter is somewhat different from the previous chapters in this book. Unlike the previous chapters that rely mostly on survey and experimental data, here we weave together existing research, a survey of journalists, and some qualitative interviews with journalists. These interviews delve into how journalists perceive their audiences, their broader perspectives on covering polarization, and how they select the voices amplified as exemplars in political stories.

We proceed as follows. First, we consider the factors that produce coverage of polarization in the first place. Then, we discuss the results of a study conducted on a sample of working journalists that tracks how these journalists perceive the American public. Then, we turn to a discussion of the voices and exemplars in political coverage. In the final sections of this chapter, however, we shift from journalists back toward the public. Here, our goal is to track the broad consequences of the types of news coverage we discuss throughout the chapter. Focusing on the "pictures in [people's] heads" (e.g. Lippmann 1922), we find differences in the ways people describe their own relationships to politics and the way they characterize the unseen others' relationships to politics. People, our results show, overestimate the prominence of partisanship and political involvement in the America.

8.1 THE JOURNALISTS

News coverage is a product of numerous decisions. Which topics are given attention? What is the particular "angle" of a story? Which sources are included? Since our goal is to consider how journalists navigate these decision points when covering polarization and partisanship, we turn to qualitative interviews with journalists. Although surveys and experiments can offer helpful evidence – indeed, we will turn to results from a survey of journalists at a later point in this chapter – the interviews offer a richer perspective about how journalists weigh the various factors that affect their work. Some of the interviews included here are from research done by the Knight Foundation (Robinson, Xia, and Zahay 2019); others were conducted by authors of this book.

In all cases, the interviews are anonymous. Indeed, the consent forms the journalists signed prior to our interviews specified that we would avoid even describing the outlets where they work. We believe this level of anonymity is important: In some of the interviews, it seemed to us that the journalist would not have shared as much information had the interview not been anonymous. We will include quotes and ideas from these interviews throughout the chapter.

8.2 JOURNALISTS AND COVERAGE OF MASS POLARIZATION

Media coverage of polarization has increased since 2000 (Klar and Krupnikov 2016; Levendusky and Malhotra 2016). Levendusky and Malhotra (2016) track patterns from 2000 to 2012; Klar and Krupnikov (2016) extend the content analysis to 2014; and in Chapter 2 of this book, we consider the patterns in 2016. There is no reason to believe that the coverage has decreased since 2016: A brief look at the patterns in 2020 suggests even greater coverage of polarization – some ushered in by the salience of partisan divides to the COVID-19 pandemic (Hart, Chinn, and Soroka 2020).

What is notable about this coverage, as Levendusky and Malhotra (2016) show and as we also find in Chapter 2, is that it is of *generalized* polarization. In other words, polarization is not invoked as a description of disagreement about a particular issue but as the state of partisan politics in America. To this point, in our content analysis of a random sample of polarization articles in 2016, we find that just over 70 percent were not about polarization *specifically* but instead noted polarization as a key contextual factor in American politics.

It should not be surprising that media actors are drawn to polarization. Contemporary American political elites are polarized, which means that polarization is at the front and center of elite political behavior and legislation (McCarty, Poole, and Rosenthal 2006; Robison and Mullinix 2016). Growing instances of political extremism by some members of the public also underscore a divided climate (Kalmoe and Mason 2019). Yet, as we already noted in

Chapter 2, the empirical evidence about the political role of affective polarization is often more nuanced than the news coverage suggests.

Take, for example, a *New York Times* poll taken months into the COVID-19 pandemic (Sanger-Katz 2020). The poll shows a partisan gap between the Democrats and Republicans – Democrats are more likely to trust medical scientists and the CDC. Although the gap exists, majorities of *both* parties do trust these experts. Among Republicans, 75% trust scientists, and 71% trust the CDC. Among Democrats, these rates are 90% and 83%. Which pattern, then, is the more important frame – that the partisan gaps in trust exist, or that the majorities of both parties support these nonpartisan expert entities? Given that the survey also highlighted vast differences in trust for then-President Donald Trump, are these smaller gaps in trust for scientists and the CDC meaningful?

Our goal here is not to adjudicate the size of the partisan gap that is most worthy of a polarization frame, nor what proportion of news coverage should be devoted to polarization. We take as a given that polarization is one of many forces shaping American politics and that mass affective polarization has significantly increased over the last several decades. But in a context of a seemingly infinite number of issues facing America, we consider why reporters may be especially drawn to stories that highlight polarization. Our interest is in the coverage of mass, rather than elite, polarization, though some of the discussion in this section could apply to elite coverage as well.

We suggest three factors that reinforce the presence of polarization coverage in the news. First, news market forces push journalists toward coverage of conflict and negativity (Soroka 2012; Trussler and Soroka 2014; Dunaway and Lawrence 2015) – something polarization stories readily provide. Second, polarization has emerged as an important "news agenda," which means that coverage of polarization will naturally beget more coverage (Boydstun 2013). Finally, this news agenda is further reinforced through social media.

8.2.1 The Newsworthiness of Polarization

Polarization is inherently newsworthy. Putting aside the levels (either elite or mass), type (ideological or affective), and scope (which groups) of polarization in America, it is a topic that is generally well-suited to media attention. Driven by consumer demands, media institutions privilege stories that highlight conflict (Patterson 1997) and negative news (Soroka 2012; Smith and Searles 2014; Trussler and Soroka 2014). These are two key components of polarization: There is conflict between partisan groups, and polarization is, generally, bad news for politics. Coverage of polarization even allows for a "dual negativity" frame: (1) disagreement and dislike between partisans and (2) polarization itself as a problem (Robison and Mullinix 2016). Thus, polarization coverage meets the professional demands of journalism; these demands are not unique to stories of polarization, and it just so happens that polarization stories fit these professional criteria especially well.

8.2.2   News Agendas

Journalists may also be drawn to stories of polarization because it has become an agenda item. News is, in many ways, self-perpetuating: As coverage of a topic increases, news organizations may come to perceive it as important enough to assign the topic as a "beat" (either formally or informally) (Boydstun 2013). Once a topic is a beat, journalists will search for stories on this particular topic (Boydstun 2013). There is some evidence of this pattern in the increasing levels of polarization coverage between 2000 and 2016 (Klar and Krupnikov 2016; Levendusky and Malhotra 2016). Of course, political divides also increased during this time period, but Levendusky and Malhotra (2016) show an increase in repeated news frames, which is suggestive of an emerging news agenda.

News agendas may emerge within a particular news organization, but they may also emerge among journalists across news organizations. Usher and Ng (2020) suggest, for example, that journalists are embedded in "microbubbles" – "silos ... with their own sets of concerns" (10). Usher and Ng (2020) are concerned about these microbubbles:

If journalists are talking to even smaller groups of journalists who share similar orientations, there is a real concern about the limitations of these epistemic communities in generating knowledge and information for the public.

We can connect this idea to coverage of polarization. So long as journalists are in networks with other journalists who believe that polarization is an important issue of the day, then polarization will be the lens through which journalists perceive citizens.

8.2.3   The Role of Social Media in Coverage of Polarization

When Usher and Ng (2020) discuss networks of journalists, they are looking at conversations on the social media platform Twitter. Twitter has increasingly become an important part of journalism (McGregor 2019; McGregor and Molyneux 2020). "If there is one academic occasion, when it is appropriate to say that Twitter is representative of the lived experience of the people using it," write Usher and Ng (2020) "the case of Beltway journalists would be it" (3). In a 2020 survey of 1,000 journalists conducted by the company, Muck Rack, for example, 85 percent said Twitter is the social network that is most valuable to them.

Even more telling is an experiment by McGregor and Molyneux (2020), in which a set of professional journalists considered the newsworthiness of a set of headlines. One group was randomly assigned to see the headlines as part of the Associated Press' (AP) wire content, and one group was randomly assigned to see the same set of headlines as shared by a set of anonymous users on Twitter. The journalists in the Twitter condition were told to imagine that these anonymous users were people whom they follow on Twitter.

McGregor and Molyneux (2020) find differences among journalists who are "high-frequency" Twitter users and those who are "low-frequency" Twitter users. The "low-frequency" journalists saw the tweets as significantly less newsworthy than the AP headlines, but the "high-frequency" journalists saw the tweets as slightly more newsworthy than the AP headlines (though the effect was not statistically significant). The more time a journalist spent on Twitter, the more likely they were to perceive tweets as a credible source of what is important.

Most of the interactions that journalists have on Twitter – for example, retweets, quote tweets – are with other journalists and political elites (Molyneux and Mourão 2019). Although Twitter offers members of the public the possibility of access to journalists, Molyneux and Mourão (2019) find that in their sample of Twitter posts retweeted by journalists, only 14.7 percent were posts by members of the public.

These networked interactions, then, can further entrench news agendas (Usher and Ng 2020). Twitter creates a "processes of monitoring, imitation, and co-orientation between different media outlets" (Harder, Sevenans, and Van Aelst 2017, 288). In the case of polarization – though not unique to polarization as a topic – this means that if some journalists are sharing stories of polarization, other journalists will be more likely to perceive polarization as an area worthy of coverage. On a broader level, these "co-orientations" between journalists "also reinforce predominant interpretations of ongoing events" (Usher and Ng 2020, 3) – for example, the understanding of contemporary American politics through the lens of partisan polarization.

8.2.4   The Role of the Public on Social Media

Journalists, research suggests, are more likely to interact with other journalists on Twitter and less likely to interact with members of the public (Molyneux and Mourão 2019) – though some journalists do value this form of engagement (Xia et al. 2020). Yet, avoiding interaction with people who are responding to the journalists' own tweets is not the same as paying no attention at all to the nonjournalist or nonelite actors on Twitter. McGregor (2019) finds that journalists use Twitter commentary from nonelite actors to track the shape of public opinion, often to characterize the political winners and losers – that is, "partisan scorekeeping." We will return to McGregor's (2019) argument when we consider the role of social media in shaping the vox populi. For now, we note that using Twitter to capture partisan scorekeeping means explicitly focusing on people who have clear, potentially strong partisan opinions.

Yet, as we write in Chapter 7, the people tweeting about politics – whose tweets can fit into the narrative of political winners and losers – form a minority; most people are not tweeting about politics (Hughes 2019), and many more people are not on Twitter at all (Guess et al. 2018). This means that when journalists "curate" these types of partisan scorekeeping stories using Twitter, as McGregor (2019) suggests they do, they are most likely to encounter the views and opinions of a group of people who may be an especially politically divided minority.

8.2.5 Journalists' Perspective

Interviews with journalists reinforce the relationship between news coverage and polarization that is suggested in the previous sections. The journalists perceive polarization as important, categorizing it as a key political issue of the day (though the interviews often suggested a blurred line between polarization at the elite level and polarization among the public). "There has been more coverage of polarization," one journalist said, "because it just feels like things have gotten much more polarized."

We also see evidence of the factors that shape polarization as a news agenda item. "Conflict is always interesting to cover," said one journalist. "'We are divided' has become a kind of easy thing to write about and to talk about, and a very obvious thing – especially in the Trump era [when] the sides were very clearly divided." Another journalist explained the presence of extreme partisan voices and divides in the news as follows:

... journalists in particular tend to think in terms of narratives and to think in terms of stories. If you're thinking about it in terms of stories it makes more sense for there to be really partisan sides, for there to be a more clearly set antagonist and protagonist – whether or not you think in those terms of course – but for there to be someone who is blocking someone's progress, someone who is working against someone else.

Also, clear from the interviews was the role of Twitter. One journalist said that Twitter was a "huge part of my job," adding "I don't know that it necessarily needs to be a huge part of my job, partly I'm just addicted to it." A different journalist noted that "muscle memory" leads them to start typing Twitter's URL whenever they open a new browser tab. Still, this journalist saw Twitter as a necessary part of news coverage:

I've been in meetings where a colleague of mine is just like on Twitter the entire time, on their computer. On one level it is deeply, deeply annoying. And on the other you can kind of understand where they are coming from ... it is to some degree a component of their jobs to try to stay abreast of what is happening and what the political conversation is and how it's evolving even throughout the day so we can assign stories and cover it in whatever way it needs to be.

Once on Twitter, the journalists mainly spoke of engaging with other journalists – as Molyneux and Mourão (2019) show. In a Knight Foundation interview, for example, a journalist explained as follows: "There's probably like 20 to 30 people who I interact with by far the most. They're often people I've accumulated over the years, depending on what I'm reporting on." Another journalist explained this as a deliberate decision to "try not to engage with people very extensively on Twitter." At the same time, journalists – both in our interviews and in the Knight Foundation interviews – underscored that they perceived Twitter as being clearly unrepresentative of the general public. "People in the real world are nothing like your Twitter feed," said one journalist in a Knight Foundation interview. "They're smart, they're open minded, they're actually polite … And so it is important to realize that your social media world is not the world. That it is not a mirror on society." When asked how they handle people on Twitter, one of the journalists we interviewed summed it up like this, "The best tactic, at least for me, is to just kind of ignore it. Which is sometimes hard."

Still, there was clear recognition that Twitter can directly shape news coverage: "There's been a lot of discussion over the Trump years in particular about Trump being addicted to Twitter," a journalist explained. "But the reality is that journalists are addicted to Twitter. And that ends up distorting a lot of things about the way coverage works." Twitter in the newsroom means that people who receive a good deal of attention on the social media platform – for example, through a viral thread on politics – may be covered in the news or invited to write an op-ed for the news outlet; this process, the journalist noted, has resulted in varying levels of success.

While social media is an important information source for journalists as they attempt to understand the public, we can think of the cues journalists receive about the state of public opinion even more broadly. As part of their jobs, journalists encounter the most polarizing voices in politics; these encounters, one of the journalists explained, have consequences:

There can be a tendency to give voice in articles mainly to folks who are really engaged and who are more partisan than the general populace. These more partisan voices that we hear whether they are local party chairs or mainly activists or whatever become emblematic of how we think of these voters overall. And so we tend to think in these extremes.

If journalistic coverage reflects, at least on some level, how journalists view politics, then coverage of mass polarization may reflect, to return to Lippmann's (1922) terms, the pictures of voters inside journalists' heads.

8.3   THE PICTURES IN JOURNALISTS' HEADS

The very nature of a political journalist's job is spending time around politics and talking to other people about politics. Some (though possibly many) of the people they encounter as part of their jobs are often extreme and polarized. One of the journalists interviewed, for example, pointed to local party leaders as people especially likely to be extreme or to connect journalists with other people who might give politically extreme comments. As Twitter has become a larger component of journalists' jobs, often at the requirement of the news organizations where the journalists work (McGregor and Molyneux 2020), these networks of political discussion have become broader (Usher and Ng 2020). Aside from other journalists and elite actors, the people journalists encounter on Twitter may also be more engaged in politics – the types of people who are most likely to harbor animosity toward the other party.

The encounters journalists have off and on Twitter may shape how they view Americans more generally. As one of the journalists we interviewed noted, the people journalists encounter in their jobs become "emblematic of how we think of these voters overall." What this suggests, then, is that journalists may imagine a populace that is highly polarized, and this perception fuels even more coverage of polarization. In the next sections, we consider how journalists view the state of polarization in America.

8.3.1 Journalists Estimate Polarization

In 2018, along with scholars Samara Klar and Kathleen Searles, we recruited a sample of working journalists from American newsrooms. In total, we recruited 697 journalists; about 94 percent reported that their main area of specialization was "government/politics," the modal journalist worked for a daily newspaper, and the median number of years spent in the field was 20. Demographically, the journalists in the sample were heavily educated and skewed male – something which others have noted about the profession (Usher, Holcomb, and Littman 2018). On characteristics such as age and race, the sample was a near-perfect reflection of other surveys of journalists (e.g. Weaver, Willnat, and Wilhoit 2019 – using a sample collected in 2013). Overall, 41.97 percent of journalists were identified as Democrats (not including leaners); for reference, 36.3 percent were identified as nonleaning Democrats in a 2017 survey by Hassell, Holbein, and Miles (2020). The difference is due to a slightly higher proportion of journalists in the Hassell, Holbein, and Miles (2020) data identifying as independent (leaning or nonleaning). We include the full characteristics of this sample in Online Appendix V7.

In this survey, we included questions designed to track journalist perceptions about the scope of mass polarization. Because perceptions are often subjective, we consider these beliefs against a baseline measure of affective polarization from previous chapters: "the marriage question." In this question, people are typically asked how happy or unhappy they would be if their child married a member of a political party. If people feel the same way about their child marrying a member of either party, then this indicates they are not polarized. But if people feel happy about their child marrying someone of their own party and unhappy with their child marrying someone from the other party, then we would say they are polarized. As in Chapters 2 and 4, this study also focuses on the amended version of the question, which adds a small caveat to the description of the future in-law: This person will rarely discuss politics (e.g. the Klar, Krupnikov, and Ryan 2018 measure). This measure now captures what we described in Chapter 2 as an *unconditional* antipathy toward the other side.

To track how journalists view the state of American politics, we asked the journalists to think about the marriage question in a particular way. In most surveys, participants are asked to report how happy or unhappy *they* would be with an in-law from a particular party. The journalists, however, were asked to consider how unhappy *others* would be under these same conditions.

Specifically, the journalists were told that researchers had asked the marriage question of a random sample of Americans. This was, of course, true; in addition to the study discussed in Chapter 4, this question had been asked of two different samples in Klar, Krupnikov, and Ryan (2018) and on a 2018 CCES module (discussed in Chapter 7). Then, the journalists were instructed to think about that random sample of Americans and offer their best *guess* of the percentage of people in that sample who were both happy when their child married someone of their own party *and* unhappy when their child married someone of the opposing party. This answer should reflect the percentage of people who the journalists believe are polarized.

The journalists were also asked for the percentage of people who expressed equal levels of happiness/unhappiness about a same-party in-law and an opposing-party in-law. This should be the percentage of people who are not polarized. The question wording noted that the two percentages did not have to equal 100; all the journalists had to do was just enter their best guesses.[5]

Since this "marriage question" has been included on a variety of surveys from 2016 to 2019, it provides a useful baseline by which to evaluate journalists' perceptions of the public. In Chapter 4, for example, we use this amended measure to demonstrate that the deeply involved are especially likely to have an unconditional concern about their child marrying someone from the opposing party. A key part of the results in Chapter 4, however, is that most people are not actually all that polarized – a pattern that replicates in Klar, Krupnikov, and Ryan (2018). In fact, 60 percent of the people in our sample feel exactly the same way about a future in-law from their own party as they do about an in-law from the opposing party. Many others have a slight preference for the in-party but are not at all unhappy with an out-party marriage. In other words, using measures that specifically focus on people's feelings about rank-and-file partisans, many people in our studies are not affectively polarized.

8.3.1.1 *How Much Polarization Do Journalists Perceive?*
As a first step, in Figure 8.1 we plot two distributions of guesses: the distribution of journalists' guesses of polarization and the distribution of guesses that

---

[5] The percentages do not need to equal 100 percent because individuals can be completely indifferent to their child marrying a member of one party and happy or unhappy with their child marrying someone from a different party. This situation is neither having equal feelings nor is it polarization.

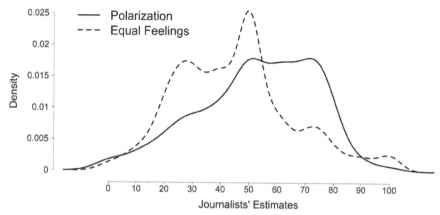

FIGURE 8.1 Distribution of journalists' estimates of public opinion on the marriage question
Source: Data from survey of journalists collected with Klar and Searles in 2018.

suggested no polarization (marked as "equal" on the figure). What is notable is that the distributions show different peaks: the polarization distribution peaks at a higher value than the non-polarized distribution. As Figure 8.1 already suggests, journalists are more likely to believe that people are unconditionally affectively polarized.

In Figure 8.2a, we present journalists' guesses of polarization levels alongside actual survey estimates of polarization levels in the public. What emerges is that journalists overestimate levels of polarization, predicting that more than 50 percent of people fall into the polarized category. None of the surveys we have ever run using this measure show a figure this high. The highest result we observe is using 2016 data (which forms the foundation of our article with Samara Klar – that is, Klar, Krupnikov, and Ryan (2018)) – and even then, the result is far from the journalists' estimate.

The journalists' estimate is 2.5 times greater than the level of polarization as measured by this marriage question in 2016 by Klar, Krupnikov, and Ryan (2018). It differs the most from study D19 where the journalists' estimate is about 40 percentage points greater. Notably, each of these baselines relies on a different sample, suggesting that this is not merely an issue of an unusual baseline due to sample recruitment.[6]

The overestimate could imply the possibility that the task was too difficult for journalists because they had to estimate a joint probability. People often have a difficult time considering probabilities (Westwood, Messing, and Lelkes 2020), and the measure asked journalists to consider the relationship between

---

[6] The four samples were recruited by: GfK (now Ipsos – this is the sample in Klar, Krupnikov, and Ryan (2018)), SSI (now Dynata), YouGov (this is the 2018 CCES sample), and Dynata (this is the sample in Chapter 4, i.e. D19).

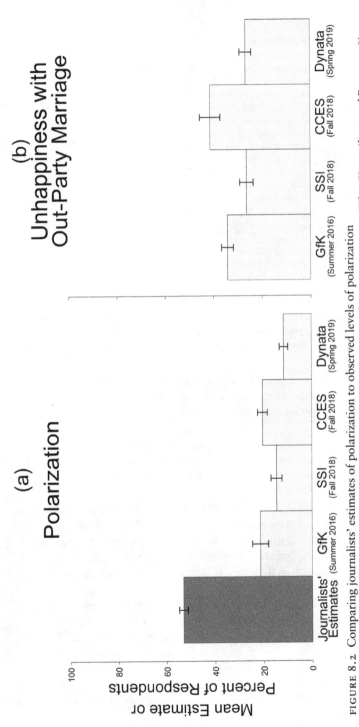

FIGURE 8.2 Comparing journalists' estimates of polarization to observed levels of polarization

Source: Data from 2018 survey of journalists with Klar and Searles, as well as GfK in summer 2016 (Klar, Krupnikov, and Ryan 2018), an unpublished SSI survey in fall 2018, the Stony Brook University module in the 2018 CCES, and D19. Error bars represent 95 percent confidence intervals.

two different probabilities. We address this possibility by relaxing the baseline of comparison. For example, it is possible that the journalists only focused on the percentage of *unhappy* Americans. In this case, a more reasonable baseline of comparison would be the proportion of people who in surveys reported they would be unhappy about their child marrying someone of the opposing party – regardless of whether they would be happy about their child marrying someone of their own party.

But if this is the case, then journalists are still overestimating the percentage of people who would be unhappy with an in-law who rarely discusses politics relative to actual survey of the public (Figure 8.2b). Certainly, the baselines here are higher but still do not match the levels of the journalists' estimates. The journalists' estimate is closest to the unhappiness level in the 2018 CCES, but even with this group, it is 13 percentage points higher.

One may also argue that the journalists received an unusual marriage question. This is a reasonable critique: Klar, Krupnikov, and Ryan (2018) modify the marriage question to include the frequency of discussion, but the original form of this measure does not (e.g. Iyengar et al. 2012). Since the results of the more traditional measure have been covered by some national news outlets, it is possible that the journalists were thinking of a measure that did not specify frequency of conversation. In other words, perhaps the sample of journalists was disadvantaged by being too knowledgeable about American politics.

Yet, even if this was case, the journalists are *still* overestimating the percentage of people who are affectively polarized. Using the traditional version of the marriage question (rather than the modified version that includes discussion), in Klar, Krupnikov, and Ryan (2018) we find that at most 30 percent *across the entire sample* report that they would be happy with an in-party in-law *and* unhappy with an out-party in-law – a 20-percentage-point difference from the journalist estimate.

Although journalists overestimate the proportion of affectively polarized people generally, it is possible that they are correct in their estimation of polarization among certain subgroups of people. Journalists are closer to the percentage of strong partisans who are polarized. For example, in Klar, Krupnikov, and Ryan (2018), strong partisans are four times as likely to be polarized as the rest of the public. Journalists' perspectives on polarization may also reflect the political divides among another group they may be likely to encounter on social media and in political coverage – the deeply involved.

As we show in Chapter 4, involvement increases affective polarization; people with higher levels of involvement are also the people who would be unhappy if their child married someone of the opposing party but happy if their child married someone of their own party. It so happens, however, that accounting for involvement brings the journalists' estimates closer to the baseline – at least at the relaxed baseline that only considers partisan animosity. Using our D19 data, we find that 42% of those who are at the highest quartile of our deep involvement scale report that they would be unhappy if their child married someone of the opposing party – 11 percentage points lower than the journalists' estimates. This proportion is significantly lower among those who are not deeply involved (21 percent report antipathy on this measure). Journalists are still overestimating polarization among the public, but the group that comes closest to journalist estimates are the deeply involved.

8.3.2   Polarized Images in the News

Journalists overestimate the level of affective polarization in the American public. They come closest, however, to guessing the level of polarization among the deeply involved. These patterns reflect a point one of our interviewees made: Journalists encounter many people who are politically extreme and very engaged; eventually, they come to see these extreme, engaged partisans as "emblematic" of other Americans. News stories of mass polarization are not only stories about the most extreme partisans but also, on a broader level, stories of those who may be most deeply involved in politics.

Covering polarization does not necessarily mean elevating the voices of the deeply involved. One can, for example, cover increasing ideological differences among political elites in Washington, and indeed, many journalists do so (Robison and Mullinix 2015). In other cases, coverage of polarization may reflect surveys that show clear, stark partisan divisions. But focusing on affective polarization among the American public is implicitly more likely to turn the attention to the political perspectives of the deeply involved. On the aggregate level, as we show in Chapter 4, it is the deeply involved who form a high percentage of those who can be classified as affectively polarized.

There is, however, another more explicit way in which the voices of the deeply involved are more likely to filter into coverage of political divides. Perhaps because they perceive Americans generally to be polarized, journalists often seek out people to "personalize" or "exemplify" a story (Levendusky and Malhotra 2016). This type of exemplification is designed to add a qualitative context to news stories, serving as a vox populi in news that often focuses on elite behavior (Tworek 2018). But these "vox pops" may further amplify people whose positions are more extreme and whose connection to politics is deeper than the average American. We turn to this idea in the next section.

8.4   ORDINARY PEOPLE IN THE NEWS

In their content analysis of polarization coverage, Levendusky and Malhotra (2016) highlight the role of exemplars of polarization. Exemplars are important because they are a way to personify an abstract idea. Sometimes, an elite actor (a politician, a head of an activist organization) can serve as an exemplar in a story, but typically research on exemplars focuses on nonelite actors in the news

(Lefevere, De Swert, and Walgrave 2012). These are "people without any specific representative function or expertise who appear to be randomly picked ... frequently appear in the news to give their opinion or tell their story" (Lefevere, De Swert, and Walgrave 2012, 103–104). Put another way, these are not people who must be included in the story due to their role, expertise, or participation in some event (e.g. protesters, people who witnessed a crime) (Bosch 2014). These people become stand-ins for the broader population or for some particular group of people, serving as a vox populi or "vox pop" (Daschmann and Brosius, 1999).

We could, of course, complicate this definition. A vox pop is a person whose opinion in a news story is included almost at random (Beckers 2017) – the classic "person on the street" interview; an exemplar, on the other hand, may be someone who is more carefully selected to represent a particular issue or experience and perhaps given more space in a story (Hinnant, Len-Ríos, and Young 2013). In practice, however, the distinction between the two is sometimes unclear. Consider the following from a *New York Times* article:

> 'More people are waking up,' said Kelly Gonzalez, who attended a Republican election party in Harlingen, in South Texas, with her husband, her 1-year-old daughter and her 7-year-old son, each of them clad in Trump gear from head to toe. In the once reliably left-leaning region, Ms. Gonzalez said her opinion of liberals – particularly young ones – had changed in the last four years. 'It's like, 'Give me this, give me that,' and they don't want to work for it,' she said.

Is Gonzalez an exemplar of a particular political orientation? Or is the interview merely a vox pop, serving as a stand-in for a broader set of opinions? Although we acknowledge that there may be some cases where exemplars and vox pop interviews obviously differ, in the following sections we will consider both as journalistic approaches with the same goal: bringing more vivid imagery and voices to often abstract news (Hinnant, Len-Ríos, and Young 2013; Levendusky and Malhotra 2016). Therefore, we will use exemplar and vox pop (and vox populi) interchangeably.

This journalistic technique has particular implications in the context of mass polarization. Vox pop that focuses on people's opinions are especially likely to be included in conflictual political coverage (Beckers, Walgrave, and Van den Bulck 2016). Indeed, as Levendusky and Malhotra (2016) find, the majority of stories about polarization included some form of exemplification. But exemplifying polarization means finding voices that are the most affectively polarized. A journalist could reasonably include Kelly Gonzalez as an example of American political divides (indeed, that is the case), but it would be more difficult to exemplify polarization with a quote like that of Ali Ahmed – "You have to have a lot less problems to worry about politics," Ahmed says in a *New York Times* story notably titled "The America that Isn't Polarized" (Tavernise and Cohn 2019).

When the goal is exemplifying polarization, the search for vox pops is more likely to lead journalists to those people who hold more extreme positions.[7] If polarization is a news agenda and if journalists, as we suggest in the previous section, overestimate the extent to which people are polarized, the vox pop that may seem to best exemplify American politics is likely to amplify very specific, very polarized voices. And, when vox pop sourcing turns to Twitter (as a number of scholars suggest is currently the case – Beckers and Harder 2016; Tworek 2018; McGregor 2019; Lukito et al. 2020; Molyneux and McGregor 2021), the voices that come to represent the populace may also be more likely to be the voices of the deeply involved.

In the following sections, we explore the role of vox pop in media coverage of polarization. First, we consider why vox pop is important, noting both the potential benefits of vox pop and its effect on perceptions of public opinion. Then, we turn to a content analysis to track the presence and shape of these voices in coverage of public opinion on politics. Next, we look more closely at research on social media and the possibility that Twitter has affected the sourcing of the "person on the street" interview. Finally, we return to our qualitative journalist interviews to consider how journalists perceive the role of vox pop and how they seek out these particular sources. Ultimately, we suggest that relying on exemplars to capture public opinion is likely to amplify discourse about political divides. Twitter can exacerbate this tendency, and it is here, then, that vox pop is especially likely to intersect with the voices of the deeply involved.

8.4.1 The Benefits of Vox Pop

The "person on the street" interview as a form of journalist coverage, explains Tworek (2018), emerged as an especially common technique after World War II. The goal, she writes, is to "highlight *ordinary people* who were personally affected by a news story or incident, to provide reactions and opinions" (emphasis in the original). These types of comments can "add a fresh angle to a tired event, color to a broader scientific study, or a local angle to a national or international story. At its best, vox pop could convey widespread feelings in a relatable way" (Tworek 2018). In the case of politics, vox pop can add a qualitative element to coverage of polls – a form of what Toff (2016) calls "public opinion storytelling" that aims to explain quantitative polling results.

There is a clear link between vox pop quotes, coverage of public opinion, and the goal of a compelling narrative. Public opinion exemplars can serve as a vivid illustration of thoughts, experiences, and beliefs that may be hidden behind survey patterns (Gaskins, Barabas, and Jerit 2019). Tworek (2018), for example, recalls the story of a woman named Brenda from Bristol, England,

---

[7] More moderate voices *generally* are less likely to be included as vox pop in political stories even in those that are not focused on polarization (Beckers and Harder 2016; Lukito et al. 2020).

whose exasperation at yet another general election became an emblem of UK voters' general political exhaustion in 2017: "You're joking! Not another one!" Brenda said to a BBC reporter who had just informed her of a coming general election. "Oh, for god's sake, honestly, I can't stand this. There's too much politics going on at the moment!"

Exemplars can also serve as "a form of democratization of the news, where citizens and their – political – views are represented" (Beckers 2018, 102). Indeed, there is evidence to suggest that journalists themselves perceive this practice as an important step to elevating certain voices. In their study of exemplification in health journalism, Hinnant, Len-Ríos, and Young (2013) find that journalists include exemplars because they believe this will be helpful to other readers. Moreover, journalists also perceived exemplars as creating more "identification" between the reader and the story (Beckers 2017; Hinnant, Len-Ríos, and Young 2013).

To this end, for example, one journalist we interviewed pointed to a recent series by a different reporter in *The Washington Post* that used many exemplars to highlight the plight of people who lost their jobs. "There is one thing to be like 'oh people can't pay their utility bills', but this person literally had their lights shut off and I'm hopeful that this resonates with people a bit more," the journalist explained. Research reinforces this point: Vivid examples are often more likely to create empathy (Krupnikov and Levine 2019). At its best, then, the use of vox pop and exemplification can draw attention to important societal problems that would have otherwise gone ignored by the populace. But at its worst, the use of exemplification can create a panic about a problem for which there is little empirical evidence (Denham 2008).

8.4.2 Vox Pop and Public Opinion

Although the vividness of exemplars and vox pop can draw attention to particular issues, a more commonly observed outcome is their effect on people's perceptions about the public opinion (Brosius and Bathelt, 1994; Zillmann and Brosius 2000). Because vox pop is "less valid but more vivid" than survey and poll results (Brosius and Bathelt 1994, 48), this type of journalism can affect how people perceive *others* (Brosius and Bathelt, 1994; Zillmann and Brosius 2000; Denham 2008).

Bosch (2014) finds that ordinary people in the news – vox pops – were perceived as a more typical American than someone who is elite. This, of course, is to be expected; vox pops are deliberately included to give ordinary people a voice (e.g., Beckers 2017; McGregor 2019). Still, Bosch's (2014) results underscore that people *do* distinguish between vox pop interviews and the more elite interviews. Perhaps due to this perceived typicality, vox pop interviews are most likely to influence people's perceptions of the state of public opinion generally (Beckers 2019; Ross and Dumitrescu 2019; see Krämer and Peter

[2020] for a meta-analysis). Notably, Beckers (2019) finds that it does not matter how the vox pop interviews are framed: Even when they are explicitly described as nonrepresentative, people still used these interviews as evidence of the shape of public opinion.

The general findings about vox pop exemplars in the news are in line with Levendusky and Malhotra's (2016) argument about the use of exemplification in the coverage of polarization. "The mass media is an important vehicle through which ordinary citizens learn about where broad collectives like 'Democrats' or 'Republicans' stand," they write (286). Exemplars in stories of polarization, they argue, will have a strong effect on how people perceive the state of polarization in America. Vox pop shapes how people perceive the typical opinion among the American public and, in the case of political coverage, how people perceive the typical Democrat and Republican. If the vox pop quotes are more likely to come from people who are more extreme – or at least more likely to express their opinions in an extreme way – then the American public will generally look more divided and extreme.

8.4.3   The Presence of Vox Pop in Polarization News

Using data from 2000 to 2012, Levendusky and Malhotra (2016) find that 70 percent of stories on polarization contain exemplars. Updating the content analysis to consider the use of vox pop in news coverage, we collected a set of *New York Times* stories from 2019 and 2020 that focused on *mass* political public opinion.[8] Although *The New York Times* is just one newspaper, scholars suggest that *The Times* often sets the agenda for other publications (Boydstun 2013). In total, 80 articles within those two years fit into our criteria of attempting to characterize mass (rather than elite) polarization.

We then coded these articles for the following set of factors. First, we considered whether they included vox pop quotes; here, we considered as vox pop anyone who was not in any way an elite. This means, for example, that we did not count people who had ever held any form of elected or nonelected political office, were organizers of any activist group, or were described as a political advisor of any sort for a party or politician; we also excluded a person who was described primarily as an "Instagram influencer."[9] Our definition of vox pop, then, follows from Beckers (2017): "an apparently randomly chosen ordinary individual without any affiliation who is interviewed by journalists for a news outlet, conveying a personal statement in a news item" (1028).

---

[8] The specific search terms used were: survey or poll, Democrat, Republican, polarized or polarization.

[9] Although we did include someone as vox pop who was described by a different profession first and as a budding Instagram influencer second.

We also coded for other means of public opinion coverage. Here, we considered whether the story included any links to quantitative polls/surveys, whether it included more extended discussion of these polls/surveys, and whether it included detailed discussion of polls/surveys. The differences between these categories are in the amount of attention given to the polls/surveys. An article may simply state that "polls show" or "according to surveys" without giving any specific details ("low details") – though the poll/survey may be hyperlinked. An article may offer more details of the surveys, specific percentages, subgroup patterns, group differences, or changes ("moderate details"). Finally, an article may focus on the types of questions asked in surveys/polls and sampling techniques ("high details"). Given the timing of our content analysis, we also coded whether the article was framed in the context of a political candidate winning or losing.

Of the 80 articles in our set, 51 had some form of vox pop/exemplar. We then extracted individual vox pop quotes from the articles that contained vox pop opinions. In total, our set of articles yielded 229 vox pop quotes. We coded these vox pop quotes for a variety of factors: whether the person invoked their own partisanship, whether they said political divides had affected their lives, whether they discussed general political divides, and whether they expressed their support for a candidate or dislike for a candidate and their feelings toward the opposing party. We also coded the general sentiment of the comment: Did the person seem hopeful or generally hopeless (or neither)?

First, we find that most of the articles did have some mention of a survey – although about 10% relied solely on vox pop to make an argument about public opinion. Moreover, articles with fewer survey details were more likely to include vox pop quotes. In total, 54.3% of articles that had moderate levels of survey details included vox pop, compared to 71.1% of articles that did not have that level of detail. Only 7.4% of the articles included high levels of survey detail – too few to consider vox pop patterns.

Next, we turn to the articles that included vox pop and focus on the comments. We present the patterns, along with example quotes, in Table 8.1. Since we noted differences in the use of vox pop by the amount of survey details in the article, we consider the possibility of these patterns in the content of vox pop as well.

What emerges most clearly in the content analysis is that these quotes are most likely to highlight political divides: 27.6 percent talked about political divisions, a higher proportion than any other category. Comparatively, few included equivocating statements – statements that pointed out both sides of an issue or noted positives and negatives of political candidates. A second pattern is that comments that speak to partisan divisions, frustration with other partisans, politics overtaking life, and hopelessness are more likely in stories that offer few survey details. In fact, these types of comments are most prominent in stories that do not mention surveys or polls at all. For example, 38.3 percent of vox pop

TABLE 8.1 *Patterns of vox pops in coverage of public opinion in 2019 and 2020*

	Example Quote	All	Low Survey Details	Moderate Survey Details
Mentions and implications of divides	"Look, I'm not some crazy Republican. I don't have flags in my yard or hit you if you like Hillary. But if Trump doesn't get it, it's over. We'll be pushed to the side. They'll be letting people in and giving them everything. We'll get squished against the wall" (Tavernise and Cohn 2019).	27.6%	33.6%	15.8%
Hopelessness	"It's been three years. I'm trying to motivate and not to throw up my hands. But I'm emotionally exhausted" (Lerer and Herndon 2020).	20.4%	28.3%	5.2%
Anger at politician or other elite	"Trump is killing us!" (Martin and Mazzei 2020).	17.5%	17.8%	17.1%
Anger at other partisans	"It's like, 'Give me this, give me that,' and they don't want to work for it" (Medina 2020).	15.8%	20.4%	6.6%
Mention of issues	"I don't like abortion, but I don't like a woman being forced to carry a baby due to a traumatic incident, so I guess I'm kind of neutral on that" (Burns and Martin 2020).	14.4%	7.5%	27.6%
Politics affecting life	"We decided not to talk about politics anymore because we couldn't come to agreements. My son is on my side, my oldest daughter is on his side, so it was causing conflict in every part of our family" (Cain Miller 2020).	12.3%	16.5%	3.95%
Equivocating statements	"I still have not made a final decision," she said. "Both of them have positive and negative things" (Epstein 2020).	6.6%	7.9%	4.0%

Results from an analysis of *New York Times* stories about political attitudes among Americans in the years 2019 and 2020.

interviews in these stories suggested that politics had affected people's personal lives.

What these patterns hint at, then, is that stories that rely mostly on vox pop to make a case are more likely to include comments that speak of deeper political divides, including divides that affect personal life. This may be because these are articles that use vox pop to make a case, rather than using vox pop to support a case made by other information. One such article, for example, speaks to political divides within marriages (Pajer 2020). Another article speaks to family divisions surrounding Trump's first impeachment (Mazzei 2019). These types of articles *depend* on quotes from ordinary people that emphasize divisions and partisanship – they could not exist otherwise.

The patterns we find are representative of previous work on vox pop use but also speak to the broader goals of characterizing public opinion (e.g., Herbst 2011). How the public feels about something can be characterized through quantitative studies (polls and surveys), but "numbers do not quench our thirst for the feel and touch of American public opinion" (Herbst 2011, 94). The voices of ordinary people are used to give shape to a sense of how the public feels even in the absence of survey data. These voices, as Herbst (2011) writes, are *also* public opinion; conversation – "talk and texture" – may be as informative as survey data about Americans' positions on important issues of the day (93).

At the same time, the voices in news stories are not a random sampling of conversations: Journalists search out voices that will best speak to a particular story angle (Hinnant, Len-Ríos, and Young 2013); in other words, they highlight *specific* conversations. To bring this back to polarization, since polarization is a news agenda, journalists will cover different angles that highlight its different implications, which means seeking out people who will reinforce the theses of division.

8.4.4 Selecting Those Who Speak

The key to vox pop interviews is that they seem like random members of the public – typical Americans who could be stand-ins for millions of other people (Beckers 2017; Tworek 2018). This, of course, does not mean that these are randomly selected members of the public. As Hinnant, Len-Ríos, and Young (2013) show in a study of health journalists, the ordinary people included as exemplars are a function of a variety of factors such as their story, their quotes, and even their demographic characteristics. "The selection of exemplars is controlled by journalists' subjective impressions when seeking to underscore certain aspects of an issue," argues Daschmann (2000, 162).

The result is that exemplars may not be representative of the particular group of people they are included to represent. Gaskins, Barabas, and Jerit (2020), for example, find that even when journalists source vox pop quotes from people who have taken part in quantitative surveys, the people who are most likely to end up as vox pop in an article are more likely to be wealthy, educated, white, and classified by the original survey interviewer as "chatty." They are also people whose words can "emphasize particular story themes" (Gaskins, Barabas, and Jerit 2020, 11). In a political context, these exemplars may also be more likely to hold extreme, polarized views (Beckers 2020).

The idea that vox pops are included to build an argument is to be expected. If a journalist's goal is to tell a narrative that is cohesive and that could grab reader attention (Hinnant, Len-Ríos, and Young 2013), it is reasonable that they would be selective in the types of quotes they include in the story. Indeed, when we return to our journalist interviews in a later section, one of the journalists will walk us through the precise relationship between story thesis and vox pop selection. At the same time, this selection effect comes with a notable tension: Vox pop can amplify the voices of certain people in the service of a "story theme," which means that other voices are excluded. This tension is exacerbated when the search for vox pop moves to Twitter.

8.4.5 Twitter on the News

Two decades ago, journalists would have to go out into the street to find a person willing to offer a quote on a news story (hence, the proverbial "person on the street" interview) (Tworek 2018). The introduction of social media – in particular Twitter – offers a new opportunity to find public opinion (McGregor 2019). As we already noted in this chapter, Twitter has become an important platform for journalists, and this is yet another example of its importance. Journalists use Twitter to track the shape and scope of public opinion on issues, but they may also use the website to find exemplars and vox pop quotes (Beckers and Harder 2016; McGregor 2019; Ross and Dumetrescu 2019; Lukito et al. 2020; Molyneux and McGregor 2020). Twitter has lowered the costs for finding exemplars and vox pops (McGregor and Molyneux 2020), and through this use of Twitter as a source of vox pop, "journalists confer[s] a sense of prevalence and legitimacy to the opinions expressed within" the tweets (Ross and Dumitrescu 2019).

Relying on Twitter, however, brings a new challenge. Let us put aside the most egregious outcome of Twitter as a source of public opinion quotes – mainstream news sources embedding tweets from fake accounts created by Russia's Information Research Agency (Lukito et al. 2020). Even if outlets avoid this particular problem and feature, as Tworek (2018) suggests, "real people," using Twitter as vox pop means highlighting a very particular set of political voices (McGregor 2019, 2020). People who post about politics on Twitter, as we show in Chapter 7, are more polarized. They are also a more educated, wealthier minority (Wojcik and Hughes 2019). As McGregor (2020) writes, "'authentic' users who engage with politics on any given social media platform are not representative of any larger public – in particular, they tend to be more partisan, polarized, and uncivil" (237).

The sample of opinions on Twitter is already different than a random sample of political opinions in America, but journalistic selection can further exacerbate these differences. Lukito et al. (2020) summarize the issue as follows:

... journalists' reliance on Twitter users implies an outsized influence of these accounts on what "public opinions" are represented through vox populi. Studies have also shown that journalists embed or quote tweets as vox populi when the tweet expresses a strong opinion or has many retweets (Beckers and Harder 2016), suggesting that *more moderate or unamplified voices are less likely to be embedded as vox populi* [emphasis added] (200).

As we show in Chapter 7, however, there is an overlap between social media use, extremity, polarization, and deep involvement. People who are deeply involved are more likely to be affectively polarized (as we show in Chapter 4), and they are also significantly more likely to post about politics on social media (as we show in Chapter 7). When journalists use Twitter to find vox populi for political stories, they are selecting not just from a group of especially polarized people (Hughes 2019) but also from a group of people who are deeply involved in politics. Characteristics of deep involvement include a concern about even the most minute political events and a need for expression, which means that the deeply involved on social media offer a treasure trove of potential vox pop quotes for any given political event. Twitter as vox populi downplays moderate voices, as Lukito et al. (2020) suggest, but it is also likely to elevate the deeply involved perspective on politics.

8.4.6 Journalist Perspectives on Vox Populi

In our interviews with journalists, we see evidence of complicated relationships with vox populi. One journalist described the process of getting these types of "person on the street" interviews as the "thing I hate most about reporting." Another journalist, however, suggested that including vox pop in stories offers an opportunity to engage with people not only for the sake of the story but also for the sake of helping people see the journalist as "a real person" and the media as "not some evil abstract entity." This journalist saw vox pop as broadly beneficial, and we will return to their perspective in the conclusion.

When asked why, as research suggests, the people represented as vox populi are often more extreme (e.g., Beckers and Harder 2016), one of the interviewed journalists explained that it is because "they're the easiest to find":

If you are covering say a rally or something like that, it is easier to see the one loud person that is holding up a sign or chanting, or leading a chant, or festooned with incendiary buttons, than it is to see someone who might be not so extreme or is perhaps more representative of a larger swath of people.

Another journalist reflected on the idea that Gaskins, Barabas, and Jerit (2020) suggest – that vox pop interviews are deliberately selected to suit a story theme.

It has happened countless, countless, countless times in my career that I will get a story idea from an editor saying go report on this or that ... So you would go out in search of vox pops that supported the thesis or the notion that the editor had sent you out to find. So, this is something that we all wrestle with as reporters and anyone who says they don't wrestle with it is lying to you. You have a preconceived notion of what the story will say and then you go out and find the people to confirm your story. It happens all the time that an editor will say 'we are doing a story on polarization in whatever state, so we need a quote'.

So, it's not like 'go talk to people and find out what they say and then come up with a thesis and write the story.' 'It's 'here is the idea, get me a quote that backs this up.' And, that's something I've dealt with many, many times ... You're basically just stopping someone on the street and hoping they are going to say something to you that backs up your thesis. And if they say something different, well then you can use that as the 'to be sure.' So here's our story, but then we have the 'to be sure' and then we hit the theme again in the end.[10] You're allowed varying views and differences of opinion in things, but only within a very narrow band of what the conceit of the story will be.

So, you know, if you go and interview a bunch of people and they say 'I don't think things are that polarized' well then that doesn't really back up [the story].

This perspective clarifies the relationship between polarization as a news agenda and the exemplars that appear in stories. When the goal of the story is to highlight polarization – for example, couples on the verge of divorce due to partisanship and people who have unfriended people on social media – that is a pre-existing thesis, and the voices that will serve this thesis are *only* those who have actually lost friends and relationships due to partisanship.

We also see evidence of some reliance on Twitter. One journalist mentioned what they termed a "cattle call" on Twitter for sources: "[H]ey I'm interested in talking to such and such people, or who are some folks in such and such county that I should be looking at." One can easily find examples of these calls on Twitter; the account "Help A Reporter Out" (run by an organization that attempts to connect journalists with sources) makes regular requests for people who can offer comments on a certain topic.

The journalist also reinforced the connection between attention on Twitter and attention from the news that Beckers and Harder (2016) find in their research. This journalist explained:

Sometimes you'll notice someone on Twitter has taken off in some way, you know, they seem to be generating a lot of retweets or you'll notice other journalists tend to be paying a lot of attention to them and so maybe you think that they should be on your radar, and then you reach out to them as well.

This Twitter effect is not specific to quotes that will be used as vox pop or exemplars but, as we noted in a previous section, may also apply to more elite voices.

[10] Academic readers will recognize the "to be sure" quote as the journalistic equivalent of the "but see" citation.

There was also recognition that this reliance on Twitter for vox pop can shape the types of voices amplified. The journalist (quoted at length earlier) spoke of a trend in reporting that leads to the selective use of vox pop quotes to exemplify a pre-existing thesis. Indeed, the journalist summed up an idea that we have now used many words to express:

And what you've seen a lot lately, now especially, which only makes this trend worse, is reporters who just go and find random people saying shit on Twitter to back up their thesis. Well Twitter . . . people say all sorts of crazy stuff, and only the people who really feel impassioned and influenced enough by polarization are the ones who actually tweet something.

So, you capture that outrage as if its representative of the public, and of course, it's not – it's just one random voice on Twitter. So, I think you really see that trend being exacerbated; we are going out to find quotes that match the conceit of the story that we already have written in our heads.

8.4.7   Whose Vox (Pop)?

The use of vox pop and exemplars is an important narrative aspect of political news (Beckers 2017; Gaskins, Barabas, and Jerit 2020). The people whose voices are included, however, are not a random sample of the public: They are people who will reinforce the main theme of a given story. When the use of vox pop intersects with a news agenda of mass polarization, it means that stories rely on exemplars of people who are polarized (e.g., Levendusky and Malhotra 2016). In turn, these exemplars and vox pops affect how people perceive others (Ross and Dumitrescu 2019); in fact, these more qualitative descriptions of public opinion may matter more than comments from experts (Beckers 2016) or surveys and polls themselves (Gaskins, Barabas, and Jerit 2020).

The interaction between polarization as an agenda and the use of exemplars is also exacerbated by the increasing reliance on Twitter as a source of vox pop (Molyneux and McGregor 2021). Reporters can easily find exemplars of polarization on Twitter: The people posting about politics on Twitter are more polarized (Hughes 2019). These people, however, are also likely to be deeply involved. When journalists use exemplars to illustrate mass polarization – especially when these voices are found on social media – they not only exemplify people who are divided but also elevate the voices of the deeply involved. Journalists do not amplify the deeply involved because they are deliberately motivated to do so. The mechanism is not deep involvement but coverage of polarization. The deeply involved are overrepresented as exemplars not because journalists seek them out for their levels of involvement but because they are disproportionately present in the ranks of the politically polarized.

People who read or watch the news do not know how difficult it may have been to find an exemplar. They do not know about the process that one of the journalists we interviewed described. They also do not stop to think about

Twitter as a potentially peculiar political ecosystem. Rather, people perceive exemplars in news stories as typical of the general populace (Bosch 2014) – and vox pops pulled from Twitter are no exception (Ross and Dumitrescu 2019). If vox pops are typical people, then the natural conclusion is that typical people are polarized (Levendusky and Malhotra 2016). The people included in the news can become what Ahler (2014) terms "easily accessible archetypes" of how a partisan or an ideologue is supposed to act.

Although our focus is on vox pop, the patterns we describe are not unique to coverage of ordinary people. In their study of media coverage of Congress members, Padgett, Dunaway, and Darr (2019) find that the most extreme members of Congress are much more likely to receive coverage than the less extreme members. The patterns Padgett, Dunaway, and Darr (2019) find suggest the dual emphasis of exemplification: Not only are the rank-and-file partisans in the news more likely to be polarized but also are the Congress members.

8.5 WHO IS A TYPICAL PARTISAN?

In 2019, we worked with co-authors, Klar, James Druckman, and Matthew Levendusky, to conduct a large, multiwave survey of Americans (Druckman et al. 2021b). In a part of this survey, we randomly assigned our participants to one of two types of questions. One group was asked how often they discuss politics and their ideological positioning. Another group was asked to guess the proportion of people who belong to the other party who frequently talk about politics and who are ideologically extreme. Key to this second measure was that we specified that people were answering questions about ordinary members of the opposing party – *not* political elites or activists. In a way, this approach was similar to the study with journalists we described in a previous section.

When asked about their own behaviors, most people report only occasionally discussing politics; they also describe themselves as quite moderate. On the other hand, when asked to guess the behaviors of the other party, like the journalists, people overestimate the prevalence of politics. Indeed, the participants in the study estimated that only 22 percent of out-partisans were moderates when in actuality the number was 51 percent. Participants also guessed that that 64 percent of out-partisans frequently talk about politics, but the reality was only 27 percent. The people in this study, it seems, pictured members of the opposing party as less moderate and more politically engaged than was actually the case; they were picturing the types of people who would be more likely to exemplify political polarization in a news story. This is, of course, the outcome that research on exemplars and vox pop would suggest: The power of exemplars is that they shape our opinion of how a typical member of a group thinks and behaves. Although exemplars are especially powerful, polarization coverage even without exemplars can have effects on the way people perceive politics (Ahler 2014).[11] Seeing stories of division can highlight to people that the other party dislikes them – suggesting that, perhaps, they too should dislike the opposing party.

8.6 POLARIZATION IN THE NEWS

We opened this chapter with a quote from John Dickerson, CBS News political analyst, *60 Minutes* correspondent, and former host of *Face the Nation*. His admonition to journalists hints at broad questions about whose voices are amplified by the news media. The images inside people's heads are the images they see in the news. And so, people who do not discuss politics that much and are not all that focused on partisanship, imagine that they are, probably, unusual. At worst, however, they imagine that they too *should* respond to political questions in a way that emphasizes how much they dislike the other party.

It would be simple to fault the media for this polarized image of America, but this would be an oversimplification.

Journalists, as both our interviews and the research we cite here suggest, are in a difficult position. The clear polarization of political elites suggests that investigation of political divides among the public is worthwhile. This focus on mass polarization is also not disingenuous – journalists believe that they are covering the correct state of the world, and indeed, many people are divided. Moreover, since academics have long tracked more and more consequences of affective polarization (Krupnikov 2019), covering political science research on the American public means covering affective polarization.

A more complicated question is the use of exemplars and vox pop. There is reason to believe that it is these aspects of news coverage that are most likely to shape how people see others (see e.g., Levendusky and Malhotra 2016; Beckers 2017; Gaskins, Barabas, and Jerit 2020; Ross and Dumitrescu 2019). In fact, prior to conducting interviews with journalists we were eager to conclude this chapter with an instructive suggestion: If journalists are going to cover polarization, they should avoid exemplars. At the very least, if journalists are going to cover partisan divides, they should avoid exemplifying millions of political partisans through one person who holds extreme fringe views.

Although we would still argue the latter point is reasonable, our interviews suggest a more complex perspective. Exemplars can elevate the voices of those who are most polarized and, potentially, most deeply involved. But, as one of the journalists we interviewed pointed out, the job of a journalist is to "tell stories." When it comes to people with extreme, fringe views, "the job of journalism," the journalist continued, "is to speak to these people and tell their stories and ... understand what is going on."

---

[11] We note, however, that Ahler (2014) addresses ideological polarization.

This is, of course, the inherent tension of exemplars. On the one hand, the vividness of exemplars can amplify voices and make fringe positions seem more prevalent and typical. The result is a perception of Americans generally as more political, more polarized, and more engaged in politics. On the other hand, journalistic narratives have the power to uncover lurking social issues that surveys and policy discussions cannot track. It is one thing to talk about policies, the journalist said, but "listen, you keep hearing about essential workers, but who are these people? What are their lives like? And I think sometimes if people can see themselves ... reflected back, that is more compelling."

This tension points to the idea that journalists are, inherently, constrained. They are constrained by editors, audiences, social media, and other journalists and by their own goals to tell a story that will be, broadly, meaningful. The journalists we interviewed spoke of struggling to engage in reporting that is accessible, that gives people a way to engage with the story, and that is not "grounded in laziness and conventional wisdom," as one journalist said. Certainly, some journalistic practices would benefit from changes – for example, reliance on tweets as vox pop seems not only to misrepresent public opinion but also to open a window to misinformation (e.g., Lukito et al. 2020). But the emerging impression is that stories focusing on mass affective polarization are a product of a broader narrative that is bigger than the journalists.

In a heavily networked environment, polarization stories are self-perpetuating. One journalist noted of a colleague who once quipped that the news was not informing people as much as giving them "ammunition." "Some of the time the reason that [a story] travels well [on social media] is because it plays into what one side or another really wants to hear," the journalist explained. So long as there are news consumers who are responsive to stories focusing on polarization, these stories will continue to exist. So long as some of these people – usually people who are, themselves, more partisan and deeply involved – share these polarization stories, people who are more casual consumers of news will see images of divided, angry partisans, suggesting that polarization in and of itself is the main political problem.

9

Middle Grove

The long-running British quiz show, *Mastermind*, has a very simple premise: Contestants sit in a chair and face the quizmaster who asks them a series of trivia questions. In the first round of an episode, the questions are all on a single subject that the contestant has chosen as his or her specialty. The specialty subject questions can be quite specific – for example, "The 7th Amendment [to the U.S. Constitution] provided for the right to a jury trial if the amount concerned in the case exceeded a certain sum of money; how much?"[1] The only way to succeed on *Mastermind* is to have dedicated a good deal of time to your specialty topic. In essence, *Mastermind* is deep involvement packaged as a game show.

But *Mastermind* also offers a useful metaphor for differentiating deep involvement from interest, attention, or caring. In 2014, a man named Clive Dunning won a semifinal of *Mastermind* with the specialty topic "The Life and Work of John Lennon." Dunning is probably more deeply involved in Lennon's work than many other people, but he is not alone in his love of Lennon's music, and he is not the only person who is inspired by Lennon's life. Clive Dunning may spend (much) more time than the average person learning about John Lennon, but he does not hold a monopoly on caring about Lennon's work.

Nobody would assume that you needed Clive Dunning-level commitment to care about the life of John Lennon, but it is much easier for people to make the error that the deeply involved are the only people who genuinely care about what happens in politics. The deeply involved, as we show in Chapter 4, are (on average) more knowledgeable and more certain about their political positions. As we demonstrate in Chapter 5, they are more likely to recall childhoods full of political discourse and more likely to surround themselves with people who are

---

[1] Readers of this book are experts in American politics and certainly know the answer is $20, but many people might not know this – including some people who skip the 7th Amendment when they teach American government.

equally involved in politics. The deeply involved are also more likely to support parents who work to transmit political values to their children. If, as we argue in Chapter 6, what we choose to teach children is the revealed preference measure of what we value, then the deeply involved place much more value on politics than the typical American.

That being said, it is a mistake to assume that deep involvement is synonymous with caring about politics. In 2020, *in the middle of a pandemic*, a greater percentage of Americans voted than in any election since the voting age was lowered to 18. That shows an amazing commitment to the political process on the part of the American public. Most of these people are not deeply involved, but this is not the same as saying that they do not care about who leads the country. One does not need to be deeply involved in politics to have ideas about what the important problems are and have preferences about how those problems should be solved. The deeply involved may spend more time than the average person following politics, but they do not have a monopoly on caring about electoral and policy outcomes.

The deeply involved have preferences and beliefs that put politics at the forefront, but the reason *others* know about these preferences and beliefs is because the deeply involved are much more likely to publicly share them. Expression of preferences and opinions, we argue in Chapter 3, is a component of deep involvement. In Chapter 7, we translate this more abstract idea into concrete behaviors: The deeply involved are much more likely to post about politics on social media. It is reasonable to make the connection between posting frequency and caring about politics – after all, why would someone constantly post about something that they do not care about?

Of course, the deeply involved care about politics. Indeed, as we argue in Chapter 3, they care about politics so much that they place importance on events that others may find minor or mundane. At issue is not the characterization of the deeply involved but the characterization of those who have lower levels of involvement. Because the deeply involved spend so much time following politics and have such a loud political voice, it is easy to equate deep involvement to caring about politics.

We hope that this book suggests that this is not the case. The people who have lower levels of involvement, as we show in Chapter 4, have clear issue preferences, and they vote. They also have clear preferences about which political elites they would like to see as representatives. While this large group does include people who have no interest in anything having to do with politics, many of those at lower levels of involvement also have high levels of knowledge about politics. They may not support parents who engage in political socialization and may not frequently post on social media about politics, but it would be a mistake to classify these people as "not caring."

One does not need to be deeply involved to care about what happens on Election Day – especially during a presidential election. One also does not need to be deeply involved to care whether Congress passes a set of policies to support Americans who are struggling during a pandemic. Rather, the distinction between the deeply involved and everyone else is about the politics that happens between elections and major crises: the myriad governing details, debates, and supposed scandals that emerge on a near-daily basis. The deeply involved are *certainly* more likely to care about these details and debates, but this is not the same as arguing that those at lower levels of involvement have little concern about what happens in American politics.

In his 1964 book, *The Symbolic Uses of Politics*, Edelman argued that politics is inherently an abstract concept. "Because politics does visibly confer wealth, take life, imprison and free people, and represent a history with strong emotional and ideological associations," Edelman wrote, "its processes become easy objects upon which to displace private emotions, especially strong anxieties and hopes" (5). To use Edelman's terms, involvement determines which emotions people ascribe to political objects. For the deeply involved, politics is likely a greater source of anxiety, but it is also likely a greater source of hope. But this does not mean that people who go about their days focused on other things are "checked out" of politics. The deeply involved know more about the minutiae of politics, but they do not have a monopoly on caring about politics, just like Clive Dunning does not have a monopoly on caring about John Lennon.

9.1   ON THE BENEFITS OF THE UNINVOLVED AND THE UNCERTAIN

> *How could a mass democracy work if all the people were deeply involved in politics?*
>
> Berelson, Lazarsfeld, and McPhee (1954)

In one sense, the deeply involved behave in the way the nation's founders intended. The founders took the unusual (at the time) step of writing down the US Constitution because they assumed people would read it, consider it, and debate it (Zink 2009). This implies that the founders believed that good citizens are politically engaged citizens. Jefferson famously said he preferred newspapers without government to government without newspapers. But in making this statement, Jefferson noted that he assumed that people would actively read the newspapers and hold their leaders accountable based on their content.

There was some acknowledgment that active participation is not possible for everyone. For example, in Federalist 68, Publius (probably Alexander Hamilton) defends the Electoral College writing that "a small number of persons ... will be most likely to possess the information and discernment requisite to such complicated investigations" as determining who the president should be. In this passage, there is an implication that the Electoral

College would be made up of the small segment of society that was deeply engaged and had a deep understanding of politics.

It is possible – and indeed it has been suggested to us by people who have read our work – that this other divide that forms of the focus of the book is not between the deeply involved and everyone else but between those individuals who have the civic competence necessary for a representative democracy and those who do not. Such a reframing, however, is a mistake that dismisses those who have lower levels of involvement. First, as we have already suggested, many of those at lower levels of involvement *do* care and are knowledgeable about politics. More importantly, however, there are often structural constraints that prevent people from becoming deeply involved. Finally, suggesting that those at lower levels of involvement have not completed their duties as citizens is assuming that political certainty is significantly more beneficial than uncertainty.

9.1.1   It Is about Time

There is a certain privilege that comes with not following politics. It is a privilege to believe that no matter what happens in government and no matter who wins the election, you and your family will be fine. It is a privilege that many people living in America do not have. For some who are uninvolved in politics, then, the implication is one of political comfort: A person may pay no attention because they believe they will succeed in *any* political outcome.

On the other hand, there is a privilege in being deeply involved as well. Spending a large part of one's day following politics, posting about politics, and thinking about politics is a luxury. "I'm a mom with three kids and sometimes I don't have the time to do the research that I need to in those races," explained Lila Haddad, an occasional voter. At the same time, Haddad clearly cares about what happens in American politics – in the interview, she described presidential elections as "really important" (Thomson-DeVeaux, Mithani, and Bronner 2020).

Deep involvement in anything takes time (Thorne and Bruner 2006), and free time is not randomly distributed – for example, unsurprisingly, people with more wealth tend to have more free time (Chatzitheochari and Arber 2012). Moreover, people with higher levels of education and income are also more likely to be employed in jobs with more standard working hours, which means they have more consistency in their schedules (Chatzitheochari and Arber 2012). In Chapter 4, we find that deep involvement correlates with higher education levels and possibly higher income. The deeply involved, as we show in Chapter 5, were also more likely to attend colleges in which a higher proportion of the student body is highly affluent. People who are deeply involved, our results suggest, may be the types of people who have the necessary combination of free time and more consistency to this time, which can make following politics easier.

There are a variety of reasons why someone may be less involved in politics. One of those reasons may be that they simply do not care. When the Knight Foundation asked nonvoters why they were not registered to vote, the most common answer given was that they did not care about politics.[2] But this pattern does not necessarily translate to the modal case among the whole public. Being deeply involved in politics requires time, and for many, time may be a difficult-to-attain luxury – or it may be time that they wish to spend in other ways on things like their family or their careers, which are no less important aspects of society.

We want to emphasize here that we are suggesting that some people may not have the time to be *deeply involved* in politics, which is not synonymous with having no time to pay *any* attention to political information. Deep involvement, as we argue in Chapter 3, is a focus on politics that is beyond just being very interested. It is the difference between a person who watches (and enjoys) a TV show when it is on and a person who devotes large parts of their week to reading about, talking about, and posting on social media about that TV show. Both people will know what happened on the show that week, but the latter person might also know numerous behind-the-scene details.

Put another way, people at lower levels of involvement are not necessarily fully disengaged from politics: Some of them, as we show in Chapter 4, have fairly high levels of political knowledge, and some of them may report having interest in political events. These people may not have the time or interest to think, read, discuss, and post about politics with some frequency on a daily basis, but we see no signs that the vast majority of those at lower levels of involvement are completely civically incompetent (though certainly, some may be). As Lupia (2016) argues, one can be civically competent through a reliance on political cues – which one can glean from more limited exposure to politics. Deep involvement, to use Lupia's terms, is neither a necessary nor sufficient condition for civic competence.

9.1.2   A Certain Uncertainty

As we show in Chapter 4, the distribution of involvement scores in our studies are similar to a Gaussian curve. Few people are entirely uninvolved, and few people are deeply involved; most people are somewhere in the middle. Those people who are deeply involved not only spend more time following politics but also much more certain that they know the correct course of action when it comes to questions of policy. In Chapter 4, we saw that when faced with conflicting scientific evidence in the middle of a deadly pandemic, for example, the deeply involved were still certain that they knew the best

---

[2] When asked the open-ended question, "Why aren't you currently registered to vote?" 29 percent of people who have a history of nonvoting gave an answer that fit into the category of "I'm not interested/Don't care" (Knight Foundation 2020, 15).

policies. Because this certainty co-occurs with a focus on politics, one could imagine that it signals a superior understanding of politics and policy.

Democracy does benefit from having some people who are deeply involved in politics and who are certain that they know the best political course of action. But the certainty that co-occurs with deep involvement should not be confused with civic competence. The deeply involved do have a clear perception of the "goodies" and "baddies" of the political world (in the words of Dinas 2014), but this is not just because they are somewhat more knowledgeable. It is also because the deeply involved are less likely to ask, "Are we the baddies?"

Chapter 1 opens with a quote from Berelson, Lazarsfeld, and McPhee (1954) – a portion of that quote is also included at the start of this section. In their study of voters in Elmira, New York, Berelson, Lazarsfled, and McPhee found that many Americans failed to live up to a political (science) ideal in their level of attention to politics. The authors, however, found this result comforting, writing "how could a mass democracy work if all the people were deeply involved in politics?" For them, a "lack of interest by some people is not without its benefits, too":

> Low interest provides maneuvering room for political shifts necessary for a complex society in a period of rapid change. Compromise might be based upon sophisticated awareness of costs and returns ... but it is more often induced by indifference. Some people are and should be highly interested in politics, but not everyone is or needs to be. Only the doctrinaire would deprecate the moderate indifference that facilitates compromise (314–315).

What is necessary for a society, Berelson, Lazarsfeld, and McPhee (1954) argued, is a distribution of involvement. Certainly, a society needs some segment of the citizenry to be deeply involved. There is a need for people who focus their attention on politics, pay attention to its minute details, and accept their role as opinion leaders within their broad social networks. The complication is, since the deeply involved are also very confident and very certain that they know the best political course of action, they are less likely to bend when faced with the beliefs of other people who are also deeply involved. So long as some people are deeply involved, there will also be a necessity for moderate indifference on the part of a portion of the public. This moderate indifference is not the same as complete disengagement or pure apathy; rather, moderate indifference is what allows for uncertainty – at least in some domains – about which policies the government should pursue.[3]

Several decades after the Elmira study, Edelman (1988) would make a similar point. Uncertainty and indifference, he argued, are often viewed by "academic

---

[3] Uncertainty should not be confused with political moderation or nonpartisanship. Lavine, Johnston, and Steenbergen (2012), for example, consider the possibility of *ambivalent* partisans. These are people who have a clear partisan side and care who wins elections but for whom partisan cues are not enough; knowing that their party supports a policy is not sufficient for these ambivalent partisans to determine whether the policy is good or bad.

political science" as "an obstacle to enlightenment" (7). Edelman, however, suggested a different interpretation: Indifference and uncertainty, he argued, can be a refuge from the claims of shrewd politicians that "a political cause serves the public interest" (8). Indifference, uncertainty and tentativeness, were, for Edelman, a necessary presence in society: "The long catalogue of political acts that have stained human history can only come from people who are sure that they are right" (5).

People's uncertainty may be frustrating, especially for someone who is very certain that they know the best course of action. Anyone who has ever visited Twitter during primary election season, for example, will be familiar with the "[Party] will definitely [win/lose] if they nominate [Candidate]" tweets; these tweets often come with frustration aimed at others who are less certain that candidate is the only "electable" person in the primary. There is also an underlying hope for what Lupia (2016) calls a "silver bullet" – the idea that if only people knew some piece of information, they would come to the correct conclusion. But as Lupia (2016) underscores, there is no silver bullet to ensure political competence. An uncertain person gaining certainty may not necessarily benefit the "better" political side, but even worse, this newfound certainty may not benefit society at large.

9.2 THE PARTISANS INSIDE OUR HEADS

> *Modern society is a society of strangers.*
>
> Petersen and Aarøe (2013, 275)

When Petersen and Aarøe write that we are living in a society of strangers, they are about to propose a puzzle. People, they argue, evolved through "intimate social experiences" in small groups. But in modern society, people constantly interact with strangers, and "our welfare is affected by people we never meet" (275). How can we reconcile people's nature as "small group social animals," Petersen and Aarøe (2013) ask, with the anonymity of mass society? The answer, they posit, is imagination. We may never meet these anonymous people, but we can picture them in our heads. The pictures we conjure in our heads, Petersen and Aarøe (2013) argue, form the basis on which we reason and think about these unseen others.

How we imagine other people affects not only how we judge these other people (Petersen and Aarøe 2013) but also how we choose to present ourselves (Klar and Krupnikov 2016). We imagine, for example, what a partisan looks like. The image we conjure in our minds affects not only whether we think partisans are "good" or "bad" but also whether we are willing to identify as partisans ourselves (Klar and Krupnikov 2016).

These images in our mind's eye (to use Petersen and Aarøe's [2013] term) are not randomly generated. Rather, how we imagine others is "pieced together out of what others have reported and what we can imagine" (Lippmann 1922, 43).

Practically speaking, it means that the images and stories around us shape our political imaginations. The stories we see in the news or repeated on social media become the building blocks that turn abstract, distant people – "typical Republican" or "classic Democrat" – into the "pictures in our heads" (Lippmann 1922, 1).

If the media (news and social) are the ultimate means by which these building blocks are delivered, then involvement is a production assistant. We do not simply mean that people who are deeply involved imagine political actors differently than those who are less involved – although that is likely very true (see Moore-Berg et al. 2020). Rather, people who are deeply involved shape the way *others* imagine politics. The deeply involved, as we show in Chapter 7, are more expressive, and their tendency for expression, as we suggest in Chapter 8, may be amplified by journalists. The deeply involved are willing to talk about politics, and they fit the dominant political narrative of division. When people imagine politically engaged partisans, they are likely imagining those who are deeply involved.

9.2.1   The Deeply Involved and Social Media

Petersen and Aarøe (2013) write that we are in a society of strangers. But social media can create a sort of imagined closeness to a much a larger group of people (Ledbetter et al. 2011; Bevan, Gomez, and Sparks 2014; Clark, Algoe, and Green 2018). As we suggest in Chapter 7, social media gives people the opportunity to connect with broader audiences – so much so that people may be "friends" with someone on social media whom they have never actual met IRL – in "real life" (Papacharissi 2012). Social media are also an answer to Petersen and Aarøe's (2013) puzzle: In a society of strangers, social media allow people to re-create more intimate social experiences – even if they are far away from those who are their closest friends (Settle 2018).

Social media also create, to use Settle's (2018) term, a "convergence of affordances," which may be ideal for deep involvement. Social media is a space where someone can both, obtain new information about politics (potentially constantly throughout the day), engage in political expression, and discuss politics with others (Settle 2018). What this means is that these platforms can engage nearly all the components that comprise deep involvement.

In Chapter 5, we introduced a woman named Stephanie who was a *Star Trek* fan. Stephanie, a participant in a study by Kozinets (2001), was embarrassed about her love for *Star Trek* until she eventually attended a *Star Trek* convention and met people who were as involved in the show as she was. After the convention, Stephanie kept in touch with her new friends through "correspondence" (Kozinets 2001, 75). Stephanie was interviewed in 1996, well before the emergence of social media in its current form, but imagine how much easier Stephanie's life would have been if social media had existed.

Every day, Stephanie could have logged on to a social media platform of her choice and interacted with many people who were just like her – it would have helped her feel less "weird or crazy" (Kozinets 2001, 74).

Social media are useful for those who are deeply involved because they give people access to others who have "the same levels of intensity" for a given topic (Thorne and Bruner 2006, 55). In turn, these interactions on social media may be even more satisfying for the deeply involved than conversations with friends and family who are less involved. But to experience these social benefits, however, one must be an active participant on social media – one must actively scroll, read through conversations, and read the (headlines and brief summaries of the) articles posted by others. Above all, however, the key to social media engagement is *expression* (Settle 2018).

Political expression "offline" could take the shape of wearing a button, putting a bumper sticker on one's car or a political sign outside one's house (e.g. Makse, Minkoff, and Sokhey 2019), but Settle (2018) characterizes these forms of expression as, largely, "passive" and "independent." A person is not going to get 1,000 visible "likes" for putting a political sign on their lawn. More active forms of expression may mean attending a protest or engaging in political discussion with others. But even these more active forms of expression still have a less clear audience response than posting something on social media. To wit, McClendon (2018) finds that people are much more likely to attend a political protest when they are reminded that they could post on social media that they attended a protest.

Put more directly, there are higher incentives for expression on social media: positive audience responses, engagement with others, and as we suggest in Chapter 8, the possibility of media coverage – that is, one's fifteen minutes of fame. There are, of course, also higher costs to social media expression. People, for example, may get sanctioned when they break with group norms (see White and Laird 2020). Expressing oneself on social media could also lead to bullying and threats (Settle 2018). Still, for many people who are deeply involved, who crave social interactions with others who are just like them, who constantly follow the political events of the day, social media becomes an important outlet for expression.

That social media platforms offer a "convergence of affordances" for people who are deeply involved means that *everyone* sees more political expression from this particular group of people. These social media posts, then, provide input for how we see others in their "mind's eye" (Petersen and Aarøe 2013). Politics is abstract, but social media posts about politics are concrete. And, for someone who is not all that involved in politics, the political posts they see on their social media timelines may be the main input into these imagined visions of politics. This, however, is the inherent tension of the interaction between deep involvement and social media. Those who are deeply involved have incentives to use social media frequently and consistently; for them, expression on social media offers the possibility of an audience, positive reinforcement, and support

(Settle 2018). But what the deeply involved share on social media may have negative implications for how others imagine politics; as we demonstrate in Chapter 7, a person who frequently posts on social media about politics seems more extreme than one who just talks a lot about politics.

As anyone who has spent an hour writing two tweets only to get ten likes and one retweet can attest, social media is fickle. Some posts will receive a tremendous amount of attention, and others receive almost none. What receives the most attention is, likely, a function of a variety of factors: content, timing, and, maybe, luck (Pressgrove, Weberling McKeever, and Jang 2018). Still, key to social media attention is the audience. What people express on social media is the function of the identities they want to project to others (Settle 2018). From the same perspective, when people share content created by others – be it posts by other social media users or news articles – it is also in the hopes of ensuring that their audience forms a positive impression of them (Kraft et al. 2020).[4] But knowing which content others will find worth sharing requires knowledge and understanding of one's audience.

For those who are deeply involved in politics, posting something that others find appealing means posting content for others who are involved in politics. The social media posts that generate results, whether consciously or subconsciously, are probably posts that reflect the preferences of that audience. Indeed, Schulz et al. (2021) find that the ideology expressed by a user on Twitter is better predicted by the expressed ideology of their Twitter followers than by the ideology that user reported in a survey. Social media is inherently social, and just as people shift how they present themselves in small groups (Klar 2014; Carlson and Settle 2016), the same outcome is likely to occur on social media.

The deeply involved may believe, as we show in Chapter 7, that they are posting on social media to inform those who are less involved. This may be the case, but it is those who are more deeply involved in politics who will be more likely to share and repost political content (Hughes 2019). One problem, of course, is that what appeals to the deeply involved may lead to images inside the heads of the less involved that make politics as a whole seem less appealing. But this is likely true of *any* political campaign: Politicians make empty valence statements because it is the only possible path to universal appeal (Milita et al. 2014).

A broader consequence of social media lies in its illusion of intimate social connection: In a society of strangers (Petersen and Aarøe 2013), social media allows us to feel like we have close social relationships with people whom we do not see on a daily, weekly, or even yearly basis (Standage 2013). But because we

---

[4] There is also the opportunity for negative attention: Someone could share something that will be so abhorrent to their audience that many people will share it so that they can send signals to others how much they hate the sentiment. This strategy for attention, however, also requires clear knowledge of one's audience.

rarely see these people in person, the only things we know about them is their social media presence. If they happen to be deeply involved in something, that topic will likely dominate their social media behavior, and because we have no other recent experiences with them, that topic will dominate our impressions of them as well. In person, people discuss different topics with different people (e.g., Settle 2018) – Stephanie, the *Star Trek* fan, for example, reported that she never discussed *Star Trek* with her family or close friends. But this is not the case on social media, where people are speaking to broad, often unseen, networks of audiences (Papacharissi 2012). Someone's daily posts about politics may appeal to their network of equally deeply involved people, but they may seem strange and even tiresome to their old camp friend from two decades ago. It is easier to imagine that we are very different from someone who is deeply involved in politics if the only thing we know about that person is that they are deeply involved in politics. Social media can bring people together, but the combination of social media and deep involvement can also push people apart.

9.2.2 Trying to Tell the Story of over 300 Million People

In Chapter 8, we described how norms surrounding news values and story sourcing may lead journalists to amplify people who are more extreme and politically vocal. Political journalists are already in networks with other political journalists (Usher and Ng 2020). Exacerbating these network effects is Twitter, where many journalists spend a large portion of their day – often at the encouragement or request of management (Molyneux and McGregor 2021). As part of their jobs and their experiences on Twitter, then, journalists are exposed to people – whether other journalists, political elites, or ordinary people – who are more extreme, partisan, and politically active. The result, as we demonstrate in Chapter 8, is that journalists overestimate the level of affective polarization among ordinary voters.

Once journalists accept that the dominant narrative for discussing the citizenry is through the lens of affective polarization, then polarization becomes a news agenda, and many news organizations will go into what Boydstun (2013) calls "patrol mode." When news organizations are in "patrol mode," they send reporters out looking for new examples and new implications of a topic that they have been covering. A reporter in patrol mode for stories of affective polarization may search for partisan gaps wherever they can find them, especially on the major story of the day.

In the fall of 2020, for example, one major story was the fall wave of the COVID-19 pandemic. During this time, CNN interviewed Jodi Doering, an emergency room nurse in South Dakota. She told CNN's Alisyn Camerota that some COVID patients' "last dying words are, 'This can't be happening to me, it's not real'." The implication of the interview was that Republicans' denial of the virus was so profound that even the people who had a severe case of the virus still believed it was a hoax. CNN contacted Doering after her Twitter post about treating COVID patients went viral: "[They] scream at you for a magic medicine and that Joe Biden is (g)oing to ruin the USA," Doering wrote.

It is not surprising that Doering's emotional tweets went viral – indeed, it is a combination of what Brady, Crockett, and Van Bavel (2020) term "moral-emotional content" and personal experience that is often most likely to be shared on social media (see also Van Bavel et al. 2021). That Doering's viral tweets resulted in an interview on CNN is also consistent with our interviews with journalists in Chapter 8. As one journalist explained:

> Sometimes you'll notice someone on Twitter has taken off in some way, you know, they seem to be generating a lot of retweets or you'll notice other journalists tend to be paying a lot of attention to them and so maybe you think that they should be on your radar, and then you reach out to them as well.

Reflecting on Doering's tweets and media interviews, David Zweig (2020) wrote a piece for *Wired* on what other nurses in South Dakota were seeing and how it compared to the environment Doering described. The nurses Zweig interviewed told him that they did not have any experiences that were similar to what Doering was discussing. "This in no way means that Doering's account is untrue," Zweig wrote, "But it provides, at minimum, some important context that was completely absent from the CNN interview and from all the media amplification that followed. Little or no effort was made to assess the *scope* of the problem that Doering so memorably described." The media attention to Doering's story, Zweig reflected, was similar to the reporting on COVID parties where individuals were supposedly exposing themselves to the virus and betting on who would get sick first. While these rumors were out there, journalist Gilad Edelman could not confirm (at least at the time of this writing) that these parties had actually ever happened.

What CNN did in booking Doering is a common occurrence in modern media: An individual Twitter user's experience was elevated to tell a broader story about the current era. The goal, likely, was to highlight that some people are ignoring the virus because of partisan polarization and that ignoring the virus has deadly consequences. If CNN, and other media outlets, assumed that a nurse's personal experience will make the danger of the virus more vivid to viewers than numbers, then they are probably right about that (Krupnikov and Levine 2019; Kubin et al. 2021; van Bavel et al. 2021). On the other hand, this elevation of single story misrepresents the experiences of many other nurses in South Dakota hospitals.

One issue with "patrol mode" method journalism is that a reporter may start with an answer rather than with a question. As one of the journalists we interviewed described it, "[Y]ou have a preconceived notion of what the story will say and then you go out and find the people to confirm your story." What this means, however, is that a news article written in patrol mode would be unlikely to communicate the nuanced results from Druckman et al. (2021a) – partisan gaps do exist in response to COVID-19 but primarily in areas with low cases and particularly among the minority of the public that is affectively polarized – because the goal is often to find clear, striking evidence of polarization, rather than conditional patterns limited to a particular group.

These types of patterns may be exacerbated when patrol mode meets Twitter. Here, journalists can find many political exemplars and opinions – though these may not be representative. Rather, when journalists turn to Twitter for public opinion, what they see are tweets written by the minority of people who are most likely to share political views on Twitter (Hughes 2019). In turn, these tweets come to shape how journalists perceive public opinion (McGregor 2019) but may also come to shape how people who never visit the platform see public opinion. CNN's interview with Doering fits within the narrative of partisan response to COVID-19. Yet, the interview is not "one nurse's" experience; it is framed – intentionally or not – as a representation of what is happening in hospitals.[5]

Although it would be easy to advise journalists to avoid Twitter when sourcing news stories, banishing Twitter does not address the underlying constraints inherent in covering politics. It is more difficult to write a news story – or an academic book – about people who are *not* extreme and who are not involved in politics. Imagine a journalist asking someone whose mother is ill with COVID-19, "Why *isn't* your mom ranting about how Joe Biden is going to destroy the country?" This question does not make any sense unless it follows from the story about a case in which someone is, in fact, doing just that.

We sympathize with journalists attempting to write about politics. In this book, we promised to talk about the whole electorate, but we often discussed the broader public only in comparison to the deeply involved. Journalists are writing stories, and people who are more extreme, more polarized, and more involved are better characters. But these people are also often unusual, and when journalists are in a patrol mode mindset with respect to partisan attitudes in the electorate, unusually conflictual voices are often most likely to be amplified. This is not unique to coverage of the electorate: A patrol mode approach to polarization has also resulted in the amplification of Congress members who are extreme at the expense of those who are more moderate (Padgett, Dunaway, and Darr 2019).

But telling journalists to break out of patrol mode approaches means undoing practices that predate even the founding of the first journalism schools in the early twentieth century. Furthermore, there is no point in making suggestions that could harm the news business' bottom line – for example, stop telling stories and just report "facts." Journalism will always be about constructing narratives and reporting on the unusual and the conflictual;

---

[5] Even if CNN had emphasized a different frame, however, research suggests this frame may not have mattered (e.g. Beckers and Harder 2016) – exemplifications and personal experiences powerfully shape how people view others (Kubin et al. 2021).

any recommendation for how journalists can better represent public opinion needs to accept these realities.

The best possible solution, suggested in a tweet, is from Ezra Klein, journalist and author of the book, *Why We're Polarized*. In response to a *New York Times* opinion piece we wrote about the research we conducted for this book, Klein tweeted, "[W]e pay too much attention to the elite left-right divide in politics and way too little attention to the interested-uninterested divide." Perhaps some journalists who are in partisan divide patrol mode could shift their efforts into interest divide patrol mode. Journalists acknowledge all the time that "Twitter is not real life," and there is no end to the stories that one could write based on that premise. None of these articles would do a good job representing public opinion, but the whole set of coverage in the aggregate would represent the complex nature of a public divided in multiple ways, some over partisanship but others over involvement.

9.3   THE CONFLICT OF POLITICS

> *But there was no way the fighting between us was 'natural.' It was crazy – a crazy situation run by crazy people.*
>
> *Dwayne, participant in the Robbers Cave study (Perry 2018, 195–196)*

In Chapter 3, we defined the concept of involvement, and as an example of deep involvement, we introduced the jazz-loving business professor, Morris B. Holbrook. On the one hand, Holbrook's commitment to his beloved art form is laudatory On the other hand, Holbrook is narrow in what he thinks is worthy in the music world – even among jazz artists – and he disdains "mass-market listeners" (Holbrook 2008, 122). Holbrook would be happy to learn that one of the five best-selling albums of the twenty-first century is a jazz record. He may be less thrilled to hear that it is *Come Away with Me* by Norah Jones – which, although released on a jazz label, won the Grammy for best *pop* album.

This is the problem of deep involvement. As we have already noted – and Berelson, Lazarsfeld, and McPhee (1954) observed many decades before us – a public made up entirely of the deeply involved would collapse as quickly as one in which everyone was tuned out. As a result, some have called our work "hopeful" because we note that there are many citizens in this country who are paying attention and who turn out to vote but who are not deeply involved.

If one was concerned that the only way to win elections in modern America is to appeal to the baser instincts of social media posters, then this book should give you hope (as should Costa 2021). But the picture we paint in this book is filled with clouds. We show, for example, that many Republicans believed senators from their party were not behaving out of principle during the first Trump impeachment trial. This did not translate, however, into support for conviction because nearly all Republicans questioned Democratic motives in the process – as did many Democrats and the majority of independents.

In work we did with co-authors, Druckman et al. (2021b), we show, when researchers attempt to measure affective polarization, they often capture an indication of fear of unpleasant conservations. At the same time, when we imply that the American public may be mischaracterized as being largely affectively polarized, it is because people's disdain for the out-party is not matched by strong positive feelings towards the in-party. The deeply involved have both aspects of affective polarization (e.g., affinity and animosity), but that makes them different. Our current era of negative partisanship – where voters' partisan preferences are more the result of opposition to the other party than support of their own – is unlikely to change given that individual politicians and media personalities benefit from stoking partisan anger (Abramowitz and Webster 2018; Webster 2020).

In Chapter 2, we also noted Costa's (2020) research, which demonstrates that voters prefer politicians who focus on policy to those who appeal to partisan conflict. Furthermore, Wolak's (2020a) research makes it clear that politicians and pundits underestimate the electorate's desire for compromise. In 2020, the presidential candidate who received the most votes in American history ran on a message of unity and, according to Ed O'Keefe of CBS News, centered his strategy on "turn[ing] off Twitter."[6] Despite this, as we write early in the Biden administration, there is little indication that a new age of bipartisanship is upon us even if there are some politicians who are trying to turn the temperature down a bit.

Although the results in this book and the research we have drawn inspiration from suggest that the shape of mass American politics is not worse than a reader may have imagined, there is also little reason for cheer. Some voters have moderate policy positions and are not "morally obstinate" (Delton, DeScioli, and Ryan 2020), but they will continue to elect extreme and uncompromising legislators because, increasingly, those are the only types of individuals who choose to run for office (Thomsen 2017). We doubt any politicians will read this book or the work we cite within it, but we are certain that the more extreme citizens will continue to contact their representatives (Broockman and Skovron 2018). The deeply involved will continue to have the largest voice on social media, and journalists will continue to amplify their more polarized thoughts, increasing the possibility that journalists and politicians will continue to misestimate public opinion (Broockman and Skovron 2018).

Imagine a world in which the music industry vastly overestimated how many consumers were like Morris Holbrook. The soundtrack of our lives would be markedly different *and much better in the eyes of Morris Holbrook*. The rest of us would choose our "favorite" artists and buy some of their records and go to some concerts, but we would be unhappy with our choices. It is difficult to

---

[6] O'Keefe reported this during live coverage the day CBS-projected President Biden's victory.

imagine, however, that the industry would allow this to continue for too long because the consumer dissatisfaction would become clear with time as sales never lived up to the projections.

Elections are much noisier signals than record sales. Did voters choose Biden because they were horrified by the previous president? Or did they choose him because his platform was, according to former President Barack Obama, "the most progressive in history"?[7] The former suggests Biden should take a very different approach to governing than the latter. If the bulk of the public that is not deeply involved prefers compromise to gridlock and wants politicians to focus on policy instead of negative partisanship, then the bulk of the public must send that clear signal to politicians. But if this book has shown anything, it has shown that sending clear signals about their preferences is the defining characteristic of the deeply involved – many of whom do not want their side to compromise. The less involved majority may be potentially less polarized, but they are also much less vocal.

9.3.1   Reconsidering the Allegory of Robbers Cave

Middle Grove is a hamlet in upstate New York; it is about seven miles away from the more famous vacation destination, Saratoga Springs. In July 1953, a group of twenty-four boys arrived at a campsite in Middle Grove for, what their parents had been promised, was a summer camp designed to "simply study the best programs and procedures for campers which will develop cooperative and spiritual living" (Perry 2018, 30). The boys arrived, spent some time together, and then were divided into two separate groups: the Panthers and the Pythons. The two groups would then spend the time at camp in a series of competitions.

Any reader who is familiar with psychology may, at this point, be a bit puzzled. The setup in the preceding paragraph sounds just like Muzafer Sherif's now famous Robbers Cave study. In the Robbers Cave study, a group of boys arrived at a summer camp and were immediately divided into two separate groups. The separation, along with a series of competitions, produced intergroup conflict: "The end result of the series of competitive contests and reciprocally frustrating encounters was that neither group wanted to have anything whatsoever to do with the other under any circumstances" wrote Sherif et al. (1988) in a book documenting the study. The Robbers Cave study is a famous example of the seeming ease with which separation and competition breeds all-consuming conflict. But the Robbers Cave study was conducted in Oklahoma in 1954, far away from and a year after the summer camp in Middle Grove, New York, and the two now-famous

---

[7] Obama made this statement during his video endorsement of his former vice-president on April 14, 2020.

groups at Robbers Cave were called the Eagles and the Rattlers, not the Pythons and the Panthers.

If Middle Grove and Robbers Cave sound similar, it is because they were the efforts of the same researcher. Sherif designed both studies: He and his researchers recruited the boys from the surrounding areas, worked as camp staff, and designed the series of competitions and "frustrating encounters" that the boys would experience during their time at camp. Each of the two studies was to have three stages. First, the boys would develop a sense of group unity – they would come to see themselves as, primarily, members of their group; second, the boys would engage in competition to produce intergroup conflict; and finally, stage three would be the reconciliation between the two groups. The key difference between Middle Grove and Robbers Cave, however, is that the Middle Grove study ended early – the researchers never got to the third stage (Perry 2018). Middle Grove never made it to stage three because stage two did not work out as expected: The group conflict between the Panthers and the Pythons never materialized.

Revisiting the two studies through old tapes of the boys at summer camp and interviews with Sherif's research assistants and the now grown-up boys who participated in the summer camps, Perry (2018) finds that Middle Grove served as a sort of template for Robbers Cave. After Middle Grove did not work out as expected, the participants for the Robbers Cave study were selected more carefully to ensure that they were competitive (Perry 2018, 155). Indeed, one of the boys chosen – identified as Red – turned out to be a bully. Red would set the tone for his group, and he would also set the tone for the animosity during the ensuing competitions.

In Middle Grove, the participants were given a chance to become friends before they were split into groups, but in Robbers Cave, the split happened immediately upon arrival at camp (Perry 2018, 157). At Robbers Cave any attempts at camaraderie were discouraged, but deliberate antagonism was to be supported, if not directly encouraged. In interviews, Sherif's research assistant recalls deliberately telling one group of boys not to invite the other to a birthday party to "stir animosity," and later, adjusting scores from the boys' competitions to ensure the most frustration (Perry 2018, 174). When the boys displayed good sportsmanship or "directed their aggression and blame towards their own" group (rather than the other group), the researchers created new "frustration episodes" (Perry 2018, 183).

The Robbers Cave study demonstrated that splitting people into groups, making those groups salient, and magnifying differences produce conflict and animosity. But Robbers Cave also demonstrates something else: Creating the now-famous conflict between the Eagles and the Rattlers *was effortful*. It required a set of carefully planned and orchestrated events (deliberately selected participants, targeted competitions, and planned "frustration episodes") and some luck (a bully). Indeed, the fragility of the result becomes especially clear in the context of the Middle Grove study one year earlier. One of the reasons why the "frustration episodes" did not work in Middle Grove is because the boys had met and become friends prior to being split up into the Panthers and the Pythons. The Middle Grove boys, Perry (2018) explains, trusted each other and instead directed their anger at the staff who they saw as trying to deliberately manipulate the competitions (which was, in fact, the case).

To many observers of American politics, the parallels between the Eagles and the Rattlers, and the Democrats and the Republicans should be clear – small differences magnified by group unity and competition (see e.g., Noel 2019). We do not disagree; the Eagles and the Rattlers seem like reasonable stand-ins for the cross-party political discourse people often observe. We would suggest, however, that American politics is better understood through the context of both studies: Robbers Cave *and* Middle Grove. Sometimes, faced with group competition and divisive efforts from elites, groups will turn on each other like the Eagles and the Rattlers. Sometimes, faced with similar group competition and similar divisive efforts, groups will direct most of their animosity at the elites, like the Panthers and the Pythons. There is a Robbers Cave and a Middle Grove in the same electorate, except, just like in Sherif's ultimate reporting of the studies, Robbers Cave is central, but Middle Grove is often a footnote.

We will belabor the comparison to Sherif's studies just a bit further. Robbers Cave offers a very clear narrative: separate groups, competition, and animosity. The idea that a group of strangers could become enemies over the course of a summer camp is both compelling and terrifying. It is more difficult to figure out what to think about Middle Grove. Yet, Robbers Cave is more interesting when understood in the context of Middle Grove. It means considering the conflict between the Eagles and the Rattlers not as something that emerged easily from group salience and competition, but rather as part of a more deliberate, effortful, and lengthy process – one in which researcher efforts intersected with unexpected group dynamics and individual predispositions.

The dominant narrative in American politics is one of partisan conflict and division. This is an evidence-based narrative: There are people whose animosity toward the other side is, as we note at various points in the book, strong, genuine, and consequential. But there are also people who direct their animosity toward political elites and people who are frustrated with partisan politics more generally. These people complicate the narrative. They may take no issue with an in-law from the opposing party, so long as that person does not really talk about politics. They are willing to have a neighbor who voted for a different presidential candidate than they did, but they are not all that open-minded about when it comes to political candidates.

Our goal is not to suggest that America is not divided in any way or that the political divisions are meaningless and easily overcome – again, this is not really a hopeful book. Rather, we want to suggest that some political divisions in America seem similar to the conflict between the Eagles and the Rattlers, but for many people, the conflict is more reflective of the Panthers and Pythons. And, just like the conflicts in both of Sherif's studies, the emergence of these divisions is often more complicated than any one dominant narrative would suggest. Competition and group salience undoubtedly reinforce conflict, but the story of American divides is also a story of the importance people place on politics and what happens when these people get the most attention. When groups are highlighted *specifically* because they are divided, then that division can seem natural and somewhat inevitable (Levendusky and Malhotra 2016). But this belief that the division is natural is the result of conscious efforts on the part of some to stoke these divisions.

The partisan divisions in American politics are profound in large part because the people who are most politically divided are also those who are most deeply involved in politics. These divisions loom large because the people who are most deeply involved loom large in American politics. It would be one thing if the loud voices of the deeply involved were "simply a superstructural indicator of what lies beneath" (Herbst 2011, 93), but, as we suggest in this book, this is not the case: There is a fundamental political divide between the deeply involved and the majority of the public. America's political divisions are inextricably linked to this other divide.

Appendix

The data in this book comes from twenty different sources – seven original surveys were collected for the book, three surveys were collected with co-authors for other studies, and nine studies were collected by other researchers and available in data archives. Three studies (D19, Q20, and YG20) are the primary sources of data for the book. In this appendix, we outline the studies, provide descriptive statistics for the three main studies, and provide the text of the various experimental treatments used in the book. More details on the studies including all question wordings are available on the book's website: www.otherdividebook.com.

A.1 SURVEYS USED IN BOOK

Original Data Collected for This Book

Participants Source	N	Period	Tables and Figures
Dynata (D19)	1564	April 2019	Figure 4.1, Figure 4.2, Figure 4.3, Figure 4.4, Figure 4.5, Figure 4.7, Figure 4.8, Figure 5.5, Figure 6.1, Figure 6.2, Figure 6.3, Figure 6.4
Qualtrics (Q20)	1586	January/ February 2020[1]	Figure 2.2, Figure 4.1, Figure 4.2, Figure 4.3, Figure 4.9, Figure 5.1, Figure 5.3, Figure 5.4, Figure 6.5, Figure 6.6

(*continued*)

---

[1] Some respondents were interviewed in March to increase the number of respondents who were racial minorities in their twenties.

(*continued*)

Participants Source	N	Period	Tables and Figures
YouGov (YG20)	1500	July 2020	Figure 4.1, Figure 4.2, Figure 4.3, Figure 4.6, Figure 4.7, Figure 4.10, Figure 4.11, Figure 6.7, Figure 6.8, Figure 7.3, Figure 7.4, Figure 7.6
SSI (Polarization Levels)	1778	November 2018	Figure 8.3
MTurk (Pre-Test)	299	April 2019	Table 4.1, Table 4.2
Lucid (Posting Frequency)	812	May 2019	Figure 7.2
MTurk (Perceptions Experiment)	796	October 2019	Figure 7.5

Data Previously Collected with Co-Authors

Original Study	N	Period	Tables and Figures
Journalists Study	698	December, 2018–January, 2019	Figure 8.1, Figure 8.2
Klar, Krupnikov, and Ryan (2018)	2,136	August 2016	Figure 8.2
Druckman et al. (2021)	5,191	August 2019	Figure 2.3

Archive Data Sets

Participants Source	N	Period	Tables and Figures
American National Election Study (Cumulative File)	36,659	1956–2016	Figure 1.1, Figure 1.2, Figure 2.1
American National Election Study (2016)	4,271	2016 (Fall)	Figure 1.2, Figure 1.4
Cooperative Congressional Election Study	60,000	2018 (Fall)	Figure 1.2, Figure 1.5

(*continued*)

(continued)

Participants Source	N	Period	Tables and Figures
Cooperative Congressional Election Study (Stony Brook Module)	1,000	2018 (Fall)	Figure 7.1, Figure 8.2
Civic Cohort Study	540	2002–2004	Table 6.1
Civic Network Study	1,228	2013	Figure 5.2
National Longitudinal Study of Freshmen	3,924	Beginning in 1999	N/A in Chapter 5, Section 5.3
NORC	1,816	2017	N/A in Chapter 7, Section 7.4.1
Pew	4,654	2016 (Winter)	Table 7.1
Pew	4,579	2016 (Summer)	N/A in Chapter 7, Section 2

A.2   DESCRIPTIVE STATISTICS IN THREE MAIN STUDIES

	D19	Q20	YG20
Women	51.4%	51.6%	52.9%
18–25	18.7%	7.7%	10.2%
Over 65	10.6%	30.4%	19.8%
White	71.0%	61.2%	66.8%
Black	12.7%	12.6%	9.8%
Hispanic	10.8%	17.7%	14.6%
College or More	39.0%	36.1%	32.3%
Less than $30 K	29.4%	23.8%	27.7%
More than $100 K	17.8%	21.4%	19.5%
Democrats	47.5%	47.2%	46.8%
Republicans	33.7%	34.9%	33.7%

A.3   EXPERIMENTAL TREATMENTS

A.3.1   Chapter 4 – COVID Policy Experiment (YG20)

Good Idea Treatment
(Respondents are asked to respond to two statements.)

We would like to ask you about some policies related to COVID-19. Please tell us if you think the following policies would be a good idea in terms of the nation's public health and economic security.

Opening all public schools in the fall.
Allowing restaurants to operate at full capacity beginning in July.

<1> I am very confident this policy would be a good idea.
<2> I am confident this policy would be a good idea.
<3> I am confident this policy would be a bad idea.
<4> I am very confident this policy would be a bad idea.
<5> I do not know if this policy would be a good idea or a bad idea.

(Responses were recoded to indicate confidence: 0 = 5, 1 = 2 or 3, and 2 = 1 or 4.)

Prediction Treatment
(Respondents are asked to respond to two statements.)
We would like to ask you about some policies related to COVID-19. Please tell us if you think the following policies are going to take place in the majority of US states.

Public schools will open in the fall.
Restaurants will operate at full capacity beginning in July.

<1> I am very confident this is going to happen in most states.
<2> I am confident this is going to happen in most states.
<3> I am confident this is not going to happen in most states.
<4> I am very confident this is not going to happen in most states.
<5> I do not know if this is going to happen in most states.

(Responses were recoded to indicate confidence: 0 = 5, 1 = 2 or 3, and 2 = 1 or 4.)

A.3.2   Chapter 6 – Parents Study 1 (D19)

Treatment 1: Make-A-Wish with Parents' Suggestion
A nine-year-old child recently had a birthday and as gifts received some money from friends and family. The child's parents have asked the child to donate one-third of this gift money.

Although the child was hesitant to donate the money, the parents convinced the child that donations are important.

The parents have suggested that the child donate the money to the Make-A-Wish Foundation.

Treatment 2: Democratic National Committee with Parents' Suggestion
A nine-year-old child recently had a birthday and as gifts received some money from friends and family. The child's parents have asked the child to donate one-third of this gift money.

Although the child was hesitant to donate the money, the parents convinced the child that donations are important.

The parents have suggested that the child donate the money to the Democratic National Committee.

Treatment 3: Republican National Committee with Parents' Suggestion
A nine-year-old child recently had a birthday and as gifts received some money from friends and family. The child's parents have asked the child to donate one-third of this gift money.

Although the child was hesitant to donate the money, the parents convinced the child that donations are important.

The parents have suggested that the child donate the money to the Republican National Committee.

Treatment 4: Make-A-Wish with Child's Decision
A nine-year-old child recently had a birthday and as gifts received some money from friends and family. The child's parents have asked the child to donate one-third of this gift money.

Although the child was hesitant to donate the money, the parents convinced the child that donations are important.

The child has decided to donate the money to the Make-A-Wish Foundation.

Treatment 5: Democratic National Committee with Child's Decision
A nine-year-old child recently had a birthday and as gifts received some money from friends and family. The child's parents have asked the child to donate one-third of this gift money.

Although the child was hesitant to donate the money, the parents convinced the child that donations are important.

The child has decided to donate the money to the Democratic National Committee.

Treatment 6: Republican National Committee with Child's Decision
A nine-year-old child recently had a birthday and as gifts received some money from friends and family. The child's parents have asked the child to donate one-third of this gift money.

Although the child was hesitant to donate the money, the parents convinced the child that donations are important.

The child has decided to donate the money to the Republican National Committee.

(All respondents answer these two questions.)

How favorable or unfavorable do you feel toward the parents in the story you just read?

<1> Extremely unfavorable
<2> Unfavorable

<3> Somewhat unfavorable
<4> Neither favorable nor unfavorable
<5> Somewhat favorable
<6> Favorable
<7> Extremely favorable

Do you agree or disagree with the following statement: If I were the child's parent, I would have made the same exact decisions as the parents in the story.

<1> Strongly agree
<2> Agree
<3> Somewhat agree
<4> Neither agree nor disagree
<5> Somewhat disagree
<6> Disagree
<7> Strongly disagree

A.3.3 Chapter 6 – Parents Study 2 (D19)

Treatment 1: Attends Game over Birthday
A nine-year-old child is part of a soccer team. The soccer team has made it to the quarterfinals of the local league. The quarterfinal game is on Saturday, and the team is expected to lose the game; the child is not a star on the team.

The child's game, however, conflicts with a grandparent's seventy-third birthday party that the parents had planned to attend. The child's parents decide that the child (along with the parents) should attend the game.

Treatment 2: Attends Birthday over Game
A nine-year-old child is part of a soccer team. The soccer team has made it to the quarterfinals of the local league. The quarterfinal game is on Saturday, and the team is expected to lose the game; the child is not a star on the team.

The child's game, however, conflicts with a grandparent's seventy-third birthday party that the parents had planned to attend. The child's parents decide that the child (along with the parents) should attend the grandparent's seventy-third birthday party.

Treatment 3: Attends Game over Pro-Choice Rally
A nine-year-old child is part of a soccer team. The soccer team has made it to the quarterfinals of the local league. The quarterfinal game is on Saturday, and the team is expected to lose the game; the child is not a star on the team.

The child's game, however, conflicts with a pro-choice rally that the parents had planned to attend. The child's parents decide that the child (along with the parents) should attend the game.

Treatment 4: Attends Pro-Choice Rally over Game

A nine-year-old child is part of a soccer team. The soccer team has made it to the quarterfinals of the local league. The quarterfinal game is on Saturday, and the team is expected to lose the game; the child is not a star on the team.

The child's game, however, conflicts with a pro-choice rally that the parents had planned to attend. The child's parents decide that the child (along with the parents) should attend the pro-choice rally.

Treatment 5: Attends Game over Pro-Life Rally

A nine-year-old child is part of a soccer team. The soccer team has made it to the quarterfinals of the local league. The quarterfinal game is on Saturday, and the team is expected to lose the game; the child is not a star on the team.

The child's game, however, conflicts with a pro-life rally that the parents had planned to attend. The child's parents decide that the child (along with the parents) should attend the game.

Treatment 6: Attends Pro-Life Rally over Game

A nine-year-old child is part of a soccer team. The soccer team has made it to the quarterfinals of the local league. The quarterfinal game is on Saturday, and the team is expected to lose the game; the child is not a star on the team.

The child's game, however, conflicts with a pro-life rally that the parents had planned to attend. The child's parents decide that the child (along with the parents) should attend the pro-life rally.

A.3.4   Chapter 6 – Parents Study 3 (Q20)

Treatment 1: Republican National Committee/Teen Girl

Consider the following scenario. A seventeen-year-old took a job waiting tables at a local restaurant as a summer job. The child's parents have asked her to donate one-tenth of her take-home pay because it is important to contribute to society. Although the child was hesitant to donate the money, she ultimately agreed with her parents to donate the money to the Republican National Committee.

Treatment 2: Democratic National Committee/Teen Girl

Consider the following scenario. A seventeen-year-old took a job waiting tables at a local restaurant as a summer job. The child's parents have asked her to donate one-tenth of her take-home pay because it is important to contribute to society. Although the child was hesitant to donate the money, she ultimately agreed with her parents to donate the money to the Democratic National Committee.

Treatment 3: Make-A-Wish/Teen Girl

Consider the following scenario. A seventeen-year-old took a job waiting tables at a local restaurant as a summer job. The child's parents have asked her to donate one-tenth of her take-home pay because it is important to contribute to society. Although the child was hesitant to donate the money, she ultimately agreed with her parents to donate the money to the Make-A-Wish Foundation.

Treatment 4: Republican National Committee/Teen Boy

Consider the following scenario. A seventeen-year-old took a job waiting tables at a local restaurant as a summer job. The child's parents have asked him to donate one-tenth of his take-home pay because it is important to contribute to society. Although the child was hesitant to donate the money, he ultimately agreed with his parents to donate the money to the Republican National Committee.

Treatment 5: Democratic National Committee/Teen Boy

Consider the following scenario. A seventeen-year-old took a job waiting tables at a local restaurant as a summer job. The child's parents have asked him to donate one-tenth of his take-home pay because it is important to contribute to society. Although the child was hesitant to donate the money, he ultimately agreed with his parents to donate the money to the Democratic National Committee.

Treatment 6: Make-A-Wish/Teen Boy

Consider the following scenario. A seventeen-year-old took a job waiting tables at a local restaurant as a summer job. The child's parents have asked him to donate one-tenth of his take-home pay because it is important to contribute to society. Although the child was hesitant to donate the money, he ultimately agreed with his parents to donate the money to the Make-A-Wish Foundation.

(All respondents answer these two questions.)

How favorable or unfavorable do you feel toward the parents in the story you just read?

<1> Extremely unfavorable
<2> Unfavorable
<3> Somewhat unfavorable
<4> Neither favorable nor unfavorable
<5> Somewhat favorable
<6> Favorable
<7> Extremely favorable

Do you agree or disagree with the following statement: If I were the child's parent, I would have made the same exact decisions as the parents in the story.

<1> Strongly agree
<2> Agree
<3> Somewhat agree
<4> Neither agree nor disagree
<5> Somewhat disagree

<6> Disagree
<7> Strongly disagree

A.3.5 Chapter 6 – Parents Study 4 (YG20)

Treatment 1: Birthday

This scenario is taking place during a time with no coronavirus outbreak, and there are no social distancing policies in place.

A fourteen-year-old child is part of a soccer team. The soccer team has made it to the quarterfinals of a local league. The quarterfinal game is on Saturday, and the team is expected to lose the game; the child is not a star on the team.

The child's game, however, conflicts with a grandparent's seventy-third birthday party that the parents had planned to attend. The child's parents decide that the child (along with the parents) should attend the grandparent's seventy-third birthday party.

Treatment 2: Voter Registration

This scenario is taking place during a time with no coronavirus outbreak, and there are no social distancing policies in place.

A fourteen-year-old child is part of a soccer team. The soccer team has made it to the quarterfinals of a local league. The quarterfinal game is on Saturday, and the team is expected to lose the game; the child is not a star on the team.

The child's game, however, conflicts with a *nonpartisan* voter registration drive in which the parents had planned to volunteer. The child's parents decide that the child (along with the parents) should attend the voter registration drive.

Treatment 3: Election Forum

This scenario is taking place during a time with no coronavirus outbreak, and there are no social distancing policies in place.

A fourteen-year-old child is part of a soccer team. The soccer team has made it to the quarterfinals of a local league. The quarterfinal game is on Saturday, and the team is expected to lose the game; the child is not a star on the team.

The child's game, however, conflicts with an election forum with local city council candidates that the parents had planned to attend. The child's parents decide that the child (along with the parents) should attend the candidate forum.

Treatment 4: Food Bank

This scenario is taking place during a time with no coronavirus outbreak, and there are no social distancing policies in place.

A fourteen-year-old child is part of a soccer team. The soccer team has made it to the quarterfinals of a local league. The quarterfinal game is on Saturday, and the team is expected to lose the game; the child is not a star on the team.

The child's game, however, conflicts with a food bank hosted by the local high school in which the parents had planned to volunteer. The child's parents decide that the child (along with the parents) should attend the food bank.

(All respondents answer these two questions.)

Keeping in mind that the story you just read happened during a time when there is no coronavirus outbreak and no social distancing policies, how favorable or unfavorable do you feel toward the parents in the story you just read?

<1> Extremely unfavorable
<2> Unfavorable
<3> Somewhat unfavorable
<4> Neither favorable nor unfavorable
<5> Somewhat favorable
<6> Favorable
<7> Extremely favorable

Keeping in mind that the story you just read happened during a time when there is no coronavirus outbreak and no social distancing policies, do you agree or disagree with the following statement: If I were the child's parent, I would have made the same exact decisions as the parents in the story.

<1> Strongly agree
<2> Agree
<3> Somewhat agree
<4> Neither agree nor disagree
<5> Somewhat disagree
<6> Disagree
<7> Strongly disagree

A.3.6 Chapter 7 – Perceptions Experiment (MTurk, October 2019)

Treatment 1: Control
Consider a forty-year-old white man who reads two national newspapers and watches local TV news five days a week.

Treatment 2: No Talk/No Post
Consider a forty-year-old white man who reads two national newspapers and watches local TV news five days a week. He does not talk about politics with his friends, family, and co-workers nor does he post about politics on social media.

Treatment 3: No Talk/Post
Consider a forty-year-old white man who reads two national newspapers and watches local TV news five days a week. He does not talk about politics with his friends, family, and co-workers but posts about politics on social media daily.

Treatment 4: Talk/No Post

Consider a forty-year-old white man who reads two national newspapers and watches local TV news five days a week. He talks frequently about politics with his friends, family, and co-workers but does not post about politics on social media.

Treatment 5: Talk/Post

Consider a forty-year-old white man who reads two national newspapers and watches local TV news five days a week. He talks frequently about politics with his friends, family, and co-workers and posts about politics on social media daily.

(All respondents answer these two questions.)

If you had to guess, how much would you say this person knows about politics?

<1> Not much at all
<2> A little less than the average person
<3> The same amount as the average person
<4> A little more than the average person
<5> A great deal

If you had to guess, what would be this person's position on most issues?

<1> Extremely liberal
<2> Liberal
<3> Somewhat liberal
<4> Moderate
<5> Somewhat conservative
<6> Conservative
<7> Extremely conservative

(Responses were recoded to indicate extremity: 0 = 4, 1 = 3 or 5, 2 = 2 or 6, and 3 = 1 or 7.)

References

Abramowitz, Alan I. and Kyle L. Saunders. 2008. "Is Polarization a Myth?" *The Journal of Politics*, 70(2): 542–555.

Abramowitz, Alan I. and Steven W. Webster. 2018. "Negative Partisanship: Why Americans Dislike Parties but Behave Like Rabid Partisans." *Political Psychology*, 39(S1): 119–135.

Ahler, Douglas. 2014. "Self-Fulfilling Misperceptions of Public Polarization." *Journal of Politics*, 76(3): 607–620.

Ahn, T. K., Robert Huckfeldt, and John Barry Ryan. 2015. *Experts, Activists, and Democratic Politics*. New York: Cambridge University Press.

Aldrich, John, David A. Lake, Jane C. Mansbridge et al. 2020. "Will the US Media Call the Right Winner on Election Night? Don't Count on It." *The Guardian*, October 7: www.theguardian.com/commentisfree/2020/oct/07/us-media-election-night-apsa

Alicke, Mark D. 2000. "Evaluating Social Comparison Targets." In Jerry Suls and Ladd Wheeler (eds.), *Handbook of Social Comparison: Theory and Research*. New York: Kluwer Academic/Plenum Press. pp.271–293.

Almond, Gabriel and Sidney Verba. 1965. *The Civic Culture: Political Attitudes and Democracy in Five Nations*. Princeton, NJ: Princeton University Press.

Anderson, Sarah E., Daniel M. Butler, and Laurel Harbridge-Yong. 2020. *Rejecting Compromise: Legislators' Fear of Primary Voters*. New York: Cambridge University Press.

American Political Science Association. 1950. "Towards a More Responsible Two-Party System: A Report of the Committee on Political Parties." *American Political Science Review*, 44(3 – Supplement): 1–96.

Aronow, Peter, Joshua Kalla, Lilla Orr, and John Ternovski. 2020. "Evidence of Rising Rates of Inattentiveness on Lucid in 2020." Working paper: https://osf.io/8sbe4/download

Auger, Giselle. 2013. "Fostering Democracy through Social Media: Evaluating Diametrically Opposed Nonprofit Advocacy Organizations' Use of Facebook, Twitter, and YouTube." *Public Relations Review*, 39: 369–376.

Badger, Emily and Quoctrung Bui. 2018. "Americans Say Their Politics Don't Define Them. But It's Complicated." *The New York Times*, October 12: www.nytimes.com/interactive/2018/10/12/upshot/us-politics-identity.html

Bail, Christopher A., Lisa P. Argyle, Taylor W. Brown et al. 2018. "Exposure to Opposing Views on Social Media Can Increase Political Polarization." *Proceedings of the National Academy of Sciences*, 115(37): 9216–9221.

Barabas, Jason, Jennifer Jerit, William Pollock, and Carlisle Rainey. 2014. "The Question(s) of Political Knowledge." *American Political Science Review*, 108(4): 840–855.

Barber, Michael and Jeremy Pope. 2019. "Does Party Trump Ideology? Disentangling Party and Ideology in America." *American Political Science Review*, 113(1): 38–54.

Bastos, Marco T. and Dan Mercea. 2016. "Serial Activists: Political Twitter beyond Influentials and the Twittertariat." *New Media and Society*, 18(10): 2359–2378.

Baumeister, Roy F. 1991. *Meanings in Life*. New York: Guilford.

Beaumont, Elizabeth. 2011. "Promoting Political Agency, Addressing Political Inequality: A Multilevel Model of Internal Political Efficacy." *The Journal of Politics*, 73(1): 216–231.

Beck, Paul Allen and M. Kent Jennings. 1982. "Pathways to Participation." *American Political Science Review*, 76(1): 94–108.

Beckers, Kathleen. 2017. "How Ordinary is the Ordinary Wo(man) on the Street? An Analysis of Vox Pop Characteristics in Television News." *Journalism Practice*, 11(8): 1026–1041.

Beckers, Kathleen. 2018. "Vox Pops in the News: The Journalists' Perspective." *Communications*, 43(1): 101–111.

Beckers, Kathleen. 2019. "What Vox Pops Say and How That Matters: Effects of Vox Pops in Television." *Journalism and Mass Communication Quarterly*, 96(4): 980–1003.

Beckers, Kathleen. 2020. "The Voice of the People in the News: A Content Analysis of Public Opinion Displays in Routine and Election News" *Journalism Studies*, 21(15), 2078–2095.

Beckers, Kathleen and Raymond A. Harder. 2016. " 'Twitter Just Exploded': Social Media As Alternative Vox Pop." Digital Journalism, 4(7): 910–920.

Beckers, Kathleen, Stefaan Walgrave, and Hilde Van den Bulck. 2018. "Opinion Balance in Vox Pop Television news." *Journalism Studies*, 19(2): 284–296.

Bekkers, René. 2005. "Participation in Voluntary Associations: Relations with Resources, Personality, and Political Values." *Political Psychology*, 26(3): 439–454.

Belk, Russel W., Güliz Ger, and Søren Askegaard. 2003. "The Fire of Desire: A Multi-Sited Inquiry into Consumer Passion." *Journal of Consumer Research*, 30(3): 326–352.

Benenson, Jodi and Inger Bergom. 2019. "Voter Participation, Socioeconomic Status, and Institutional Contexts in Higher Education." *The Review of Higher Education*, 42(4): 1665–1688.

Bennett, Linda L. M. and Stephen Earl Bennett. 1989. "Enduring Gender Differences in Political Interest: The Impact of Socialization and Political Dispositions." *American Politics Research*, 17(1): 105–122.

Berelson, Bernard, Paul Lazarsfeld, and William McPhee (1954). *Voting: A Study of Opinion Formation in a Presidential Campaign*. Chicago: University of Chicago Press.

Berinsky, Adam J. 2004. "Can We Talk? Self-Presentation and the Survey Response." *Political Psychology*, 25(4): 643–659.

Berinsky, Adam J. and Gabriel S. Lenz. 2011. "Education and Political Participation: Exploring the Causal Link." *Political Behavior*, 33(3): 357–373.

Berry, Jeffrey and Sarah Sobieraj. 2013. *The Outrage Industry: Political Opinion Media and the New Incivility*. New York: Oxford University Press.

Bevan, Jennifer L., Ruth Gomez, and Lisa Sparks. 2014. "Disclosures about Important Life Events on Facebook: Relationships with Stress and Quality of Life." *Computers in Human Behavior*, 39: 246–253.

Bloch, Peter H., Suraj Commuri, and Todd J. Arnold. 2009. "Exploring the Origins of Enduring Product Involvement." *Qualitative Market Research*, 12(1): 49–69.

Boczkowski, Pablo J., Eugenia Mitchelstein, and Martin Walter. 2011. "Convergence across Divergence: Understanding the Gap in the Online News Choices of Journalists and Consumers in Western Europe and Latin America." *Communication Research*, 38: 376–396.

Bode, Leticia. 2016. "Political News in the News Feed: Learning Politics from Social Media." *Mass Communication and Society*, 19(1): 24–48.

Bolsen, Toby and Thomas Leeper. 2013. "Self-Interest and Attention to News among Issue Publics." *Political Communication*, 30: 329–248.

Booth, Paul and Katie Booth. 2014. "The Discourse of Authenticity in the Doctor Who Fan Community." In Jason Barr and Camille D.G. Mustachio (eds.), *The Language of Doctor Who: From Shakespeare to Alien Tongues*. London: Rowman and Littlefield, pp. 259–273.

Bosch, Brandon. 2014. "Beyond Vox Pop: The Role of News Sourcing and Political Beliefs in Exemplification Effects." *Mass Communication and Society*, 17(2): 217–235.

Boudreau, Cheryl and Scott A. MacKenzie. 2014. "Informing the Electorate? How Party Cues and Policy Information Affect Public Opinion about Initiatives." *American Journal of Political Science*, 58(1): 48–62.

Bougher, Lori. 2017. "The Correlates of Discord: Identity, Issue Alignment, and Political Hostility in Polarized America." *Political Behavior*, 39(3): 731–762.

Boulianne, Shelley. 2011. "Stimulating or Reinforcing Political Interest: Using Panel Data to Examine Reciprocal Effects between News Media and Political Interest." *Political Communication*, 28(2): 147–162.

Bowman, Nicholas A. and Michael N. Bastedo. 2011. "Anchoring Effects in World University Rankings: Exploring Biases in Reputation Scores." *Higher Education*, 61: 431–444.

boyd, danah. 2010. "Social Network Sites as Networked Publics: Affordances, Dynamics, and Implications." In Zizi Papacharissi (ed.), *A Networked Self: Identity, Community, and Culture on Social Network Sites*. New York: Routledge, pp. 39–58.

Boydstun, Amber E. 2013. *Making the News: Politics, the Media, and Agenda Setting*. Chicago: University of Chicago Press.

Bradshaw, Alan. 2012. "Interview with Morris Holbrook." *Royal Holloway University of London Marketing Blog*, June 28: http://royalhollowaymarketing.blogspot.com/2012/06/interview-with-morris-holbrook.html

Brady, Henry E., Sidney Verba, and Kay Lehman Schlozman. 1995. "Beyond SES: A Resource Model of Political Participation." *American Political Science Review*, 89 (2): 271–294.

Brady, William J., M. J. Crockett1, and Jay J. Van Bavel. 2020. "The MAD Model of Moral Contagion: The Role of Motivation, Attention, and Design in the Spread of Moralized Content Online." *Perspectives on Psychological Science*, 15(4): 978–1010.

Brennan, Jason. 2016. "Trump Won Because Voters are Ignorant, Literally." *Foreign Policy*, November 10: https://foreignpolicy.com/2016/11/10/the-dance-of-the-dunces-trump-clinton-election-republican-democrat/

Bright, Jonathan. 2016. "The Social News Gap: How News Reading and News Sharing Diverge." *Journal of Communication*, 66: 343–365.

Brosius, Hans-Bernd and Anke Bathelt. 1994. "The Utility of Exemplars in Persuasive Communications." *Communication Research*, 21(2): 48–78.

Broockman, David E. and Christopher Skovron. 2018. "Bias in Perceptions of Public Opinion among Political Elites." *American Political Science Review*, 112(3): 542–563.

Broockman, David E., Joshua L. Kalla, and Sean J. Westwood. 2021. "Does Affective Polarization Undermine Democratic Norms or Accountability? Maybe Not." Working paper: 10.31219/osf.io/9btsq

Burns, Alexander and Jonathan Martin. 2020. "Trump Struggles on GOP Turf As Women Favor Biden." *The New York Times*, September 25: Section A Page 1.

Burns, Nancy, Kay Schlozman, and Sidney Verba. 2001. *The Private Roots of Public Action: Gender, Equality, and Political Participation.* Cambridge, MA: Harvard University Press.

Burrow, Anthony and Nicolette Rainone. 2017. "How Many *Likes* Did I Get?: Purpose Moderates Links between Positive Social Media Feedback and Self-Esteem." *Journal of Experimental Social Psychology*, 69: 232–236.

Buttice, Matthew, Robert Huckfeldt, and John Barry Ryan. 2009. "Political Polarization and Communication Networks in the 2006 Congressional Elections." In Jeffery J. Mondak and Donna-Gene Mitchell (eds.), *Fault Lines: Why the Republicans Lost Congress*. New York: Routledge, pp. 42–60.

Cain Miller, Claire. 2020. "More Partisanship But Happier Couples?" *The New York Times*, October 27: Section A Page 14.

Campbell, Angus, Philip E. Converse, Warren E. Miller, and Donald E. Stokes. 1960. *The American Voter*. Chicago: University of Chicago Press.

Cappella, Joseph N. 1985. "Production Principles for Turn-Taking Rules in Social Interaction: Socially Anxious vs. Socially Secure Persons." *Journal of Language and Social Psychology*, 4: 193–212.

Carlson, Taylor N. 2018. "Modeling Political Information Transmission as a Game of Telephone." *The Journal of Politics*, 80(1): 348–352.

Carlson, Taylor N. 2019. "Through the Grapevine: Informational Consequences of Interpersonal Political Communication." *American Political Science Review*, 113(2): 325–339.

Carlson, Taylor and Jaime Settle. 2016. "Political Chameleons: An Exploration of Conformity in Political Discussions." *Political Behavior*, 38(4): 817–859.

Chatzitheochari, Stella and Sara Arber. 2012. "Class, Gender and Time Poverty: A Time-Use Analysis of British Workers' Free Time Resources." *The British Journal of Sociology*, 63(3): 451–471.

Chen, M. Keith and Ryne Rohla. 2018. "The Effect of Partisanship and Political Advertising on Close Family Ties." *Science*, 360(6392): 1020–1024.

Choi, Sujin. 2014. "Flow, Diversity, Form, and Influence of Political Talk in Social-Media-Based Public Forums." *Human Communication Research*, 40: 209–237.

Cisneros, J. David and Thomas K. Nakayama. 2015. "New Media, Old Racisms: Twitter, Miss America, and Cultural Logics of Race." *Journal of International and Intercultural Communication*, 8(2): 108–127.

Claassen, Ryan L. and John Barry Ryan. 2016. "Social Desirability, Hidden Biases, and Support for Hillary Clinton." *PS*, 49(4): 730–735.

Clark, Jenna L., Sara B. Algoe, and Melanie C. Green. 2018. "Social Network Sites and Well-Being: The Role of Social Connection." *Current Directions in Psychological Science*, 27(1): 32–37.

Cohen, Jacob. 1988. *Statistical Power Analysis for the Behavioral Sciences*, Second Edition. New York: Lawrence Earlbaum Associates.

Cohn, Nate and Kevin Quealy. 2019. "The Democratic Electorate on Twitter Is Not the Actual Democratic Electorate." *The New York Times*, April 9: www.nytimes.com /interactive/2019/04/08/upshot/democratic-electorate-twitter-real-life.html

Connors, Elizabeth C. 2020. "The Social Dimension of Political Values." *Political Behavior*, 42(3): 961–982.

Connors, Elizabeth C., Yanna Krupnikov, and John Barry Ryan. 2019. "How Transparency Affects Survey Responses." *Public Opinion Quarterly*, 83(S1): 185–209.

Conover, Pamela Johnston, Donald D. Searing and Ivor M. Crewe. 2002. "The Deliberative Potential of Political Discussion." *British Journal of Political Science*, 32(1): 21–62.

Converse, Philip. 1962. "Information Flow and the Stability of Partisan Attitudes." *Public Opinion Quarterly*, 26(4): 578–599.

Converse, Phillip. 1964. "The Nature of Belief Systems In Mass Publics." In David Apter (ed.), *Ideology and Discontent*. New York: Free Press of Glencoe, pp. 206–261.

Coppock, Alexander and Oliver A. McClellan. 2019. "Validating the Demographic, Political, Psychological, and Experimental Results Obtained from a New Source of Online Survey Respondents." *Research & Politics*, https://doi.org/10.1177 /2053168018822174

Coppock, Alexander, Thomas J. Leeper, and Kevin J. Mullinix. 2018. "Generalizability of Heterogeneous Treatment Effect Estimates Across Samples." *Proceedings of the National Academic of Sciences of the United States of America*, 115(49): 12441–12446.

Cornwall, Gail. 2020. "The Right Way to Talk About Politics with Your Kids, According to Experts." *Good Housekeeping*, August 24: www.goodhousekeeping.com/life/ parenting/a32811769/talking-to-kids-about-politics/

Cornwell, Susan, David Morgan and Richard Cowen. 2020. "Trump Impeachment Trial Opens as Watchdog Faults White House on Ukraine." *Reuters*. Retrieved from https://fr.reuters.com/article/uk-usa-trump-impeachment-idUKKBN1ZF18Q

Costa, Mia. 2021. "Ideology, Not Affect: What Americans Want From Political Representation." *American Journal of Political Science*, 65(2): 342–358.

Dafoe, Allan, Baobao Zhang, and Devin Caughey. 2018. "Information Equivalence in Survey Experiments." *Political Analysis*, 26(4): 399–416.

Dalton, Russell. 1980. "Reassessing Parental Socialization: Indicator Unreliability Versus Generational Transfer." *American Political Science Review*, 74(2): 421–431.

Darling, Nancy and Laurence Steinberg. 1993. "Parenting Style as Context: An Integrative Model." *Psychological Bulletin*, 113(3): 487–496.

Daschmann, Gregor. 2000. "Vox Pop & Polls: The impact of Poll Results and Voter Statements in the Media on the Perception of a Climate of Opinion." *International Journal of Public Opinion Research*, 12: 160–181.

Daschmann, Gregor and Hans-Bernd Brosius. 1999. "Can a Single Incident Create an Issue? Exemplars in German Television Magazine Shows." *Journalism and Mass Communication Quarterly*, 76(1): 35–51.

Davis, Robert and Lee Phillip McGinnis. 2016. "Conceptualizing Excessive Fan Consumption Behavior." *Journal of Retailing and Consumer Services*, 28: 252–262.

de Zúñiga, Homero Gil, Logan Molyneux,and Pei Zheng. 2014. "Social Media, Political Expression, and Political Participation: Panel Analysis of Lagged and Concurrent Relationships." *Journal of Communication*, 64(4): 612–634.

de Zúñiga, Homero Gil, Sebastián Valenzuela, and Brian E. Weeks. 2016. "Motivations for Political Discussion: Antecedents and Consequences on Civic Engagement." *Human Communication Research*, 42(4): 533–552.

Dean, Jonathan. 2017. "Politicising Fandom." *British Journal of Politics and International Relations*, 19(2): 408–424.

Delton, Andrew W., Peter DeScioli, and Timothy J. Ryan. 2020. "Moral Obstinacy in Political Negotiations." *Political Psychology*, 41(1): 3–20.

Denham Bryan E. 2008. "Folk Devils, News Icons and the Construction of Moral Panics." *Journalism Studies*, 9(6): 945–961.

Dias, Nicholas and Yphtach Lelkes. 2021. "The Partisan Roots of Affective Polarization: Disentangling Partisanship from Policy Positions." *American Journal of Political Science*. https://doi.org/10.1111/ajps.12628

Dickerson, John. 2020. *The Hardest Job in the World: The American Presidency.* New York: Random House.

Dickerson, Mary Dee and James W. Gentry. 1983. "Characteristics of Adopters and Non-Adopters of Home Computers." *Journal of Consumer Research*, 10(2): 225–235.

Diehl, Trevor, Alberto Ardèvol-Abreu and Homero Gil de Zúñiga. 2019. "How Engagement with Journalists on Twitter Reduces Public Perceptions of Media Bias." *Journalism Practice*, 13(8): 971–975.

Dimmock, James A. and J. Robert Grove. 2005. "Relationship of Fan Identification to Determinants of Aggression." *Journal of Applied Sport Psychology*, 17(1): 37–47.

Dinas, Elias. 2013. "Opening 'Openness to Change': Political Events and the Increased Sensitivity of Young Adults." *Political Research Quarterly*, 66(4): 868–882.

Dinas, Elias. 2014. "Why Does the Apple Fall Far from the Tree? How Early Political Socialization Prompts Parent-Child Dissimilarity." *British Journal of Political Science*, 44(4): 827–852.

Dionísio, Pedro, Carmo Leal and Luiz Mountinho. 2008. "Fandom Affiliation and Tribal Behaviour: A Sports Marketing Application." *Qualitative Marketing Research: An International Journal*, 11(1): 17–39.

Doosje, Bertjan, Russell Spears, Naomi Ellemers and Willem Koomen. 1999. "Perceived Group Variability in Intergroup Relations: The Distinctive Role of Social Identity." *European Review of Social Psychology*, 10(1): 41–74.

Downs, Anthony. 1957. *An Economic Theory of Democracy.* New York: Harper and Row.

Druckman, James N. and Matthew Levendusky. 2019. "What Do We Measure When We Measure Affective Polarization?" *Public Opinion Quarterly*, 83(1): 114–122.

Druckman, James N., Samara Klar, Yanna Krupnikov, Matthew Levendusky, and John Barry Ryan. 2020. "How Affective Polarization Shapes Americans' Political Beliefs: A Study of Response to the COVID-19 Pandemic." *Journal of Experimental Political Science*, DOI: 10.1017/XPS.2020.28

Druckman, James N., Samara Klar, Yanna Krupnikov, Matthew Levendusky, and John Barry Ryan. 2021a. "Affective Polarization, Local Contexts, and Public Opinion in America." *Nature Human Behaviour*, 5: 28–38

Druckman, James N., Samara Klar, Yanna Krupnikov, Matthew Levendusky, and John Barry Ryan. 2021b. "(Mis-)Estimating Affective Polarization." *The Journal of Politics*. https://doi.org/10.1086/715603

Duggan, Maeve and Aaron Smith. 2016. "The Political Environment on Social Media." *Pew Report*, October 25: www.pewresearch.org/internet/2016/10/25/the-political-environment-on-social-media/

Dunaway, Johanna and Regina G. Lawrence. 2015. "What Predicts the Game Frame? Media Ownership, Electoral Context, and Campaign News." *Political Communication*, 32(1): 43–60.

Dunaway, Johanna L., Kathleen Searles, Mingxiao Sui, and Newly Paul. 2018. "News Attention in a Mobile Era." *Journal of Computer-Mediated Communication*, 23 (2):107–124.

Edelman, Murray. 1964. *The Symbolic Uses of Politics*. Urbana, IL: University of Illinois Press.

Edelman, Murray. 1988. *Constructing the Political Spectacle*. Chicago: University of Chicago Press.

Edrington, Candice L. and Nicole Lee. 2018. "Tweeting a Social Movement: Black Lives Matter and its use of Twitter to Share Information, Build Community, and Promote Action." *Journal of Public Interest Communications*, 2(2): 289–306.

Eiser, J. Richard., Thomas Stafford, John Henneberry and Philip Catney. 2009. "'Trust me, I'm a Scientist (Not a Developer)': Perceived Expertise and Motives as Predictors of Trust in Assessment of Risk from Contaminated Land." *Risk Analysis*, 29(2): 288–297.

Ellemers, Naomi and Wendy Van Rijswijk. 1997. "Identity Needs Versus Social Opportunities: The Use of Group-Level and Individual-Level Identity Management Strategies." *Social Psychology Quarterly*, 60(1): 52–65.

Ellemers Naomi, Russell Spears and Bertjan Doosje. 2002. "Self and Social Identity." *Annual Review of Psychology*, 53: 161–186.

Epstein, Reid. 2020. "Wild Card in Wisconsin: Virus in a Purple Region." *The New York Times*, October 31: Section A Page 15.

Eulau, Heinz and Peter Schneider. 1956. "Dimensions of Political Involvement." *Public Opinion Quarterly*, 20(1): 128–142.

Eveland, Jr., William P., Alyssa C. Morey, and Myiah J. Hutchens. 2011. "Beyond Deliberation: New Directions for the Study of Informal Political Conversation from a Communication Perspective." *Journal of Communication*, 61: 1082–1103.

Fan, Rui, Ali Varameshb, Onur Varolc, et al. 2018. "Does Putting Your Emotions Into Words Make You Feel Better? Measuring the Minute-Scale Dynamics of Emotions from Online Data." Working paper: https://arxiv.org/pdf/1807.09725.pdf

Fandos, Nicholas. 2020. "A Step-by-Step Guide to Trump's Impeachment Trial." *The New York Times*, January 14: Section A, Page 16.

Fandos, Nicholas, Erin Schaff and Emily Cochrane. 2021. "'It Didn't Feel Real': Covering Politics One Moment, and Chaos the Next." *The New York Times*, January 8: Section A, Page 15.

Federico, Christopher M. and Corrie V. Hunt. 2013. "Political Information, Political Involvement, and Reliance on Ideology in Political Evaluation." *Political Behavior*, 35 (1): 89–112.

Fiorina, Morris P. 1990. "Information and Rationality in Elections." In John A. Ferejohn and James H. Kuklinski (eds.), *Information and Democratic Processes*. Urbana: University of Illinois Press, pp. 329–342.

Fiorina, Morris P. 2016. "The Political Parties Have Sorted." Hoover Institution Essays on Contemporary American Politics, Series No. 3. www.hoover.org/sites/default/files/research/docs/fiorina_3_finalfile.pdf

Fiorina, Morris. 2017. *Unstable Majorities: Polarization, Party Sorting and Political Stalemate*. Stanford, CA: Hoover Institution Press.

Fox, Richard L. and Jennifer L. Lawless. 2014. "Uncovering the Origins of the Gender Gap in Political Ambition." *American Political Science Review*, 108(3): 499–519.

Francis, Lizzy. 2017. "7 Fathers on Why They Take Their Kids to Protests." Fatherly.com, www.fatherly.com/love-money/7-dads-on-why-they-take-their-kids-to-protests/

Freelon, Deen. 2015. "Discourse Architecture, Ideology, and Democratic Norms in Online Political Discussion." *New Media & Society*, 17(5): 772–791.

Freelon, Deen, Charlton McIlwain and Meredith Clark. 2018. "Quantifying the Power and Consequences of Social Media Protest." *New Media & Society*, 20 (3): 990–1011.

Fry, Richard and Anthony Cilluffo. 2019. "A Rising Share of Undergraduates Are From Poor Families, Especially at Less Selective. Colleges." Pew Research Center Report. https://www.pewresearch.org/social-trends/2019/05/22/a-rising-share-of-undergraduates-are-from-poor-families-especially-at-less-selective-colleges/

Galais, Carolina and Blais, André and Bowler, Shaun. 2014. "Is Political Interest Absolute or Relative?" APSA 2014 Annual Meeting Paper, Available at SSRN: https://ssrn.com/abstract=2455573

Galston, William. 2004. "Civic Education and Political Participation." *PS: Political Science and Politics*, 37(2): 263–266.

Galuszka, Patryk. 2015. "New Economy of Fandom." *Popular Music and Society*, 38 (1): 25–43.

Garrett, Kristin N. and Alexa Bankert. 2020. "The Moral Roots of Partisan Division: How Moral Conviction Heightens Affective Polarization." *British Journal of Political Science*, 50(2): 621–640.

Gaskins, Ben, Jason Barabas, and Jennifer Jerit. 2020. "Qualitative Quotes: The Prevalence and Effects of Survey Respondent Exemplars in Political News Coverage." *The International Journal of Press/Politics*, 25(1): 96–114.

Gawronski, Bertram and Galen V. Bodenhausen. 2006. "Associative and Propositional Processes in Evaluation: An Integrative Review of Implicit and Explicit Attitude Change." *Psychological Bulletin*, 132(5): 692–731.

Gerson, Michael. 2019. "Politics is Religion and the Right is Getting Ready for the End Times." *The Washington Post*, March 18: www.washingtonpost.com /opinions/the-left-was-about-salvation-the-right-is-about-the-end-times/2019/03/ 18/2cd16898-49b8-11e9-9663-00ac73f49662_story.html

Glasser, William. 1976. *Positive Addiction*. Oxford, England: Harper & Row.

Gnolek, Shari L., Vincenzo T. Falciano and Ralph W. Kuncl. 2014. "Modeling Change and Variation in U.S. News & World Report College Rankings: What Would It Really Take to Be in the Top 20?" *Research in Higher Education*, 55: 761–779.

Goffman, Erving. 1959. *The Presentation of Self in Everyday Life*. New York: Anchor.

Gray, Jonathan. 2003. "New Audiences, New Textualities: Anti-Fans and Non-Fans." *International Journal of Cultural Studies*, 6(1): 64–81.

Green, Donald, Bradley Palmquist and Eric Shickler. 2002. *Partisan Hearts and Minds: Political Parties and the Social Identities of Voters*. New Haven, CT: Yale University Press.

Green, Emma. 2018. "Politics as the New Religion for Progressive Democrats." *The Atlantic*, www.theatlantic.com/politics/archive/2018/10/poll-shows-activism-highest-among-non-religious-democrats/572674/

Greene, Steven. 1999. "Understanding Party Identification: A Social Identity Approach." *Political Psychology*, 20(2): 393–403.

Greenstein, Fred I. 1965. *Children and Politics*. New Haven, CT: Yale University Press.

Groenendyk, Eric. 2013. *Competing Motives in the Partisan Mind: How Loyalty and Responsiveness Shape Party Identification and Democracy*. New York: Oxford University Press.

Groenendyk, Eric. 2018. "Competing Motives in a Polarized Electorate: Political Responsiveness, Identity Defensiveness, and the Rise of Partisan Antipathy." *Advances in Political Psychology*, 39(S1): 159–171.

Groenendyk, Eric. 2019. "Of Two Minds, But One Heart: A Good 'Gut' Feeling Moderates the Effect of Ambivalence on Attitude Formation and Turnout." *American Journal of Political Science*, 63(2): 368–384.

Groenendyk, Eric, Michael W. Sances, and Kirill Zhirkov. 2020. "*Intra*party Polarization in American Politics." *The Journal of Politics*, 82(4): 1616–1620.

Grusec, Joan E. Jacqueline J. Goodnow, and Leon Kuczynski. 2000. "New Directions in Analyses of Parenting Contributions to Children's Acquisition of Values." *Child Development*, 71(1): 205–211.

Guess, Andrew M., Brendan Nyhan, Benjamin Lyons and Jason Reifler. 2018. "Avoiding the Echo Chamber About Echo Chambers: Why Selective Exposure to Like-Minded Political News is Less Prevalent Than You Think." Knight Foundation White Paper. https://kf-site-production.s3.amazonaws.com/media_elements/files/000/000/133/original/Topos_KF_White-Paper_Nyhan_V1.pdf

Guess, Andrew M., Brendan Nyhan, and Jason Reifler. 2020. "Exposure to Untrustworthy Websites in the 2016 US Election." *Nature Human Behaviour*, 4: 472–480.

Guschwan, Matthew. 2011. "Fans, Romans, Countrymen: Soccer Fandom and Civic Identity in Contemporary Rome." *International Journal of Communication*, 5: 1990–2013.

Gutmann, Amy. 1980. "Children, Paternalism, and Education: A Liberal Argument." *Philosophy & Public Affairs*, 9(4): 338–358.

Gutmann, Amy. 1995. "Civic Education and Social Diversity." *Ethics*, 105(3): 557–579.

Hall, Judith A., Jason D. Carter, and Terrence G. Horgan. 2000. "Gender Differences in Nonverbal Communication of Emotion." In A. H. Fischer (ed.), *Gender and Emotion: Social Psychological Perspectives*. New York: Cambridge University Press, pp. 97–117.

Harbridge, Laurel, Neil Malhotra and Brian F. Harrison. 2014. "Public Preferences for Bipartisanship in the Policymaking Process." *Legislative Studies Quarterly*, 39(3): 327–355.

Harder, Raymond A., Julie Sevenans, Peter Van Aelst. 2017. "Intermedia Agenda Setting in the Social Media Age: How Traditional Players Dominate the News Agenda in Election Times." *The International Journal of Press/Politics*, 22(3): 275–293.

Hart, Joshua, Elizabeth Nailling, George Y. Bizer and Caitlyn K. Collins. 2015. "Attachment Theory as a Framework for Explaining Engagement with Facebook." *Personality and Individual Differences*, 77: 33–40.

Hart, P. Sol, Sedona Chinn, and Stuart Soroka. 2020. "Politicization and Polarization in COVID-19 News Coverage." *Science Communication*, 42(5): 679–697.

Hasell, Ariel. 2020. "Shared Emotion: The Social Amplification of Partisan News on Twitter." *Digital Journalism*. https://doi.org/10.1080/21670811.2020.1831937

Hassell, Hans G., John B. Holbein and Matthew R. Miles. 2020. "There is no Liberal Media Bias in Which News Stories Political Journalist Choose to Cover." *Science Advances*, 6(14): eaay9344.

Hatemi, Peter and Christopher Ojeda. 2021. "The Role of Child Perception and Motivation in Political Socialization." *British Journal of Political Science*, 51(3): 1097–1118.

Herbst, Susan. 2011. "(Un)Numbered Voices? Reconsidering the Meaning of Public Opinion in a Digital Age." In Kirby Goidel (ed.), *Political Polling in the Digital Age: The Challenge of Measuring and Understanding Public Opinion*, Baton Rouge, LA: LSU Press, pp. 85–98.

Hersh, Eitan. 2020. *Politics is For Power: How To Move Beyond Political Hobbyism, Take Action, and Make Real Change*. New York: Scribner.

Hersh, Eitan and Yair Ghitza. 2018. "Mixed partisan households and electoral participation in the United States." *PLOS One*. https://doi.org/10.1371/journal.pone.0203997

Hersh, Richard H. 1999. "Generating Ideals and Transforming Lives: A Contemporary Case for the Residential Liberal Arts College." *Daedalus*, 128(1): 173–194.

Hetherington, Marc J. 2001. "Resurgent Mass Partisanship: The Role of Elite Polarization." *The American Political Science Review*, 95(3): 619–631.

Hetherington, Marc and Thomas Rudolph. 2015. *Why Washington Won't Work: Polarization, Political Trust, and the Governing Crisis*. Chicago: University of Chicago Press.

Hetherington, Marc J. and Jonathan D. Weiler. 2009. *Authoritarianism and Polarization in American Politics*. New York: Cambridge University Press.

Hibbing, John R. and Elizabeth Theiss-Morse. 2002. *Stealth Democracy: Americans' Beliefs about How Government Should Work*. New York: Cambridge University Press.

Hill, Ronald Paul and Harold Robinson. 1991. "Fanatic Consumer Behavior: Athletics as a Consumption Experience." *Psychology & Marketing*, 8(2): 79–99.

Hills, Matthew. 2002. *Fan Cultures*. London: Routledge.

Hillygus, D. Sunshine. 2005. "The Missing Link: Exploring the Relationship between Higher Education and Political Engagement." *Political Behavior*, 27(1): 25–47.

Hinnant, Amanda, María E. Len-Ríos, and Rachel Young. 2013. "Journalistic Use of Exemplars to Humanize Health News." *Journalism Studies*, 14(4): 539–554.

Hoffman, Lindsay H., Philip Edward Jones, and Dannagal Goldthwaite Young. 2013. "Does My Comment Count? Perceptions of Political Participation in an Online Environment." *Computers in Human Behavior*, 29(6): 2248–2256.

Holbein, John and D. Sunshine Hillygus. 2020. *Making Young Voters: Converting Civic Attitudes into Civic Actions*. New York: Cambridge University Press.

Holbrook, Morris B. 1987. "An Audiovisual Inventory of Some Fanatic Consumer Behavior: the 25-Cent Tour of a Jazz Collector's Home." In Melanie Wallendorf and Paul Anderson (eds.), *Advances in Consumer Research Volume 14*. Provo, UT: Association for Consumer Research, pp. 144–149.

Holbrook, Morris B. 2008. *Playing the Changes on the Jazz Metaphor: An Expanded Conceptualization of Music, Management, and Marketing-Related Themes*. Hanover, MA: Now Publishers.

Holbrook, Allyson K., Melanie C. Green, and Jon A. Krosnick. 2003. "Telephone Versus Face-to-Face Interviewing of National Probability Samples with Long Questionnaires: Comparisons of Respondent Satisficing and Social Desirability Response Bias." *Public Opinion Quarterly*, 61(1): 79–125.

Holt, Douglas B. 1995. "How Consumers Consume: A Typology of Consumption Practices." *Journal of Consumer Research*, 22(1): 1–16.

Housley, William, Helena Webb, Meredydd Williams, et al. 2018. "Interaction and Transformation on Social Media: The Case of Twitter Campaigns." *Social Media + Society*: https://doi.org/10.1177/2056305117750721.

Huber, Gregory A. and Neil Malhotra. 2017. "Political Homophily in Social Relationships: Evidence from Online Dating Behavior." *The Journal of Politics*, 79 (1): 269–283.

Huckfeldt, Robert. 2001. "The Social Communication of Political Expertise." *American Journal of Political Science*, 45(2): 425–438.

Huckfeldt, Robert. 2007. "Unanimity, Discord, and the Communication of Public Opinion." *American Journal of Political Science*, 51(4): 978–995.

Huckfeldt, Robert, Jeffrey Levine, William Morgan, and John Sprague. 1999. "Accessibility and the Political Utility of Partisan and Ideological Orientations." *American Journal of Political Science*, 43(3): 888–911.

Huckfeldt, Robert, Jeanette Mendez, and Tracy Osborn. 2004. "Disagreement, Ambivalence and Engagement: The Political Consequences of Heterogeneous Networks." Political Psychology, 26: 65–96.

Huckfeldt, Robert and John Sprague. 1995. *Citizens, Politics, and Social Communication: Information and Influence in an Election Campaign*. New York: Cambridge University Press.

Huddy, Leonie and Nadia Khatib. 2007. "American Patriotism, National Identity, and Political Involvement." *American Journal of Political Science*, 51(1): 63–77.

Huddy, Leonie, Lilliana Mason, and Lene Aarøe. 2015. "Expressive Partisanship: Campaign Involvement, Political Emotion, and Partisan Identity." *American Political Science Review*, 109(1): 1–17.

Hughes, Adam. 2019. "A Small Group of Prolific Users Account for a Majority of Political Tweets Sent by U.S. Adults." Pew Research Center Fact Tank. https://www.pewresearch.org/fact-tank/2019/10/23/a-small-group-of-prolific-users-account-for-a-majority-of-political-tweets-sent-by-u-s-adults/

Hutchings, Vincent L. 2005. *Public Opinion and Democratic Accountability: How Citizens Learn about Politics*. Princeton, NJ: Princeton University Press.

Ishizuka, Patrick. 2019. "Social Class, Gender, and Contemporary Parenting Standards in the United States: Evidence from a National Survey Experiment." *Social Forces*, 98 (1): 31–58.

Iyengar, Shanto, Tobias Konitzer and Kent Tedin. 2018. "The Home as a Political Fortress: Family Agreement in an Era of Polarization." *The Journal of Politics*, 80 (4): 1326–1338.

Iyengar, Shanto and Masha Krupenkin. 2018. "The Strengthening of Partisan Affect." *Advances in Political Psychology*, 39(1): 201–218.

Iyengar, Shanto, Yphtach Lelkes, Matthew Levendusky, Neil Malhotra, and Sean Westwood. 2019. "The Origins and Consequences of Affective Polarization in the United States." *Annual Review of Political Science*, 22(1): 129–146.

Iyengar, Shanto, Gaurav Sood and Yphtach Lelkes. 2012. "Affect, Not Ideology: A Social Identity Perspective on Polarization." *Public Opinion Quarterly*, 76(3): 405–431.

Iyengar, Shanto and Sean J. Westwood. 2015. "Fear and Loathing across Party Lines: New Evidence on Group Polarization." *American Journal of Political Science*, 59(3): 690–707.

Jackson, Sarah J., Moya Bailey and Brooke Foucault Welles. 2020. *#HashtagActivism: Networks of Race and Gender Justice.* Cambridge, MA: MIT Press.

Janoff-Bulman, Ronnie and Cynthia McPherson Frantz. 1997. "The Impact of Trauma on Meaning: From Meaningless World to Meaningful Life." In Mick Power and Chris Brewin (eds.), *The Transformation of Meaning in Psychological Therapies: Integrating Theory and Practice.* Hoboken: John Wiley & Sons, pp. 91–106.

Japutra, Arnold, Yuksel Ekinci, and Lyndon Simkin. 2017. "Self-Congruence, Brand Attachment and Compulsive Buying." *Journal of Business Research*, 99: 456–463.

Jefferson, Hakeem. 2020. "The Curious Case of Black Conservatives: Construct Validity and the 7-point Liberal-Conservative Scale." Working paper: https://papers.ssrn.com/sol3/papers.cfm?abstract_id=3602209

Jennings, M. Kent and Gregory B. Markus. 1988. "Political Involvement in the Later Years: A Longitudinal Survey." *American Journal of Political Science*, 32(2): 302–316.

Jennings, M. Kent and Richard G. Niemi. 1968. "The Transmission of Political Values from Parent to Child." *American Political Science Review*, 62(1): 169–184.

Jennings, M. Kent and Richard G. Niemi. 1981. *Generations and Politics: A Panel Study of Young Adults and Their Parents.* Princeton, NJ: Princeton University Press.

Jennings, M. Kent, Laura Stoker and Jake Bowers. 2009. "Politics across Generations: Family Transmission Reexamined." *The Journal of Politics*, 71(3): 782–799.

Jost, John, Jack Glaser, Arie Kruglanski and Frank Sulloway. 2003. "Political Conservatism as Motivated Social Cognition." *Psychological Bulletin*, 129(3): 339–375.

Kahne, Joseph, Nam-Jin Lee and Jessica Timpany Feezell. 2012. "Digital Media Literacy Education and Online Civic and Political Participation." *International Journal of Communication*, 6: 1–24.

Kalmoe, Nathan and Lilliana Mason. 2019. "Lethal Mass Partisanship: Prevalence, Correlates & Electoral Contingencies." Paper presented at the National Capital Area Political Science Association American Political Workshop.

Kam, Cindy D. and Maggie Deichert. 2020. "Boycotting, Buycotting, and the Psychology of Political Consumerism." *The Journal of Politics*, 82(1): 72–88.

Kam, Cindy D. and Carl L. Palmer. 2008. "Reconsidering the Effects of Education on Political Participation." *The Journal of Politics*, 70(3): 612–631.

Karpowitz, Christopher and Jeremy Pope. 2020. American Family Survey Summary Report: Life During a Pandemic. https://media.deseret.com/media/misc/pdf/afs/2020-AFS-Final-Report.pdf

Kashdan, Todd B. and Paul Silvia. 2009. "Curiosity and Interest: The Benefits of Thriving on Novelty and Challenge." In Shane J. Lopez and C.R. Snider (eds.), *Oxford Handbook of Positive Psychology*. New York: Oxford University Press, pp. 367–374.

Katz, Elihu. 1957. "The Two Step Flow of Communication: An Up-to-Date Report on an Hypothesis." *Public Opinion Quarterly*, 21(1): 67–81.

Katz, Elihu and Paul Lazarsfeld. 1955. *Personal Influence*. New York: Free Press.

Kim, Hyun Suk. 2015. "Attracting Views and Going Viral: How Message Features and News-Sharing Channels Affect Health News Diffusion." *Journal of Communication*, 65: 512–534.

Kingzette, Jon. 2020. "Who Do You Loathe? Feelings toward Politicians vs. Ordinary People in the Opposing Party." *Journal of Experimental Political Science*. DOI: 10.1017/XPS.2020.9

Kingzette, Jon, James N. Druckman, Samara Klar, et al. 2021. "How Affective Polarization Undermines Support for Democratic Norms." *Public Opinion Quarterly*. https://doi.org/10.1093/poq/nfab029

Klar, Samara. 2014. "Partisanship in a Social Setting." *American Journal of Political Science*, 58(3): 687–704.

Klar, Samara and Yanna Krupnikov. 2016. *Independent Politics: How American Disdain for Parties Leads to Political Inaction*. New York: Cambridge University Press.

Klar, Samara, Yanna Krupnikov and John Barry Ryan. 2018. "Affective Polarization or Partisan Disdain? Untangling a Dislike for the Opposing Party from a Dislike of Partisanship." *Public Opinion Quarterly*, 82(2): 379–390.

Klar, Samara, Thomas Leeper and Joshua Robison. 2020. "Studying Identities with Experiments: Weighing the Risk of Posttreatment Bias against Priming Effects." *Journal of Experimental Political Science*, 7(1): 56–60.

Klofstad, Casey A. Scott D. McClurg, and Meredith Rolfe. 2009. "Measurement of Political Discussion Networks: A Comparison of Two 'Name Generator' Procedures." *Public Opinion Quarterly*, 73(3): 462–483.

Knight Foundation. 2020. "The 100 Million Project: The Untold Story of American Non-Voters." https://knightfoundation.org/wp-content/uploads/2020/02/The-100-Million-Project_KF_Report_2020.pdf

Kozinets, Robert V. 2001. "Utopian Enterprise: Articulating the Meanings of *Star Trek*'s Culture of Consumption." *Journal of Consumer Research*, 28(1): 67–88.

Kraft, Patrick W, Yanna Krupnikov, Kerri Milita, John Barry Ryan and Stuart Soroka. 2020. "Social Media and the Changing Information Environment: Sentiment Differences in Read versus Circulated Content." *Public Opinion Quarterly*, 84(S1): 195–215.

Krämer, Benjamin and Christina Peter. 2020. "Exemplification Effects: A Meta-Analysis." *Human Communication Research*. 46(2–3): 192–221.

Krauss, Robert M., Yihsiu Chen, and Purnima Chawla. 1996. "Nonverbal Behavior and Nonverbal Communication: What do Conversational Hand Gestures Tell Us?" *Advances in Experimental Social Psychology*, 28: 389–450.

Kreiss, Daniel. 2014. "Seizing the Moment: The Presidential Campaigns' Use of Twitter During the 2012 Electoral Cycle." *New Media and Society* 18(8): 1473–1490.

Krosnick, Jon A. 1991. "Response Strategies for Coping with the Cognitive Demands of Attitude Measures in Surveys." *Applied Cognitive Psychology*, 5(3): 213–236.

Krosnick, Jon A., Sowmya Narayan, and Wendy R. Smith. 1996. "Satisficing in Surveys: Initial Evidence." *New Directions for Evaluation*, 70: 29–44.

Krupnikov, Yanna. 2019. "Overcoming Biases and Bridging Gaps: The Democratic Dilemma's Perspective of Hope." *PS: Political Science & Politics*, 52(4): 634–637.

Krupnikov, Yanna and Adam Seth Levine. 2019. "Political Issues, Evidence, and Citizen Engagement: The Case of Unequal Access to Affordable Health Care." *The Journal of Politics*, 81(2): 385–398.

Krupnikov, Yanna, H. Hannah Nam and Hillary Style. 2021. "Convenience Samples in Political Science Experiments." in James N. Druckman and Donald P. Green (eds). *Advances in Experimental Political Science*. New York: Cambridge University Press, pp. 165–183.

Kudrnáč, Aleš and Pat Lyons. 2017. "Parental Example as Motivation for Turnout among Youths." *Politcal Studies*, 65(1): 43–63.

Kubin, Emily, Curtis Puryear, Chelsea Schein and Kurt Gray. 2021 "Personal Experiences Bridge Moral and Political Divides Better than Facts." *PNAS*, 118(6): e2008389118.

Kutlaca Maja, van Zomeren Martjin, and Epstude Kai. 2020. "Friends or Foes? How Activists and Non-Activists Perceive and Evaluate Each Other." *PLoS ONE*, 15(4): e0230918, https://doi.org/10.1371/journal.pone.0230918

Kwong, Matt. 2018. "In A Divided US, Therapists Treating Anxiety Are Hearing the Same Name Over and Over: Donald Trump." *CBC.com*, July 28: www.cbc.ca/news/world/trump-anxiety-disorder-mental-health-political-divide-us-1.4762487

Langmuir, Molly. 2018. "Donald Trump is Destroying My Marriage." *New York Magazine*, November 27: https://nymag.com/intelligencer/2018/11/donald-trump-is-destroying-my-marriage.html

LaRose, Robert. 2010. "The Problem of Media Habits." *Communication Theory*, 20: 194–222.

Lasswell, Harold D. 1936. *Politics: Who Gets What, When, How*. New York: McGraw-Hill.

Lavine, Howard G., Christopher D. Johnston, and Marco R. Steenbergen. 2012. *The Ambivalent Partisan: How Critical Loyalty Promotes Democracy*. New York: Oxford University Press.

Lawless, Jennifer L. and Richard L. Fox. 2010. *It Still Takes A Candidate: Why Women Don't Run for Office*. New York: Cambridge University Press.

Lawson, Caitlin E. 2018. "Platform Vulnerabilities: Harassment and Misogynoir in the Digital Attack on Leslie Jones." *Information, Communication & Society*, 21: 818–833.

Ledbetter, Andrew M., Joseph P. Mazer, Jocelyn M. DeGroot, et al. 2011. "Attitudes Toward Online Social Connection and Self-Disclosure as Predictors of Facebook Communication and Relational Closeness." *Communication Research*, 38(1): 27–53.

Lefevere, Jonas, Knut De Swert, and Stefaan Walgrave. 2012. "Effects of Popular Exemplars in Television News." *Communication Research*, 39(1): 103–119.

Leighley, Jan. 1991. "Participation as a Stimulus of Political Conceptualization." *The Journal of Politics*, 53(1): 198–211.

Lerer, Lisa and Astead W. Herndon. 2020. "Why The Turnout In Iowa Has Some Democrats Worried." *The New York Times,* February 10: Section A Page 19.

Levendusky, Matthew. 2009. *The Partisan Sort.* Chicago: University of Chicago Press.

Levendusky, Matthew S. and Neil Malhotra. 2016. "(Mis)Perceptions of Partisan Polarization in the American Public." *Public Opinion Quarterly,* 80(S1): 387–91.

Lewis, Justin and Stephen Cushion. 2009. "The Thirst To Be First: An Analysis of Breaking News Stories and Their Impact on the Quality of 24-hour News Coverage in the UK." *Journalism Practice,* 3(3): 304–318.

Lewis, Justin, Sanna Inthorn and Karin Wahl-Jorgensen. 2005. *Citizens or Consumers? What the Media Tell Us About Political Participation.* New York: Open University Press.

Lippmann, Walter. 1922. *Public Opinion.* New York: Harcourt, Brace.

Litman, Jordan A. and Charles D. Spielberger. 2003. "Measuring Epistemic Curiosity and Its Diversive and Specific Components." *Journal of Personality Assessment,* 80 (1): 75–86.

Litt, Eden. 2012. "Knock, Knock. Who's There? The Imagined Audience." *Journal of Broadcasting & Electronic Media,* 56(3): 330–345.

Litt, Eden and Eszter Hargittai. 2016. "The Imagined Audience on Social Network Sites." *Social Media & Society,* 2(1): 1–12.

Lockwood, Penelope and Ziva Kunda. 1997. "Superstars and Me: Predicting the Impact of Role Models on the Self." *Journal of Personality and Social Psychology,* 73(1): 91–103.

Lukito, Josephine Jiyoun Suk, Yini Zhang, Larissa Doroshenko, Sang Jung Kim, Min-Hsin Su, Yiping Xia, Deen Freelon, and Chris Wells. 2020. "The Wolves in Sheep's Clothing: How Russia's Internet Research Agency Tweets Appeared in U.S. News as Vox Populi." *The International Journal of Press/Politics,* 25(2): 196–216.

Lupia, Arthur. 2016. *Uninformed: Why People Seem to Know So Little about Politics and What We Can Do about It.* New York: Oxford University Press.

Lupia, Arthur and Mathew McCubbins. 1998. *The Democratic Dilemma: Can Citizens Learn What They Need to Know?* New York: Cambridge University Press.

Lupton, Robert, Smallpage, Steven and Enders, Adam. 2020. "Values and Political Predispositions in the Age of Polarization: Examining the Relationship between Partisanship and Ideology in the United States, 1988–2012." *British Journal of Political Science,* 50(1): 241–260.

Ma, Will W. K. and Albert Chan. 2014. "Knowledge Sharing and Social Media: Altruism, Perceived Online Attachment Motivation, and Perceived Online Relationship Commitment." *Computers in Human Behavior,* 39: 51–58.

MacKinnon, Amy and Robbie Gramer. 2019. "In Historic Vote, House Impeaches Trump Over Ukraine Scandal." *Foreign Policy,* December 18: https://foreignpolicy.com/2019/12/18/house-representatives-historic-vote-impeach-trump-ukraine/

Mahler, Jonathan. 2016. "In Sunset of the Baby Boom Generation, the Election Reawakens an Old Divide." *The New York Times,* November 7: Section A Page 15.

Makse, Todd, Scott L. Minkoff and Anand E. Sokhey. 2019. *Politics on Display: Yard Signs and the Politicization of Social Spaces.* New York: Oxford University Press.

Martherus, James L., Andres G. Martinez, Paul K. Piff, and Alexander G. Theodoridis. 2021. "Party Animals? Extreme Partisan Polarization and Dehumanization." *Political Behavior,* 43: 517–540.

Martin, Jonathan and Nate Cohn. 2016. "Electoral Map a Reality Check to a Trump Bid." *The New York Times*, April 3: Section A Page 1.

Martin, Jonathan and Patricia Mazzei. 2020. "A Tight Trump-Biden Race in Florida: Here Is The State of Play" *The New York Times*, September 15: Section A Page 1.

Marwick, Alice E. and danah boyd. 2011. "I Tweet Honestly, I Tweet Passionately: Twitter Users, Context Collapse, and the Imagined Audience." *New Media and Society*, 13: 114–133.

Mason, Lilliana. 2015. "'I Disrespectfully Agree': The Differential Effects of Partisan Sorting on Social and Issue Polarization." *American Journal of Political Science*, 59 (1):128–45.

Mason, Lilliana. 2018. *Uncivil Agreement*. Chicago: University of Chicago Press.

Mazzei, Patricia. 2019. "Impeachment Divides a Nation, a District and a Dinner Table" *The New York Times*, December 19: Section A Page 20.

McCarty Nolan, Keith T. Poole and Howard Rosenthal. 2006. *Polarized America: The Dance of Ideology and Unequal Riches*. Cambridge, MA: MIT Press

McClendon, Gwyneth H. 2018. *Envy in Politics*. Princeton, NJ: Princeton University Press.

McDevitt, Michael. 2018. "Political Socialization and Child Development." In William Outhwaite and Stephen Turner (eds.), *The SAGE Handbook of Political Sociology*. London: SAGE, pp.797–811.

McDevitt, Michael and Spiro Kiousis. 2015. "Active Political Parenting: Youth Contributions During Election Campaigns." *Social Science Quarterly*, 96(1): 19–33.

McGregor, Shannon. 2019. "Social Media as Public Opinion: How Journalists use Social Media to Represent Public Opinion." *Journalism*, 20(8): 1070–1086.

McGregor, Shannon. 2020. "'Taking the Temperature of the Room': How Political Campaigns Use Social Media to Understand and Represent Public Opinion" *Public Opinion Quarterly*, 84(S1): 236–256

McGregor, Shannon and Logan Molyneux. 2020. "Twitter's Influence on News Judgment: An Experiment Among Journalists" *Journalism*, 21(5)597–613.

Mead, George H. 1934. *Mind, Self and Society*. Chicago: University of Chicago Press.

Medina, Jennifer. 2020. "How Democrats Missed Trump's Appeal to Latino Voters." *The New York Times*, November 9: Section A Page 1.

Mendelberg, Tali, Katherine McCabe and Adam Thal. 2017. "College Socialization and the Economic Views of Affluent Americans." *American Journal of Political Science*, 61 (3): 606–623.

Mendelberg, Tali, Vittorio Mérola, Tanika Raychaudhuri, and Adam Thal. 2020. "When Poor Students Attend Rich Schools: Do Affluent Social Environments Increase or Decrease Participation?" *Perspectives on Politics*, 1–17. DOI: 10.1017/S1537592720000699

Meraz, Sharon and Zizi Papacharissi. 2013. "Networked Gatekeeping and Networked Framing on #Egypt." *The International Journal of Press/ Politics*, 18(2): 138–166.

Mettler, Suzanne and Eric Welch. 2004. "Civic Generation: Policy Feedback Effects of the GI Bill on Political Involvement over the Life Course." *British Journal of Political Science*, 34(3): 497–518.

Milita, Kerri, John Barr Ryan, and Elizabeth N. Simas. 2014. "Nothing to Hide, Nowhere to Run, or Nothing to Lose: Candidate Position-Taking in Congressional Elections." *Political Behavior*, 36(2): 427–449.

Mill, John Stuart. 1956. *On Liberty*. New York: Bobbs-Merrill.

Miller, Kevin P., Marilynn B. Brewer and Nathan L. Arbuckle. 2009. "Social Identity Complexity: Its Correlates and Antecedents." *Group Processes and Intergroup Relations*, 12(1): 79–94.

Miller, Joanne M., Kyle Saunders, and Christina E. Farhart. 2016. "Conspiracy Endorsement as Motivated Reasoning: The Moderating Roles of Political Knowledge and Trust." *American Journal of Political Science*, 60(4): 824–844.

Mimms, Sarah. 2014. "Chuck Schumer: Passing Obamacare in 2010 Was a Mistake." *The Atlantic*, November25: www.theatlantic.com/politics/archive/2014/11/chuck-schumer-passing-obamacare-in-2010-was-a-mistake/449700/

Minozzi, William, Hyunjin Song, David M. J. Lazer, Michael A. Neblo, and Katherine Ognyanova. 2020. "The Incidental Pundit: Who Talks Politics with Whom, and Why?" *American Journal of Political Science*, 64(1): 135–151.

Minson, Julia and Benoît Monin. 2012. "Do-Gooder Derogation: Disparaging Morally Motivated Minorities to Defuse Anticipated Reproach." *Social Psychological and Personality Science*, 3(2): 200–207.

Mittal, Banwari. 1995. "A Comparative Analysis of Four Scales of Consumer Involvement." *Psychology & Marketing*, 12(7): 663–682.

Molyneux, Logan and Shannon C. McGregor. 2021. "Legitimating a platform: evidence of journalists' role in transferring authority to Twitter." *Information, Communication & Society*, DOI: 10.1080/1369118X.2021.1874037

Molyneux, Logan and Rachel R. Mourão. 2019. "Political Journalists' Normalization of Twitter: Interaction and New Affordances." *Journalism Studies*, 20(2): 248–266.

Monin, Benoît, Pamela Sawyer and Michael Marquez. 2008. "The Rejection of Moral Rebels: Resenting those Who do the Right Thing." *Journal of Personality and Social Psychology*, 95(1): 76–93.

Montgomery, Jacob M., Brendan Nyhan, and Michelle Torres. 2018. "How Conditioning on Posttreatment Variables Can Ruin Your Experiment and What to Do about It." *American Journal of Political Science*, 62(3): 760–775.

Moore-Berg, Samantha L, Lee-Or Ankori-Karlinsky, Boaz Hameiri and Emile Bruneau. 2020. "Exaggerated Meta-Perceptions Predict Intergroup Hostility between American Political Partisans." *Proceedings of the National Academy of Sciences*, 117(26): 14864–14872, DOI: 10.1073/pnas.2001263117

Morrell, Michael E. 2003. "Survey and Experimental Evidence for a Reliable and Valid Measure of Internal Political Efficacy." *Public Opinion Quarterly*, 67(4): 589–602.

Morsbach, Sarah K. and Ronald Prinz. 2006. "Understanding and Improving the Validity of Self-Report of Parenting." *Clinical Child and Parenting Psychology Review*, 9(1): 1–21.

Muller, Dominique and Fabrizio Butera. 2007. "The Focusing Effect of Self-Evaluation Threat in Coaction and Social Comparison." *Journal of Personality and Social Psychology*, 93(2): 194–211.

Munar, Ana María and Jens Kr. Steen Jacobsen. 2014. "Motivations for Sharing Tourism Experiences through Social Media." *Tourism Management*, 43: 46–54.

Najle, Mazine and Robert P. Jones. 2019. "American Democracy in Crisis: The Fate of Pluralism in a Divided Nation." PRRI Research Report. https://www.prri.org/research/american-democracy-in-crisis-the-fate-of-pluralism-in-a-divided-nation/

Neundorf, Anja, Richard Niemi, and Kaat Smets. 2016. "The Compensation Effect of Civic Education on Political Engagement: How Civics Classes Make Up for Missing Parental Socialization." *Political Behavior*, 38(4): 921–949.

Neundorf, Anja and Kaat Smets. 2017. "Political Socialisation and the Making of Citizens" Oxford Handbooks Online. DOI: 10.1093/oxfordhb/978019993 5307.013.98

Newcomb, Theodore M. 1943. *Personality and Social Change; Attitude Formation in a Student Community*. New York: Dryden Press.

Newcomb, Theodore M., Kathryn E. Koenig, Richard Flacks, and Donald P. Warwick. 1967. *Persistence and Change: Bennington College and Its Students after Twenty-Five Years*. New York: John Wiley & Sons.

Niemi, Richard G., Stephen C. Craig, and Franco Mattei. 1991. "Measuring Internal Political Efficacy in the 1988 National Election Study." *American Political Science Review*, 85(4): 1407–1413.

Niemi, Richard and Jane Junn. 1998. *Civic Education: What Makes Students Learn*. New Haven, CT: Yale University Press.

Noel, Hans. 2019. "Ideology and Its Discombobulations." *The Journal of Politics*, 81 (3): e57–e61.

Noel, Hans and Brendan Nyhan. 2011. "The "Unfriending" Problem: The Consequences of Homophily in Friendship Retention for Causal Estimates of Social Influence." *Social Networks*, 33(3): 211–218.

Ognyanova, Katherine. 2020. "Contagious Politics: Tie Strength and the Spread of Political Knowledge." *Communication Research*, https://doi.org/10.1177 /0093650220924179

Oliver, J. Eric and Thomas J. Wood. 2014. "Conspiracy Theories and the Paranoid Style(s) of Mass Opinion." *American Journal of Political Science*, 58(4): 952–966.

Ondercin, Heather and Mary Kate Lizotte. 2020. "You've Lost That Loving Feeling: How Gender Shapes Affective Polarization." *American Politics Research*, https://doi .org/10.1177/1532673X20972103

Orr, Lilla V. and Gregory A. Huber. 2020. "The Policy Basis of Measured Partisan Animosity in the United States." *American Journal of Political Science* 64(3): 569–86.

Ottoni-Wilhelm, Mark, David B. Estell and Neil H. Perdue. 2014. "Role-Modeling and Conversations About Giving in the Socialization of Adolescent Charitable Giving and Volunteering." *Journal of Adolescence*, 37(1): 53–66.

Oxley, Zoe, Mirya R. Holman, Jill S. Greenlee, Angela L. Bos and J. Celeste Lay. 2020. "Children's Views of the American Presidency." *Public Opinion Quarterly*, 84(1): 141–157.

Padgett, Jeremy Johanna L Dunaway, and Joshua P Darr. 2019. "As Seen on TV? How Gatekeeping Makes the U.S. House Seem More Extreme." *Journal of Communication*, 69 (6): 696–719.

Pajer, Nicole. 2020. "Can Love Survive This Election?" *The New York Times*, August 25: https://www.nytimes.com/2020/08/25/fashion/weddings/can-love-relationships-survive-this-election.html

Panning, Jennifer. 2017. "Trump Anxiety Disorder: The Trump Effect on the Mental Health of Half of the Nation and Special Populations." In Bandy Lee, (ed.), *The Dangerous Case of Donald Trump: 27 Psychiatrists and Mental Health Experts Assess a President*. New York: Thomas Dunne Books, pp. 235–243.

Papacharissi, Zizi. 2010. *A Private Sphere: Democracy in a Digital Age.* Malden, MA: Polity Press.

Papacharissi, Zizi. 2012. "Without You, I'm Nothing: Performances of the Self on Twitter." *International Journal of Communication,* 6: 1989–2006.

Park, Crystal L. 2010. "Making Sense of the Meaning Literature: An Integrative Review of Meaning Making and Its Effects on Adjustment to Stressful Life Events." *Psychological Bulletin,* 136(2): 257–301.

Park, Chang Sup. 2013. "Does Twitter Motivate Involvement in Politics? Tweeting, Opinion Leadership, and Political Engagement." *Computers in Human Behavior,* 29 (4): 1641–1648.

Parker, Christopher S. and Matt A. Barreto. 2014. *Change They Can't Believe In: The Tea Party and Reactionary Politics in America.* Princeton, NJ: Princeton University Press.

Patterson, Thomas E. 1997. "The News Media: An Effective Political Actor?" *Political Communication,* 14(4): 445–455.

Pegoraro, Ann. 2013. "Sport Fandom in the Digital World." In Paul M. Pederson, (ed.), *Routledge Handbook of Sport Communication.* Routledge, pp. 248–258.

Penney, Joel. 2016. "Motivations for Participating in 'Viral Politics': A Qualitative Case Study of Twitter Users and the 2012 US Presidential Election." *Convergence: The International Journal of Research into New Media Technologies,* 22(1): 71–87.

Perry, Gina. 2018. *The Lost Boys: Inside Muzafer Sherif's Robbers Cave Experiment.* London, UK: Scribe Publications.

Petersen, Michael Bang and Lene Aarøe. 2013. "Politics in the Mind's Eye: Imagination as a Link between Social and Political Cognition." *American Political Science Review,* 107(2): 275–293.

Pew 2019. "National Politics on Twitter Small Share of U.S. Adults Produce Majority of Tweets." Pew Report. www.pewresearch.org/politics/2019/10/23/national-politics-on-twitter-small-share-of-u-s-adults-produce-majority-of-tweets/#those-who-tweet-about-politics-differ-from-those-who-avoid-the-topic-or-tweet-infrequently

Peyton, Kyle, Gregory Huber and Alexander Coppock. 2020. "The Generalizability of Online Experiments Conducted During The COVID-19 Pandemic." Working Paper: 10.31235/osf.io/s45yg

Pietryka, Matthew T. and Donald A. DeBats. 2017. "It's Not Just What You Have, but Who You Know: Networks, Social Proximity to Elites, and Voting in State and Local Elections." *American Political Science Review,* 111(2): 360–378.

Preece, Jessica. 2016. "Mind the Gender Gap: An Experiment on the Influence of Self-Efficacy on Political Interest." *Politics & Gender,* 12(1): 198–217.

Pressgrove, Geah, Brooke Weberling McKeever and S. Mo Jang. 2018. "What is Contagious? Exploring Why Content Goes Viral on Twitter: A case study of the ALS Ice Bucket Challenge." *International Journal of Nonprofit and Voluntary Sector Marketing,* 23: e1586.

Prior, Markus. 2007. *Post-Broadcast Democracy: How Media Choice Increases Inequality In Political Involvement and Polarizes the Electorate.* New York: Cambridge University Press.

Prior, Markus. 2010. "You've Either Got It or You Don't? The Stability of Political Interest Over the Life Cycle." *The Journal of Politics,* 72(3): 747–766.

Prior, Markus. 2019. *Hooked: How Politics Captures People's Interest.* New York: Cambridge University Press.

Pye, Lucian W. 1959. "Political Modernization and Research on the Process of Political Socialization." *Items*, 13: 25–28.

Quinn, Kelly. 2016. "Contextual Social Capital: Linking the Contexts of Social Media Use to Its Outcomes." *Information, Communication & Society*, 19(5): 582–600.

Rainie, Lee and Barry Wellman. 2012. *Networked: The New Social Operating System*. Cambridge, MA: MIT Press.

Raychaudhuri, Tanika. 2018. "The Social Roots of Asian American Partisan Attitudes." *Politics, Groups, and Identities*, 6(3): 389–410.

Renninger, Ann and Suzanne Hidi, 2011. "Revisiting the Conceptualization, Measurement and Generation of Interest." *Educational Psychologist*, 46(3): 168–184.

Riesman, David and Nathan Glazer. 1950. "Criteria for Political Apathy." In Alvin W. Gouldner, (ed.), *Studies in Leadership*. New York: Harper and Brothers, pp. 505–559.

Robinson, Sue, Yiping Xia and Megan Zahay. 2019. "Public Political Talk on Twitter and Facebook: The View from Journalists." Knight Foundation Report. https://knightfoundation.org/wp-content/uploads/2019/12/KF-Twitter-Report-Part2.pdf

Robison, Joshua and Kevin J. Mullinix. 2016. "Elite Polarization and Public Opinion: How Polarization is Communicated and Its Effects." *Political Communication*, 33(2): 261–282.

Rogowski, Jon and Joseph Sutherland. 2016. "How Ideology Fuels Affective Polarization." *Political Behavior*, 38(3): 485–508.

Rosenberg, Howard and Charles Feldman. 2008. *No Time To Think: The Menace of Media Speed and the 24-hour News Cycle*. New York: Continuum.

Rosenstone, Stephen J. and John Mark Hansen. 1993. *Mobilization, Participation, and Democracy in America*. New York: Macmillan Publishing Company

Ross, Andrew R. N. and Delia Dumitrescu. 2019. "'Vox Twitterati' Investigating the Effects of Social Media Exemplars in Online News Articles." *New Media & Society*, 21(4): 962–983.

Rubin, Bonnie Miller. 2020. "A Lesson in Civics or Indoctrination? Deciding Whether to Bring Kids to Political Protests." *The Washington Post*, March 5: www.washingtonpost.com/lifestyle/2020/03/05/lesson-civics-or-indoctrination-deciding-whether-bring-kids-political-protests/

Rubin, Rebecca, Elizabeth M. Perse and Carole E. Barbato. 1988. "Conceptualization and Measurement of Interpersonal Communication Motives." *Human Communication Research*, 14(4): 602–628.

Rudolph, Thomas J., Amy Gangl, and Dan Stevens. 2000. "The Effects of Efficacy and Emotions on Campaign Involvement." *The Journal of Politics*, 62(4): 1189–1197.

Rudy, Duane and Joan E. Grusec. 2001. "Correlates of Authoritarian Parenting in Individualist and Collectivist Cultures and Implications for Understanding the Transmission of Values." *Journal of Cross-Cultural Psychology*, 32(2): 202–212.

Russo, Silvia and Håkan Stattin. 2017. "Stability and Change in Youth's Political Interest." *Social Indicators Research*, 132(2): 643–658.

Ryan, John Barry. 2011. "Accuracy and Bias in Perceptions of Political Knowledge." *Political Behavior*, 33(2): 335–356.

Saleem, Hajra, Jawaria Rahman, Nida Aslam, Salikh Murtazaliev and Safeera Khan. 2020. "Coronavirus Disease 2019 (COVID-19) in Children: Vulnerable or Spared? A Systematic Review." *Cureus*, 12(5): e8207.

Sanger-Katz, Margot. 2020 "On Coronavirus, Americans Still Trust the Experts." *New York Times*, June 27: www.nytimes.com/2020/06/27/upshot/coronavirus-americans-trust-experts.html#:~:text=In%20the%20Times%20survey%2C%2084, and%2083%20percent%20among%20Democrats.

Sapiro, Virginia. 2004. "Not Your Parents' Political Socialization: Introduction for a New Generation." *Annual Review of Political Science*, 7: 1–23.

Shulman, Hillary C. and Timothy R. Levine. 2012. "Exploring Social Norms as a Group-Level Phenomenon: Do Political Participation Norms Exist and Influence Political Participation on College Campuses?" *Journal of Communication*, 62(3): 532–552.

Schulz, William Small, Andrew M. Guess, Pablo Barberá, et al. 2021. "(Mis)representing Ideology on Twitter: How Social Influence Shapes Online Political Expression." Working Paper available at https://csdp.princeton.edu/sites/csdp/files/media/schulzguess_spirals_csdp.pdf

Segesten, Anamaria Dutceac and Michael Bossetta. 2017. "A Typology of Political Participation Online: How Citizens used Twitter to Mobilize during the 2015 British General Elections." *Information, Communication & Society*, 20(11): 1625–1643.

Seregina, Anastasia and John W. Schouten. 2017. "Resolving Identity Ambiguity through Transcending Fandom." *Consumption Markets & Culture*, 20(2): 107–130.

Settle, Jaime E. 2018. *Frenemies: How Social Media Polarizes America*. New York: Cambridge University Press.

Settle, Jaime and Taylor Carlson. 2019. "Opting Out of Political Discussion." *Political Communication*, 36(3): 476–496.

Sherif, Muzafer, O. J. Harvey, B. Jack White, William R. Hood and Carolyn W. Sherif. 1988. *The Robber's Cave Experiment: Intergroup Conflict and Cooperation*. Middletown, CT: Wesleyan University Press.

Silvia, Paul. 2005. "What is Interesting? Exploring the Appraisal Structure of Interest." *Emotion*, 5(1): 89–102.

Smith, Glen and Kathleen Searles. 2014. "Who Let the (Attack) Dogs Out? New Evidence for Partisan Media Effects." *Public Opinion Quarterly*, 78(1): 71–99.

Sokhey, Anand E. and Paul A. Djupe. 2011. "Interpersonal Networks and Democratic Politics." *PS: Political Science and Politics*, 44(1): 55–59.

Soroka, Stuart N. 2012. "The Gatekeeping Function: Distributions of Information in Media and the Real World." *The Journal of Politics* 74(2): 514–528.

Spears, Russel, Bertjan Doosje and Naomi Ellemers. 1997. "Self-Stereotyping in the Face of Threats to Group Status and Distinctiveness: the Role of Group Identification." *Personality and Social Psychology Bulletin*, 23: 538–553

Spry, Amber. 2018. *Identity in American Politics: A Multidimensional Approach to Study and Measurement*. Doctoral Dissertation, Columbia University.

Standage, Tom. 2013. *Writing on the Wall: Social Media – the First 2,000 Years*. New York: Bloomsbury.

Stewart, Emily. 2019. "The Incredibly Absurd Trump/CNN SharpieGate Feud, Explained." *Vox.com*, September 6: www.vox.com/policy-and-politics/2019/9/6/20851971/trump-hurricane-dorian-alabama-sharpie-cnn-media

Stockton, Nick. 2017. "The New FOMO: Who Cares About My Friends? I'm Missing the News." *Wired Magazine*, September: www.wired.com/2017/08/fomo/.

Stoker, Laura and Jackie Bass. 2011. "Political Socialization: Ongoing Questions and New Directions." In George C. Edwards III, Lawrence R. Jacobs, and Robert

Y. Shapiro (eds.), *The Oxford Handbook of American Public Opinion and the Media*. New York: Oxford University Press, pp. 453–470.

Strömbäck, Jesper, Monika Djerf-Pierre and Adam Shehata (2013). "The Dynamics of Political Interest and News Media Consumption: A Longitudinal Perspective" *International Journal of Public Opinion Research*, 25(4): 414–435.

Stromer-Galley, Jennifer. 2002. "New Voices in the Public Sphere: A Comparative Analysis of Interpersonal and Online Political Talk." *Javnost-The Public*, 9(2): 23–41.

Strother, Logan, Spencer Piston, Ezra Golberstein, Sarah E. Gollust and Daniel Eisenberg. 2021. "College Roommates have a Modest but Significant Influence on Each Other's Political Ideology." *Proceedings of the National Academy of Sciences*, 118(2): e2015514117.

Suls, Jerry, René Martin and Ladd Wheeler. 2002. "Social Comparison: Why, With Whom, and With What Effect?" *Current Directions in Psychological Science*, 11(5): 159–163.

Sunstein, Cass R. 2002. "The Law of Group Polarization." *The Journal of Political Philosophy*, 10(2): 175–195.

Taber, Charles S. and Milton Lodge. 2006. "Motivated Skepticism in the Evaluation of Political Beliefs." *American Journal of Political Science*, 50(3): 755–769.

Taylor, Jessica. 2017. "Republicans and Democrats Don't Agree, Or Like Each Other – And its Worse Than Ever." NPR, October 5: https://www.npr.org/2017/10/05/555685136/republicans-and-democrats-dont-agree-dont-like-each-other-and-its-worst-than-eve

Tavernise, Sabrina and Nate Cohn. 2019. "Moderate Majority with Other Things to Worry About." *The New York Times*, September 24: Section A Page 11.

Thomas, Nancy and Margaret Brower. 2017. "Politics 365: Fostering Campus Climates for Student Political Learning & Engagement" *Institute for Democracy and Higher Education Report*. https://tischcollege.tufts.edu/sites/default/files/Politics%20365.pdf

Thompson, Dondrea. 2002. "The Politics of Display or the Display of Politics? Cultural Policy and the Museo del Hombre Dominicano." *Museum Anthropology*, 25(2): 38–49.

Thomsen, Danielle. 2017. *Opting Out of Congress: Partisan Polarization and the Decline of Moderate Candidates*. New York: Cambridge University Press.

Thomson-DeVeaux, Amelia, Jasmine Mithani, and Laura Bronner. 2020. "Why Many Americans Don't Vote: And Why for Some, This Year Could Be Different." *Five Thirty Eight*, October 26: https://projects.fivethirtyeight.com/non-voters-poll-2020-election/

Thorne, Scott and Gordon C. Bruner. 2006. "An Exploratory Investigation of the Characteristics of Consumer Fanaticism" *Qualitative Market Research*, 9(1): 51–72.

Thorson, Emily. 2014. "Beyond Opinion Leaders: How Attempts to Persuade Foster Political Awareness and Campaign Learning." *Communication Research*, 41(3): 353–374.

Toff, Benjamin J. 2016. *The Blind Scorekeepers: Journalism, Polling, and the Battle to Define Public Opinion in American Politics*. Doctoral dissertation, University of Wisconsin–Madison, Madison, WI.

Torre, Jared B. and Matthew D. Lieberman. 2018. "Putting Feelings Into Words: Affect Labeling as Implicit Emotion Regulation." *Emotion Review*, 10(2): 116–124.

Trussler, Marc and Stuart Soroka. 2014. "Consumer Demand for Cynical and Negative News Frames." *The International Journal of Press/Politics*, 19(3): 360–379.

Turner, John C. and Katherine Reynolds. 2012. "Self-Categorization Theory." In Paul Van Lange, Arie Kruglanski and E. Tory Higgins (eds.), *Handbook of Theories of Social Psychology: Volume Two*. London: SAGE, pp. 399–417.

Turner, Julius. 1951. "Responsible Parties: A Dissent from the Floor." *American Political Science Review*, 45(1): 143–152.

Tworek, Heidi. 2018. "Tweets are the New Vox Populi." *Columbia Journalism Review*, March 27: https://www.cjr.org/analysis/tweets-media.php

Usher, Nikki and Yee Man Margaret Ng. 2020. "Sharing Knowledge and 'Microbubbles': Epistemic Communities." *Social Media + Society*, 6(2): https://doi.org/10.1177/2056305120926639

Usher, Nikki, Jesse Holcomb, and Justin Littman. 2018. "Twitter Makes it Worse: Political Journalists, Gendered Echo Chambers, and the Amplification of Gender Bias." *The International Journal of Press/Politics*, 23(3): 324–344.

Valentino, Nicholas, Krysha Gregorowicz, and Eric W. Groenendyk. 2009. "Efficacy, Emotions and the Habit of Participation." *Political Behavior*, 31(3): 307–330.

Van Bavel, Jay J., Diego A. Reinero, Victoria Spring, Elizabeth A. Harris, and Annie Duke. 2021. "Speaking My Truth: Why Personal Experiences can Bridge Divides but Mislead." *PNAS*, 118(8): e2100280118.

van Deth, Jan W., Simone Abendschön and Meike Vollmar. 2011. "Children and Politics: An Empirical Reassessment of Early Political Socialization." *Political Psychology* 32(1): 147–174.

Van Duyn, Emily. 2018. "Hidden Democracy: Political Dissent in Rural America." *Journal of Communication*, 68: 965–987.

Vázquez-Arroyo, Antonio Y. 2013. "How Not to Learn From Catastrophe: Habermas, Critical Theory and the 'Catastrophization' of Political Life." *Political Theory*, 41(5): 738–765.

Verba, Sidney, Kay Lehman Schlozman and Henry Brady. 1995. *Voice and Equality: Civic Volunteerism in American Politics*. Cambridge, MA: Harvard University Press.

Vromen, Ariadne, Michael Andrew Xenos and Brian Loader. 2013. *The Civic Network: A Comparative Study of the Use of Social Media for Enhancing Young People's Political Engagement, Australia, United Kingdom, & United States*. Ann Arbor, MI: Inter-university Consortium for Political and Social Research [distributor], 2018-05-04. https://doi.org/10.3886/ICPSR37023.v1

Wagner, Claudia, Vera Liao, Peter Pirolli, Les Nelson and Markus Strohmaier. 2012. "It's Not in Their Tweets: Modeling Topical Expertise of Twitter Users." *International Conference on Privacy, Security, Risk and Trust and 2012 International Conference on Social Computing*, Amsterdam, pp. 91–100, DOI: 10.1109/SocialCom-PASSAT.2012.30.

Wakefield Research Study. 2017. "The Trump Effect on American Relationships." www.wakefieldresearch.com/blog/2017/05/10/new-wakefield-research-study-trump-effect-american-relationships

Wallace, Julian. 2018. "Modelling Contemporary Gatekeeping: The rise of individuals, algorithms and platforms in digital news dissemination." *Digital Journalism*, 6(3): 274–293.

Walsh, Katherine Cramer. 2004. *Talking about Politics: Informal Groups and Social Identity in American Life*. Chicago: University of Chicago Press.

Watson, Kathryn. 2019 "Trump Displays Seemingly Edited Map of Hurricane Dorian Projected Path." *CBS News*, September 4: www.cbsnews.com/news/trump-hurricane-map-briefing-today-shows-dorian-tracker-seemingly-altered-with-black-pen-or-sharpie-marker-2019-09-04/

Weaver, David H., Lars Willnat and G. Cleveland Wilhoit. 2019. "The American Journalist in the Digital Age: Another Look at U.S. News People." *Journalism & Mass Communication Quarterly*, 96(1): 101–130.

Webster, Steven. 2020. *American Rage: How Anger Shapes Our Politics*. New York: Cambridge University Press.

Webster, Steven and Alan Abramowitz. 2017. "The Ideological Foundations of Affective Polarization in the U.S. Electorate." *American Politics Research*, 45(4): 621–647.

Weinschenk, Aaron and Christopher Dawes. 2021. "Civic Education in High School and Voter Turnout in Adulthood." *British Journal of Political Science*, https://doi.org/10.1017/S0007123420000435

Wells, Chris, Yini Zhang, Josephine Lukito and Jon C. W. Pevehouse. 2020. "Modeling the Formation of Attentive Publics in Social Media: The Case of Donald Trump." *Mass Communication and Society*, 23(2): 181–205.

West, Emily A. and Shanto Iyengar. 2020. "Partisanship as a Social Identity: Implications for Polarization." *Political Behavior*, https://doi.org/10.1007/s11109-020-09637-y

Westwood, Sean, Solomon Messing, and Yphtach Lelkes. 2020. "Projecting Confidence: How the Probabilistic Horse Race Confuses and Demobilizes the Public" *The Journal of Politics* 82:4, 1530–1544.

Westwood, Sean J. and Erik Peterson. 2020. "The Inseparability of Race and Partisanship in the United States." *Political Behavior*, https://link.springer.com/article/10.1007/s11109-020-09648-9

Westwood, Sean J., Erik Peterson, and Yphtach Lelkes. 2019. "Are There Still Limits on Partisan Prejudice?" *Public Opinion Quarterly*, 83(3): 584–597.

White, Ismail and Chryl Laird. 2020. *Steadfast Democrats: How Social Forces Shape Black Political Behavior*. Princeton, NJ: Princeton University Press.

Whitesides, John. 2017. "From Disputes to a Breakup – Wounds Still Raw After U.S. Election." *Reuters*, February 7: https://www.reuters.com/article/uk-usa-trump-relationships-insight-idUKKBN15M13P

Williams, Rebecca. 2013. "'Anyone who Calls Muse a Twilight Band will be Shot on Sight': Music, Distinction, and the 'Interloping Fan' in the Twilight Franchise." *Popular Music and Society*, 36(3): 327–342.

Wojcik, Stefan and Adam Hughes. 2019. "Sizing Up Twitter Users." Pew Research Center: https://www.pewresearch.org/internet/wp-content/uploads/sites/9/2019/04/twitter_opinions_4_18_final_clean.pdf

Wolak, Jennifer. 2009. "Explaining Change in Party Identification in Adolescence." *Electoral Studies*, 28(4): 575–583.

Wolak, Jennifer. 2020a. *Compromise in an Age of Party Polarization*. New York: Oxford University Press.

Wolak, Jennifer. 2020b. "Conflict Avoidance and Gender Gaps in Political Engagement." *Political Behavior*. DOI: 10.1007/s11109-020-09614-5

Wolak, Jennifer and Carey E. Stapleton. 2020. "Self-Esteem and the Development of Partisan Identity." *Political Research Quarterly*, 73(3): 609–622.

Woudstra, Kristy. 2017. "Why I won't take my kids to protests" *Today's Parent*. www.todaysparent.com/family/parenting/why-i-wont-take-my-kids-to-protests/

Xia, Yiping, Sue Robinson, Megan Zahay and Deen Freelon. 2020 "The Evolving Journalistic Roles on Social Media: Exploring 'Engagement' as Relationship Building between Journalists and Citizens" *Journalism Practice*, 14(5): 556–573

Xu, Weiai Wayne and Miao Feng. 2014. "Talking to the Broadcasters on Twitter: Networked Gatekeeping in Twitter Conversations with Journalists." *Journal of Broadcasting & Electronic Media*, 58(3): 420–437.

Yair, Omer. 2020. "A Note on the Affective Polarization Literature." Working paper available at: https://papers.ssrn.com/sol3/papers.cfm?abstract_id=3771264.

Yoo, Sung Woo, Ji Won Kim, and Homero Gil de Zúñiga. 2017. "Cognitive Benefits for Senders: Antecedents and Effects of Political Expression on Social Media." *Journalism & Mass Communication Quarterly*, 94(1): 17–37.

Zillmann, Dolf and Hans-Bernd Brosius. 2000. *Exemplification in Communication: The Influence of Case Reports on the Perception of Issues*. New York, NY: Routledge.

Zink, James. 2009. "The Language of Liberty and Law: James Wilson on America's Written Constitution." *American Political Science Review*, 103(3): 442–455.

Zmigrod, Leor, Peter Jason Rentfrow and Trevor Robbins. 2019. "The Partisan Mind: Is Extreme Political Partisanship Related to Cognitive Inflexibility?" *Journal of Experimental Psychology: General*. http://dx.doi.org/10.1037/xge0000661

Zweig, David. 2020. "Are COVID Patients Gasping 'It Isn't Real' As They Die?" *Wired*, November 19: www.wired.com/story/are-covid-patients-gasping-it-isnt-real-as-they-die/

Index

CPSIA information can be obtained
at www.ICGtesting.com
Printed in the USA
BVHW072025190122
62664484BV00002B/13